Communications
in Computer and Information Science　1068

Commenced Publication in 2007
Founding and Former Series Editors:
Phoebe Chen, Alfredo Cuzzocrea, Xiaoyong Du, Orhun Kara, Ting Liu,
Krishna M. Sivalingam, Dominik Ślęzak, Takashi Washio, Xiaokang Yang,
and Junsong Yuan

Editorial Board Members

More information about this series at http://www.springer.com/series/7899

Vinícius Rosa Cota · Dante Augusto Couto Barone ·
Diego Roberto Colombo Dias ·
Laila Cristina Moreira Damázio (Eds.)

Computational Neuroscience

Second Latin American Workshop, LAWCN 2019
São João Del-Rei, Brazil, September 18–20, 2019
Proceedings

 Springer

Editors
Vinícius Rosa Cota (iD)
Federal University of São João Del-Rei
São João Del-Rei, Brazil

Dante Augusto Couto Barone (iD)
Federal University of Rio Grande do Sul
Porto Alegre, Brazil

Diego Roberto Colombo Dias (iD)
Federal University of São João Del-Rei
São João Del-Rei, Brazil

Laila Cristina Moreira Damázio (iD)
Federal University of São João Del-Rei
São João Del-Rei, Brazil

ISSN 1865-0929   ISSN 1865-0937 (electronic)
Communications in Computer and Information Science
ISBN 978-3-030-36635-3   ISBN 978-3-030-36636-0 (eBook)
https://doi.org/10.1007/978-3-030-36636-0

This Springer imprint is published by the registered company Springer Nature Switzerland AG
The registered company address is: Gewerbestrasse 11, 6330 Cham, Switzerland

Preface

The human brain is the most complex object of the universe known to man. Almost a hundred billion neurons making trillions of synaptic contacts in an astounding number of possible combinations is only one important part of this system, that also includes glia and other cells with multifaceted effects in neural function. This tremendous complexity makes it incredibly challenging to fully understand the nervous system and deliver robust treatment to its dysfunctions – a winning candidate for the ultimate frontier of science. To overcome this immense challenge, a fruitful endeavor is to approach the study of the brain by multi and interdisciplinary science. With the benefit of exponential development in computer sciences and technologies, and also the comprehensive accumulated knowledge on the nuts and bolts of the nervous system, a new era of highly collaborative transdisciplinary science is blooming.

Neuroscientists can now simulate from molecules to neuronal cells, circuits, and maybe the whole brain in *in silico* experiments of computational neuroscience overcoming limitations of *in vivo* and *in vitro* preparations. At the same time, computer science can also benefit from neuroscience by incorporating neurobiological knowledge of how the brain learns and performs cognitive tasks into software and hardware to generate artificial intelligence and machine learning. Finally, the dialogue between the biological milieu and the digital world has enabled the direct communication between brain and machine, making it possible to develop groundbreaking technologies to treat myriad brain disorders and to enhance function, while at the same time giving rise to entire novel biohybrid systems of neuroengineering.

Computational neuroscience, artificial intelligence, and neuroengineering have, thus, become hot topics attracting scientists from different departments in a new front of strong interdisciplinarity. This reunion of minds and talents must be fostered by, among other initiatives, the opportunity to gather people in vibrant scientific meetings. Thus, the goal behind the biannual Latin American Workshop on Computational Neuroscience (LAWCN) series is to provide scientists – established or in training – with an inspiring opportunity to get together and exchange experiences and ideas that may foster new avenues of interdisciplinary brain investigation and induce the formation of robust collaborative networks of researchers. Particularly, there is a prevalent interest in integrating the academic community of Latin America, whose collaboration networks are not fully developed when compared, for instance, with those involving European nations and the USA. Moreover, the LAWCN workshop aims at congregating neuroscientists coming from different backgrounds, particularly in the areas of computational neuroscience, neuroengineering, artificial intelligence, and neurosciences in general to foster high impact interdisciplinary science.

The second edition of the workshop (LAWCN 2019) was held with great success in the historic city of São João Del-Rei, Minas Gerais, Brazil, during September 18–20, 2019. During these labor-intensive 3 days, participants had the opportunity to listen to the brilliant lectures from 8 world-class scientists from Brazil and abroad (Italy,

Norway, Colombia, and Ecuador), and also to attend the presentation of accepted papers in 15-minute sessions or accepted posters in a 2-hour session. New ideas, collaborations, and friendships were cemented during our coffee-breaks and social events, served with exquisite local cuisine and an inspiring atmosphere in the historic city surrounded by beautiful nature.

All manuscripts submitted were reviewed in a single-blind fashion by at least 3 experienced reviewers from our Program Committee, comprised of members from 18 different countries located on 4 different continents. The papers found in this volume (1068) of Springer's *Communications in Computer and Information Science* (CCIS) were among the top 20 of accepted papers, and thus represent science of excellence performed in different multidisciplinary centers of investigation across Latin America. They encompass all areas of the event. While being highly interdisciplinary, they have been grouped under the areas of artificial intelligence, machine learning, and related topics; complex systems and complex networks; computational neuroscience of learning and memory; neural signal processing; software and hardware implementations in neuroscience; brain-machine interfaces and neurostimulation; and seizure prediction.

LAWCN 2019 was organized by the Laboratory of Neuroengineering and Neuroscience (LINNce – Laboratório Interdisciplinar de Neuroengenharia e Neurociências) of the Federal University of São João Del-Rei (UFSJ – Universidade Federal de São João Del-Rei), ranked second in the Category Normalized Citation Index (CNCI) – a measurement of international research impact – as assessed by the recently published report from Clarivate Analytics, entitled "Research in Brazil: funding excellence," regarding Brazilian science in the period of 2013–2018. The conference was supported by the Electrical Engineering Graduate Program (PPGEL/CEFET-MG – UFSJ), the Provost Office for Research and Graduate Programs (PROPE – Pró-reitoria de Pesquisa e Pós-graduação/UFSJ), the Office for International Affairs (ASSIN – Assessoria Internacional/UFSJ), the Online Education Center of UFSJ (NEAD – Núcleo de Ensino à Distância/UFSJ), and the Academic League of Medical Anatomy (LIAC – Liga de Anatomia Clínica). Financial aid was provided by PROPE, Coordenação de Aperfeiçoamento de Pessoal de Nível Superior (CAPES), and the International Brain Research Organization – Latin American Regional Committee (IBRO-LARC). The event was also sponsored by UNIMED São João Del-Rei, YED, and CONECTA MG. NEUROMODEC was the advertising partner of the conference worldwide. Last but not least, Springer Nature has become a key collaborator of LAWCN as the publisher of our top papers in the very reputable book series CCIS.

To all these organizations, to the keynote speakers, to the authors, and to all the participants, we, the editors of CCIS volume 1068, would like express our most heartfelt gratitude for helping us put together an awesome event and this excellent book. Thank you!

September 2019

Vinícius Rosa Cota
Dante Augusto Couto Barone
Diego Roberto Colombo Dias
Laila Cristina Moreira Damázio

Organization

Editor

Vinícius Rosa Cota   Federal University of São João del-Rei (UFSJ), Brazil

Co-editors

Dante Augusto Couto Barone   Federal University of Rio Grande do Sul (UFRGS), Brazil

Diego Roberto Colombo Dias   Federal University of São João del-Rei (UFSJ), Brazil

Laila C. Moreira Damázio   Federal University of São João del-Rei (UFSJ), Brazil

Organized By

Federal University of São João Del-Rei, Brazil

Conference Chairs

Vinícius Rosa Cota (Chair)   Federal University of São João del-Rei (UFSJ), Brazil

Dante Augusto Couto Barone (Co-chair)   Federal University of Rio Grande do Sul (UFRGS), Brazil

Organizing Committee

Álvaro César de Oliveira Penoni   Federal University of São João del-Rei (UFSJ), Brazil

Christian Puhlmann Brackmann   Federal Institute of Education, Science and Technology Farroupilha (IFFAR), Brazil

Dárlinton Barbosa Feres Carvalho   Federal University of São João del-Rei (UFSJ), Brazil

Diego Roberto Colombo Dias   Federal University of São João del-Rei (UFSJ), Brazil

Eduardo Oliveira Teles   Federal Institute of Bahia, Brazil

Erivelton Geraldo Nepomuceno   Federal University of São João del-Rei (UFSJ), Brazil

Erika Lorena Fonseca Costa de Alvarenga   Federal University of São João del-Rei (UFSJ), Brazil

Guillermo Cecchi   IBM T. J. W. Research Center, USA

Jaime Andres Riascos Salas   Corporación Universitaria Autónoma de Nariño, Colombia

Jasiara Carla de Oliveira	Federal University of São João del-Rei (UFSJ), Brazil
Jim Jones da Silveira Marciano	Federal University of São João del-Rei (UFSJ), Brazil
Laila Cristina Moreira Damázio	Federal University of São João del-Rei (UFSJ), Brazil
Leonardo Chaves Dutra da Rocha	Federal University of São João del-Rei (UFSJ), Brazil
Paulo Rogério de Almeida Ribeiro	Federal University of Maranhão (UFMA), Brazil
Reginaldo Coimbra Vieira	Federal University of São João del-Rei (UFSJ), Brazil
Rodrigo Alejandro Sierra Ordoñez	University of Szeged, Hungary
Sen Cheng	Ruhr University Bochum, Germany

Program Committee Chair

Vinícius Rosa Cota	Federal University of São João del-Rei (UFSJ), Brazil

Program Committee

Alan Talevi	National University of La Plata, Argentina
Antônio Carlos Roque da Silva Filho	São Paulo University (USP), Brazil
Carlos Dias Maciel	São Paulo University (USP), Brazil
Carlos Madrigal	Metropolitan Technological Institute, Colombia
César Collazos	University of Cauca, Colombia
Cleiton Lopes Aguiar	Federal University of Minas Gerais (UFMG), Brazil
Cleo Billa	Federal University of Rio Grande (FURG), Brazil
Cristiane Queixa Tilelli	Federal University of São João del-Rei (UFSJ), Brazil
Daniel Margulies	National Centre for Scientific Research (CNRS), France
Daniel de Castro Medeiros	Federal University of Minas Gerais (UFMG), Brazil
Dante Augusto Couto Barone	Federal University of Rio Grande do Sul (UFRGS), Brazil
Diego Hernán Peluffo-Ordóñez	Yachay Tech University, Ecuador
Diego Roberto Colombo Dias	Federal University of São João del-Rei (UFSJ), Brazil
Dimitris Kugiumtzis	Aristotle University of Thessaloniki, Greece
Eduardo Mazoni Andrade Marçal Mendes	Federal University of Minas Gerais (UFMG), Brazil
Erivelton Geraldo Nepomuceno	Federal University of São João del-Rei (UFSJ), Brazil
Flávio Afonso Gonçalves Mourão	Federal University of Minas Gerais (UFMG), Brazil
Fransciso Sotres Bayón	National Autonomous University of Mexico, Mexico

Gabriel Mindlin	Buenos Aires University, Argentina
Gabriela Castellano	State University of Campinas (UNICAMP), Brazil
Gloria Mercedes Diaz Cabrera	Metropolitan Technological Institute, Colombia
Guillermo Cecchi	IBM T.J. Watson Research Center, USA
Hu Danqing	Mayo Clinic, USA
Ives Cavalcante Passos	Federal University of Rio Grande do Sul (UFRGS), Brazil
Jaime Andres Riascos Salas	Federal University of Rio Grande do Sul (UFRGS), Brazil
Jasiara Carla de Oliveira	Federal University of São João del-Rei (UFSJ), Brazil
Jean Faber Ferreira de Abreu	Federal University of São Paulo (UNIFESP), Brazil
Jim Jones da Silveira Marciano	Federal University of São João del-Rei (UFSJ), Brazil
Jim Torresen	University of Oslo, Norway
Jose Donoso	Ruhr University Bochum, Germany
Juan David Martinez Vargas	Metropolitan Technological Institute, Colombia
Juan Verdejo-Román	University of Granada, Spain
Juliana Valencia-Aguirre	Metropolitan Technological Institute, Colombia
Laila Cristina Moreira Damázio	Federal University of São João del-Rei (UFSJ), Brazil
Leonardo Bonato Félix	Federal University of Viçosa (UFV), Brazil
Lubomir Kostal	Czech Academy of Science, Czech Republic
Leonardo Duque	Metropolitan Technological Institute, Colombia
Marcelo Pias	Federal University of Rio Grande (FURG), Brazil
Márcio Flávio Dutra Moraes	Federal University of Minas Gerais (UFMG), Brazil
Michela Chiappalone	Italian Institute of Technology, Italy
Patricio Orio	University of Valparaíso, Chile
Patrick Forcelli	Georgetown University, USA
Pedro Almeida	University of Lisboa, Portugal
Premsyl Jiruska	The Czech Academy of Sciences, Czech Republic
Radek Janca	Czech Technical University, Czech Republic
Reihold Scherer	University of Essex, UK
Rodrigo Alejandro Sierra Ordoñez	University of Szeged, Hungary
Salvador Dura-Bernal	SUNY Downstate, USA
Sen Cheng	Ruhr University Bochum, Germany
Sidarta Tollendal Gomes Ribeiro	Federal University of Rio Grande do Norte (UFRN), Brazil
Stiliyan Kalitzin	Foundation Epilepsy Institute in The Netherlands, The Netherlands
Thomas Walther	Ruhr University Bochum, Germany

Keynote Speakers

Diego Hernán Peluffo-Ordóñez	Yachay Tech University, Ecuador
Gabriela Castellano	State University of Campinas (UNICAMP), Brazil
Hector Julián Tejada Herrera	Federal University of Sergipe (UFS), Brazil
Ives Cavalcante Passos	Federal University of Rio Grande do Sul (UFRGS), Brazil
Jim Torresen	University of Oslo, Norway
Márcio Flávio Dutra Moraes	Federal University of Minas Gerais (UFMG), Brazil
Michela Chiappalone	Italian Institute of Technology, Italy
Sidarta Tollendal Gomes Ribeiro	Federal University of Rio Grande do Norte (UFRN), Brazil

Organization

Universidade Federal
de São João del-Rei

Laboratório Interdisciplinar de
Neuroengenharia e Neurociências

Support

Sponsors and Funding

Contents

Neural Signal Processing

Software and Hardware Implementations in Neuroscience

Brain-Computer Interfaces and Neurostimulation

Seizure Prediction

Artificial Intelligence, Machine Learning, and Related Topics

Application of Machine Learning Approaches to Identify New Anticonvulsant Compounds Active in the 6 Hz Seizure Model

S. Goicoechea[1,2] (ID), M. L. Sbaraglini[1], S. R. Chuguransky[1] (ID),
J. F. Morales[1], M. E. Ruiz[1] (ID), A. Talevi[1,2] (ID),
and C. L. Bellera[1,2(✉)] (ID)

[1] Laboratory of Bioactive Research and Development (LIDeB),
Department of Biological Sciences, Faculty of Exact Sciences,
University of La Plata (UNLP), La Plata, Buenos Aires, Argentina
{sofiagoicoechea, cbellera}@biol.unlp.edu.ar
[2] CCT La Plata, Consejo Nacional de Investigaciones Científicas y Técnicas
(CONICET), Buenos Aires, Argentina

Abstract. Epilepsy is the second most common chronic brain disorder, affecting 65 million people worldwide. According to the NIH's Epilepsy Therapy Screening Program, evaluation of potential new antiepileptic drug candidates begins with assessment of their protective effects in two acute seizure models in mice, the Maximal Electroshock Seizure test and the 6 Hz test. The latter elicits partial seizures through an electrical stimulus of 44 mA, at which many clinically established anti-seizure drugs do not suppress seizures. The inclusion of this "high-hurdle" acute seizure assay at the initial stage of the drug identification phase is intended to increase the probability that agents with improved efficacy will be detected. In this work, we have used machine learning approximations to develop *in silico* models capable of identifying novel anticonvulsant drugs with protective effects in the 6 Hz seizure model. Linear classifiers based on Dragon conformation-independent descriptors were generated through an in-house routine in R environment and validated through standard validation procedures. They were later combined through different ensemble learning schemes. The best ensemble comprised the 29 best-performing models combined using the MIN operator. With the objective of finding new drug repurposing opportunities (i.e. identifying second or further therapeutic indications, in our case anticonvulsant activity, in existing drugs), such model ensemble was applied in a virtual screening campaign of DrugBank and Sweetlead databases. 28 approved drugs were identified as potential protective agents in the 6 Hz model. The present study constitutes an example of the use of machine learning approximations to systematically guide drug repurposing projects.

Keywords: Machine learning · Ensemble learning · 6 Hz seizure model · Anticonvulsant drugs · Virtual screening · Epilepsy · Drug repurposing

---

Electronic supplementary material The online version of this chapter (https://doi.org/10.1007/978-3-030-36636-0_1) contains supplementary material, which is available to authorized users.

V. R. Cota et al. (Eds.): LAWCN 2019, CCIS 1068, pp. 3–19, 2019.
https://doi.org/10.1007/978-3-030-36636-0_1

1   Introduction

Epilepsy is the second most common chronic brain disorder characterized by recurrent and spontaneous seizures, that affect 65 million all ages people in the world [1]. Around thirty percent of epileptic patients do not respond to clinically established anticonvulsants, a condition known as refractory or intractable epilepsy [2].

Drug repositioning represents an interesting strategy to expedite the development of new medications [3]. This approach consists in searching second or further medical uses for experimental, approved, discontinued and shelved drugs. Computer-aided drug repurposing provides a rational framework to identify repurposing opportunities with minimal investment of time and resources [4].

The 6 Hz psychomotor seizure model of partial seizures in mice uses electrical stimulation by low-frequency (6 Hz) rectangular pulses of 0.2-ms duration delivered through corneal electrodes for 3 s [5], to induce seizures that are reminiscent of the psychomotor ones occurring in human limbic epilepsy. It is currently included in the initial phase of drug screening of the NIH's Epilepsy Therapy Screening Program (ETPS) [6].

This model has been able to identify drugs that are not active in conventional animal models, such as levetiracetam (which has a novel mechanism of action and is effective in treating a wide range of seizures including partial onset refractory epilepsy, a type of epilepsy usually difficult to control by drug therapy). It has been thus suggested as a screening tool to evaluate new antiepileptic drugs (AEDs) with potential activity against refractory seizures [7].

In this work, we have developed *in silico* models capable of discriminating active from inactive compounds in the 6 Hz model. Such models have been then applied in a virtual screening campaign oriented to find drug repurposing opportunities.

2   Methods

2.1   Data Set Compilation and Splitting

90 compounds evaluated in the 6 Hz seizure model were compiled from literature [8–42] and conformed a balanced dataset which includes 44 active compounds (>75% protection at doses ≤ 30 mg/kg) and 46 inactive compounds (no protection up to doses of 100 mg/kg). This dataset was later used to obtain training and test sets to calibrate and validate the models, respectively. It was curated using Standardizer Instant JCHEM v. 16.9.12.0. The molecular diversity of the dataset (both within and between the Active and Inactive classes) can be appreciated in the heatmaps of Fig. 1, which shows, for each pair of compounds in the dataset, the Tanimoto distances calculated using extended connectivity fingerprints with a maximum diameter of 4 (ECFP_4). Such heatmaps were built using Gitools v. 2.3.1 [43] and Tanimoto distances were calculated employing ScreenMD - Molecular Descriptor Screening v. 5.5.0.1. (ChemAxon 2011).

A)   B)   C)

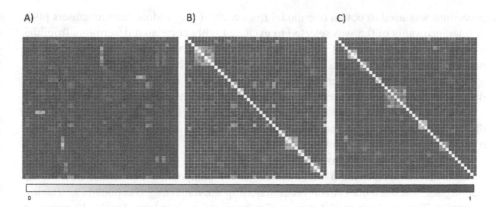

0   1

Fig. 1. Heatmaps of dissimilarity for the whole database and within each database category. (A) Active compounds vs. inactive compounds; (B) active compounds vs. active compounds; (C) inactive compounds vs. inactive compounds.

Following previous studies suggesting that rational sampling of the training and test sets lead to models of enhanced predictivity [44, 45] we chose to resort to a clustering approach to partition the dataset representatively. We used a combined hierarchical and non-hierarchical procedure [46]: the LibraryMCS v16.10.10.0 (ChemAxon 2016) hierarchical clustering approach based in the Maximum Common Substructure (MCS) was first applied, and the resulting clusters were then optimized using the k-means algorithm (Statistica 10 Cluster Analysis Module, Statsoft Inc. 2011). Such combined clustering procedure was performed in an independent manner for the Active and Inactive classes to obtain a balanced training set (30 active compounds and 30 inactive compounds). The remaining compounds were assigned to the test set (14 active and 16 inactive compounds). The molecular structures of the training and test set compounds are presented as Supplementary Material.

2.2 Descriptor Calculation and Modelling

Molecular descriptors are numerical variables that reflect different aspects of the molecular structure. The values of 3668 conformation-independent (0D–2D) descriptors were computed with Dragon 6.0 software. A random subspace approach [47, 48] was then used to explore the descriptor space: 1000 random subsets of 200 descriptors each were generated, and one model was trained from each subset. The random subspace approximation causes the models not to over-focus on features that display high explanatory power in the training set. It can also be useful when handling datasets that suffer from small sample size and large dimensionality (i.e. large feature space) (a quite frequent scenario in the drug discovery field) and when the feature space includes redundant features.

A binary variable associated to each dataset class (active and inactive compounds) was used as dependent variable. Such variable was assigned observed values of 1 for compounds within the Active class and observed values of 0 for compounds in the Inactive class. A semi-correlation approach using a Forward Stepwise feature selection procedure was used to obtain one model from each of the random feature subsets [49]. A tolerance value of 0.5 was selected to exclude highly correlated descriptors from the models. A minimum ratio of 10 between the number of training set examples and the number of descriptors was used in order to reduce the chances of overfitting.

An in-house script in R environment was used for all data analysis. The R package data table (https://cran.r-project.org/package=data.table) was used to handle datasets.

Standard validation approaches, including stratified Leave-Group-Out cross validation, randomization test and external validation, were applied to assess the models' robustness and predictive ability.

Regarding the Leave-Group-Out cross-validation, in each cross-validation round, random subsets comprising 5 active and 5 inactive compounds were removed from the training set, and the model was regenerated using the remaining compounds as training examples. The resulting model was used to predict the class label for the 10 removed compounds. The procedure was repeated 10 times, removing each of the training set compounds at least once. The results were informed as the average percentage of good classifications (accuracy) across the folds, and this was compared with the accuracy of the model for the original training set and also, as advised by Gramatica [50], with the No-Model error rate or risk (NOMER%), i.e. the error provided in absence of model.

In the case of randomization, the class label was randomized across the compounds in the training set. The training set with the randomized dependent variable was then used to train new models from the descriptor selection step. Such procedure was repeated 10 times within each descriptor subset and the average accuracy and the 95% confidence interval for the accuracy of the randomized models were calculated. It is expected that the randomized models will perform poorly compared to the real ones.

At last, the predictivity of each individual model was assessed through external validation, using the 30-compound test set. A diversity of statistical parameters commonly used to assess the performance of classificatory models [50, 51] were estimated for both the training and test sets: sensitivity (Se, i.e. true positive rate), specificity (Sp, i.e. true negative rate), accuracy (Acc. overall percentage of good classifications), positive and negative predictivity and the F-measure.

2.3 Ensemble Learning

An ensemble of classifiers is a set of classifiers whose individual decisions are combined in some way (e.g. through voting, or averaging their scores) to classify new examples; interestingly, ensembles are often much more accurate and provide better generalization than the individual classifiers [47, 52]. There are different reasons that explain the enhanced performance and predictivity of model ensembles [52]. The first is statistical: a learning algorithm can be viewed as a search in a hypothesis space to identify the best hypothesis in it. The learning algorithm can find several different hypotheses that all give the same or similar accuracy on the training data; by constructing an ensemble out of all (or some) of these accurate classifiers, the algorithm can average their votes or score and reduce the risk of choosing the wrong one. A second reason is computational: many learning algorithms work by performing some form of local search that might get stuck in local optima. An ensemble built by running the local search from several different starting points provides a better approximation to the true (unknown) function than any of the individual classifiers. There are many methods for constructing ensembles, but essentially they comprise enumerating and weighting all possible hypotheses, manipulating the training examples (as in bagging), manipulating the input features (as in the already described random subspace approach), manipulating the output targets (as in boosting) and injecting randomness.

As described below, two retrospective virtual screening campaigns were used to evaluate the performance of individual models and model ensembles. The first retrospective experiment enabled evaluating the performance of individual models and bestow the basis to decide which individual classifiers would be selectively combined in the model ensemble and what operator would be used to combine them. The second retrospective virtual screening was used to validate the performance of the chosen model ensemble.

The best individual classifiers were selected and combined using the area under the ROC curve metric (AUCROC) in the first retrospective virtual screening experiment as criterion of performance. Systematic combinations of the 2–100 best performing classifiers were analyzed. Four combination schemes were applied to obtain a combined score (Fig. 3): MIN operator; Average Score; Average Ranking and Average Voting. AUCROCs were obtained with the pROC package [53]; the DeLong method was used to obtain 95% confidence intervals. BEDROC and RIE (1%) were also computed [54]. For that purpose, we have resorted to the R package enrichvs (enrichment assessment of virtual screening approaches) [55] and the online tool ROCKER [56].

2.4 Retrospective Virtual Screening

Truchon and Bayly [54] demonstrated that the AUCROC metric is dependent on the ratio of actives/inactives, and its standard deviation converges to a constant value when small yield of actives (Ya) of the screened library are used (Ya below 0.05 seems to provide more robust results). A reasonably small Ya also ensures that the saturation effect is constant or absent. A high number of decoys (1000 or higher) and a small Ya contribute to a controlled statistical behaviour. Consequently, we performed retrospective virtual screening campaigns to better estimate the enrichment provided by the individual models and the model ensembles. For this, we have dispersed 14 active compounds from the test set among a large number of paired decoys (putative inactive compounds) provided by the enhanced Directory Useful Decoys (DUD-E) [57]. The first library subjected to retrospective virtual screening consisted in the 14 active compounds with 700 presumed inactive ones (decoys). This library has been denominated DUD-E A library. The second library subjected to retrospective virtual screening is comprised by the 14 active compounds plus 3500 decoys and was named DUD-E B library. DUD-E A was used to estimate the performance of the individual models in a true virtual screening experiment and to train the ensemble (i.e. to decide which individual models would be included and how they would be combined). DUD-E B was only used to validate the performance of the best model ensemble.

2.5   Building Positive Predictive Value Surfaces and Choosing an Adequate Score Threshold Value

A practical concern when implementing *in silico* screening campaigns is to predict the actual probability that a hit will confirm its predicted activity when submitted to experimental testing (Positive Predictive Value, PPV). Estimation of such probability is however precluded due to its dependency on the Ya of the screened library, which is not known *a priori* (Eq. 1):

$$PPV = \frac{SeYa}{SeYa + (1 - Sp)(1 - Ya)} \tag{1}$$

Equation (1) was applied to build PPV surfaces. In order to choose an optimal score cutoff value to select predicted hits in prospective virtual screening experiments, 3D plots illustrating the interplay between PPV, the Se/Sp ratio and Ya were built for each individual model and for each model ensemble [58]. Using the DUD-E A and DUD-E B databases, Se and Sp were computed in all the range of possible cutoff score values. Since controlled statistical behavior is observed for database sizes of about 1000 compounds or more and Ya below 0.05, we can reasonably assume that the ROC curve and derived metrics will be similar when applying the models to classify other large chemical databases with low Ya. Taking into consideration that in real virtual screening applications Ya is ignored a priori but invariably low, Ya was varied between 0.001 and 0.010. The R package plotly (https://cran.r-project.org/package=plotly) was used to obtain all the PPV graphs. Visual analysis of the resulting PPV surfaces allowed us to select a score threshold value with a desired range of PPV.

2.6   Virtual Screening

Based on visual inspections of the resulting of PPV surface graphs, the best model ensemble was used in a prospective virtual screening application. We used a 29-model ensemble using the MIN operator to combine the scores of the individual models, choosing 0.3505 as score threshold. Such threshold corresponds to a Se/Sp ratio of 0.793. It was checked that every hit belonged to the applicability domain of the ensemble model which assigned the minimum score. The leverage approach was used to assess if a hit belongs to the applicability domain, using 3d/n as cutoff value, where d is the number of descriptors in the correspondent model and n is the number of compounds in the training set.

We used the 29-model ensemble to screen two databases: (a) DrugBank 5.0.0, an online database containing extensive information about the US Food and Drug Administration (FDA) approved, experimental, nutraceutical, illicit and investigational drugs [59]; (b) Sweetlead, a curated database of drugs approved by other international regulatory agencies, compounds isolated from traditional medicinal herbs, and regulated chemicals [60]. Both databases were curated using Standardizer version 16.9.12.0 (ChemAxon 2016). We applied the following actions to generate homogeneous representations of the molecular structure for the virtual screen: (1) Strip salts; (2) Remove Solvents; (3) Clear Stereo; (4) Remove Absolute Stereo; (5) Aromatize; (6) Neutralize;

(7) Add Explicit Hydrogens; and (8) Clean 2D. Additionally, duplicated structures were removed using Instant JCHEM v.17.2.6.0.

The general protocol used for building and validating our individual models and model ensembles has been included in Fig. 2.

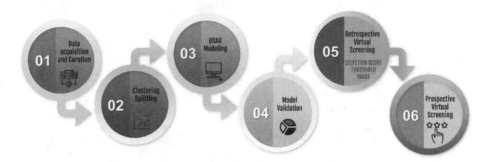

Fig. 2. Computational flowchart for cheminformatics analysis using ensemble learning

3   Results

Ligand-Based Model Development, Validation and Virtual Screening

We resorted to a computationally inexpensive (conformation-independent) ligand-based approach to obtain 1000 individual linear classifiers by applying a random subspace approximation. The individual models were externally validated by using an independent test set and, for a more realistic performance assessment, by retrospective screening of pilot databases, where a small proportion of known active compounds was dispersed among a high number of decoys (putative inactive compounds). Table 1 shows the enrichment metrics of the five individual classifiers that displayed the best performance on the training set, test set and DUD-E A library.

Table 1. Values of the AUCROC metric for the best five individual models.

Model	Training set	Test set	DUDE-A	DUDE-B
191	**0.790 (± 0.0570)**	**0.690 (± 0.100)**	**0.855 (± 0.0426)**	**0.829 (± 0.0460)**
208	0.886 (± 0.0405)	0.884 (± 0.0598)	0.844 (± 0.0397)	0.823 (± 0.0434)
586	0.787 (± 0.0580)	0.862 (± 0.0694)	0.837 (± 0.0521)	0.830 (± 0.0518)
051	0.851 (± 0.0493)	0.871 (± 0.0694)	0.836 (± 0.0507)	0.818 (± 0.0538)
902	0.770 (± 0.0405)	0.786 (± 0.0841)	0.835 (± 0.0372)	0.801 (± 0.0411)

The best individual model included the following features:

Model 191: **Class** = 0.46645 - 0.71571 * **B02[O-O]** - 0.24724 * **CATS2D_00_PP** + 0.02305 * **SM13_EA (dm)**

$F_{(3,56)}$ = 7.821188 $p < 0.0002$

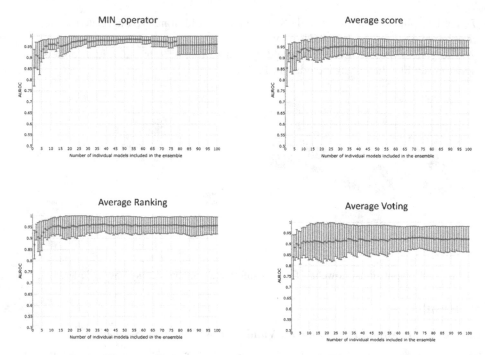

Fig. 3. AUCROC metric vs. the number of combined models in the DUDE-A database (a) MIN operator; (B) Average score; (C) Average ranking; (D) Average voting.

Dragon's nomenclature for the molecular descriptors has been kept in the previous expression. **B02[O-O]** represents the presence/absence of an O-O pair at topological distance 2; **CATS2D_00_PP** refers to the CATS (Chemically Advanced Template Search) 2D Positive-Positive at lag 00; and **SM13_EA (dm)** corresponds to the spectral moment of order 13 from edge adjacency matrix, weighted by dipole moment.

Whereas the performance of the best individual classifiers was acceptable, we resorted to ensemble learning to obtain meta-classifiers with improved accuracy, enhanced enrichment parameters and a more robust behavior. The expectations on the model combination approach were confirmed statistically, showing clear statistical differences in comparison to the best individual model. Figure 3 shows the influence of the number of models included in the ensemble on the AUCROC metric.

The MIN, RANKING and AVERAGE combination schemes exhibited similar classificatory ability and enrichment behavior on the test set, DUDE-A and DUDE-B libraries.

We chose to move to the prospective virtual screening experiment using the ensemble obtained by combining the 29 best-performing individual models using the MIN operator, which was statistically superior to the best individual model on DUDE-A ($p < 0.01$) and DUDE-B ($p < 0.05$) and provided better results than other combination schemes in terms of the deviation associated to the estimated enrichment parameters. Table 2 shows the enrichment metrics for the 29-model ensembles obtained by different combination schemes.

Table 2. Values of metrics for the 29-model ensemble

29-model ensemble	Training set		DUDE-A			DUDE-B		
	AUCROC	BEDROC	AUCROC	BEDROC	$RIE_{1\%}$	AUCROC	BEDROC	$RIE_{1\%}$
MIN-operator	**0.951**	**0.999**	**0.983**	**0.841**	**36.22**	**0.975**	**0.752**	**64.43**
Average score	0.942	0.998	0.951	0.627	14.49	0.946	0.646	35.80
Average ranking	0.940	0.998	0.959	0.721	28.98	0.938	0.664	50.11
Average voting	0.941	0.998	0.916	0.572	14.49	0.887	0.525	28.64

We decided to optimize the score cutoff value by resorting to analysis of PPV surfaces [57]. With the help of these surfaces, the evolution of the most relevant metric for our purposes, the PPV value, can be visually (or, eventually, mathematically) optimized as a function of the Se/Sp ratio across a range of Ya values. We built such surfaces using the data from the retrospective screening of DUDE-A. The strongest assumption of our approach is that the Se/Sp value observed for a given score during this retrospective screening experiment will hold when screening other databases (e.g., the ones screened in prospective virtual screening applications). This is of course not necessarily true. However, since the AUCROC values obtained for the DUD-E libraries are unequivocally high (always above 0.9 for the individual models and very close to the perfect value of 1 for the ensembles) while on the other hand the DUD-E database Ya ratio (quite below 0.05) and size (>1000 compounds) speak of a controlled statistical behavior, we believe it is a reasonable assumption in the present setting.

Using the PPV surface, we chose 0.35 as score threshold to be used in our virtual screening of DrugBank and Sweetlead; such score is associated to a Se/Sp ratio of 0.793 for the 29-model ensemble based on the MIN operator and to PPV value $\geq 20\%$ for a Ya of 0.01 (Fig. 4). This means that if Ya in the real virtual screen was 0.01, we would have to submit about five predicted hits to experimental testing in order to find one confirmed hit. The virtual screen using the previous score cutoff value resulted in 57 hits, with 28 of them corresponding to approved drugs (Table 3 shows the top-scoring hits, their original indication, their score and predicted PPV value).

It should be noted that, whereas almost all the hits (with the exception of lacosamide, which is an already known anticonvulsant, and the benzodiazepine flurazepam) constitute valid options as starting points (novel scaffolds) to develop new AEDs though hit-to-lead and lead optimization strategies, not all of them are identically attractive as repurposing prospects, especially considering that epilepsy is a chronic condition that requires chronic medication. When considering a repurposing candidate, one should take into account its original indication (is it compatible with the intended new one?) and also the dose compatibility between the previous and the new indication (which depends on the effective concentrations required in each case, but also possibly on pharmacokinetic considerations: i.e. the drug levels reached in different organs may vary) [61, 62]. Systemic medications are more favorable as repurposing candidates for

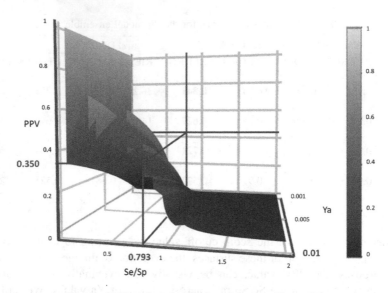

Fig. 4. PPV surface for the best 29-ensemble model.

systemic ailments. New therapeutic indications requiring equal or lower doses than the ones used for the original indication represent a more straightforward repurposing opportunity.

For instance, anticancer agents in Table 3 (sonidegib, doxifluridine) can be regarded as poor repurposing candidates due to their unfavorable safety profile (for instance, common side effects include muscle spasms, hair loss, fatigue, abdominal pain, nausea, headache, and weight loss).

Table 3. Top-scoring hits, their original indication, their score and predicted PPV value

Name	MIN Score	PPV% (Ya=0.01)	Structure	Original indication
Flibanserin	0.6185	33.43		Hypoactive Sexual Desire Disorder in Women
Sonidegib	0.5601	50.10		Antineoplastic Agent

(continued)

Table 3. *(continued)*

Flurazepam	0.4952	55.66		Hypnotic

Lacosamide	0.4683	45.56		Anticonvulsant

Etidocaine	0.4537	50.10		Local anesthetic

Leflunomide	0.4142	47.48		Disease-modifying antirheumatic drug

Bupivacaine	0.3907	42.96		Local anesthetic or analgesia for surgery

Doxifluridine	0.3857	39.23		Treatment of stomach cancer

(continued)

Table 3. *(continued)*

Floxuridine	0.3788	39.24		Antineoplastic antimetabolite
Triflupromazine	0.3783	39.23		Management of psychoses. Also to control nausea and vomiting

4   Conclusions

We have implemented a machine learning study to build ligand-based linear models capable of discriminating between active and inactive anticonvulsant drugs in the 6 Hz seizure test, one of the primary in vivo screens of ETSP. Using a random subspace strategy and Dragon conformation-independent models, we have obtained satisfactory individual classifiers, whose statistical behavior has though been improved by ensemble learning. The best performing ensemble was used in a prospective virtual screening experiment on DrugBank and Sweetlead databases, leading to 29 approved hits which are straightforward drug repurposing candidates. We will experimentally examine their activity in the 6 Hz model in the near future.

It should be highlighted that, whereas very valuable as a primary screen for AEDs with distinctive pharmacological profile, such as levetiracetam or brivaracetam, the 6 Hz models is still an acute seizure model with adequate throughput, but it is not a model of epilepsy, and it provides limited, insufficient evidence for a translational analysis. Animal models of seizure should be complemented with (more complex and low-throughput) animal models of epilepsy to grasp a better understanding of the perspective of a drug candidate as a treatment for human epilepsy, as suggested by the EPTS itself [6].

Virtual screening and computer-guided drug repurposing are excellent strategies to expedite the development of innovative medications, by exploiting previous knowledge on the pharmacological, toxicological and pharmacokinetic data of known drugs, and also by rescuing abandoned/shelved and discontinued drugs and drug candidates.

Acknowledgments. The authors would like to thank the following public and non-profit organisations: National University of La Plata (UNLP) and Argentinean National Council of Science and Technological Research (CONICET).

Funding. Support was received from the National University of La Plata (UNLP) [grant X729].

References

1. World Health Organization: Fact Sheet Epilepsy. https://www.who.int/news-room/fact-sheets/detail/epilepsy
2. Xia, L., Ou, S., Pan, S.: Initial response to antiepileptic drugs in patients with newly diagnosed epilepsy as a predictor of long-term outcome. Front. Neurol. **8**, 658 (2017). https://doi.org/10.3389/fneur.2017.00658
3. Corsello, S.M., et al.: The Drug Repurposing Hub: a next-generation drug library and information resource. Nat. Med. **23**, 405–408 (2017). https://doi.org/10.1038/nm.4306
4. Talevi, A.: Drug repositioning: current approaches and their implications in the precision medicine era. Expert. Rev. Precis. Med. Drug Dev. **3**, 49–61 (2018). https://doi.org/10.1080/23808993.2018.1424535
5. Barton, M.E., Klein, B.D., Wolf, H.H., White, H.S.: Pharmacological characterization of the 6 Hz psychomotor seizure model of partial epilepsy. Epilepsy Res. **47**, 217–227 (2001). https://doi.org/10.1016/S0920-1211(01)00302-3
6. Löscher, W.: Critical review of current animal models of seizures and epilepsy used in the discovery and development of new antiepileptic drugs. Seizure **20**(5), 359–368 (2011). https://doi.org/10.1016/j.seizure.2011.01.003
7. Vyskovsky, R., Schwarz, D., Janousova, E., Kasparek, T.: Random subspace ensemble artificial neural networks for first-episode Schizophrenia classification. In: Proceedings of the 2016 Federated Conference on Computer Science and Information Systems (Gdansk: FedCSIS), pp. 317–321 (2016). https://doi.org/10.15439/2016f333
8. Kamiński, K., Wiklik, B., Obniska, J.: Synthesis and anticonvulsant activity of new N-phenyl-2-(4-phenylpiperazin-1-yl) acetamide derivatives. Med. Chem. Res. **24**(7), 3047–3061 (2015). https://doi.org/10.1007/s00044-015-1360-6
9. Dawidowski, M., Lewandowski, W., Turło, J.: Synthesis of new perhydropyrrolo [1, 2-a] pyrazine derivatives and their evaluation in animal models of epilepsy. Molecules **19**(10), 15955–15981 (2014). https://doi.org/10.3390/molecules191015955
10. Coleman, N., et al.: The riluzole derivative 2-amino-6-trifluoromethylthio-benzothiazole (SKA-19), a mixed K_{Ca}^2 activator and Na_V blocker, is a potent novel anticonvulsant. Neurotherapeutics **12**(1), 234–249 (2015). https://doi.org/10.1007/s13311-014-0305-y
11. Obniska, J., Chlebek, I., Kamiński, K., Bojarski, A.J., Satała, G.: Synthesis, anticonvulsant activity and 5-HT1A/5-HT7 receptors affinity of 1-[(4-arylpiperazin-1-yl)-propyl]-succini-mides. Pharmacol. Rep. **64**(2), 326–335 (2012)
12. Xian-Qing, D., Ming-Xia, S., Guo-Hua, G., Shi-Ben, W., Zhe-Shan, Q.: Synthesis and anticonvulsant evaluation of some new 6-(substituted-phenyl) thiazolo [3, 2-b][1, 2, 4]triazole derivatives in mice. Iran. J. Pharm. Res. **13**(2), 459–469 (2014)
13. Byrtus, H., Obniska, J., Czopek, A., Kamiński, K., Pawłowski, M.: Synthesis and anticonvulsant activity of new N-Mannich bases derived from 5-cyclopropyl-5-phenyl- and 5-cyclopropyl-5-(4-chlorophenyl)-imidazolidine-2, 4-diones. Bioorg. Med. Chem. **19**(20), 6149–6156 (2011). https://doi.org/10.1016/j.bmc.2011.08.017

14. Florek-Luszczki, M., Wlaz, A., Luszczki, J.J.: Interactions of levetiracetam with carbamazepine, phenytoin, topiramate and vigabatrin in the mouse 6 Hz psychomotor seizure model – A type II isobolographic analysis. Eur. J. Pharmacol. **723**, 410–418 (2014). https://doi.org/10.1016/j.ejphar.2013.10.063

15. Dawidowski, M., Turło, M.: Multicomponent synthesis and anticonvulsant activity of monocyclic 2, 6-diketopiperazine derivatives. Med. Chem. Res. **23**(4), 2007–2018 (2014). https://doi.org/10.1007/s00044-013-0800-4

16. Ugale, V.G., Bari, S.B.: Structural exploration of quinazolin-4 (3H)-ones as anticonvulsants: rational design, synthesis, pharmacological evaluation, and molecular docking studies. Arch. Pharm. **349**(11), 864–880 (2016). https://doi.org/10.1002/ardp.201600218

17. Tomaciello, F., Leclercq, K., Kaminski, R.M.: Resveratrol lacks protective activity against acute seizures in mouse models. Neurosci. Lett. **632**, 199–203 (2016). https://doi.org/10.1016/j.neulet.2016.09.002

18. Sałat, K., et al.: Novel, highly potent and in vivo active inhibitor of GABA transporter subtype 1 with anticonvulsant, anxiolytic, antidepressant and antinociceptive properties. Neuropharmacol. **113**(Pt A), 331–342 (2017). https://doi.org/10.1016/j.neuropharm.2016.10.019

19. Gunia-Krzyżak, A., et al.: Structure-anticonvulsant activity studies in the group of (E)-N-cinnamoyl aminoalkanols derivatives monosubstituted in phenyl ring with 4-Cl, 4-CH$_3$ or 2-CH$_3$. Bioorg. Med. Chem. **25**(2), 471–482 (2017). https://doi.org/10.1016/j.bmc.2016.11.014

20. Zolkowska, D., Dhir, A., Krishnan, K., Covey, D.F., Rogawski, M.A.: Anticonvulsant potencies of the enantiomers of the neurosteroids androsterone and etiocholanolone exceed those of the natural forms. Psychopharmacol. (Berl). **231**(17), 3325–3332 (2014). https://doi.org/10.1007/s00213-014-3546-x

21. Shekh-Ahmad, T., et al.: Enantioselective pharmacodynamic and pharmacokinetic analysis of two chiral CNS-active carbamate derivatives of valproic acid. Epilepsia **55**(12), 1944–1952 (2014). https://doi.org/10.1111/epi.12857

22. Kamiński, K., Wiklik, B., Obniska, J.: Synthesis, anticonvulsant properties, and SAR analysis of differently substituted pyrrolidine-2, 5-diones and piperidine-2, 6-diones. Arch. Pharm. (Weinheim) **347**(11), 840–852 (2014). https://doi.org/10.1002/ardp.201400179

23. Orellana-Paucar, A.M., et al.: Insights from zebrafish and mouse models on the activity and safety of ar-turmerone as a potential drug candidate for the treatment of epilepsy. PLoS ONE **8**(12), e81634 (2013). https://doi.org/10.1371/journal.pone.0081634

24. Nieoczym, D., Socała, K., Jedziniak, P., Olejnik, M., Wlaź, P.: Effect of sildenafil, a selective phosphodiesterase 5 inhibitor, on the anticonvulsant action of some antiepileptic drugs in the mouse 6-Hz psychomotor seizure model. Prog. Neuropsychopharmacol. Biol. Psychiatry **47**, 104–110 (2012). https://doi.org/10.1016/j.pnpbp.2013.08.009

25. Dawidowski, M., Wilczek, M., Kubica, K., Skolmowski, M., Turło, J.: Structure-activity relationships of the aromatic site in novel anticonvulsant pyrrolo [1, 2-a]pyrazine derivatives. Bioorg. Med. Chem. Lett. **23**(22), 6106–6110 (2013). https://doi.org/10.1016/j.bmcl.2013.09.022

26. Shaikh, M.F., Tan, K.N., Borges, K.: Anticonvulsant screening of luteolin in four mouse seizure models. Neurosci. Lett. **550**, 195–199 (2013). https://doi.org/10.1016/j.neulet.2013.06.065

27. Buenafe, O.E., et al.: Tanshinone IIA exhibits anticonvulsant activity in zebrafish and mouse seizure models. ACS. Chem. Neurosci. **4**(11), 1479–1487 (2013). https://doi.org/10.1021/cn400140e

28. Kumar, D., Kumar Sharma, V., Kumar, R., Singh, T., Singh, H., Singh, A.D., Roy, R.K.: Design, synthesis and anticonvulsant activity of some new 5, 7-dibromoisatin semicarbazone derivatives. EXCLI J. **12**, 628–640 (2013)

29. Wlaz, A., Kondrat-Wrobel, M.W., Zaluska, K., Kochman, E., Rekas, A.R., Luszczki, J.J.: Synergistic interaction of levetiracetam with gabapentin in the mouse 6 Hz psychomotor seizure model – A type II isobolographic analysis. Curr. Issues Pharm. Med. Sci. **28**(3), 204–207 (2015). https://doi.org/10.1515/cipms-2015-0073

30. Shandra, A., Shandra, P., Kaschenko, O., Matagne, A., Stöhr, T.: Synergism of lacosamide with established antiepileptic drugs in the 6-Hz seizure model in mice. Epilepsia **54**(7), 1167–1175 (2013). https://doi.org/10.1111/epi.12237

31. Ahsan, M.J., Khalilullah, H., Yasmin, S., Singh Jadav, S., Stables, J.P.: Synthesis and anticonvulsant evaluation of 2-(substituted benzylidene/ethylidene)-N-(substituted phenyl) hydrazinecarboxamide analogues. Med. Chem. Res. **22**(6), 2746–2754 (2013). https://doi.org/10.1007/s00044-012-0271-z

32. Tripathi, L., Kumar, P.: Augmentation of GABAergic neurotransmission by novel N-(substituted)-2-[4-(substituted) benzylidene] hydrazinecarbothioamides—a potential anticonvulsant approach. Eur. J. Med. Chem. **64**, 477–487 (2013). https://doi.org/10.1016/j.ejmech.2013.04.019

33. Ulloora, S., Shabaraya, R., Ranganathan, R., Adhikari, A.V.: Synthesis, anticonvulsant and anti-inflammatory studies of new 1, 4-dihydropyridin-4-yl-phenoxyacetohydrazones. Eur. J. Med. Chem. **70**, 341–349 (2013). https://doi.org/10.1016/j.ejmech.2013.10.010

34. Zuliani, V., Rivara, M.: In vivo screening of diarylimidazoles as anticonvulsant agents. Med. Chem. Res. **21**(11), 3428–3434 (2011). https://doi.org/10.1007/s00044-011-9869-9

35. Kumar, P., Shrivastava, B., Pandeya, S.M., Tripathi, L., Stables, J.P.: Design, synthesis, and anticonvulsant evaluation of some novel 1, 3 benzothiazol-2-yl hydrazones/acetohydrazones. Med. Chem. Res. **21**(9), 2428–2442 (2012). https://doi.org/10.1007/s00044-011-9768-0

36. Hebeisen, S., et al.: Eslicarbazepine and the enhancement of slow inactivation of voltage-gated sodium channels: a comparison with carbamazepine, oxcarbazepine and lacosamide. Neuropharmacology **89**, 122–1235 (2015). https://doi.org/10.1016/j.neuropharm.2014.09.008

37. Ahsan, M.J., Khalilullah, H., Stables, J.P., Govindasamy, J.: Synthesis and anticonvulsant activity of 3a, 4-dihydro-3H-indeno [1, 2-c] pyrazole-2-carboxamide/carbothioamide analogues. J. Enzyme Inhib. Med. Chem. **28**(3), 644–650 (2013). https://doi.org/10.3109/14756366.2012.663364

38. Tosh, D.K., et al.: Structural sweet spot for A1 adenosine receptor activation by truncated (N)-methanocarba nucleosides: receptor docking and potent anticonvulsant activity. J. Med. Chem. **55**(18), 8075–8090 (2012)

39. Mishra, R.K., Baker, M.T.: *Ortho* Substituent effects on the anticonvulsant properties of 4-hydroxy-trifluoroethyl phenols. Bioorg. Med. Chem. Lett. **22**(17), 5608–5611 (2012). https://doi.org/10.1016/j.bmcl.2012.07.001

40. Wang, D.D., Englot, D.J., Garcia, P.A., Lawton, M.T., Young, W.L.: Minocycline and tetracycline-class antibiotics are protective against partial seizures in vivo. Epilepsy Behav. **24**(3), 314–318 (2012). https://doi.org/10.1016/j.yebeh.2012.03.035

41. Dawidowski, M., Herold, F., Chodkowski, A., Kleps, J.: Synthesis and anticonvulsant activity of novel 2, 6-diketopiperazine derivatives. Part 2: Perhydropyrido [1, 2-a] pyrazines. Eur. J. Med. Chem. **48**, 347–353 (2012). https://doi.org/10.1016/j.ejmech.2011.11.032

42. Gasior, M., Socała, K., Nieoczym, D., Wlaź, P.: Clavulanic acid does not affect convulsions in acute seizure tests in mice. J. Neural. Transm. **119**(1), 1–6 (2012). https://doi.org/10.1007/s00702-011-0662-1

43. Perez-Llamas, C., Lopez-Bigas, N.: Gitools: analysis and visualisation of genomic data using interactive heat-maps. PLoS ONE **6**, e19541 (2011). https://doi.org/10.1371/journal.pone.0019541
44. Golbraikh, A., Shen, M., Xiao, Z., Xiao, Y.D., Lee, K.H., Tropsha, A.: Rational selection of training and test sets for the development of validated QSAR models. J. Comput. Aided Mol. Des. **17**, 241–253 (2003). https://doi.org/10.1023/A:1025386326946
45. Martin, T.M., et al.: Does rational selection of training and test sets improve the outcome of QSAR modeling? J. Chem. Inf. Model. **52**, 2570–2578 (2012). https://doi.org/10.1021/ci300338w
46. Everitt, B.S., Landau, S., Leese, M., Stahl, D.: Cluster Analysis, 5th edn. Wiley, West Sussex (2011)
47. El Habib Daho, M., Chikh, M.A.: Combining bootstrapping samples, random subspaces and random forests to build classifiers. J. Med. Imaging Health Inf. **5**, 539–544 (2015). https://doi.org/10.1166/jmihi.2015.1423
48. Yu, G., Zhang, G., Domeniconi, C., Yu, Z., You, J.: Semi-supervised classification based on random subspace dimensionality reduction. Pattern Recogn. **45**, 1119–1135 (2012). https://doi.org/10.1016/j.patcog.2011.08.024
49. Toropova, A.P., Toropov, A.A.: CORAL: binary classifications (active/inactive) for drug-induced liver injury. Toxicol. Lett. **268**, 51–57 (2017). https://doi.org/10.1016/j.toxlet.2017.01.011
50. Gramatica, P.: On the development and validation of QSAR models. Methods Mol. Biol. **930**, 499–526 (2013). https://doi.org/10.1007/978-1-62703-059-5_21
51. Roy, K., Mitra, I.: On various metrics used for validation of predictive QSAR models with applications in virtual screening and focused library design. Comb. Chem. High Throughput Screen. **14**(6), 450–474 (2011). https://doi.org/10.2174/138620711795767893
52. Dietterich, T.G.: Ensemble methods in machine learning. In: Kittler, J., Roli, F. (eds.) MCS 2000. LNCS, vol. 1857, pp. 1–15. Springer, Heidelberg (2000). https://doi.org/10.1007/3-540-45014-9_1
53. Robin, X., et al.: pROC: an open-source package for R and S + to analyze and compare ROC curves. BMC Bioinf. **12**, 77 (2011). https://doi.org/10.1186/1471-2105-12-77
54. Truchon, J.F., Bayly, C.L.: Evaluating virtual screening methods: good and bad metrics for the "early recognition" problem. J. Chem. Inf. Model. **47**, 488–508 (2007). https://doi.org/10.1021/ci600426e
55. Yabuuchi, H., et al.: Analysis of multiple compound–protein interactions reveals novel bioactive molecules. Mol. Syst. Biol. **7**, 472, 1–12 (2011). https://doi.org/10.1038/msb.2011.5
56. Lätti, S., Niinivehmas, S., Pentikäinen, O.T.: Rocker: open source, easy-to-use tool for AUC and enrichment calculations and ROC visualization. J. Cheminformatics **8**(1), 45 (2016). https://doi.org/10.1186/s13321-016-0158-y
57. Mysinger, M.M., Carchia, M., Irwin, J.J., Shoichet, B.K.: Directory of useful decoys, enhanced (DUD-E): better ligands and decoys for better benchmarking. J. Med. Chem. **55**(14), 6582–6594 (2012). https://doi.org/10.1021/jm300687e
58. Alberca, L.N., et al.: Cascade ligand-and structure-based virtual screening to identify new trypanocidal compounds inhibiting putrescine uptake. Front. Cell. Infect. Microbiol. **8**, 173 (2018). https://doi.org/10.3389/fcimb.2018.00173
59. Law, V., et al.: DrugBank 4.0: shedding new light on drug metabolism. Nucleic Acids Res. **42**, D1091–D1097 (2014). https://doi.org/10.1093/nar/gkt1068
60. Novick, P.A., Ortiz, O.F., Poelman, J., Abdulhay, A.Y., Pande, V.S.: SWEETLEAD: an in silico database of approved drugs, regulated chemicals, and herbal isolates for computer-aided drug discovery. PLoS ONE **8**(11), e79568 (2013). https://doi.org/10.1371/journal.pone.0079568

61. Talevi, A., Carrillo, C., Comini, M.: The thiol-polyamine metabolism of *Trypanosoma cruzi*: molecular targets and drug repurposing strategies. Curr. Med. Chem. **26** (2019). https://doi.org/10.2174/0929867325666180926151059

62. Oprea, T.I., Overington, J.P.: Computational and practical aspects of drug repositioning. Assay Drug Dev. Technol. **13**, 299–306 (2015). https://doi.org/10.1089/adt.2015.29011. tiodrrr

Motor Learning and Machine Learning: Predicting the Amount of Sessions to Learn the Tracing Task

Eduardo Dorneles Ferreira de Souza[1], Moisés Rocha dos Santos[2] (ID),
Lucas Cléopas Costa da Silva[1], Alexandre César Muniz de Oliveira[1],
Areolino de Almeida Neto[1], and Paulo Rogério de Almeida Ribeiro[1(✉)] (ID)

[1] Federal University of Maranhão, Av. dos Portugueses, 1966 Bacanga, São Luís,
Maranhão, Brazil
eduardo.dorneles.fs@gmail.com, lcleopark99@gmail.com
{alexandre.cesar,areolino.neto}@ufma.br, paulo.ribeiro@ecp.ufma.br
[2] Instituto de Ciências Matemáticas e de Computação, University of São Paulo,
São Carlos, SP, Brazil
mmrsantos@usp.br

Abstract. Motor activities are the main way of interacting with the world. Therefore, loss of ability to perform some of these activities, e.g. as a result of a neurological disease, is a serious injury to the individual. The present work aims to propose an approach to estimate the number of sessions required to learn a motor task. In the literature, there are many works on motor learning, mostly looking for ways to decrease the time of skill acquisition or motor rehabilitation. However, few works concentrate on trying to estimate the training time needed to achieve certain motor performance. In the experiment, three sessions - one session per day - were performed for each participant, whose purpose was to predict in which tracing task session the participant would reach a certain error based on their profile and initial performance. The classification models were: Algorithm K-Neighbors Nearer (KNN), Neural Network Multi Layer Perceptron (MLP), Decision Tree (AD) and Support Vector Machine (SVM). They were compared using three metrics, namely: Accuracy, F1-Score and Cohen Kappa coefficient. MLP, SVM and AD, had similar results for Accuracy and Cohen Kappa coefficient, but better than KNN, whereas for the F1-Score MPL performed better than all. This work showed the possibility of estimating the number of sessions to achieve a certain performance using prediction algorithms. This finding suggests that a similar approach may be used to estimate the amount of training a patient requires to rehabilitate.

Keywords: Motor skill learning · Machine learning · Tracing task

1 Introduction

A considerable part of our daily lives is dedicated to learn new motor skill such as walking, writing, driving, practicing sports, and so on. Motor tasks are the

© Springer Nature Switzerland AG 2019
V. R. Cota et al. (Eds.): LAWCN 2019, CCIS 1068, pp. 20–29, 2019.
https://doi.org/10.1007/978-3-030-36636-0_2

main way to interact with the world that surround us. For this reason, losing the ability to perform any kind of these motor tasks because of a neurological disease is a serious loss to an individual [10].

When a subject is damaged by a neurological disease, he or she must acquire a new motor skill that may activate the muscles to accomplish a motor task with better performance [6]. However, the training sessions might require days, months, or even years - depending on the task complexity and the subject damage - to achieve a desirable performance.

Even though there are several works on motor learning, mainly related to improvement features, there is a lack on prediction of motor learning acquisition. However, prediction algorithms have been applied with success in several different research fields, such as sciences, health sciences, technology and logistic [5]. A massive amount of data is generated everyday, thus, applications to process those data may aid decision making. These prediction algorithms enable new analysis, building of new patterns and new associations to problems heretofore dealt only by field experts.

For instance, machine learning algorithms has been applied to predict daily activities of post-stroke patients. Similarly, in [14], it was created a model to predict the independence level of patients on his/her activities of daily living after stroke. Additionally, a prediction model was proposed to evaluate how stroke progresses, which has the Functional Independence Measure (FIM) as its metric [17]. FIM can be estimated by patient's features [16].

Despite these works, there is no work that estimates motor learning. Thus, this work combines machine learning algorithms and motor learning tasks to estimate the amount of sessions a subject has to perform to learn a motor task.

The present work is organized as follows: Sect. 2 presents Material and Methods, where the criteria for the subjects, experimental design, and classification models are described; Sect. 3 shows the results obtained with the models, as well as a comparison among them; and Sect. 4 presents the conclusion and the directions for further work.

2   Materials and Methods

2.1   Participants

Initially 15 healthy volunteers, whom were students and professors from Federal University of Maranhão (UFMA), were invited to be subject on the experiment. All participants signed a permission to authorize the use of their collected data for research purposes whereas at the same time this work maintains the confidentiality of the participants.

Furthermore, before start the experiment all participants answered the Edinburgh Handedness Inventory. Only participants having right-handedness (Laterality Quotient equals or greater than 61) [3] are considered on this experiment. Additionally, the participants answered a Portuguese translated version of the *Beck Depression Inventory"* [1], this inventory identify depression symptoms in participants that may affect the result of the experiment. As a result, every participant that obtained score bigger than 12 was excluded of this study. Also, participants were asked if they already had any neurological disorder that would provoke changes in their motor performance. At the end of all scheduled experiment sessions only 8 subjects completed the experiment and had their data analyzed. The participants selection criteria are similar to paper [10].

Table 1 shows some aspects - number of participants, mean age and standard deviation, Edinburgh Handedness Inventory mean score and its standard deviation, and male percentage - of the subjects of the current work and other similar works [10,11].

Table 1. Comparison of participants general data with similar works

Experiment	Number of participants	Age $\pm\sigma$	Edinburgh $\pm\sigma$	Male (%)
Current work	8	23.88 ± 4.94	75.19 ± 26.32	62.50
Reis et al. [11]	12	32.00 ± 3.00	–	58.33
Prichard et al. [10]	18	25.70 ± 4.60	93.4 ± 10.7	38.90

2.2 Experimental Design

A software to acquire the images and metrics for the tracing task was developed [2] and it is based on the experiment of [10], which proposed the tracing task as a motor learning task. The technologies used to develop the software were the Pygame Framework [15] made with the Python language [12].

During the experiment, with the software running, the participant must trace a series of words (each word representing a trial) holding a stylus pen with the left hand (the non-dominant hand) over the graphic tablet as depicted on Fig. 1. The chosen words are all from Brazilian Portuguese containing at least 3 up to 5 letters collected from the free database by Invoke IT[1]. Furthermore, the words printed on screen by the software are in the cursive font League Script[2].

For each trial the extracted metric is the percentage error from the difference of both template and the traced images. However, a margin of error is taken into account, i.e. both images (template and traced) are blurred with a gaussian kernel of 50×50 pixels size and 12 pixels of standard deviation.

The experiment is conducted in three consecutive days, where each day is a session, thus three sessions in total, and each session is composed by nine blocks, with each block having ten trials. Therefore, a participant must complete in 1 session, daily session, 9 blocks of 10 trials. For each trial the necessary time to trace a letter was fixed to 10 s, consequently the time to complete a trial was set to $10 \times word_{length}$ seconds.

---

[1] https://invokeit.wordpress.com/frequency-word-lists/.
[2] www.theleagueofmoveabletype.com.

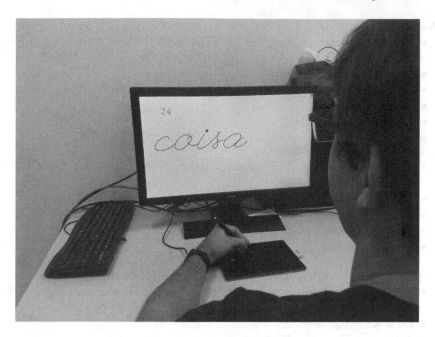

Fig. 1. Representation of a trial in the tracing task software. The Portuguese word *"coisa"* (the word means "thing") is displayed, the participant must move the stylus pen touching the graphic tablet to control the cursor on screen while he or she traces the word. The percentage error, between the desired and actual trace, is computed to measure the participant skill.

Once the experiment was completed the acquired data were formatted to "comma separated values" (CSV) file in order to be analyzed and processed. The CSV format was chosen because of its simplicity and wide use for data analysis. The CSV file contained participant's age, gender, percentage error of session 1, the percentage error of current session and the number of current session.

2.3   Classification Models

The prediction methods used in this work are provided by Python "SciKit Learn" library [9]. This library provides a variety of machine learning techniques and evaluation techniques. This library is widely used in academic research because it has many machine learning algorithms implemented.

The bests prediction models for the collected data were built using *"Grid Search"* algorithm, which performs an exhaustive search to select the bests parameters for each machine learning classifier inside of a limited search space. The selected parameters were:

- **K-nearest neighbours**
  - Prediction variables: Age, gender, First Session Mean Error, Current Session Mean Error;
  - Class Variable: Session;
  - Number of neighbours: 9;
  - Distance measure: Euclidian;
  - Algorithm: *"Ball Tree"*;

- **Support Vector Machine**
  - Prediction variables: Age, gender, First Session Mean Error, Current Session Mean Error;
  - Class Variable: Session;
  - C penalty factor: 64;
  - *'Coef0'* independent kernel term: 0;
  - Kernel: Sigmoid;

- **Multi layer Perceptron Artificial Neural Network**
  - Prediction variables: Age, gender, First Session Mean Error, Current Session Mean Error;
  - Class Variable: Session;
  - Activation Function: Rectified linear unit;
  - Hidden Layer: 100 neurons;
  - Epochs: 5000
  - Learning ratio: 0.01;
  - Solver: Quasi-Newton method;

- **Decision Tree**
  - Prediction variables: Age, gender, First Session Mean Error, Current Session Mean Error;
  - Class Variable: Session;
  - Splitting Criteria: Entropy;
  - Minimum samples in each splitting: 64;
  - Splitting method: *"Best"*;

To evaluate the prediction models performance, the k-folds cross validation [8] was applied with 10 folds. This approach was used to keep the training set balanced as possible [4,7]. As evaluation metrics of the classifiers there are: Accuracy, F1-Score and Cohen Kappa coefficient. These metrics are calculated from the Confusion Matrix.

Additionally, in order to compare the prediction among the models (Neural Network Multi Layer Perceptron, Support Vector Machine, K-Nearest Neighbors and Decision Tree) an Analysis of variance (ANOVA) was carried out for each metric (Accuracy, F1-Score and Cohen Kappa coefficient) with the model prediction being the factor, as well as the Tukey's Post Hoc Test.

3   Results

Figure 2 and Table 2 show the performance of classification models for the accuracy metric. Four different classification models were used: Neural Network Multi Layer Perceptron (MLP); Support Vector Machine (SVM) with kernel RBF; K-Nearest Neighbors (KNN); and Decision Tree (AD).

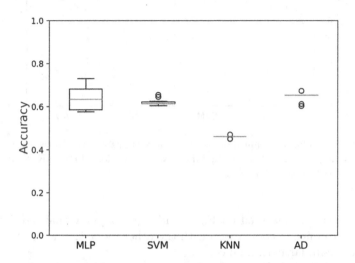

Fig. 2. Accuracy of classification models. The models are Neural Network Multi Layer Perceptron (MLP); Support Vector Machine (SVM) with kernel RBF; K-Nearest Neighbors (KNN); and Decision Tree (AD).

Table 2. Experimental accuracy results

Model	Max	Mean	Min	Std
MLP	0.7307	0.6384	0.5769	0.0549
KNN	0.4715	0.4605	0.4515	0.0056
SVM	0.6553	0.6223	0.6053	0.0156
AD	0.6738	0.6468	0.6038	0.0211

As one can see on Fig. 2 and Table 2, mean accuracy for MLP, SVM and AD were similar whereas KNN model presented the worst performance in contrast to the others models. It is worth mentioning that MLP accuracy maximum value was superior when compared with the other classifiers.

Figure 3 and Table 3 show the performance of classification models for F1-score metric and the four different classification models MLP, SVM, KNN and AD.

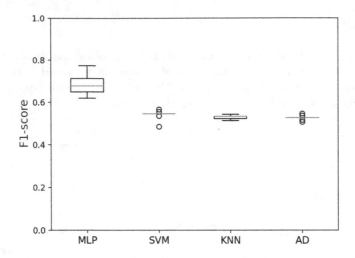

Fig. 3. F1-score of classification models. The models are Neural Network Multi Layer Perceptron (MLP); Support Vector Machine (SVM) with kernel RBF; K-Nearest Neighbors (KNN); and Decision Tree (AD).

F1-score results, presented on Fig. 3 and Table 3, show that MLP obtained the best performance in comparison with the other models, whereas SVM, KNN and AD had a similar performance.

Figure 4 and Table 4 show the performance of classification models for Cohen Kappa coefficient metric and the four different classification models MLP, SVM, KNN and AD.

Cohen Kappa coefficient results, presented Fig. 4 and Table 4, show that on average MLP SVM and AD had a similar performance. However, the maximum performance was obtained with MLP (0.4615). The KNN had again the worst performance, it had negative values and because of these negative values it is not shown on Fig. 4.

Furthermore, in order to compare the classifiers, an ANOVA for each metric was carried out and depicted on Table 5. It is worth emphasizing that each row on Table 5 is an ANOVA for a metric among the models, where model (MLP, SVM, KNN and AD) is the factor, as well as one can see that all metrics were statically significant different ($p < 0.01$), i.e. the classifier had different performance for the metrics. Once there is difference between the model for each metric, the Tukey's Post Hoc Test was applied to detect the best model as shown on Table 6.

Table 6 indicate that MLP, SVM and AD, had similar results, for Accuracy, i.e. they were not statically significant different. Similarly, SVM and AD were not statically significant different for Accuracy. On the other hand, KNN was, statically significant, the worst classifier. Reasonable performance of the KNN technique was expected due to past results obtained with simulated data [13]. However, in real data, the KNN model result was poor.

Table 3. Experimental F1-score results

Model	Max	Mean	Min	Std
MLP	0.7741	0.6841	0.6206	0.0497
KNN	0.5433	0.5283	0.5133	0.0097
SVM	0.5654	0.5414	0.4854	0.0211
AD	0.5463	0.5263	0.5063	0.0105

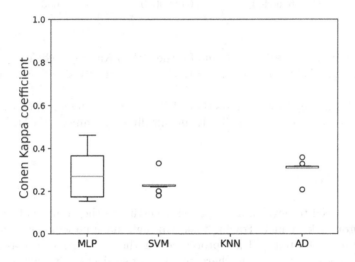

Fig. 4. Cohen Kappa coefficient of classification models. The models are Neural Network Multi Layer Perceptron (MLP); Support Vector Machine (SVM) with kernel RBF; K-Nearest Neighbors (KNN); and Decision Tree (AD).

Table 4. Experimental Cohen Kappa coefficient results

Model	Max	Mean	Min	Std
MLP	0.4615	0.2769	0.1538	0.1099
KNN	0	−0.0779	−0.0969	0.0099
SVM	0.3307	0.2317	0.1807	0.0387
AD	0.3576	0.3056	0.2076	0.0014

Table 5. Analysis of variance of experimental classification models

Metric	Df	Df.res	Sum Sq	Sum Sq.res	Mean Sq	p-value
Accuracy	3	36	0.233	0.033	0.077	<0.001
F1-score	3	36	0.174	0.028	0.058	<0.001
Kappa	3	36	0.943	0.136	0.314	<0.001

Table 6. Post Hoc Test - Tukey multiple comparisons of means

Models	p-value (Accuracy)	p-value (F1-score)	p-value (Kappa)
KNN-AD	0.0000000	0.9984802	0.0000000
MLP-AD	0.9274347	0.0000000	0.7239393
SVM-AD	0.2960432	0.6248643	0.0506931
MLP-KNN	0.0000000	0.0000000	0.0000000
SVM-KNN	0.0000000	0.7224017	0.0000000
SVM-MLP	0.6465444	0.0000000	0.3690339

Similar results, Table 6, were found for the Cohen Kappa coefficient, i.e. MLP, SVM and AD, had similar results, and KNN was, statically significant, the worst classifier.

For the F1-Score, Table 6 shows that MLP was, statically significant, the best model, and there were no statically significant difference among SVM, KNN and AD.

4   Conclusion

This article aimed to develop an approach to estimate the number of sessions to learn a motor task, namely tracing task, through machine learning algorithms. The data were collected and pre-processed for the application of classification algorithms. These data include characteristics of subjects, e.g. age and gender, and motor performance characteristics as tracing error.

The results show that it is possible to predict the amount of sessions a subject requires to achieve a certain performance based on initial motor practice. Four different approaches were used - MLP, SVM KNN, and AD - and their results with three different metrics - Accuracy, F1-Score and Cohen Kappa coefficient - were compared. MLP, SVM and AD, had similar results for Accuracy and Cohen Kappa coefficient, but better than KNN, whereas for the F1-Score MPL performed better than all.

Future works will be devoted to employ this setup for more subjects, predict the amount of sessions a patient requires to rehabilitate, as well as explore new features and other machine learning models.

Acknowledgment. The authors acknowledge FAPEMA for the financial support for this research specially for scholarship, Proc. UNIVERSAL-01294/16 and Proc. 2019/10012-2, Fundação de Amparo à Pesquisa do Estado de São Paulo (FAPESP).

References

1. Beck, A.T., Ward, C.H., Mendelson, M., Mock, J., Erbaugh, J.: An inventory for measuring depression. Arch. Gen. Psychiatry **4**(6), 561–571 (1961)
2. Carvalho, M.B.F.: Evaluate plataform of automatic motor learning skill, monograph (Computer Engineering), UFMA (Federal Uniersvity of Maranhão), São Luís, Brazil (2018)
3. Espírito-Santo, H., Pires, C.F., Garcia, I.Q., Daniel, F., Silva, A.G., Fazio, R.L.: Preliminary validation of the portuguese edinburgh handedness inventory in an adult sample. Appl. Neuropsychol. Adult **24**(3), 275–287 (2017)
4. Hahne, J.M., et al.: Linear and nonlinear regression techniques for simultaneous and proportional myoelectric control. IEEE Trans. Neural Syst. Rehabil. Eng. **22**(2), 269–279 (2014)
5. Jordan, M.I., Mitchell, T.M.: Machine learning: trends, perspectives, and prospects. Science **349**(6245), 255–260 (2015)
6. Kitago, T., Krakauer, J.W.: Motor learning principles for neurorehabilitation. Handb. Clin. Neurol. **110**, 93–103 (2013)
7. Lemm, S., Blankertz, B., Dickhaus, T., Müller, K.R.: Introduction to machine learning for brain imaging. Neuroimage **56**(2), 387–399 (2011)
8. Norvig, P., Russell, S.: Inteligência Artificial, vol. 1, 3 edn. Elsevier, Brasil (2014)
9. Pedregosa, F., et al.: Scikit-learn: machine learning in python. J. Mach. Learn. Res. **12**, 2825–2830 (2011)
10. Prichard, G., Weiller, C., Fritsch, B., Reis, J.: Effects of different electrical brain stimulation protocols on subcomponents of motor skill learning. Brain Stimulation **7**(4), 532–540 (2014)
11. Reis, J., et al.: Noninvasive cortical stimulation enhances motor skill acquisition over multiple days through an effect on consolidation. Proc. Nat. Acad. Sci. U.S.A. **106**(5), 1590–1595 (2009)
12. Rossum, G.: Python reference manual. Technical report, Amsterdam, The Netherlands (1995)
13. Santos, M.R., et al.: Machine learning to estimate the amount of training to learn a motor skill. In: Duffy, V.G. (ed.) HCII 2019. LNCS, vol. 11581, pp. 198–209. Springer, Cham (2019). https://doi.org/10.1007/978-3-030-22216-1_15
14. Sato, A., Fujita, T., Ohashi, Y., Yamamoto, Y., Suzuki, K., Otsuki, K.: A prediction model for activities of daily living for stroke patients in a convalescent rehabilitation ward. J. Allied Health Sci. **7**(1), 1–6 (2016)
15. Shinners, P.: Pygame. http://pygame.org/ (2011)
16. Sonoda, S., Saitoh, E., Nagai, S., Okuyama, Y., Suzuki, T., Suzuki, M.: Stroke outcome prediction using reciprocal number of initial activities of daily living status. J. Stroke Cerebrovasc. Dis. **14**(1), 8–11 (2005)
17. Tsuji, T., Liu, M., Sonoda, S., Domen, K., Chino, N.: The stroke impairment assessment set: its internal consistency and predictive validity. Arch. Phys. Med. Rehabil. **81**(7), 863–868 (2000)

Kernel-Spectral-Clustering-Driven Motion Segmentation: Rotating-Objects First Trials

O. Oña-Rocha[1,2], J. A. Riascos-Salas[3,7(✉)], I. C. Marrufo-Rodríguez[4], M. A. Páez-Jaime[4], D. Mayorca-Torres[5], K. L. Ponce-Guevara[6], J. A. Salazar-Castro[7], and D. H. Peluffo-Ordóñez[1,4]

[1] Universidad Técnica del Norte, Ibarra, Ecuador
[2] Universidad de las Fuerzas Armadas - ESPE, Sangolquí, Ecuador
[3] SDAS Research Group, Ibarra, Ecuador
[4] Yachay Tech University, Urcuquí, Ecuador
[5] Universidad Mariana, Pasto, Colombia
[6] Universidade Federal de Pernambuco, Recife, Brazil
[7] Corporación Universitaria Autónoma de Nariño, Pasto, Colombia
`jarsalas@inf.ufrgs.br`
`https://sdas-group.com/`

Abstract. Time-varying data characterization and classification is a field of great interest in both scientific and technology communities. There exists a wide range of applications and challenging open issues such as: automatic motion segmentation, moving-object tracking, and movement forecasting, among others. In this paper, we study the use of the so-called kernel spectral clustering (KSC) approach to capture the dynamic behavior of frames - representing rotating objects - by means of kernel functions and feature relevance values. On the basis of previous research works, we formally derive a here-called tracking vector able to unveil sequential behavior patterns. As a remarkable outcome, we alternatively introduce an encoded version of the tracking vector by converting into decimal numbers the resulting clustering indicators. To evaluate our approach, we test the studied KSC-based tracking over a rotating object from the COIL 20 database. Preliminary results produce clear evidence about the relationship between the clustering indicators and the starting/ending time instance of a specific dynamic sequence.

Keywords: Kernels · Motion tracking · Spectral clustering

1 Introduction

Today, the analysis of dynamic (also known as time-varying) data is a great-of-interest and highly-relevant topic within areas such as: data science, automation

O. Oña-Rocha—This work is supported by SDAS Research Group (www.sdas-group.com).

© Springer Nature Switzerland AG 2019
V. R. Cota et al. (Eds.): LAWCN 2019, CCIS 1068, pp. 30–40, 2019.
https://doi.org/10.1007/978-3-030-36636-0_3

and pattern recognition - benefiting then several scientific and technology fields. Among its remarkable applications, it is worth mentioning: motion segmentation [1], video analysis [2], and object tracking [3]. In this connection, the theoretical approaches that have shown to be a significant tool for dealing with dynamic data are the matrix spectral techniques along with graph-cut approaches. Specifically, the so-called kernel spectral clustering (KSC), introduced in [4], is a well-reputed state-of-the-art method. KSC - broadly speaking - is a generalization of a weighted, kernelized version of principal component analysis within a non-supervised, least-squares-support-vector-machines framework. Furthermore, in a previous work [5], we demonstrated the usefulness of KSC - powered by a feature relevance analysis [6] - for dealing with time-varying data problems. Particularly, the segmentation of a sequence of moving level curves into motion clusters was studied.

In this work, from such previous studies, we explore the use of the KSC-based tracking approach to segment into meaningful motion stages a sequence of frames describing rotating objects. A noticeable contribution of this work is the possibility to validate an afore-introduced approach for estimating a tracking vector, by means of an encoded version thereof. Such an encoding procedure is carried out so that clustering indicators matrix is converted into a vector holding decimal numbers, and therefore the clustering membership is truly unveiled. Experiments are carried out over a sequence of frames of a rotating object from the COIL 20 [7]. Clustering parameters, such as the number of clusters, type of kernel function, and kernel parameters are empirically set. Obtained results proves that the explored tracking vector is able to automatically identify motion stages in a sequence of frames (video) of of objects submitted to a rotational movement.

The remaining of this paper is structured as follows: Sect. 2 briefly outlines the KSC formulation and its general use for unsupervised grouping. Then, in Sect. 3, both the already-developed KSC-based tracking and the novel encoded tracking vector are explained. Sections 4 and 5 holds the experimental setup and results, respectively. Finally, in Sect. 6 the concluding remarks are drawn.

2   Kernel Spectral Clustering

Spectral clustering techniques have successfully been used for separating a dataset into a K disjoint subsets [8]. The Kernel Spectral Clustering (KSC) [4] consists in using a Least-Squares Support Vector Machine (LS-SVM) as a clustering technique. For further statements, consider the notation described in Table 1.

Given a set of N data points $\boldsymbol{X} = \{\boldsymbol{x}\}_{i=1}^{N}$, being $\boldsymbol{x}_i \in \mathbb{R}^d$ the i-th data point, and $\boldsymbol{X} \in \mathbb{R}^{N \times d}$ the data matrix, it is possible to assume a latent variable $\boldsymbol{E} \in \mathbb{R}^{N \times n_e}$ as $\boldsymbol{E} = \boldsymbol{\Phi W} + \mathbf{1}_N \otimes \boldsymbol{b}^\top$ as a model for the projections with $\boldsymbol{\Phi} = \left(\phi(\boldsymbol{x}_1)^\top, \ldots, \phi(\boldsymbol{x}_N)^\top\right)^\top$, $\boldsymbol{\Phi} \in \mathbb{R}^{N \times d_h}$ being the high dimensional representation of the input data such that $\phi(\cdot)$ is the function that maps data from the original dimension to a higher one d_h, i.e., $\phi(\cdot) : \mathbb{R}^d \to \mathbb{R}^{d_h}$; meanwhile, the weighting

Table 1. Mathematical notation

Notation	Description
$\boldsymbol{A}^{\top}$	Transpose of the vector or matrix $\boldsymbol{A}$
$\boldsymbol{I}_n$	n-dimensional identity matrix
$\boldsymbol{1}_n$	n-dimensional ones vector
$\phi(\cdot)$	Feature mapping function
$\mathcal{K}(\cdot,\cdot)$	Kernel function
$\boldsymbol{\Omega} = [\mathcal{K}(\boldsymbol{x}_i, \boldsymbol{x}_j)]$	Kernel matrix
$\otimes$	Kronecker product
$\mathrm{tr}(\cdot)$	Trace operator
$\mathrm{sgn}(\cdot)$	Sign function
$\circ$	Hadammard product

factor matrix is defined by $\boldsymbol{W} = (\boldsymbol{w}^{(1)}, \cdots, \boldsymbol{w}^{(n_e)})$, $\boldsymbol{W} \in \mathbb{R}^{d_h \times n_e}$; and $\boldsymbol{b} = [b_1, \ldots, b_{n_e}]$ the vector that contains the bias terms, $\boldsymbol{b} \in \mathbb{R}^{n_e}$ with n_e as the number of considered support vectors.

Then, following a LS-SVM [4] formulation, the primal formulation of KSC optimization problem can be expressed in matrix terms [9], as follows:

$$\min_{E,W,b} \quad \frac{1}{2N} \mathrm{tr}(\boldsymbol{E}^{\top}\boldsymbol{V}\boldsymbol{E}\boldsymbol{\Gamma}) - \frac{1}{2}\mathrm{tr}(\boldsymbol{W}^{\top}\boldsymbol{W}); \quad \text{s.t.} \quad \boldsymbol{E} = \boldsymbol{\Phi}\boldsymbol{W} + \boldsymbol{1}_N \otimes \boldsymbol{b}^{\top} \quad (1)$$

Being $\boldsymbol{\Gamma} = \mathrm{Diag}([\gamma_1, \ldots, \gamma_{n_e}])$ the diagonal matrix composed by the regularization terms. For solving KSC problem, it is necessary to form the corresponding Lagrangian of previous problem, as follows:

$$\mathcal{L}(\boldsymbol{E}, \boldsymbol{W}, \boldsymbol{\Gamma}, \boldsymbol{A}) = \frac{1}{2N}\mathrm{tr}(\boldsymbol{E}^{\top}\boldsymbol{V}\boldsymbol{E}) - \frac{1}{2}\mathrm{tr}(\boldsymbol{W}^{\top}\boldsymbol{W}) - \mathrm{tr}(\boldsymbol{A}^{\top}(\boldsymbol{E} - \boldsymbol{\Phi}\boldsymbol{W} - \boldsymbol{1}_N \otimes \boldsymbol{b}^{\top}))$$

with $\boldsymbol{A} \in \mathbb{R}^{N \times n_e}$ as the matrix formed by the Lagrange multiplier vectors such that $\boldsymbol{A} = [\boldsymbol{\alpha}^{(1)}, \cdots \boldsymbol{\alpha}^{(n_e)}]$, where $\boldsymbol{\alpha}^{(l)} \in \mathbb{R}^N$ denotes the l-th vector of Lagrange multipliers.

Consequently, we define the Karush-Kuhn-Tucker (KKT) conditions by solving the partial derivatives on $\mathcal{L}(\boldsymbol{E}, \boldsymbol{W}, \boldsymbol{\Gamma}, \boldsymbol{A})$. Then, the optimization problem defined in the Eq. (1) becomes a dual problem: $\boldsymbol{A}\boldsymbol{\Lambda} = \boldsymbol{V}\boldsymbol{H}\boldsymbol{\Phi}\boldsymbol{\Phi}^{\top}\boldsymbol{A}$, by eliminating the primal variables, where $\boldsymbol{\Lambda} = \mathrm{Diag}(\lambda_1, \ldots, \lambda_{n_e})$ is a diagonal matrix formed by the eigenvalues $\lambda_l = N/\gamma_l$; $\boldsymbol{H} \in \mathbb{R}^{N \times N}$ is the centering matrix define as

$$\boldsymbol{H} = \boldsymbol{I}_N - 1/(\boldsymbol{1}_N^{\top}\boldsymbol{V}\boldsymbol{1}_N)\boldsymbol{1}_N\boldsymbol{1}_N^{\top}\boldsymbol{V}. \quad (2)$$

Additionally, in order to satisfying the condition $\boldsymbol{b}^{\top}\boldsymbol{1}_N = 0$ resulting from KKT conditions, the bias vector $\boldsymbol{b}$ can be chosen as a centering vector (i.e. with zero mean) as follows:

$$b_l = -1/(\boldsymbol{1}_N^{\top}\boldsymbol{V}\boldsymbol{1}_N)\boldsymbol{1}_N^{\top}\boldsymbol{V}\boldsymbol{\Omega}\boldsymbol{\alpha}^{(l)}. \quad (3)$$

Moreover, the kernel matrix $\boldsymbol{\Omega} = [\Omega_{ij}] = \mathcal{K}(\boldsymbol{x}_i, \boldsymbol{x}_j), i, j \in [N]$, is created applying the kernel trick $\boldsymbol{\Omega} \in \mathbb{R}^{N \times N}$ with $\boldsymbol{\Omega} = \boldsymbol{\Phi}\boldsymbol{\Phi}^\top$. Likewise, the matrix $\boldsymbol{A}$ turns into the eigenvectors, resulting in a set of projections calculated by means of the following formula:

$$E = \boldsymbol{\Omega}A + 1_N \otimes b^\top \tag{4}$$

Considering that the kernel matrix is mathematically equivalent to the similarity matrix used in conventional graph-based clustering methods, and considering $\boldsymbol{V} = \boldsymbol{D}^{-1}$ with $\boldsymbol{D} = \mathrm{Diag}(\boldsymbol{\Omega}1_N)$, $\boldsymbol{D} \in \mathbb{R}^{N \times N}$ begin the degree matrix; thus, it is possible to infer that the $K - 1$ eigenvectors composed by the largest eigenvalues are cluster indicators and therefore, $n_e = K - 1$ [10]. Afterward, the eigenvectors can be codified based on that both each cluster has a single and unique coordinate system in the $K - 1$-dimensional eigenspace; and two points, of the same orthant in the corresponding eigenspace, belong to the same cluster [10]. Therefore, we obtain the code book

$$\widetilde{E} = \mathrm{sgn}(E), \tag{5}$$

by binaryzing the rows of the projection matrix E (using the the sign function $\mathrm{sgn}(\cdot)$), and therefore its corresponding rows become codewords enabling the the formation of the holding-similar-samples clusters according to the minimal Hamming distance. Following the pseudo-code (Algorithm 1) to perform KSC is shown.

Algorithm 1. Kernel spectral clustering: $[A, \Lambda, \widetilde{E}] = \mathrm{KSC}(\boldsymbol{X}, \mathcal{K}(\cdot, \cdot), K)$

1: **Input**: K, $\boldsymbol{X}$, $\mathcal{K}(\cdot, \cdot)$
2: Form the kernel matrix $\boldsymbol{\Omega}$ such that $\Omega_{ij} = \mathcal{K}(\boldsymbol{y}_i, \boldsymbol{x}_j)$
3: Calculate matrix $\boldsymbol{H}$ and b as stated in equations (2) and (3), respectively.
4: Compute the eigendecomposition from the dual the problem: $A\Lambda = \boldsymbol{V}\boldsymbol{H}\boldsymbol{\Omega}A$
5: Determine E through $E = \boldsymbol{\Omega}A + 1_N \otimes b^\top$
6: Form the training codebook by binarizing $\widetilde{E} = \mathrm{sgn}(E)$

7: **Output**: $A, \Lambda, \widetilde{E}$

---

3 Time-Varying Data Analysis via KSC

3.1 KSC-Based Tracking

Following the work done by Wolf and Shashua [11], which introduces a function regarding a non-negative matrix for a relevance analysis, along with the developments presented in [6], we build an optimization problem for obtaining the ranking values for samples instead of features. Focusing on the task of interest, we define the non-negative matrix as $\boldsymbol{\Omega}$ and the data matrix $\boldsymbol{X}$ is formed taking each row as a frame, i.e., $\boldsymbol{x}_i$ represents the coordinates vectors of the i-th frame. More specifically, by considering a sequence of N_f, denoted as $\{\boldsymbol{\mathcal{X}}^{(0)}, \ldots, \boldsymbol{\mathcal{X}}^{(N_f-1)}\}$, the whole (frame) data matrix will be then $\boldsymbol{X} = (\boldsymbol{x}_1^\top, \ldots, \boldsymbol{x}_{N_f}^\top)^\top$, such that $\boldsymbol{x}_t = \text{vec}(\boldsymbol{\mathcal{X}}^{(t)})$, where $t \in \{1, \ldots, N_f\}$ and $\text{vec}(\cdot)$ is a vectorization operator.

Thus, the Eq. (4) becomes an energy maximization problem, stated as follows:

$$\max_{U} \text{tr}(\boldsymbol{U}^\top \boldsymbol{\Omega}^\top \boldsymbol{\Omega U}); \quad \text{s.t.} \quad \boldsymbol{U}^\top \boldsymbol{U} = \boldsymbol{I}_{n_e}. \tag{6}$$

The orthonormal rotation matrix $\boldsymbol{U} \in \mathbb{R}^{N \times n_e}$ is formulated such that the linear transformation of kernel matrix is in the form $\boldsymbol{Z} = \boldsymbol{\Omega U}, \boldsymbol{Z} \in \mathbb{R}^{N \times n_e}$. Following the procedure described in Sect. 2, it is possible to formulate that $\text{tr}(\boldsymbol{U}^\top \boldsymbol{\Omega}^\top \boldsymbol{\Omega U}) = \text{tr}(\boldsymbol{\Lambda}^2)$ and therefore a suitable solution for the problem is $\boldsymbol{U} = \boldsymbol{A}$. So, the ranking vector $\boldsymbol{\eta} \in \mathbb{R}^N$, as explained in [6], can be expressed as a linear combination of vectors $\boldsymbol{\alpha}^{(l)}$:

$$\boldsymbol{\eta} = \sum_{l=1}^{n_e} \lambda_l \boldsymbol{\alpha}^{(l)} \circ \boldsymbol{\alpha}^{(l)}. \tag{7}$$

Subsequently, the ranking factor η_i can be seen as a single value representing a unique frame in a sequence. In such vein, $\boldsymbol{\eta}$ becomes a tracking vector.

3.2   Encoded Tracking Vector

In this section we describe the proposed encoding approach for comparing frame tracking given by the original approach. This encoding approach is inspired by the procedure explained in [12].

As discussed in [5,13], given the KKT conditions applied to the dual formulation of the KSC problem, the clusters can directly be recognized, as the geometrical location of projected data points $\boldsymbol{E}$ in every single orthant represents an unique cluster. In other words, clusters can be encoded with binary indicators as expressed in Eq. (5). Consequently, we can obtain crisp values from the cluster indicators as the rows $\tilde{\boldsymbol{e}}_i$ ($\forall i, i \in \{1, \ldots, N\}$) of matrix $\tilde{\boldsymbol{E}}$ can be directly converted from binary to decimal numbers. Nonetheless, here it is preferred to constraint such a conversion as the maximum resulting number will be the expected number of clusters. Then, binary codes are converted into decimal numbers upon order of appearing, from 1 to K to reach the encoded tracking vector $\tilde{\boldsymbol{\eta}} \in \mathbb{R}^d$.

So, to exemplify our encoding approach, let us consider the following example with $n_e = 4$:

$$\boldsymbol{E} = \begin{pmatrix} 2.7 & 2.1 & -0.4 & 4.1 \\ 4.3 & 2.5 & -0.5 & -1.3 \\ 2.3 & 1.5 & -0.5 & 4.3 \\ 1.3 & -1.5 & -0.5 & 2.3 \\ 1.3 & 2.5 & -0.5 & 4.3 \end{pmatrix},$$

yielding an encoded matrix in the form:

$$\widetilde{E} = \begin{pmatrix} 1 & 1 & -1 & 1 \\ 1 & 1 & -1 & -1 \\ 1 & 1 & -1 & 1 \\ 1 & -1 & -1 & 1 \\ 1 & 1 & -1 & 1 \end{pmatrix}, \tag{8}$$

and therefore its $\widetilde{\eta}$ will correspondingly be given by:

$$\widetilde{\eta} = \begin{pmatrix} 1 \\ 1 \\ 2 \\ 3 \\ 1 \end{pmatrix}.$$

3.3 KSC-Based Tracking Algorithm

The steps for calculating the proposed KSC-based tracking (KSCT) vectors are summarized in Algorithm 2.

Algorithm 2. KSCT: $[\eta, \widetilde{\eta}] = \text{KSCT}\left(\{X^{(0)}, \ldots, X^{(N_f - 1)}\}, K\right)$

Input: Number of clusters K, a frame sequence $\{\mathcal{X}^{(1)}, \ldots, \mathcal{X}^{(N_f)}\}$, a kernel function $\mathcal{K}(\cdot, \cdot)$

1. Form the frame matrix $X = [x_1^{\top}, \ldots, x_{N_f}^{\top}]$ such that $x_t = \text{vec}(\mathcal{X}^{(t)})$
2. Apply KSC over X with K to get the eigenvalues $\Lambda = \text{Diag}(\lambda_1, \ldots, \lambda_{\tilde{n}_e})$ and eigenvectors
   $A = [\alpha^{(1)}, \cdots, \alpha^{(\tilde{n}_e)}]$: $[A, \Lambda, \widetilde{E}] = \text{KSC}(X, \mathcal{K}(\cdot, \cdot), K)$
3. Compute $\eta = \sum_{\ell=1}^{\tilde{n}_e} \lambda_\ell \alpha^{(\ell)} \circ \alpha^{(\ell)}$ with $\tilde{n}_e = K - 1$
4. Normalize η as $\eta \leftarrow \eta / \max |\eta|$
5. Obtain $\widetilde{\eta}$ by encoding into decimal numbers $\widetilde{E}$

Output: Tracking vectors $\eta, \widetilde{\eta}$

---

4 Experimental Setup

4.1 Database

For experiments, we use an object of the well-known database COIL 20 introduced in [7], which is an image bank consisting of 72 gray-level images of 20 different objects placed at different angles (72) - rotated at every 5 degrees. Specifically, we pick the object # 4 as shown in Fig. 1. The 72 images (one per angle/pose) $\mathbb{I}$ are in size 128×128 pixels, which are firstly re-scaled at a 50 %, yielding then final RGB images as $\boldsymbol{\mathcal{X}}^{(t)} \in \mathbb{R}^{64 \times 64}$, being $t \in \{0, \dots, 71\}$. Subsequently, a data matrix is formed by vectoryzing the RGB images. Therefore, the number of data points is $N = 64 \times 64 \times 3 = 12288$, as well as the number of variables is $d = 72$ (being the same number as N_f), which means that the data matrix to be clustered is $\boldsymbol{X} \in \mathbb{R}^{12288 \times 72}$.

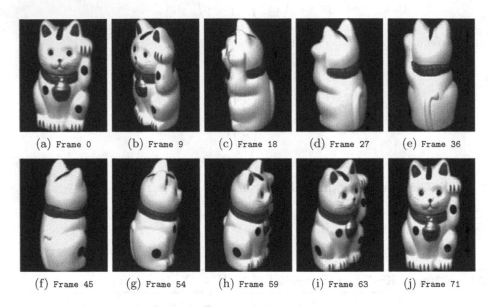

(a) Frame 0   (b) Frame 9   (c) Frame 18   (d) Frame 27   (e) Frame 36

(f) Frame 45   (g) Frame 54   (h) Frame 59   (i) Frame 63   (j) Frame 71

Fig. 1. Some instances of object # 4 frames from COIL 20 database.

4.2   Clustering and Kernel Settings

The number of clusters is set to be $K = 4$. The considered kernel function is the conventional Gaussian kernel defined as: $\Omega_{ij} = \exp(-\|\boldsymbol{x}_i - \boldsymbol{x}_j\|_2^2/(2\sigma^2))$, where $\|\cdot\|$ denotes the Euclidean norm and the scale parameter σ is set empirically as 30.

5   Results and Discussion

For analyzing the sequence of frames arranged into matrix $\boldsymbol{X}$, we first apply KSC. Then, with the KSC outcomes, the vector $\boldsymbol{\eta}$ is calculated using the Eq. (7). From Fig. 2, we can observe the process of the dynamic behaviour captured by the KSC-based tracking, as follows: Fig. 2(a) and (b) shows the plotting of the original tracking vector $\boldsymbol{\eta}$ and the encoded version $\widetilde{\boldsymbol{\eta}}$, respectively. In Fig. 2(c), the reference labelling vector is shown, which is obtained directly from the values of $\widetilde{\boldsymbol{\eta}}$.

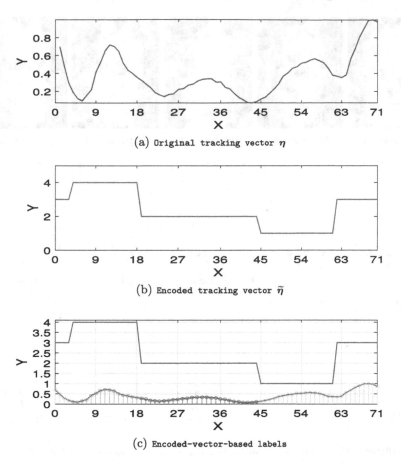

(a) Original tracking vector η

(b) Encoded tracking vector $\widetilde{\eta}$

(c) Encoded-vector-based labels

Fig. 2. Original and encoded tracking vector plotting. It is depicted the plotting of vectors η and $\widetilde{\eta}$ along the 72 frames for Object # 4 from COIL 20 database in Figs. 2(a) and (b), respectively. Figure 2(c) is the overlapped representation of the vectors η and $\widetilde{\eta}$, while the area under the curve is colored to highlight the motion-stage-based labelling regarding $\widetilde{\eta}$.

From the plotting of η, it can be seen that its shape is multimodal-like. By comparing vector $\widetilde{\eta}$ with η, it can be readily noticed that each mode of the η plotting corresponds to a different cluster, i.e. a motion stage in the context of video analysis. Such correspondence can be attributed to the fact that the eigenvectors $\boldsymbol{\alpha}^{(l)}$ point out the direction where samples exhibit the most variability measured in term of the generalized inner product ($\boldsymbol{\Phi}^{\top}\boldsymbol{\Phi}$). In this connection, kernel functions take place and enable the estimation of the inner of high-dimensional representation spaces, wherein resulting clusters are assumed to be linearly separable. The direct connection between the tracking vector η

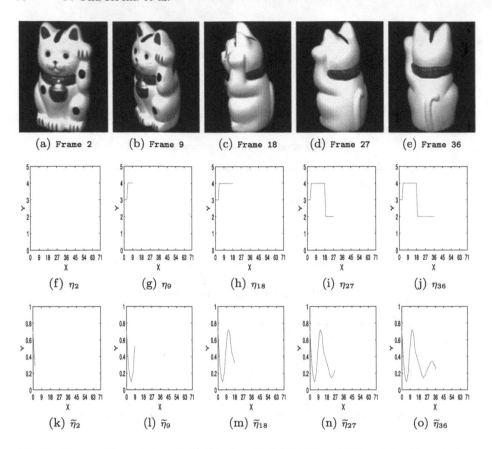

Fig. 3. Object #4 tracking original frames (2, 9, 18, 27 and 36) and tracking vectors.

and the partition of natural movements from Object #4 can be plainly appreciated in Figs. 3 and 4, where the top row shows representative frames per cluster while middle row and bottom row depicts the corresponding evolution of the η and $\tilde{\eta}$ curve, respectively.

As noticed, each mode between inflections forms a concave curve in the plotting, which means that another natural cluster within the sequence has appeared. Such cluster splitting can even be determined by simple inspection. Besides, the encoding vector allows then for validating the premise that vector η is able to divide the sequence of frames into natural motion stages (clusters), when the clustering settings are appropriate. An instance of the motion segmentation effect is depicted in the video available at: https://sdas-group.com/gallery/.

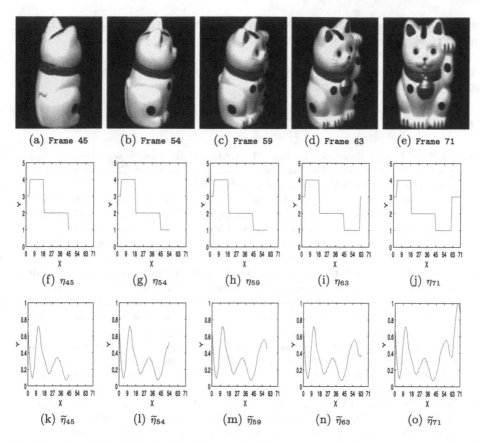

(a) Frame 45   (b) Frame 54   (c) Frame 59   (d) Frame 63   (e) Frame 71

(f) η_{45} (g) η_{54} (h) η_{59} (i) η_{63} (j) η_{71}

(k) $\tilde{\eta}_{45}$ (l) $\tilde{\eta}_{54}$ (m) $\tilde{\eta}_{59}$ (n) $\tilde{\eta}_{63}$ (o) $\tilde{\eta}_{71}$

Fig. 4. Object #4 tracking original frames (45, 54, 59, 63 and 71) and tracking vectors.

6   Conclusions

The dynamic point of view of the greatly wide field of data analysis entails a complex and difficult issue to tackle, since the input data vary along the time. Even more, the intrinsic dynamics - involved during the movement itself - adds more complexity to the subsequent data processing task. On this regard, one of the challenging open issues is the automatic motion segmentation - which can be readily evaluated over rotating objects. In this sense, we have proved that KSC method represents a powerful, suitable tool.

In this work, the use of non-supervised approaches is preferred since, in real-world video applications, an enough amount of labelling is infeasible or prohibitive. Notwithstanding, the disadvantage of working on rotating objects analysis within unsupervised settings is that no automatic motion segmentation can directly be generated by means of a tracking function (here-called tracking vector). At this point, to overcome this obstacle, we have introduced a clustering-indicators-based encoding procedure, so that the quality of the original multi-modal tracking vector can be measured.

Acknowledgments. Authors acknowledge the SDAS Research Group (www.sdas-group.com) for its valuable support.

References

1. Sandhu, M., Upadhyay, S., Krishna, M., Medasani, S.: Motion segmentation using spectral clustering on Indian road scenes. In: The European Conference on Computer Vision (ECCV) Workshops, September 2018
2. Huang, W., Zhang, P.: A novel framework to localize moving targets in video surveillance systems via spectral clustering. Proc. Comput. Sci. **147**, 480–486 (2019). 2018 International Conference on Identification, Information and Knowledge in the Internet of Things. http://www.sciencedirect.com/science/article/pii/S1877050919302996
3. Aamer, B., et al.: Self-tuning spectral clustering for adaptive tracking areas design in 5G ultra-dense networks. arXiv e-prints, arXiv:1902.01342, February 2019
4. Alzate, C., Suykens, J.: A weighted kernel PCA formulation with out-of-sample extensions for spectral clustering methods. In: International Joint Conference on Neural Networks, 2006. IJCNN 2006, pp. 138–144. IEEE (2006)
5. Oña-Rocha, O.R., et al.: Automatic motion segmentation via a cumulative kernel representation and spectral clustering. In: Yin, H., et al. (eds.) IDEAL 2017. LNCS, vol. 10585, pp. 406–414. Springer, Cham (2017). https://doi.org/10.1007/978-3-319-68935-7_44
6. Peluffo Ordoñez, D.H., Lee, J.A., Verleysen, M., Rodriguez, J.L., Castellanos-Dominguez, G.: Unsupervised relevance analysis for feature extraction and selection. A distance-based approach for feature relevance. In: 3rd International Conference on Pattern Recognition Applications and Methods (ICPRAM 2014) (2015)
7. Nene, S.A., Nayar, S.K., Murase, H.: Columbia object image library, COIL-20, Technical report (1996)
8. Langone, R., Mall, R., Alzate, C., Suykens, J.A.K.: Kernel spectral clustering and applications. In: Celebi, M.E., Aydin, K. (eds.) Unsupervised Learning Algorithms, pp. 135–161. Springer, Cham (2016). https://doi.org/10.1007/978-3-319-24211-8_6
9. Diego Peluffo-Ordóñez, E. M.-O.: Theoretical developments for interpreting kernel spectral clustering from alternative viewpoints. Adv. Sci. Technol. Eng. Syst. J. **2**(3), 1670–1676 (2017). https://astesj.com/v02/i03/p208/
10. Alzate, C., Suykens, J.A.K.: Multiway spectral clustering with out-of-sample extensions through weighted Kernel PCA. IEEE Trans. Pattern Anal. Mach. Intell. **32**(2), 335–347 (2010)
11. Wolf, L., Shashua, A.: Feature selection for unsupervised and supervised inference: the emergence of sparsity in a weight-based approach. J. Mach. Learn. Res. **6**, 1855–1887 (2005). http://portal.acm.org/citation.cfm?id=1046920.1194906
12. Alzate, S.J.C.: Highly sparse kernel spectral clustering with predictive out-of-sample extensions (2010)
13. Peluffo-Ordóñez, D.H., García-Vega, S., Álvarez-Meza, A.M., Castellanos-Domínguez, C.G.: Kernel spectral clustering for dynamic data. In: Ruiz-Shulcloper, J., Sanniti di Baja, G. (eds.) CIARP 2013. LNCS, vol. 8258, pp. 238–245. Springer, Heidelberg (2013). https://doi.org/10.1007/978-3-642-41822-8_30

A New Granular Approach
for Multivariate Forecasting

Petrônio Cândido de Lima e Silva[1,3(✉)] [iD], Carlos Alberto Severiano Jr.[2,3] [iD],
Marcos Antônio Alves[3] [iD], Miri Weiss Cohen[5] [iD],
and Frederico Gadelha Guimarães[3,4] [iD]

[1] Instituto Federal do Norte de Minas Gerais - Campus Januária,
Januária, Brazil
petronio.candido@ifnmg.edu.br
[2] Instituto Federal de Minas Gerais - Campus Sabará,
Sobradinho, Brazil
[3] Machine Intelligence and Data Science Lab (MINDS UFMG),
Belo Horizonte, Brazil
[4] Department of Electrical Engineering,
Universidade Federal de Minas Gerais, UFMG,
Belo Horizonte, Brazil
[5] Department of Software Engineering, Braude College of Engineering,
Karmiel, Israel
http://www.minds.eng.ufmg.br/

Abstract. The research for computationally cheaper, scalable and explainable machine learning methods for time series analysis and forecasting has grown in recent years. One of these developments is the Fuzzy Time Series (FTS), simple and fast methods to create readable and accurate forecasting models. However, as the number of variables increase the complexity of these models becomes impractical. This work proposes the $\mathcal{FIG}$-FTS, a new approach to enable multivariate time series to be tackled as univariate FTS methods using composite fuzzy sets to represent each Fuzzy Information Granule (FIG). $\mathcal{FIG}$-FTS is flexible and highly adaptable, allowing the creation of weighted high order forecasting models capable to perform multivariate forecasting for many steps ahead. The proposed method was tested with Lorentz Attractor chaotic time series and the GEFCom 2012 electric load forecasting contest data, considering different forecasting horizons. The results showed that the Mean Average Percentual Error of the models was at about 2% and 4% for one step ahead, and for a prediction horizon of 48 h, the MAPE is at about 10%.

Keywords: Fuzzy Time Series · Fuzzy Information Granule · Multivariate time series

1 Introduction

Accurate forecasting of complex dynamics systems, as several natural and social processes, is a challenging task specially when the underlying system is composed

© Springer Nature Switzerland AG 2019
V. R. Cota et al. (Eds.): LAWCN 2019, CCIS 1068, pp. 41–58, 2019.
https://doi.org/10.1007/978-3-030-36636-0_4

by many interacting variables. Many techniques were employed to tackle these systems along the years, from classical statistical tools to newer machine learning algorithms.

Among them, Fuzzy Time Series (FTS) methods [30] have been drawing more attention and relevance in recent years due to many studies reporting its good accuracy coupled with simplicity, versatility and computational performance. FTS forecasting methods produce data driven and non-parametric models with human readable representations of the time series patterns, making its knowledge transferable, auditable, easily reusable and updatable. Examples of successful applications are shown in energy load forecasting [18, 20–22], stock index prices prediction [17, 24, 31], seasonal time series [7, 25] among others.

In FTS methods, the fuzzy sets are used to split the Universe of Discourse of the time series. This works as a feature extraction layer – the fuzzyfication process, whose output enables the identification of temporal patterns and the induction of rules that describe the behavior of data. The fuzzy sets are also used as a final layer that aids to reconstruct the original UoD from the predicted features, a process known as defuzzyfication.

Despite the existing approaches in the literature, dealing with multivariate and spatio-temporal time series was always a challenging task for FTS methods, specially because of the complexity growth of the rules as the dimension increases. An important gap in the literature is the absence of multiple input and multiple output (MIMO) methods - the majority of FTS literature consists of basically univariate forecasting methods.

A possible approach is to transform the multivariate data into univariate data by using Fuzzy Information Granules (FIG) [37]. In this work, each FIG acts as a multivariate fuzzy set, or a composition of individual fuzzy sets from different variables. This approach allows to replace a vector (the values of one data point) by a scalar (the identification of the FIG with the highest membership of that data point). Following this approach, this work introduces the Fuzzy Information Granular Fuzzy Time Series ($\mathcal{FIG}$-FTS), a new method that is able to tackle multivariate time series. It begins by partitioning the Universe of Discourse of each individual variable. Then the crisp values of each variable are fuzzyfied and the corresponding fuzzy sets are combined to create one Fuzzy Information Granule, such that it can be used as a reference of all data points in that same region. This incremental approach creates the FIGs on demand, according to the training data, and its sensibility can be controlled using the method's hyperparameters.

The remainder of this work is organized as follows: in Sect. 2, the main concepts of Fuzzy Time Series and Fuzzy Information Granules are introduced, in Sect. 3, the procedures for training and multivariate forecasting are detailed. In Sect. 4 computational experiments are performed to evaluate the effectiveness of the model, using artificial and real time series. Finally, in Sect. 5, the main findings of the research are summarized.

2   Preliminaries

2.1   Fuzzy Time Series

Fuzzy Time Series (FTS) were introduced in [30] to deal with vague and impre-
cise knowledge in time series data. Given a univariate time series $Y \in \mathbb{R}^1$, and its
individual values $y(t) \in Y$, for $t = 0, 1, \ldots, T$, the Universe of Discourse (UoD)
U is delimited by the known bounds of Y, such that $U = [\min(Y), \max(Y)]$.
A linguistic variable $\tilde{A}$ is defined upon U, where the linguistic terms are fuzzy
sets A_i, for $i = 1 \ldots k$ and k is the number of partitions, each one with its own
membership function (MF) μ_{A_i}, where $\mu : U \to [0, 1]$. This step is called UoD
partitioning.

There are several categories of FTS methods, varying mainly by their *order*
and time-variance. The order is the number of time-delays (lags) that are used
in modeling the time series. Given the time series data F, First Order models
need $F(t - 1)$ data to predict $F(t)$, while Higher Order models require $F(t -
1), \ldots, F(t - p)$ data to predict $F(t)$. After [30], Conventional FTS (CFTS) was
proposed in [4] in order to simplify the training and forecasting procedures,
also generating more readable rules. The Weighted FTS (WFTS), proposed in
[36], adds weights to the rules to prioritize the recent ones. The more recent,
the greater the weight of the rule. Trend Weighted FTS (TWFTS) [6] applies
three different weights based on a trend component which can be ascending,
descending or linear. Exponentially Weighted FTS (EWFTS) [16] is very similar
to the WFTS, but uses exponential relation of weights. High order methods can
be found on [20]. A method to generate prediction intervals is proposed in [24]
and a probabilistic forecasting method is proposed in [25]. In [27] is presented the
Probabilistic Weighted FTS (PWFTS), a weighted high order method capable
to produce point, interval and probabilistic forecasts. A combination of FTS
methods and convolutional neural networks is presented in [19]. A method to
tackle non-stationary and heteroskedastic time series is proposed in [1].

Multivariate time series are sets of sequential vectors of the form $Y \in \mathbb{R}^n$
where $n = |\mathcal{V}|$ and $\mathcal{V}$ is the set of attributes of Y. Each vector $y(t) \in Y$ contains
all attributes $\mathcal{V}_i \in \mathcal{V}$ and there is a temporal dependence between these data
points such that their temporal ordering – given by the time index $t \in T$ – must
be respected. There are, in the FTS literature, some methods for multivariate
time series, such as [2] and [5]. In [23] is proposed the Weighted Multivariate FTS
(WMVFTS) a scalable first order multivariate FTS with weighted rules. However, there are noticeable gaps in the literature regarding a more general framework for multivariate FTS: (a) multi-step forecasting; (b) multivariate forecast;
(c) weighted and high order multivariate methods.

2.2   Fuzzy Information Granules

The concept of Fuzzy Information Granules (FIG) was first proposed in [37] as
a way to define entities that represent subsets (or granules) of a wider domain.
There are some works in the FTS literature where this concept is mixed with

the partition of the Universe of Discourse, as discussed in [3,11], but there are several ways to define FIG in the literature.

For univariate time series it is common to define a FIG as representative set of sub-samples of the data, so each FIG is a common temporal pattern as in [35]. The construction of this kind of FIG usually employs the clustering of sub-sequences, as in [12]. In [33,34] we can find a univariate fuzzy time series approach whose FIGs are a combination of unequal partitioning of the UoD and prototype sub-sequences.

For multivariate time series FIGs are usually represented as hyper-boxes or multidimensional clusters in the feature space, as in [15,28]. In [28], a multivariate fuzzy time series method is presented, which uses a bio-inspired optimization method to create FIGs by iteratively adjusting the interval lengths of each variable.

Other non-FTS granular approaches can also be found in the literature, as the Granular Functional Forecasting (GFM), proposed in [12], a univariate forecasting method based on Takagi-Sugeno fuzzy system where FIGs are created using clustering methods. In [9], the authors propose the fuzzy set based granular evolving modeling (FBeM) approach for time series prediction, later extended in [29] for spatio-temporal data.

There are some notable drawbacks in the previous methods, namely: (a) the absence of multivariate forecast (MIMO); (b) the use of optimization methods to create the FIGs, which makes the learning process computationally expensive; (c) the absence of multivariate FTS methods that could provide both weighted and high order characteristics. To fix these drawbacks this work proposes the $\mathcal{FIG}$-FTS method, a weighted and high-order FTS method that will be discussed in the next sections.

3   The Fuzzy Information Granular Fuzzy Time Series Method

$\mathcal{FIG}$-FTS is a high order multivariate forecaster of type Multiple Input/Multiple Output (MIMO), where all variables are both targets and explanatory variables. It works as a wrapper that transforms a crisp multivariate time series into a fuzzyfied univariate time series.

Given an n-variate time series $Y(t) = (Y_1(t), \ldots, Y_n(t)), t = 0, 1, \ldots$, corresponding variables $\mathcal{V}_i$ are defined for each Y_i. The resulting fuzzy time series F is then composed by data points $f(t) \in F$ that represent a sequence of fuzzy information granules $\mathcal{G}_i$. Each granule contains a set of fuzzy linguistic variables $\widetilde{\mathcal{V}}_i$ related to each variable $\mathcal{V}_i$.

The $\mathcal{FIG}$-FTS is composed of the training and forecasting procedures, described in Sects. 3.1 and 3.2, and contains the hyper-parameters listed on Table 1. These hyper-parameters give more versatility and flexibility to the method, allowing it to control the sensibility of the fuzzyfication, the number of generated rules and the overall accuracy of the model.

The training procedure performs partition, fuzzyfication and rule induction stages and is responsible to create a model $\mathcal{M}$. The final $\mathcal{FIG}$-FTS model $\mathcal{M}$ consists of a set of variables $\mathcal{V}$, a fuzzy linguistic variable $\widetilde{\mathcal{V}}_i$ for each $\mathcal{V}_i \in \mathcal{V}$, a fuzzy information granule set $\mathcal{FIG}$ and a set of high order weighted fuzzy rules over the information granules $\mathcal{G}_i \in \mathcal{G}$.

In the training method the partitioning of each variable is independent from the others. Each variable has its own linguistic variable $\widetilde{\mathcal{V}}_i$. For this it is necessary to inform, for each chosen variable $\mathcal{V}_i \in \mathcal{V}$ on Y, the hyper-parameters k_i, μ and α. The order of the model is controlled by the parameter Ω and the lag indexes are controlled by the parameter L.

Table 1. $\mathcal{FIG}$-FTS hyper-parameters

Alias	Parameter	Type	Description
k_i	Number of partitions	$\mathbb{N}^+$	The number of fuzzy sets that will be created in the linguistic variable $\widetilde{\mathcal{V}}_i$
μ	Membership function	$\mu : U \to [0,1]$	A function that measure the membership of a value $y \in U$ to a fuzzy set
α	α-cut	$[0,1]$	The minimal membership grade to take account on fuzzyfication process
Ω	Order	$\mathbb{N}^+$	The number of past lags used in the precedent of each fuzzy rule
L	Lags		A vector of the past lag indexes, with length Ω and $1 \leq L[i] < L[i+1]$ for $t = 0..\Omega$
κ	k-nearest neighbors	$\mathbb{N}^+$	The number of nearest neighbors that the spatial index search on $\mathcal{FIG}$ during the fuzzyfication process

The global linguistic variable $\mathcal{FIG}$ is the union of all Fuzzy Information Granules $\mathcal{G}_i$, which in turn are the combination of one fuzzy set for each variable, such that $\mathcal{G}_i = \{A_j^{\mathcal{V}_i}\}$, $\forall \mathcal{V}_i \in \mathcal{V}$ and its membership function is given by $\mu_{\mathcal{G}_i} = \bigcap \mu_{A_j^{\mathcal{V}_i}}$, where $\bigcap$ is the minimum T-norm. The $\mathcal{FIG}$ set is indexed by the midpoints of its internal fuzzy sets, enabling optimized spatial search using KD-trees. With the linguistic variable $\mathcal{FIG}$ the fuzzyfication process transforms each multivariate data point $y(t) \in Y$ into a $\mathcal{G}_i \in \mathcal{FIG}$, such that $f(t) = \mathcal{G}_i$.

The forecasting procedure, explained in Subsect. 3.2, aims to produce a point estimate $\widehat{y}(t+1)$ for each variable $\mathcal{V}$, given an input sample Y, using the linguistic variable $\mathcal{FIG}$ and the induced fuzzy rules on model $\mathcal{M}$.

The rule matching procedure can become computationally expensive as the size of the rule base $\mathcal{M}$ grows. Because of this it is advisable that implementations of this model use spatial trees [13] to index the rules with the midpoints of each fuzzy set on their LHS, optimizing the search for applicable rules during the forecasting step. This work used the KD-tree implementation of the Scipy Spatial package[1].

The global parameter κ is related with the spatial index search on $\mathcal{FIG}$, and indicates how many $\mathcal{G}_i \in \mathcal{FIG}$ are returned for a given crisp multivariate data point. This parameter has influence on the sensibility and the diversity of the rules considered during the forecasting procedure, such that as κ increases more rules will be accounted on. If $\kappa = 1$, just the closest rule (the rule with the highest membership degree) will be used.

In the next sections the training and forecasting procedures are detailed and, finally, the overall method features are discussed.

3.1   Training Procedure

Stage 1 *Partitioning*:

(a) *Defining $U_{\mathcal{V}_i}$*: The Universe of Discourse $U_{\mathcal{V}_i}$ defines the sample space, i.e., the known bounds of the variable $\mathcal{V}_i$, such that $U_{\mathcal{V}_i} = [\min(Y^{\mathcal{V}_i}) - D_1, \max(Y^{\mathcal{V}_i}) + D_2]$, where $D_1 = \min(Y^{\mathcal{V}_i}) \times 0.2$ and $D_2 = \max(Y^{\mathcal{V}_i}) \times 0.2$ are used to extrapolate the known bounds as a security margin, $\forall \mathcal{V}_i \in \mathcal{V}$ (Fig. 1).

(b) *$U_{\mathcal{V}_i}$ Partitioning*: Split $U_{\mathcal{V}_i}$ in k_i intervals U_j with midpoints c_j, for $j = 0..k_i$, where all the intervals have the same length;

(c) *Define the linguistic variable $\tilde{\mathcal{V}}_i$*: For each interval $U_j \in U_{\mathcal{V}_i}$ create an overlapping fuzzy set $A_j^{\mathcal{V}_i}$, with the membership function

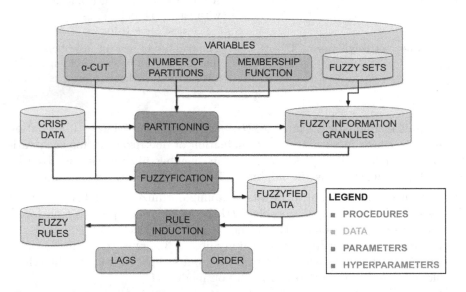

Fig. 1. $\mathcal{FIG}$-FTS training procedure and its components

---

[1] https://docs.scipy.org/doc/scipy/reference/spatial.html. Access in 2019-04-29.

$\mu_{A_j^{\mathcal{V}_i}}(y_{\mathcal{V}_i}(t))$, where $y_{\mathcal{V}_i}(t)$ is the value of the $\mathcal{V}_i$ variable on instance $y(t) \in Y$. The midpoint of the fuzzy set $A_j^{\mathcal{V}_i}$ will be c_j, the lower bound $l_j = c_{j-1}$ and the upper bound $u_j = c_{j+1} \forall j > 0$ and $j < k_i$, and $l_0 = \min U_{\mathcal{V}_i}$, $l_k = \max U_{\mathcal{V}_i}$. Each fuzzy set $A_j^{\mathcal{V}_i}$ is a linguistic term of the linguistic variable $\widetilde{\mathcal{V}}_i$;

Stage 2 *Fuzzyfication*:

Transform the original numeric time series Y into a fuzzy time series F, where each data point $f(t) \in F$ is a $\mathcal{G}_i \in \mathcal{FIG}$. For each $y(t) \in Y$ the following steps must be executed:

(a) *Individual variable fuzzyfication*: For each variable $\mathcal{V}_i \in \mathcal{V}$, find the linguistic terms $A_j^{\mathcal{V}_i} \in \widetilde{\mathcal{V}}_i$, where the fuzzy membership is greater than the predefined α-cut, i.e., $f_{\mathcal{V}_i}(t) = \{A_j^{\mathcal{V}_i} \mid \mu_{A_j^{\mathcal{V}_i}}(y_{\mathcal{V}_i}(t)) \geq \alpha_i \forall A_j^{\mathcal{V}_i} \in \widetilde{\mathcal{V}}_i\}$;

(b) *Search in $\mathcal{FIG}$*: For each combination of fuzzy sets $A_j^{\mathcal{V}_i}$ in $f_{\mathcal{V}_i}(t)$ verify if there is a $\mathcal{G}_i \in \mathcal{G}$ where $\mathcal{G}_i \supset \{A_j^{\mathcal{V}_i}\}, \forall A_j^{\mathcal{V}_i} \in f_{\mathcal{V}_i}(t)$. If it exists, then the fuzzyfied value of $y(t)$ is $\mathcal{G}_i$. This search is performed with KD-trees, comparing the midpoints of the fuzzyfied data and the midpoints of the fuzzy sets in the $\mathcal{FIG}$.

(c) *Create new $\mathcal{G}_i$ in $\mathcal{FIG}$*: If no $\mathcal{G}_i$ was found in the previous step, new ones are added to $\mathcal{FIG}$. For each combination of fuzzy sets $A_j^{\mathcal{V}_i}$ in $f_{\mathcal{V}_i}(t)$ create a fuzzy information granule $\mathcal{G}_i$ such that $\mathcal{G}_i = \{A_j^{\mathcal{V}_i}\}, \forall A_j^{\mathcal{V}_i} \in f_{\mathcal{V}_i}(t)$ and $\mu_{\mathcal{G}_i} = \bigcap \mu_{A_j^{\mathcal{V}_i}}$. The created $\mathcal{G}_i$ is then the fuzzyfied value of $y(t)$.

Stage 3 *Rule Induction*:

(a) *Generate the high order temporal patterns*: The fuzzy temporal patterns have format $\mathcal{G}_{i0}, ..., \mathcal{G}_{i\Omega} \rightarrow \mathcal{G}_{ij}$, where the precedent (or Left Hand Side) is $f(t - L(\Omega)) = \mathcal{G}_{i0}$, $f(t - L(\Omega - 1)) = \mathcal{G}_{i1}$, ..., $f(t - L(0)) = \mathcal{G}_{i\Omega}$, and the consequent (or RHS) is $f(t + 1) = \mathcal{G}_{ij}$.

(b) *Generate the rule base*: Select all temporal patterns with the same precedent and group their consequent sets creating a rule with the format $\mathcal{G}_{i0}, ..., \mathcal{G}_{i\Omega} \rightarrow w_k \cdot \mathcal{G}_{ik}, w_j \cdot \mathcal{G}_{ij}, ...$, where the LHS is $f(t - L(\Omega)) = \mathcal{G}_{i0}$, $f(t - L(\Omega - 1)) = \mathcal{G}_{i1}$, ..., $f(t - L(0)) = \mathcal{G}_{i\Omega}$ and the RHS is $f(t + 1) \in \{\mathcal{G}_k, \mathcal{G}_j, ...\}$ and the weights $w_j, w_k, ...$ are the normalized frequencies of each temporal pattern such that:

$$w_i = \frac{|\mathcal{G}_i|}{|RHS|} \quad \forall \mathcal{G}_i \in RHS \tag{1}$$

where $|\mathcal{G}_i|$ is the number of occurrences of $\mathcal{G}_i$ on temporal patterns with the same precedent LHS and $|RHS|$ is the total number of temporal patterns with the same precedent LHS. Each rule can be understood as the weighted set of possibilities which may happen on time $t + 1$ (the consequent) when a certain precedent $\mathcal{G}_{i0}, ..., \mathcal{G}_{i\Omega}$ is identified on previous L lags (the precedent).

3.2 Forecasting Procedure

Step 1 *Fuzzyfication*: Find all $\mathcal{G}_{i\Omega}, ..., \mathcal{G}_{i0} \in \mathcal{FIG}$ which is close to the sample $y(t - \Omega), ..., y(t)$, such that $\mu_{\mathcal{G}_{it}}(y(t)) > 0$.

Step 2 *Rule matching*: Select κ rules in $\mathcal{M}$ where the LHS match the $\mathcal{G}_{i\Omega}, ..., \mathcal{G}_{i0}$ values found in the previous step. The rule activation μ_j is shown below, using the minimum function as T-norm.

$$\mu_j = \bigcap_{t \in L\ i \in \mathcal{FIG}} \mu_{\mathcal{G}_{it}} \tag{2}$$

Step 3 *Rule mean points*: For each selected rule $q = 0..\kappa$, compute the mean point mp_q of each variable $\mathcal{V}_i \in \mathcal{V}$ as below, where c_j is the c parameter of the $\mu_{A_j^{\mathcal{V}_i}}$ function from fuzzy set $A_j^{\mathcal{V}_i}$:

$$mp_q^{\mathcal{V}_i} = \sum_{j \in \mathcal{V}} w_j \cdot c_j \tag{3}$$

Step 4 *Defuzzyfication*: For each variable $\mathcal{V}_i \in \mathcal{V}$, compute the forecast as the weighted sum of the rule mid-points mp_q by their membership grades μ_q for each selected rule j:

$$\hat{y}^{\mathcal{V}_i}(t + 1) = \frac{\sum_{q=0..\kappa} \mu_q \cdot mp_q^{\mathcal{V}_i}}{\sum_{q=0..\kappa} \mu_q} \tag{4}$$

Step 5 *Forecasting horizon*: Given the number m of steps ahead to forecast (the forecast horizon), repeat the Steps 1 to 4 m times, appending the output $\hat{y}$ of the previous Step 4 at the end of the $y(t)$ input for the next Step 1.

3.3 Method Discussion

In contrast with other machine learning approaches, $\mathcal{FIG}$-FTS learning method is not a stochastic heuristic procedure and has no convergence issues, it is a deterministic data driven method whose cost is linear with the data input size and the parsimony of the model, hereafter defined as the number of rules of the trained model $\mathcal{M}$.

The main insight of the $\mathcal{FIG}$-FTS is that the linguistic variables $A_{\mathcal{V}_i}$ work as feature extraction layers and each fuzzy information granule $\mathcal{G}$ is a small cluster prototype of these features, simplifying the representation of temporal patterns and aiding pattern identification and rule induction. Each $\mathcal{G}$ also helps the multivariate defuzzyfication process, working as a final output layer for the model.

The learning procedure of $\mathcal{FIG}$-FTS is controlled by its hyper-parameters that directly affect its accuracy and parsimony. The number of partitions of each variable k_i affects the number of rules directly, given the maximum number of rules (in the worst case) is a Cartesian product of the fuzzy sets $A_j^{\mathcal{V}_i} \in \tilde{\mathcal{V}}_i$, for each $\mathcal{V}_i \in \mathcal{V}$. The α_i-cut, on the other hand, controls the fuzzyfication sensibility by eliminating, in the rule induction stage, values with lower membership grades. It reduces the number of rules by preventing the capture of spurious patterns, generated by insignificant memberships or noise. The α_i-cut also enhances the forecasting process by eliminating lower related rules on rule search.

There is a non-linear relationship between the number of rules and the model accuracy, also related to the well known bias-variance trade off. Too few fuzzy sets makes the model underfit, being incapable of learning the time series patterns, while using too many fuzzy sets makes the model overfit and start learning the time series noise. The optimal number of k_i must be optimized for each problem, balancing the accuracy and the parsimony, also affecting the computational performance due to the rule matching in the forecasting procedure.

The parameter κ has influence on the forecasting accuracy. There is also a balance between the use of too few or too many rules on forecasting procedure, such that too few rules may not have enough patterns to describe the correct time series behavior and too many may bring patterns that are not closely related with the current behavior.

The best values of the hyper-parameters are intrinsically related with each time series characteristics and must be empirically determined. The authors recommend the following values to start the hyper-parameter optimization: $\Omega = 2$, $L = [1, 2]$, $\kappa = 2$, $k_i = 35 \ \forall \ \widetilde{\mathcal{V}}_i \in \mathcal{V}$. However, it is mandatory to remember that all these values may have a great variation according to each time series.

In the next section the empirical results of the proposed method are presented, showing its effectiveness for complex artificial and natural dynamic processes.

4 Computational Experiments

This section aims to evaluate the out-of-sample performance of the proposed method using artificial and real datasets, namely, the Lorentz chaotic attractor and the Global Energy Forecasting Competition 2012. The chosen experimental datasets reflect the demand for forecasting tools of complex dynamic processes with interacting factors which can be challenging to predict as the forecasting horizon increases. The hyper-parameters k, α and μ of each variable were chosen using a grid search, where the search spaces are presented on Table 2 and the Ω, L and κ values were kept constant using the reference values given in Sect. 3.3. Once the best parameters were established, the response of Ω and κ were measured on intervals $\Omega \in [1, 3]$ and $\kappa \in [1, 3]$.

Table 2. Hyper-parameters search spaces used on grid search

Parameter	Search space
k	$[10, 200]$
μ	Triangular, Trapezoidal, Gaussian
α	$\{0, .05, .15, .2, .25, .3, .35, .4, .45, .5\}$

The proposed method and the computational experiments were implemented with the Python programming language (version 3.6), using pyFTS library [26] infrastructure and all the experiments can also be found on a permanent link[2] for research reproducibility.

The accuracy measure chosen to evaluate the out-of-sample results was the Mean Average Percentual Error (MAPE) that expresses the error as a percentage of the correct value, and it is detailed in Eq. (5). A rolling window cross validation methodology [32] was applied, using a data window length of 80% of the dataset total length, where 90% of it was used for training and the remaining 10% is used for testing, with a sliding increment of 5% of the data window, and all measurements were performed out of sample.

$$MAPE = n^{-1} \sum_{t=0}^{n} \left| \frac{y(t) - \hat{y}(t)}{y(t)} \right| \tag{5}$$

The first test dataset is the Lorentz Attractor, proposed in [10] defined by Eq. (6) and illustrated in Fig. 2. It is a three-variable chaotic system with high sensibility to its initial values and even small variations can induce great perturbations few steps ahead[3]. This dataset contains 5000 samples, where the parameters are $a = 10.0$, $b = 28.0$, $c = 8.0/3.0$, the differential step is 0.01 and the initial values are $x = 0.1$, $y = 0$ and $z = 0$.

$$\begin{aligned} \dot{x} &= a(y - x) \\ \dot{y} &= x(b - z) - y \\ \dot{z} &= xy - cz \end{aligned} \tag{6}$$

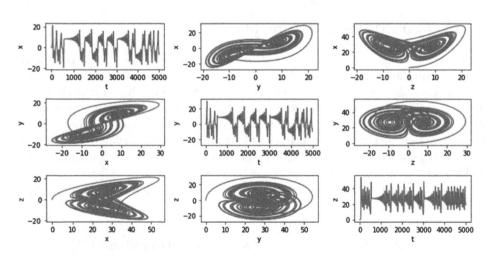

Fig. 2. The Lorentz Map dataset

---

[2] http://bit.ly/fig-fts-experiments.

[3] It is necessary to warn that simulations of chaotic systems contains accumulated errors, caused by discretization and limited numerical precision, and the propagation of these errors creates a divergence from the true orbit, as discussed in [14].

In the experiments the partitioning of Lorentz Attractor for the best model is complex, as shown in Table 3. This reflects the sensibility of the generating process, where minimal perturbations affect all the system behavior in short term. The sensibility of the Ω and κ parameters, also the parsimony of the models are described in Table 4. It is possible to note with these results, and the sample on Fig. 3, that the median errors for the X, Y and Z variables are respectively 1.56%, 3.09% and 1.23% for one step ahead. The errors increase as the forecasting horizon increases and hit 21%, 45% and 5% for 100 steps ahead. The model accuracy has a great variance between the variables reflecting the impact of the interactions of each variable and the differences on the velocities of its changing rates. This is, however, a known property of the chaotic systems that make them hard to predict even in short forecasting horizons.

Table 3. Lorentz Attractor best model hyper-parameters

Parameter	Variables	Value
k	x	120
	y	180
	z	144
μ	x, y, z	Gaussian
α	x, y, z	0.0
Ω	Global	2
L	Global	[1,2]
κ	Global	3

The Global Energy Forecasting Competition 2012 is defined in [8], and illustrated in Fig. 4. This dataset contains 39432 instances with hourly time granularity, from February of 2004 to July of 2008. It contains the variables timestamp, energy load and temperature, and the objective is to use the timestamp and temperature as explanatory variables to predict the energy load.

In the experiments the partitioning of GEFCom'12 for the best model is very simple when compared to the Lorentz Attractor, as shown in Fig. 5 and Table 5. The sensibility of the Ω and κ parameters, also the parsimony of the models are described in Table 6. It is possible to note with these results, and the sample in Fig. 6, that the median error for the Load variable is 4.5% and for the temperature variable is 2.7% for one step ahead. The errors increase as the forecasting horizon increases and hit 12% and 10% for 100 steps ahead. As occurred with the Lorentz Attractor, the model accuracy varies between the variables and the prediction horizon considered. The above values reflect a good accuracy for short and very short term load forecasting (between 24 h and 72 h).

Finally, the experiments showed the applicability of the proposed method on the forecasting of complex dynamical processes with interacting factors, with

Table 4. Accuracy and parsimony results for the Lorentz Attractor by order, number of nearest neighbors, variable and forecasting horizon.

Ω	$|\mathcal{M}|$	κ	$\mathcal{V}_i$	MAPE by forecasting horizon				
				1	25	50	75	100
1	14, 849	1	x	1.63	2.80	30.58	25.02	21.79
			y	3.95	25.85	19.53	15.12	27.36
			z	1.412	1.12	2.12	4.75	5.74
		2	x	1.58	2.82	17.21	14.77	12.22
			y	3.65	15.98	22.90	16.58	24.14
			z	1.19	0.87	2.28	3.56	3.80
		3	x	1.51	2.90	15.10	14.22	18.48
			y	3.26	12.97	27.98	22.04	31.14
			z	0.87	0.92	2.40	4.72	4.70
2	167, 840	1	x	1.60	2.04	27.95	24.63	22.64
			y	3.98	25.04	25.99	21.31	27.44
			z	1.33	1.54	2.01	4.84	5.06
		2	x	1.56	5.58	16.74	14.20	12.80
			y	3.13	25.02	30.08	21.86	60.19
			z	1.38	1.43	3.10	5.62	5.71
		3	x	1.65	5.67	16.78	14.21	12.14
			y	3.17	21.54	29.99	21.56	48.70
			z	1.38	1.99	2.15	3.34	3.66
3	1, 546, 844	1	x	1.73	28.54	44.80	32.27	49.11
			y	4.53	53.34	43.68	38.23	65.44
			z	1.14	5.55	18.14	16.83	18.33
		2	x	1.80	28.54	44.80	32.27	49.11
			y	3.09	55.82	45.66	39.50	67.48
			z	1.32	5.55	17.81	16.83	18.33
		3	x	1.83	29.81	46.43	33.34	50.50
			y	4.15	54.99	44.99	39.08	66.79
			z	1.23	5.55	18.33	16.83	18.33

Table 5. GEFCom'12 best model hyper-parameters

Parameter	Variables	Value
k	Hour	24
	Temperature	10
	Load	15
μ	Hour	Triangular
	Temperature, Load	Gaussian
α	Hour	0.25
	Temperature, Load	0.3
Ω	Global	1
L	Global	[1]
κ	Global	3

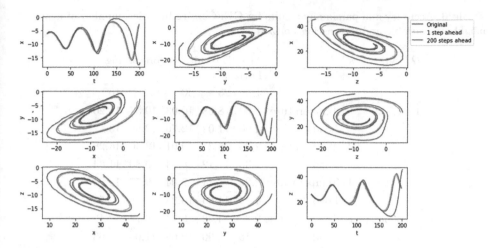

Fig. 3. Sample of $\mathcal{FIG}$-FTS best model for Lorentz Attractor, for one and many steps ahead

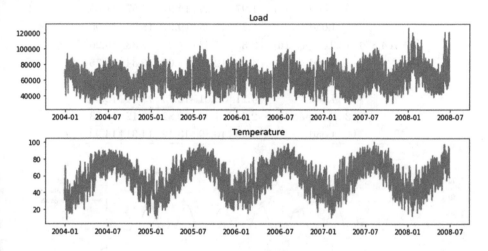

Fig. 4. GEFCom'12 dataset

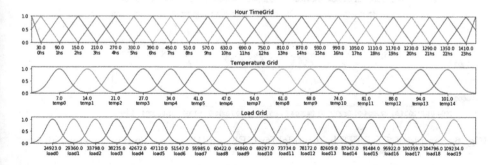

Fig. 5. GEFCom'12 partitioning scheme

Table 6. Accuracy and parsimony results for GEFCom'12 by order, number of nearest neighbors, variable and forecasting horizon.

Ω	$|\mathcal{M}|$	κ	$\mathcal{V}_i$	MAPE results by forecasting horizon				
				1	25	50	75	100
1	2,542	1	Temperature	3.00	8.58	10.03	10.57	11.26
			Load	4.60	11.02	12.70	12.86	13.12
		2	Temperature	2.76	5.31	10.01	13.46	16.28
			Load	4.38	12.12	8.94	9.80	11.84
		3	Temperature	2.26	7.14	9.04	9.77	11.75
			Load	4.49	11.65	10.83	11.88	12.58
2	34569.0	1	Temperature	2.83	4.38	6.74	9.74	12.12
			Load	5.15	9.90	12.05	11.05	12.63
		2	Temperature	2.33	11.08	13.63	16.29	18.67
			Load	4.97	9.63	9.68	8.83	11.34
		3	Temperature	1.97	7.29	14.97	12.57	11.36
			Load	4.20	15.79	19.27	18.36	18.05
3	164,876	1	Temperature	3.30	7.83	10.91	16.38	15.26
			Load	4.28	12.15	14.00	15.34	16.75
		2	Temperature	2.92	7.94	11.46	8.41	9.14
			Load	4.21	12.01	12.79	12.11	12.46
		3	Temperature	2.24	7.93	10.82	10.12	12.53
			Load	4.49	10.89	13.12	14.31	14.93

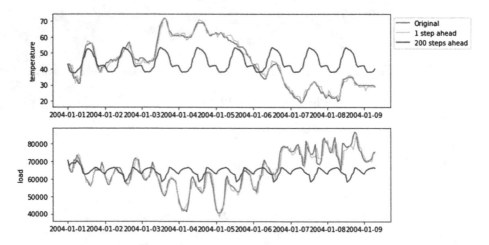

Fig. 6. Sample of $\mathcal{FIG}$-FTS best model for GEFCom'12, for one and many steps ahead

accurate results from short to medium term. In the next section the main findings of this work are summarized and discussed. Finally, future research directions are pointed out.

5   Conclusion

Fuzzy Time Series are data driven and non parametric forecasting methods with model readability, simplicity and accuracy. But even such methods have difficulty handling multivariate time series data of complex dynamical systems.

This work proposed the Fuzzy Information Granular Fuzzy Time Series method ($\mathcal{FIG}$-FTS), an approach that incorporates Fuzzy Information Granules (FIG) to the FTS methodology in order to simplify the processing of the multivariate crisp data. First, individual Universe of Discourse partitioning schemes are provided for each variable and then Fuzzy Information Granules $\mathcal{G}_i$ are created as combinations of the fuzzy sets of the variables. Each $\mathcal{G}$ is created on demand, on the fuzzyfication phase, by selecting one fuzzy set of each variable. After that, each multivariate data point can be replaced by an univariate one, identified with a corresponding $\mathcal{G}$.

This approach enabled the creation of a high order weighted method for multivariate forecasting, where each $\mathcal{G}$ contains information about all variables. It is also used to forecast all of them, for one or more steps ahead.

This work performed computational experiments to assess the $\mathcal{FIG}$-FTS method performance, and applied the proposed method to model and forecast the Lorentz Attractor, a complex dynamic and chaotic process with three interacting variables. The results showed that the Mean Average Percentual Error (MAPE) of the models vary between 1% and 4% (depending on the variable) for one step ahead. Chaotic processes are hard to forecast, even for short term, and for a prediction horizon of 100 steps ahead the MAPE increases up to 41% in the worst case.

A real dataset was also employed to asses the model performance, namely the Global Energy Forecasting Competition 2012, with four years of temperature and energy load data. The results showed that the Mean Average Percentual Error of the models was at about 2% and 4% for one step ahead, and for a prediction horizon of 48 h, the MAPE is at about 10%.

The hyperparameters of the $\mathcal{FIG}$-FTS method allow it to be very flexible and adaptable to several real-world scenarios. Future research will extend the proposed method to embody more complex hyper-parameter optimization methods and comparisons with other modelling approaches in the literature.

Acknowledgements. This work has been supported by CAPES, CNPq and FAPEMIG funding agencies in Brazil, and the PBQS program of the IFNMG - Campus Januária institution.

References

1. Alves, M.A., Silva, P.C.D.L., Severiano, C.A.J., Vieira, G.L., Guimaraes, F.G., Sadaei, H.J.: An extension of nonstationary fuzzy sets to heteroskedastic fuzzy time series. In: 26th European Symposium on Artificial Neural Networks, Computational Intelligence and Machine Learning, Bruges (2018)
2. Askari, S., Montazerin, N.: A high-order multi-variable fuzzy time series forecasting algorithm based on fuzzy clustering. Expert Syst. Appl. **42**(4), 2121–2135 (2015). https://doi.org/10.1016/j.eswa.2014.09.036
3. Chen, M.Y., Chen, B.T.: A hybrid fuzzy time series model based on granular computing for stock price forecasting. Inf. Sci. (2015). https://doi.org/10.1016/j.ins.2014.09.038
4. Chen, S.M.: Forecasting enrollments based on fuzzy time series. Fuzzy Sets Syst. **81**(3), 311–319 (1996). https://doi.org/10.1016/0165-0114(95)00220-0
5. Chen, S.M., Tanuwijaya, K.: Multivariate fuzzy forecasting based on fuzzy time-series and automatic clustering techniques. Expert Syst. Appl. **38** (2011). https://doi.org/10.1016/j.eswa.2011.02.098
6. Cheng, C.H., Chen, T.L., Teoh, H.J., Chiang, C.H.: Fuzzy time-series based on adaptive expectation model for TAIEX forecasting. Expert Syst. Appl. **34**, 1126–1132 (2008). https://doi.org/10.1016/j.eswa.2006.12.021
7. Guney, H., Bakir, M.A., Aladag, C.H.: A novel stochastic seasonal fuzzy time series forecasting model. Int. J. Fuzzy Syst. **20**(3), 729–740 (2018). https://doi.org/10.1007/s40815-017-0385-z
8. Hong, T., Pinson, P., Fan, S.: Global energy forecasting competition 2012. Int. J. Forecast. **30**(2), 357–363 (2014). https://doi.org/10.1016/j.ijforecast.2013.07.001
9. Leite, D., Gomide, F., Ballini, R., Costa, P.: Fuzzy granular evolving modeling for time series prediction. In: IEEE International Conference on Fuzzy Systems, pp. 2794–2801 (2011). https://doi.org/10.1109/FUZZY.2011.6007452
10. Lorenz, E.N.: Deterministic nonperiodic flow. J. Atmos. Sci. **20**, 130–141 (1963)
11. Lu, W., Pedrycz, W., Liu, X., Yang, J., Li, P.: The modeling of time series based on fuzzy information granules. Expert Syst. Appl. (2014). https://doi.org/10.1016/j.eswa.2013.12.005
12. Magalhães, M.H., Ballini, R., Gomide, F.A.C.: Granular models for time-series forecasting. In: Handbook of Granular Computing, chap. 45, pp. 949–967. Wiley (2008). https://doi.org/10.1002/9780470724163.ch45, https://onlinelibrary.wiley.com/doi/abs/10.1002/9780470724163.ch45
13. Muja, M., Lowe, D.G.: Scalable nearest neighbor algorithms for high dimensional data. IEEE Trans. Pattern Anal. Mach. Intell. **36**(11), 2227–2240 (2014). https://doi.org/10.1109/TPAMI.2014.2321376
14. Nepomuceno, E.G., Mendes, E.M.A.M.: On the analysis of pseudo-orbits of continuous chaotic nonlinear systems simulated using discretization schemes in a digital computer. Chaos, Solitons Fractals **95**, 21–32 (2017). https://doi.org/10.1016/j.chaos.2016.12.002,http://www.sciencedirect.com/science/article/pii/S0960077916303551
15. Reyes-Galaviz, O.F.: Granular Fuzzy Models: Construction, Analysis, and Design. Ph.D. thesis, Department of Electrical and Computer Engineering, University of Alberta (2016)
16. Sadaei, H.J., Enayatifar, R., Abdullah, A.H., Gani, A.: Short-term load forecasting using a hybrid model with a refined exponentially weighted fuzzy time series and an improved harmony search. Int. J. Electr. Power Energy Syst. **62**, 118–129 (2014). https://doi.org/10.1016/j.ijepes.2014.04.026

17. Sadaei, H.J., Enayatifar, R., Lee, M.H., Mahmud, M.: A hybrid model based on differential fuzzy logic relationships and imperialist competitive algorithm for stock market forecasting. Appl. Soft Comput. J. **40**, 132–149 (2016). https://doi.org/10. 1016/j.asoc.2015.11.026
18. Sadaei, H.J., Guimarães, F.G., Silva, C.J.D., Lee, M.H., Eslami, T.: Short-term load forecasting method based on fuzzy time series, seasonality and long memory process. Int. J. Approximate Reasoning **83**, 196–217 (2017). https://doi.org/10. 1016/j.ijar.2017.01.006
19. Sadaei, H.J., de Lima e Silva, P.C., Guimarães, F.G., Lee, M.H.: Short-term load forecasting by using a combined method of convolutional neural networks and fuzzy time series. Energy **175**, 365–377 (2019). https://doi.org/10.1016/j.energy.2019.03. 081, http://www.sciencedirect.com/science/article/pii/S0360544219304852
20. Severiano, C.A.C., Silva, P.P.C.L., Sadaei, H.J.H., Guimarães, F.F.G.: Very short-term solar forecasting using fuzzy time series. In: 2017 IEEE International Conference on Fuzzy Systems. Naples (2017). https://doi.org/10.1109/FUZZ-IEEE.2017. 8015732
21. Silva, G.C., Alexandre, D., Vieira, G., Silva, J.L.R., Lisboa, A.C., Vieira, D.A.G., Saldanha, R.R.: Fuzzy time series applications and extensions: analysis of a short term load forecasting challenge. In: International conference on Time Series and Forecasting (ITISE 2018), vol. 770, Granada (2018). https://www.researchgate. net/publication/327756074
22. Silva, G.C., Silva, J.L.R., Lisboa, A.C., Vieira, D.A.G., Saldanha, R.R.: Advanced fuzzy time series applied to short term load forecasting. In: 4th IEEE Latin American Conference on Computational Intelligence, IEEE, Guadalajara (2017)
23. de Lima e Silva, P.C., de Oliveira e Lucas, P., Guimarães, F.G.: A distributed algorithm for scalable fuzzy time series. In: Miani, R., Camargos, L., Zarpelão, B., Rosas, E., Pasquini, R. (eds.) GPC 2019. LNCS, vol. 11484, pp. 42–56. Springer, Cham (2019). https://doi.org/10.1007/978-3-030-19223-5_4
24. Silva, P., Sadaei, H.J., Guimarães, F.: Interval forecasting with fuzzy time series. In: IEEE Symposium Series on Computational Intelligence (IEEE SSCI 2016), Athens (2016). https://doi.org/10.1109/SSCI.2016.7850010
25. Silva, P.C.D.L., Alves, M.A., Severiano Jr, C.A., Vieira, G.L., Guimarães, F.G., Sadaei, H.J.: Probabilistic forecasting with seasonal ensemble fuzzy time-series. In: XIII Brazilian Congress on Computational Intelligence, Rio de Janeiro (2017)
26. Silva, P.C.D.L., Lucas, P.O., Sadaei, H.J., Guimarães, F.G.: pyFTS: Fuzzy Time Series for Python (2018). https://doi.org/10.5281/zenodo.597359
27. Silva, P.C.L., Sadaei, H.J., Ballini, R., Guimaraes, F.G.: Probabilistic forecasting with fuzzy time series. IEEE Trans. Fuzzy Syst. 1 (2019). https://doi.org/10.1109/ TFUZZ.2019.2922152, https://ieeexplore.ieee.org/document/8734764/
28. Singh, P., Dhiman, G.: A hybrid fuzzy time series forecasting model based on granular computing and bio-inspired optimization approaches. J. Comput. Sci. **27**, 370–385 (2018). https://doi.org/10.1016/j.jocs.2018.05.008
29. Soares, E.A., Camargo, H.A., Camargo, S.J., Leite, D.F.: Incremental gaussian granular fuzzy modeling applied to hurricane track forecasting. In: 2018 IEEE International Conference on Fuzzy Systems (FUZZ-IEEE) (2018). https://www. researchgate.net/publication/326731587
30. Song, Q., Chissom, B.S.: Fuzzy time series and its models. Fuzzy Sets Syst. **54**(3), 269–277 (1993). https://doi.org/10.1016/0165-0114(93)90372-O

31. Talarposhti, F.M., Sadaei, H.J., Enayatifar, R., Guimarães, F.G., Mahmud, M., Eslami, T.: Stock market forecasting by using a hybrid model of exponential fuzzy time series. Int. J. Approximate Reasoning **70**, 79–98 (2016). https://doi.org/10.1016/j.ijar.2015.12.011
32. Tashman, L.J.: Out-of-sample tests of forecasting accuracy: an analysis and review. Int. J. Forecast. **16**(4), 437–450 (2000). https://doi.org/10.1016/S0169-2070(00)00065-0
33. Wang, L., Liu, X., Pedrycz, W., Shao, Y.: Determination of temporal information granules to improve forecasting in fuzzy time series. Expert Syst. Appl. **57**, 1–8 (2014). https://doi.org/10.1016/j.eswa.2013.10.046
34. Wang, W., Pedrycz, W., Liu, X.: Time series long-term forecasting model based on information granules and fuzzy clustering. Eng. Appl. Artif. Intell. (2015). https://doi.org/10.1016/j.engappai.2015.01.006
35. Yang, D., Dong, Z., Hong, L., Lim, I., Liu, L.: Analyzing big time series data in solar engineering using features and PCA. Sol. Energy **153**, 317–328 (2017). https://doi.org/10.1016/j.solener.2017.05.072
36. Yu, H.K.: Weighted fuzzy time series models for TAIEX forecasting. Phys. A **349**(3), 609–624 (2005). https://doi.org/10.1016/j.physa.2004.11.006
37. Zadeh, L.A.: Fuzzy sets and information granularity. In: Fuzzy Sets, Fuzzy Logic, and Fuzzy Systems, pp. 433–448 (1996). https://doi.org/10.1142/9789814261302_0022

Interactive Analysis of the Discussion from a Virtual Community on Neuroscience

Rafael José de Alencar Almeida[1,2]($\boxtimes$) ,
and Dárlinton Barbosa Feres Carvalho[2]

[1] IF Sudeste MG, Barbacena, Brazil
rafael.alencar@ifsudestemg.edu.br
[2] Universidade Federal de São João del-Rei, São João del-Rei, Brazil
darlinton@acm.org

Abstract. Social media on the Internet has been promoting disruptive transformations in the society, enabling new possibilities for knowledge construction. Nowadays, researchers can fastly gather a large number of discussions from a virtual community of interest for analysis. This paper presents the study of a relevant community on neuroscience, with more than 43,000 registered members. The research method employs a process based on Grounded Theory and Knowledge Discovery in Databases (KDD), using a tool crafted to support interactively and iteratively use of data mining algorithms such as topic modeling and sentiment analysis. From the analysis of 2,927 posts and 19,227 comments, the results reveal the most prominent subject regards Alzheimer's disease, followed by general acknowledgments and requests for help whether concerning symptom assessment, examination results analysis, and medical advice. Most of the identified topics have a positive polarity, indicating that interactions are predominantly friendly. Negative feelings emerged from controversial topics, being mostly non-technical or speculative subjects such as mind control techniques, help with MRI results, answers to medical advice, and theories about consciousness. The findings reinforce the feasibility of such studies and show useful insights regarding the community interest in neuroscience.

Keywords: Neuroscience · Virtual community · Analysis

1 Introduction

Widespread Internet access, fueled by the popularization of mobile devices, has been promoting disruptive social transformations, enabling new possibilities for knowledge construction. In this context, social media—such as forums, blogs, and social network sites—stand out because of the emergence of online communities, with a continuous and intense exchange of information and experiences among users on the most varied themes and aspects of their lives [10].

© Springer Nature Switzerland AG 2019
V. R. Cota et al. (Eds.): LAWCN 2019, CCIS 1068, pp. 59–78, 2019.
https://doi.org/10.1007/978-3-030-36636-0_5

In the context of scientific research, social media has the potential to accelerate the pace of biomedical research and scientific dissemination through online collaboration, discussions, and faster sharing of information [7]. Just as successful experiences on web-mediated collaboration (e.g., [6]), neuroscience researchers, students, and enthusiasts have been building strong virtual communities for discussion [7]. The topics of interest in these communities range from specific themes like Pain Research Forum, Schizophrenia Research Forum and Alzheimer's Research Forum to general discussions involving experts and enthusiasts, such as Reddit Neuroscience Community.

The scope of the use of social media and the abundance of data produced on discussions has fostered new possibilities of scientific investigation, usually looking for a comprehensive understanding of the arguments in these communities [20]. Through research oriented to the data available on online communities, it becomes possible to identify recurring subjects in the discussions, controversial or questionable topics and even emerging issues—providing an overview of the relevant discussion themes and yet revealing concerns to guide future researches.

However, the manual analysis of the data produced in virtual communities for scientific discussions proves impracticable, both due to the large volume of text being read and the increasing flow of new posts. To reduce the time consumed in the process and to enable the production of new knowledge from the analysis of virtual communities, it is necessary to develop innovations in computer science research [24]. In this sense, various studies have been developed applying computational techniques of data mining to support the analysis of virtual communities in several areas of knowledge. From the literature, we point out the challenge of selecting the content to be analyzed [2], analysis of the sentiments expressed in the discussions [23], and automatic visual summarization and analysis of the results [27].

Data mining techniques enable the automatic identification of patterns and relationships implicit in large volumes of data, which may lead to new knowledge [13]. This purpose establishes the field known as Knowledge Discovery in Databases (KDD), an iterative process with the involvement of a specialist in the domain of the analyzed problem, which aims to extract useful knowledge of large volumes of data [11]. The KDD process consists of five main steps that lead to discovering of new knowledge: selection, preprocessing, transformation, data mining and interpretation/evaluation (Fig. 1).

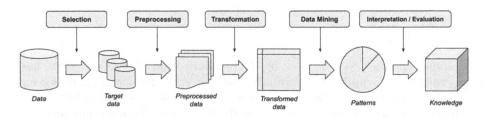

Fig. 1. The Knowledge Discovery in Database (KDD) process.

Since KDD process strongly relies on parameter choices for the data mining tools, this kind of studies requires multiple expertises to guarantee the research quality [9]. Beyond the knowledge on the studied domain, usually advanced computer science skills are required to conduct the research. Unfortunately, the cooperation of multiple specialists throughout the entire process is a hurdle that prevents domain experts from conducting analyses effectively. Thus, to overcome the struggles regarding the parameters fine-tuning, we have created an interactive tool to enable domains experts to use cutting-edge data mining algorithms and comfortably explore the available settings through a graphical interface tailored to aid at discussion forum analysis.

For the present research, we employ the proposed interactive tool that combines data mining techniques for analysis of an online community on neuroscience. The tool allows researchers to perform interactive and iterative exploratory analysis, covering all stages of the KDD process, with automatic summarization of prominent subjects, sentiment analysis of the discussions and graphic visualization of results.

As exploratory and data-driven research, the present study employs KDD with the methodological approach known as Grounded Theory, which is based on the collection and systematic and rigorous analysis of data, for the construction of theories that answer the proposed research questions [12]. For the research questions regarding the analyzed neuroscience community, we sought to investigate the characterization of the main subjects discussed, their polarity and their interest over time. So, they are formulated as follows:

RQ1: What are the main characteristics of the subjects most frequently discussed in the community?

RQ2: What are the emerging issues and those that have been losing community interest over time?

RQ3: What are and how are characterized the subjects, in which there is a strong predominance of feelings in the community?

Accordingly, we hope the results of this research brings an overall understanding of the discussions on the Neuroscience Reddit Community. The identification of recurring subjects in the community reveal its main interests, and given its size, this interest can be regarded as a broad interest of the neuroscience community at large. The results can also provide support at developing better scientific communications. Moreover, significant concerns can be used to guide future researches.

The rest of this paper is structured as follows. Section 2 presents the related work to this research. Next, Sect. 3 details the methodology employed in this study. As a result, the analyzed data is described in Sect. 4. Section 5 presents the results of community analysis, answering the research questions. Finally, Sect. 6 concludes this article with the final remarks.

2   Related Work

Different techniques of data mining have been applied in research involving analysis of virtual communities related to the health area, covering several topics such as drug addiction [16], cancer [4] and medication use [1]. Considering the full range of suitable data mining techniques, Fan and Gordon [10] present an overview of the process of social media analysis, describing the main data mining techniques fitted to the context and used in this work: modeling topics, sentiment analysis and visual analysis.

Topic modeling techniques make it possible to automatically summarize the main subjects (i.e., topics) from extensive text datasets, tackling the main challenge of social media research, which consists in the analysis of the massive content discussed. In this unsupervised data mining technique, community posts from a virtual community are automatically grouped into semantically related assortments [18], which are identified and characterized by their most relevant terms defined in the analysis.

Abdellaoui et al. [1] leverage the topic modeling technique to analyze messages from public forums mentioning certain drugs, seeking to assemble the results into semantic topics in order to identify those related to non-compliance with the instructions prescribed by the physician for further examination. Based on the same principles regarding the analysis of relevant subjects from a large text dataset by topic modeling, this work extends this approach, employing an interactive tool to better explorer the clustering parameters and integrating topic modeling with other data mining techniques, such as the sentiment analysis.

In sentiment analysis, the polarity of the opinions, emotions, and feelings manifested by the users in the virtual community is evaluated automatically through computational analysis of the written language [25]. Zheng et al. [29] demonstrate the potential of this technique, applying it to analyze feelings in the investigation of the impacts and working dynamics of support groups in virtual communities on diseases—being able to automatically segment thousands of posts as positive or negative for further scrutiny, in a way that would be impossible to do manually. In the present work, the sentiment analysis is combined with the topic modeling. This combination intents to determine the polarity of the sentiments involved in each prominent subject (i.e., topic) discussed in the community, and to characterize those in which there is a strong predominance of feelings.

The results generated by the combination of topic modeling techniques and sentiment analysis enable the automatic discovery of relevant topics for study in large volumes of data. However, to fully exploit the potential of this approach, the results need to be understandable and explorable. This process requires specialists to vary the parameters of the data mining tools and assess the quality of the results.

Chen et al. [3] investigate the use of graphical visualizations of the topic modeling result applied to a virtual community on health issues involved in the use of electronic cigarettes, proposing that visual representations of the topics allow their better understanding and comparison. This work employs this design principle. The interactive tool presents the analysis results as graphical visualizations for each identified topic, describing the distribution of the most common terms, the sentiments predominance and the user interest in the discussions over time (i.e., posts frequency).

Besides, to enable practical analysis by researchers from any area of knowledge, this approach requires simple and easy interactivity of the data mining tools, allowing a researcher to visually configure the techniques and their parameters - without the need for programming knowledge. Mindful to the challenge of data mining models operation requiring unattainable expertise for potential end-users, Choo et al. [5], Hu et al. [14] and Zou and Hou [30] contribute with user-oriented and visually-oriented topic modeling proposals. These ideas are extended in the present work, in which the interface of the interactive tool seamless blends the technique of sentiment analysis with the topic modeling, besides allowing the customization and interactivity to all stages of the KDD process, and not only for the topic modeling setup.

Finally, it is worth noting the work from De Choudhury et al. [8], which explored the potential of using the social media platform Reddit on the analysis of a forum on mental health. Descriptive statistics of texts, temporal analysis of postings, and content assortment by topic modeling are used to identify issues related to social support and advice in the community. Just as the work from Choudhury et al., this study uses as a data source for investigation the Reddit discussion forum on neuroscience, looking for unveiling insights regarding the conversations as well as answering the proposed research questions.

3   Methodology

3.1   Data Source

With an active community, growing popularity and forums publicly available for access [28], the Reddit platform presents itself as a relevant virtual space for discussions and a potential source of data for studies. The present paper analyzes the neuroscience community of the Reddit platform: "Neuroscience: your brain on reddit" (https://www.reddit.com/r/neuro/). This community has 43,000 registered members, with various profiles, such as doctors, researchers, enthusiasts, and patients. Their discussions cover the most varied topics related to neuroscience - making possible a vast panorama about the area.

A forum on a particular subject on the platform is called subreddit, and its subscribed users can add posts including text, images, and links. Posts may receive comments from users, creating a hierarchical structure of discussion - including the possibility of comments in response to other comments. Users can also vote positively or negatively on a post or comment, producing scores that allow them to evaluate their popularity and relevance.

The Reddit web interface allows the users to filter the featured posts from a subreddit into three categories based on the scoring system generated by users' votes according to the following criteria:

1. Top: posts with the highest amount of positive feedback from the community throughout its lifetime, indicating topics that have aroused the users' interest and have been widely viewed and discussed;

2. Hot: posts that receive large amounts of positive feedback and comments, in a short period, indicating emerging issues with high interest;
3. Controversial: posts that received many comments and votes, but with similar amounts of positive and negative votes, indicating contentious or controversial subjects.

For gathering the dataset used in this study, a web crawler in Python language was developed to collect all the posts and their respective comments from each of the three prominent categories of the neuroscience community. The total of 22,154 records was retrieved from this community.

3.2   Data Processing

Two main techniques of the data mining field were combined to perform automatic knowledge extraction for the exploratory analysis of the collected data: topic modeling and sentiment analysis. For the topic modeling, which consists in identifying the main semantic subjects discussed in the community, the Non-Negative Matrix Factor (NMF) technique [17] was used, which usually produces coherent topics for different datasets [22].

The texts of each topic had their overall sentiment investigated through the VADER tool - Valence Aware Dictionary and sEntiment Reasoner [15], a lexicon optimized to analyze feelings associated with social media texts. For each topic, the tool calculates the valency and intensity of its terms based on a weighted dictionary, generating numerical values or three sentiments classes: positive, negative and neutral. Because the studied community has discussions predominantly of technical nature, the expected type of greater prominence is neutral. Thus, for the leading sentiment evaluation, the neutral class was disregarded, resulting in only positive or negative assessments.

The execution of these two techniques are supported by a web tool for interactive data analysis developed by the authors, combining the data mining techniques and visualization of the generated results. The goal is to aid researchers to conduct the study in the entire process of analysis by controlling all five steps of the KDD process involved in mining:

- Step 1 - Selection: allows to select the input dataset and define whether the analysis will be applied only to the posts - covering the general subjects discussed - or to the posts and their comments - investigating the specificities of each subject;
- Step 2 - Preprocessing: this stage handles the text normalization, with standardization of uppercase and lowercase letters, and removal of accents and redundancies. Besides, researchers can define which stopwords—words that are common in most texts, but with minimal semantic value—have to be removed and also control the grammar classes to be considered in the analysis (part-of-speech tagging). Such way allows to refine the analyzes, for instance,

filtering out words from the text to only remain verbs to identify intentions or nouns or adjectives to define entities and opinions;

- Step 3 - Transformation: at this stage, the pre-processed textual data are transformed into suitable representations that can be used by data mining algorithms. The term frequency-inverse document frequency (TF-IDF) format is used, which comprises a numerical matrix where each line represents a document, and a column represents each term. The matrix generation procedure determines the terms values from their specific frequency in each text in relation to their general rate throughout the corpus. Since in this representation there is loss of the original order of the terms in the documents, the developed tool supports the use of grouped words (i.e., n-grams) allowing the data mining algorithms to deal with sequences of common terms such as "good morning" and "don't like";
- Step 4 - Mining: In this step, the data mining algorithms process the transformed data. At the beginning of the process, the topic modeling extracts the main semantic subjects. Next, the sentiment analysis evaluates each topic. Statistical analysis is the last processing of generating results for visualization. The developed tool allows easy control for the granularity of extracted items by letting researches explicitly define the number of topics to be generated. A topic modeling setup to obtain fewer topics favors to capture a global discussion arrangement, revealing the most frequent terms of each big discussion group, while configurations with larger amounts of topics promote the identification of a more specific discussion interest;
- Step 5 - Interpretation and evaluation: In this final step of the KDD process, the knowledge produced by the application of the data mining algorithms are interpreted and evaluated by the researcher. This process is carried out by analyzing the statistics and graphs produced, combined with the theoretical background of the researcher. If the result is not satisfactory, the researcher can return to the KDD process and modify the parameters of one or more steps in an iterative and interactive process.

3.3 Data Analysis

The investigation of the research questions defined in this work involves the exploratory analysis of the community, seeking to characterize the main subjects discussed, their temporal evolution and their associated feelings. Due to the iterative, exploratory and data-oriented character of the proposed research, we used the Grounded Theory (GT) research method - whose use in Information Systems researches has gradually increased over the years, as qualitative research generally becomes more prevalence [26].

Like KDD, GT is characterized by a circular process, where the researcher seeks meanings in the data through the continuous collection, coding, and comparative analysis. This technique consists of conducting the data analysis process as a constant comparison of data instances to be categorized in search of meaning [26]. This process is performed iteratively until reaching the theoretical saturation, in which the identified categories begin to stabilize, and new analyzes do not bring new results.

This research process is seamlessly supported by the developed tool to answer the proposed research questions. Besides, it is possible to observe several similarities between GT and data mining research - mainly involving topic modeling techniques. As Muller et al. [21] point out, both processes are grounded in the data, being repeatedly performed until achieving saturation on the interpretation and construction of theories—crucially requiring human understanding and judgment at each iteration. Figure 2 illustrates the iterative process of data analysis performed through the use of the developed tool.

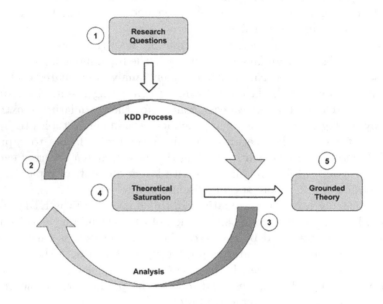

Fig. 2. The analysis process performed in this study.

4   Dataset Description

For the present research, three datasets, collected from the Reddit discussion forum on neuroscience using the "top", "hot" and "controversial" filters, were stored as CSV files - comma separated values. The dataset top.csv contains the posts and comments with the highest amount of positive feedback from the community throughout its existence, representing lasting discussions and considered highly relevant by the members. It has 9146 lines, of which 970 are posts and 8176 are comments, produced by 3033 users. Table 1 describes some supplementary dataset statistics:

The second collected dataset, hot.csv, is composed of posts that have had high rates of positive votes and comments in a short period, representing emerging posts that arouse rapid interest in the community. This dataset has 5661

Table 1. Statistics from the top.csv dataset.

	Average	SD	Min	Max
Comments/posts	9,46	7,29	1	29
Posts/authors	0,32	1,55	0	53
Comments/authors	2,69	13,94	0	735
Posts/day	23,66	43,02	0	153
Comments/day	199,41	412,57	0	1786
Words/posts	16,53	9,11	4	54
Words/comments	49,22	67,99	1	979

lines, containing 979 posts and 4682 comments, with 1711 users involved. Table 2 describes some supplementary dataset statistics:

Table 2. Statistics from the hot.csv dataset.

	Average	SD	Min	Max
Comments/posts	6,28	5,92	1	35
Posts/authors	0,57	2,29	0	58
Comments/authors	2,74	5,73	0	115
Posts/day	23,46	45,46	0	142
Comments/day	126,54	214,59	5	772
Words/posts	13,20	7,75	3	50
Words/comments	61,05	83,15	1	962

The third dataset, controversial.csv, contains posts with high interaction within the community, but with a related amount of positive and negative votes, denoting public disagreement. There are 7347 lines, of which 978 are posts, and 6369 are comments. The number of users involved is 2661. Table 3 describes some supplementary dataset statistics:

Table 3. Statistics from the controversial.csv dataset.

	Average	SD	Min	Max
Comments/posts	7,63	6,56	1	31
Posts/authors	0,37	1,54	0	70
Comments/authors	2,39	10,90	0	537
Posts/say	22,23	40,18	0	149
Comments/day	144,75	259,61	0	920
Words/posts	13,31	7,83	3	63
Words/comments	62,93	85,43	1	1242

Although they come from the same community forum, the three datasets have significant differences from the statistics of their posts and comments. In the hot.csv dataset records, there are more posts and comments from the same author, indicating that individual users are more likely to follow the lead discussions and are more active in the community. The controversial dataset, by its controversial nature, has on average more comments per post and day than in the hot dataset, but still, these are smaller than in the top dataset. As it represents the discussions that have developed more quickly in the community, the dataset hot.csv has comments every day, unlike the dataset top.csv and even the controversial.csv, that also has posts with high interaction in a short period - but still have days without comments.

Regarding the size of the texts, the discussions with the highest number of positive votes (i.e., top.csv) have in average posts with several more words than the average from the other datasets, indicating that top posts seem to qualify and describe better their message. Besides, these discussions generally have shorter and more objective comments, with fewer words than compared to comments from the other two datasets. It is also interesting to note that the post and comment with more words are part of the controversial.csv dataset, and all datasets have comments with only one word - most of the cases being kudos.

Because all three datasets come from the same forum, there may be postings and comments shared among them, such as posts that have a high amount of positive votes fastly reached, granting it a place in the top and in the hot datasets too. Figure 3 shows the number of texts in common between the three datasets, indicating that the most significant intersection of data is located between the fast emerging discussions and the controversial ones, sharing 1174 records.

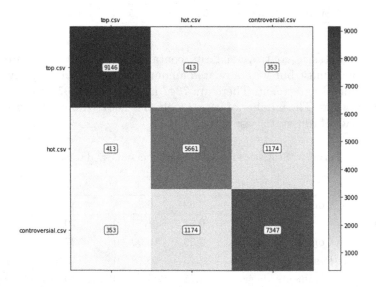

Fig. 3. The intersection of records between the datasets collected for analysis.

5   Community Analysis

This section presents the exploratory analysis of the community from the Reddit platform on neuroscience, seeking to answer the proposed research questions. The datasets gathered were analyzed with the help of the interactive data mining tool developed by the authors; accordingly to the Grounded Theory research method presented in the previous section. Through the production of a series of exploratory clusters of semantic topics, community discussion patterns were investigated, iteratively adjusting the data mining parameters of the KDD process. The results obtained at each iteration assessment concerns their capacity to respond to research questions. At each iteration, the research was refined to reveal better patterns of discussions and their relationships, to the point where no relevant new knowledge was produced—theoretical saturation.

Tables 4, 5, and 6 present the ten most relevant semantic topics selected for the final analysis of each of the three analyzed datasets (i.e., top.csv, hot.csv, and controversial.csv). Each row of the tables shows a topic with its main terms automatically identified by the tool, followed by a short description inferred and manually annotated by the authors, the volume of posts and comments over time, and the predominant polarity concerning positive and negative feelings.

> **RQ1: What are the main characteristics of the subjects most frequently discussed in the community?**

The exploration and characterization of the subjects discussed more frequently in the community makes it possible to draw an overview of the virtual community. In order to answer RQ1, the identification of items relevant for this analysis took into account:

1. Those who appear in more than one of the datasets analyzed, sharing descriptive terms of their topics and representing the same general subject;
2. Sub-topics of the same general subject, present in one or more datasets;
3. Subjects unique to a single dataset, but that show themselves constant or recurring in the graph of your timeline.

The first frequent subject observed in the research relates to Alzheimer's, a degenerative brain disease. Discussions about this disease are present in all three datasets analyzed, all with an increasing volume of posts over time in the community. In the discussion datasets with most positive feedback (i.e., top.csv) and high interest (i.e., hot.csv), users' interactions are characterized by more technical issues, using words such as "amyloid", "protein", "neurobiology", other related diseases (terms: "parkinsons" and "huntingtons"), treatment (terms: "symptoms", "drug", and "restores") and prevention (term: "prevent"). Now in the controversial.csv dataset, the discussion on Alzheimer's seems to be more speculative, with prominent terms related to hypotheses and personal opinions of the participants, such as indicated by "hypothesis" and "think."

Another frequent topic are acknowledgments, which were identified by the tool as semantic subjects characteristic of datasets top.csv and hot.csv. These

Table 4. Topic analysis of the top.csv dataset.

Terms	Description	Activity over time	Predominant Sentiment
Brain, human, cells, activity, project, neurons, regions, changes, part, new	Human brain		Positive
thanks, sharing, lot, amazing, check, posting, much, post, wow, fantastic	Acknowledgment		Positive
Research, am, phd, doing, lab, school, labs, funding, years, animal	Neuroscience research		Positive
Study, explained, brainpost, humans, new, psychiatry, stimulation, effects, rewards, rats	Discussions about published studies		Positive
Memory, learning, work, loss, enhances, alters, view, does, dopamine, restores	Studies about memory		Positive
Alzeheimers, disease, amyloid, protein, disorder, huntingtons, parkinsons, drug, restores, prevent	Alzheimer		Positive
Mri, gif, data, xpost, neuro, look, based, imaging, animated, showing	Magnetic resonance imaging (MRI)		Positive
Neuroscience, society, computacional, disorders, books, carees, school, university, professor, students	Academic area		Positive
Neuroscientist, books, life, interview, thoughts, prof, own, slice, scientist, drugs	Neuroscientists		Positive
Good, book, molecular, free, online, computational, neurobiology, basic, introductory, suggestions	Book suggestions		Positive

Table 5. Topic analysis of the hot.csv dataset.

Terms	Description	Activity over time	Predominant Sentiment
Thanks, interesting, cool, answer, helpful, replay, advice, lot, man, yeah	Acknowledgements		Positive
Brain, damage, injury, blood, cells, oxygen, hypoxia, cause, activity, areas	Brain damage		Positive
New, study, explained, brainpost, humans, psychiatry, molecular, mice, rats, journal	New published studies		Positive
Dopamine, seretonin, receptors, effects, release, drugs, reward, reuptake, long, cause	Studies on dopamine and serotonin		Positive
Neuroscience, computational, programs, phd, neuro, resources, server, perceptual, abstracts, lab	Academic area		Positive
Feeling, fast, neuro, nerve, caffeine, odd, getting, minutes, thing, understand	Fast feelings		Positive
Disease, alzheimers, parkinsons, patients, protein, neurobiology, amyloid, roundtable, dollar, symptoms	Alzheimer's disease and Parkinson's disease		Positive
Time, weird, perception, memories, symptoms, sensation, periods, change, taking, short	Unusual perceptions of time		Negative
Mind, effect, stress, thought, behavior, body, fast, state, neuro, analysis	Effects of fatigue		Positive
Help, mouse, need, neuralgia, club, mri, behaviour, journal, report, cant	Help with studies involving mice		Positive

Table 6. Topic analysis of the controversial.csv dataset.

Terms	Description	Activity over time	Predominant Sentiment
New, eeg, meditation, neuroscientists, activity, company, psychostimulants, transcendental, optogenetics, cells	Meditation electroencephalography		Positive
Neuroscience, psychology, field, phd, cognitive, degree, masters, computational, learn, program	Career in neuroscience		Positive
Doctor, see, go, talk, symptoms, ask, neurologist, medical, advice, said	Search for medical advice		Negative
Memory, working, memories, recall, longterm, information, problems, loss, hippocampus	Memory working		Positive
Help, need, please, am, someone, find, understand, symptoms, try, sounds	Search for help		Positive
Science, article, read, post, love, link, cognitive, interesting, title, results	Discussions regarding scientific articles		Positive
Dissease, alzheimers, prevent, problem, hypothesis, stress, think, pdf, effects, exercise	Prevention of Alzheimer's		Positive
Consciousness, theory, know, neuro, serotonin, light, quantum, solving, state, beliefs	Theories about consciousness		Negative
Mind, control, ways, has, reading, efect, technologies, blown, conscious, drug	Mind control		Negative
Mri, scan, tell, look, got, results, head, has, neurologist, ct	Requests for help with MRI scan results		Negative

subjects have a relatively uniform distribution over the timeline of the community activities, and high positive content, with terms like "amazing", "wow", "fantastic", "interesting", "cool", "helpful". Based on the words used to describe the topics, it is possible to distinguish what users are acknowledging: shares, posts, answers, aids, and advice. It is also interesting to note that this topic of acknowledgment does not appear in the controversial.csv dataset, indicating that in controversial discussions there is less collaboration and empathy among users - reducing the community advantages.

A recurring subject that receives high community engagement relates to strange perceptions of time, identified in the hot.csv dataset as two topics. In the first, there are specific discussions about the effect named by the participants as "Fast Feeling" (terms: "feeling", "fast" and "neuro"), where several users share experiencing the passage of time more quickly than usual. There is a positive bias in the polarity of the discussions, with participants demonstrating an interest in understanding the effect, but not perceiving it as bad or harmful. The second topic of the subject is more comprehensive about the phenomena discussed (terms "time", "weird" and "perception"), and presents a predominantly negative polarity in the analysis of feelings, with the users describing the phenomena as symptoms of some problem.

The academic area in neuroscience is another identified topic of continuous interest in the community, appearing as a topic in all three datasets. In top.csv, the subject is mainly related to studying in the area (terms: "school", "university", "professor", and "students"), while in hot.csv the discussions have a more significant focus in the computational area (terms: "computational", "programs", "server" and "resources"). Then in the controversial.csv dataset, there are fewer discussions on this subject over time, being the focus more related to the field of psychology - terms: "psychology", "field", "cognitive."

Related to the academic subject, another common topic in the community refers to discussions about scientific publications - which appears in the analysis of the three datasets. However, while in the top.csv and hot.csv datasets we have the topics indicating that the focus is the explanation of new studies (terms "new", "study" and "explained") in the dataset controversial.csv the discussion seems to be shallow, as noted by the terms "read", "title", "interesting" and "love".

Subtopics of research on neuroscience also appear as subjects of discussion frequent in all datasets, covering themes such as brain, memory, dopamine, serotonin, stress effect and laboratory research with rats - all topics with a prevalence of positive sentiment. Regarding the topic of research with mice, identified in the dataset hot.csv, it is interesting to note that in addition to being a matter that usually has answers in a short period, its graph of occurrences over time shows that it is the most persistent topic throughout the community discussion.

Other common questions involving requests of help or advice relate to symptom evaluation (terms: "help", "need", "please", "understand" and "symptoms"), analysis of MRI scan results (terms: "mri", "scan", "tell" and "look"), and response to the search for medical advice (terms: "doctor", "see", "go", "talk", "symptoms") - all present in the dataset controversial.csv.

Regarding the number of posts over time, there is a smaller amount of subjects that are losing interest than those that have been gaining prominence. Discussion topics related to sharing free books for download ("good", "book", "free" and "online") show a clear drop in the volume of community discussion over time. Through the analysis of samples from the discussion on this topic, it is possible to observe this behavior is due to users' awareness concerning policies against piracy.

RQ2: What are the emerging issues and those that have been losing community interest over time?

The temporal evolution analysis of the main subjects discussed in the community allows identifying and characterizing those who are losing or gaining interest - enabling to direct research to the themes of emerging importance. This analysis answers RQ2. The sparkline generated by the tool allows a summary of the number of activities (i.e., comments and postings) of each topic over time. For the selection of subjects for analysis, we exclude those topics whose graphs present constant or recurrent occurrences over time.

Discussions on Alzheimer's disease are not only one of the most discussed issues in the community, but also a subject of growing interest. This result is consistent with statistics that indicate the growth of disease cases over the years [19], which promotes the interest of people and also reinforces the need for research and scientific discussions about the disease.

Other topics that are gaining increasing interest are related to discussions on studies on neuroscience, with the presence of this specific topic (terms: "study" and "explained"), and subtopics such as brain damage, dopamine and serotonin, stress effects, effects of meditation, and theory of consciousness. There are also some emerging issues with less technical and more personal manifestations, such as reports of unfamiliar perception of time, and requests for help, advice, and discussion about a career in neuroscience.

In addition to the growing interest of the community in specific topics on neuroscience, it is interesting to note that there are emerging discussions with a large number of positive votes - dataset top.csv - on remarkable neuroscientists. They cover many aspects, such as their work, lifestyle, and ideas (terms: "neuroscientist", "books", "life", "interview" and "thoughts").

Discussions sharing MRI images and data (terms: "mri", "gif" and "data") have been recurrent for a long time, but there are indications of loss of interest in the community. Then the discussions related to mind control (terms: "mind", "control" and "ways") have shown a peak of recent community interest, but now they have been losing their volume of posts, reinforced by the various criticisms of users regarding this dark theme.

RQ3: What are and how are characterized the subjects, in which there is a strong predominance of feelings in the community?

As a community of predominantly technical discussions, the predominant polarity of all posts in sentiment analysis is neutral. However, considering only the perceived diametral sentiments on the positive and negative feelings, it is observed that their values vary accordingly to the discussions, thus identifying the overall prevailing community's opinion for each subject.

All subjects in the dataset with the top-rated posts (top.csv) present positive value in the sentiment analysis, indicating that a friendly and positive sentiment characterizes well-evaluated discussions. In the hot.csv dataset, which gathers well-voted subjects with fast replies, only one topic has the prevalence of negative feelings. On this subject, where users describe unusual time perceptions (terms "time", "weird" and "perception"), the reason for the negative polarity prevalence in the sentiment analysis is related more to how users describe their perceptions.

As expected, the dataset of controversial discussions (controversial.csv) has the highest incidence of subjects with the prevalence of negative feelings. Because of its polemical nature, this predominance is caused by how the community reacts to certain ideas and behaviors in the topics. The subject of mind control, which has already been mentioned before as a remarkable negative topic that has losing interest over time, features with other three topics some important topics worthwhile to mention regarding this matter. However, on the contrary to the mind control topic, the other three subjects have been increasingly appearing in the discussions. Two of them are related: requests for help with MRI results (terms: "mri", "scan", "tell" and "look"), and response to the search for medical advice (terms: "doctor", "see", "go", "talk" and "symptoms")—both focused on criticism that certain issues would be more relevant to a medical professional rather than to a public online community. Finally, the last relevant subject from the controversial dataset is related to discussions about theories of consciousness (terms "consciousness" and "theory"), which for its fascinating but speculative character produces long discussions involving beliefs (term: "know").

6   Concluding Remarks

This study explored new possibilities for data-oriented scientific research in the context of social media. This paper presents the analysis of a relevant online community on neuroscience. Data mining and visualization techniques were used to identify and characterize prominent semantic subjects in the midst of thousands of posts and comments - which would be impracticable through manual reading and analysis. Moreover, the research process, which involves iteratively tuning and refining algorithm parameters and comparing the results, were conducted employing an interactive tool specially developed to support this process.

The analytical process was applied to three datasets collected from the Reddit community on neuroscience, each referring to one aspect of the discussions: best feedback (i.e., top), with high interest over a short period (i.e., hot) and controversial. The identified subjects cover various topics in neuroscience, ranging from technical discussions and analysis of recent articles to requests for help and speculation about the functioning of consciousness. Grounded Theory methodological approach was used to answer the proposed research questions, through a systematic and rigorous analysis of the data.

The first research question sought to investigate the main issues most frequently discussed in the community. The most prominent subject is Alzheimer's disease, being discussed in the three analyzed datasets, with various interests such as prevention, diagnosis, treatment, and related conditions. Acknowledgments and requests for help are also recurring topics, whether concerning symptom assessment, examination results analysis, and medical advice. Another identified personal manifestation regards the unusual perceptions of time, with participants sharing experiences of strange effects they witnessed, such as Fast Feeling. The academic field and career in neuroscience is also a relevant topic to the community, with discussions related to universities, laboratory research, and analysis of published articles. Other related topics identified were: brain, memory, dopamine, serotonin, stress effect and laboratory research with rats.

The objective of the second research question was the identification and characterization of emerging subjects as well as those that have been losing interest in the community over time. Discussions on studies in neuroscience have been showing growing interest, with topics such as career, Alzheimer's, brain damage, dopamine and serotonin, effects of stress, effects of meditation and theory of consciousness. Advice, help requests, and experience reports also feature a growing volume of posts, indicating community openness for more personal and less technical discussions. Only three subjects has noticeable and recent loss of interest: book suggestions, magnetic resonance imaging (MRI), and mind control.

The third research question evaluated subjects with a strong predominance of feelings, with positive or negative polarity. It was noticed that most of the identified topics have a positive polarity, indicating that interactions are predominantly friendly. Most negative feelings emerged from topics belonging to the controversial dataset, with many interactions but a similar proportion of positive and negative feedbacks. In general, these topics are non-technical or speculative subjects such as mind control techniques, help with MRI results, answers to medical advice, and theories about consciousness.

The consistency of the topics identified by the analysis and the answers provided to the research questions are evidence of the achievement of applying KDD through the proposed tool with Grounding Theory to the study of a virtual community, especially providing useful insights from automatically processing a large volume of discussions. As future work, this analytical process can be used to study other virtual communities on neuroscience, such as the Alzheimer Research Forum, comparing the subjects that emerge in each one. Another research front is to understand better the usability challenges of the developed data mining tool, experimenting its use with neuroscience researchers who are not computer science experts.

References

1. Abdellaoui, R., Foulquié, P., Texier, N., Faviez, C., Burgun, A., Schück, S.: Detection of cases of noncompliance to drug treatment in patient forum posts: topic model approach. J. Med. Internet Res. **20**(3), e85 (2018)
2. Carvalho, D., Marcacini, R., Lucena, C., Rezende, S.: A process to support analysts in exploring and selecting content from online forums. Soc. Netw. **3**(02), 86 (2014)
3. Chen, A.T., Zhu, S.H., Conway, M.: What online communities can tell us about electronic cigarettes and hookah use: a study using text mining and visualization techniques. J. Med. Internet Res. **17**(9), e220 (2015)
4. Cho, H., Silver, N., Na, K., Adams, D., Luong, K.T., Song, C.: Visual cancer communication on social media: an examination of content and effects of# melanomasucks. J. Med. Internet Res. **20**(9), e10501 (2018)
5. Choo, J., Lee, C., Reddy, C.K., Park, H.: UTOPIAN: user-driven topic modeling based on interactive nonnegative matrix factorization. IEEE Trans. Vis. Comput. Graphics **19**(12), 1992–2001 (2013)
6. Clark, T., Kinoshita, J.: Alzforum and SWAN: the present and future of scientific web communities. Briefings Bioinf. **8**(3), 163–171 (2007)
7. Das, S., et al.: Pain research forum: application of scientific social media frameworks in neuroscience. Front. Neuroinf. **8**, 21 (2014)
8. De Choudhury, M., De, S.: Mental health discourse on reddit: self-disclosure, social support, and anonymity. In: Eighth International AAAI Conference on Weblogs and Social Media (2014)
9. Debuse, J., de la Iglesia, B., Howard, C., Rayward-Smith, V.: Building the KDD roadmap. In: Roy, R. (eds.) Industrial Knowledge Management, pp. 179–196. Springer, London (2001). https://doi.org/10.1007/978-1-4471-0351-6_12
10. Fan, W., Gordon, M.D.: The power of social media analytics. Commun. ACM **57**(6), 74–81 (2014)
11. Fayyad, U., Piatetsky-Shapiro, G., Smyth, P.: The KDD process for extracting useful knowledge from volumes of data. Commun. ACM **39**(11), 27–34 (1996)
12. Glaser, B.G., Strauss, A.L.: Discovery of Grounded Theory: Strategies for Qualitative Research. Routledge (2017)
13. Han, J., Pei, J., Kamber, M.: Data Mining: Concepts and Techniques. Elsevier (2011)
14. Hu, Y., Boyd-Graber, J., Satinoff, B., Smith, A.: Interact. Top. Model. Mach. Learn. **95**(3), 423–469 (2014)
15. Hutto, C.J., Gilbert, E.: VADER: a parsimonious rule-based model for sentiment analysis of social media text. In: Eighth International AAAI Conference on Weblogs and Social Media (2014)
16. Kim, S.J., Marsch, L.A., Hancock, J.T., Das, A.K.: Scaling up research on drug abuse and addiction through social media big data. J. Med. Internet Res. **19**(10), e353 (2017)
17. Lee, D.D., Seung, H.S.: Learning the parts of objects by non-negative matrix factorization. Nature **401**(6755), 788 (1999)
18. Liu, B.: Sentiment analysis and opinion mining. Synth. lect. Hum. Lang. Technol. **5**(1), 1–167 (2012)
19. Matthews, K.A., et al.: Racial and ethnic estimates of alzheimer's disease and related dementias in the united states (2015–2060) in adults aged⩾ 65 years. Alzheimer's Dement. **15**(1), 17–24 (2019)

20. Meshi, D., Tamir, D.I., Heekeren, H.R.: The emerging neuroscience of social media. Trends Cogn. Sci. **19**(12), 771–782 (2015)
21. Muller, M., Guha, S., Baumer, E.P., Mimno, D., Shami, N.S.: Machine learning and grounded theory method: convergence, divergence, and combination. In: Proceedings of the 19th International Conference on Supporting Group Work, pp. 3–8. ACM (2016)
22. O'callaghan, D., Greene, D., Carthy, J., Cunningham, P.: An analysis of the coherence of descriptors in topic modeling. Expert Syst. Appl. **42**(13), 5645–5657 (2015)
23. Qiu, B., et al.: Get online support, feel better-sentiment analysis and dynamics in an online cancer survivor community. In: 2011 IEEE Third International Conference on Privacy, Security, Risk and Trust and 2011 IEEE Third International Conference on Social Computing, pp. 274–281. IEEE (2011)
24. Shneiderman, B., Preece, J., Pirolli, P.: Realizing the value of social media requires innovative computing research. Commun. ACM **54**(9), 34–37 (2011)
25. Song, Y., Pan, S., Liu, S., Zhou, M.X., Qian, W.: Topic and keyword re-ranking for LDA-based topic modeling. In: Proceedings of the 18th ACM Conference on Information and Knowledge Management, pp. 1757–1760. ACM (2009)
26. Urquhart, C., Fernández, W.: Using grounded theory method in information systems: the researcher as blank slate and other myths. In: Willcocks, L.P., Sauer, C., Lacity, M.C. (eds.) Enacting Research Methods in Information Systems: Volume 1, pp. 129–156. Springer, Cham (2016). https://doi.org/10.1007/978-3-319-29266-3_7
27. Vasconcellos-Silva, P.R., Carvalho, D., Lucena, C.: Word frequency and content analysis approach to identify demand patterns in a virtual community of carriers of hepatitis C. Interact. J. Med. Res. **2**(2), e12 (2013)
28. Weninger, T., Zhu, X.A., Han, J.: An exploration of discussion threads in social news sites: a case study of the reddit community. In: 2013 IEEE/ACM International Conference on Advances in Social Networks Analysis and Mining (ASONAM 2013), pp. 579–583. IEEE (2013)
29. Zheng, K., Li, A., Farzan, R.: Exploration of online health support groups through the lens of sentiment analysis. In: Chowdhury, G., McLeod, J., Gillet, V., Willett, P. (eds.) iConference 2018. LNCS, vol. 10766, pp. 145–151. Springer, Cham (2018). https://doi.org/10.1007/978-3-319-78105-1_19
30. Zou, C., Hou, D.: LDA analyzer: a tool for exploring topic models. In: 2014 IEEE International Conference on Software Maintenance and Evolution, pp. 593–596. IEEE (2014)

Complex Systems and Complex Networks

Influence of Contact Network Topology on the Spread of Tuberculosis

Eduardo R. Pinto[1], Erivelton G. Nepomuceno[2],
and Andriana S. L. O. Campanharo[3(✉)]

[1] Institute of Biosciences, Postgraduate Program in Biometrics,
São Paulo State University (UNESP), Botucatu, São Paulo, Brazil
eduardo.pinto@unesp.br
[2] Department of Electrical Engineering,
Federal University of São João del-Rei (UFSJ),
São João del-Rei, Minas Gerais, Brazil
nepomuceno@ufsj.edu.br
[3] Institute of Biosciences, Department of Biostatistics,
São Paulo State University (UNESP), Botucatu, São Paulo, Brazil
andriana.campanharo@unesp.br

Abstract. This paper presents the influence of the complex networks topology on the spread of Tuberculosis with the use of the Individual-Based Model (IBM). Five complex network models were used with the IBM, namely, random, small world, scale-free, modular and hierarchical models. For every model, we applied the usual topological properties available in literature for the characterization of complex networks. Afterwards, we verified the topological effect of the contact networks in the evolution of tuberculosis and it was observed that different contact networks result in different epidemic thresholds (β^*) for the spread of tuberculosis. More specifically, we noted that networks that have greater heterogeneity of connections need a lower β^*, however when the value of the infection rate (β) is large, the number of individuals infected are similar. It is believed that this observation may contribute to actions to reduce and eradicate the disease.

Keywords: Tuberculosis · Topological effect · Complex networks · Individual-Based Model · Complex systems

1   Introduction

Tuberculosis (TB) is an infectious-contagious disease, transmitted by *Mycobacterium tuberculosis* (Mtb), it is one of the deadliest diseases in the world [11]. In 2015, approximately 70,000 new cases of tuberculosis and around 4,500 deaths were diagnosed in Brazil [11]. TB is transmitted when a person with active tuberculosis (pulmonary tuberculosis) expels, whilst speaking, sneezing or coughing, droplets of saliva composed of Mtb organisms that can be aspirated by other

© Springer Nature Switzerland AG 2019
V. R. Cota et al. (Eds.): LAWCN 2019, CCIS 1068, pp. 81–88, 2019.
https://doi.org/10.1007/978-3-030-36636-0_6

individuals who share the same environment, contaminating them. Poor nutrition, lack of hygiene, smoking, alcoholism or any other factor that causes low organic resistance, may also promote the establishment of tuberculosis [11].

Considering such scenario, methods that can help prevent tuberculosis, in order to reduce its incidence and reduce costs, have become essential. Several mathematical models have been proposed to infer relevant information about tuberculosis, for example, the epidemiological impact of vaccines, which and how many individuals should be vaccinated, projections on the number of infected and others [13].

Recent studies have shown that complex networks are a natural support for the study of epidemics spreading rate [1,3]. In tuberculosis modeling through a complex network, each of its nodes represents an individual and each pair of edges represents the interactions between two nodes. IBM's in combination with complex networks have been increasingly used in the modeling of infectious processes [13]. The IBM consists of a discrete structure in which interactions occur among a certain number of individuals, whose behavior is determined by a set of characteristics that stochastically evolve in time [5,14].

Among the numerous works in the area, we highlight the research developed by Pastor-Satorras and collaborators [12]. In an extensive paper, the authors develop the epidemics spreading rate analysis through the perspective of complex networks. When comparing with this study and other developments, the present study brings two contributions: the specific analysis of tuberculosis and the comparison of several topologies on the threshold for the rupture of a disease variation. We believe that this study can contribute to a better understanding of the disease and its consequences may influence more effective practices of tuberculosis control and eradication.

2 Theoretical Foundation

2.1 Compartmental Model

The compartmental model developed by Moreno *et al.* [6] has been proposed to simulate the dynamics of tuberculosis. In order to reach the main features of the epidemiological system, the population has been divided into three compartments: susceptible (S), exposed (E) and infected (I). This model can be expressed by the following system of nonlinear ordinary differential equations:

$$
\begin{cases}
\dfrac{dS}{dt} = \mu N - \dfrac{\beta I\, S}{N} - \mu S, & S(0) = S_0 \geq 0, \\[2mm]
\dfrac{dE}{dt} = q\dfrac{\beta I\, S}{N} + \rho I - \left(\gamma + \dfrac{\delta I}{N} + \mu\right) E & E(0) = E_0 \geq 0, \\[2mm]
\dfrac{dI}{dt} = (1-q)\dfrac{\beta I\, S}{N} + \left(\gamma + \dfrac{\delta I}{N}\right) E - (\rho + \mu)I & I(0) = I_0 \geq 0,
\end{cases}
\tag{1}
$$

where q is the proportion of susceptible individuals who contract the bacillus agent but do not develop tuberculosis and $\mu, \beta, \gamma, \delta$ and ρ are the birth/death, infection, latency, exogenous infection and relapse rates, respectively [6].

2.2   Individual-Based Model

Based on the premises used in the differential equations model described in Sect. 2.1, a set of characteristics was proposed for the dynamics of tuberculosis with the use of the IBM [13]. These characteristics are as follows:

- $C_1 \in [0, 1, 2]$: The state of an individual regarding to the epidemic, i.e. the individual may be in the state susceptible (0), exposed (1) or infected (2), respectively.
- C_2 : Individual's age in years. Δt is added to the age in each transition. At $t = 0$, $C_2 = 0$.
- C_3 : Maximum age in which the individual will live. The birth age of an individual is given by:

$$C_3 = -\mu_{ibm} \log(a_u), \tag{2}$$

where μ_{ibm} is the life expectancy of the population and a_u is a random variable uniformly distributed between 0 and 1.
- C_4 : Time (in years) in which an individual is exposed. At $t = 0$, $C_4 = 0$.
- C_5 : Maximum time that an individual remains in the exposed state and it is obtained by

$$C_5 = -\rho_{ibm} \log(a_u), \tag{3}$$

where ρ_{ibm} is the exposure period.
- C_6 : Time (in years) in which an individual is infected. At $t = 0$, $C_6 = 0$.
- C_7 : Maximum time in which an individual remains in the infected state and it is obtained by

$$C_7 = -\gamma_{ibm} \log(a_u), \tag{4}$$

where γ_{ibm} is the infected period.

C_4 to C_7 are unnecessary for susceptible individuals, therefore we consider that these cases are equal to zero $\forall t$. The number of susceptible, exposed and infected individuals at a given time t, are denoted by $S(t), E(t)$ and $I(t)$, respectively. We used a constant population size given by $N = S(t) + E(t) + I(t)$ for all $t \geq 0$. Moreover, the transitions between the epidemiological states are discrete and defined according to the categories between the compartments [7,8].

2.3   Complex Networks

A complex network $R = (V, E)$ is described by a set of V vertices and a set of E edges, where $E = \{\{a, b\} \mid a, b \in V\}$ [10]. Several models of complex networks have been proposed in the literature in order to synthesize patterns of connections found in many real networks to better understand the implications of those. The complex network models used in this work are briefly given as follows.

The random model (RAN), proposed by Erdös-Rényi [4], is a network model based on random connections in which all pairs of vertices have the same probability p to be connected. Therefore, this type of network has a highly homogeneous structure. Watts and Strogatz [15] observed that the connections of several real networks were not completely regular nor random, but between these two extremes. They then proposed the small world model (SMW) that was able to produce highly clustered networks with short path characteristics between their vertices [15]. Barabási and Albert [1] mapped the topology of the connections between the WWW (World-Wide Web) pages and found out that, besides presenting the small world phenomenon, its degree distribution was not random, but scale-free. That is, the probability $P(k)$ of a vertex to be connected to k other vertices was given by $P(k) \approx k^{-\gamma}$. They then proposed the scale-free model (SCF) that was able to produce networks with such characteristics. The majority of the social, biological and technological networks has a modular structure, i.e. edges densely distributed between vertices belonging to the same group (module) and sparsely distributed between vertices in different groups. In this sense, Newman [9] proposed a modular model (MOD) that was capable of producing networks with such characteristics. Several real networks, such as social, metabolic and protein interaction networks are scaled-free and high clustered. Since the scale-free network model described here produces low clustered networks, we used the hierarchical model (HIE), proposed by Dodds *et al.* [2], that is able to produce networks with such real properties. A network produced by a hierarchical model has a tree-like structure, i.e. its vertices are organized hierarchically from top to bottom [2].

3 Results

Considering that the IBM is discrete and, based on the parameters of the SEI model previously described in Sect. 2.1, the following rules can be established

$$\begin{cases} \beta_{ibm} = \beta_{sei} \Delta t, \\ \delta_{ibm} = \delta_{sei} \Delta t, \\ \mu_{ibm} = 1/\mu_{sei}, \\ \gamma_{ibm} = 1/\gamma_{sei}, \\ \rho_{ibm} = 1/\rho_{sei}. \end{cases} \tag{5}$$

With the use of Eq. 5, it is possible to build the equivalence between the SEI model and the IBM, in such way that, on average, their solutions will present similar behaviors [8]. Figure 1(a) presents the number of susceptibles, exposed and infected individuals of the SEI model (black lines) in an epidemic state (basic reproduction number $\mathcal{R}_0 > 1$) for $q = 0.9$, $\gamma_{sei} = 0.0027$, $\rho_{sei} = 0.0083$, $\mu_{sei} = 1/70$, $\delta_{sei} = 0.0026$ and $\beta_{sei} = 0.07$ and the average number of susceptibles, exposed and infected individuals of the IBM for $\gamma_{ibm} = 1/0.0027$, $\rho_{ibm} = 1/0.0083$, $\mu_{ibm} = 70$, $\delta_{ibm} = 0.00026$, $\beta_{ibm} = 0.007$ and $\Delta t = 0.1$, over 10 different realizations. Figure 1(b) presents the number of susceptibles, exposed and infected individuals of the SEI model (black lines) in a non-epidemic state ($\mathcal{R}_0 < 1$) for $q = 0.9$, $\gamma_{sei} = 0.0027$, $\rho_{sei} = 0.0083$, $\mu_{sei} = 1/70$, $\delta_{sei} 0.0026$ and $\beta_{sei} = 0.13$ and the average number of susceptibles, exposed and infected individuals of the IBM for $\gamma_{ibm} = 1/0.0027$, $\rho_{ibm} = 1/0.0083$, $\mu_{ibm} = 70$,

$\delta_{ibm} = 0.00026$, $\beta_{ibm} = 0.013$ e $\Delta t = 0.1$ ($\mathcal{R}_0 < 1$), over 10 different real-izations. In both models, $N = 10,000$, $S(0) = 9,200$, $E(0) = 200$ and $I(0) = 600$ were considered.

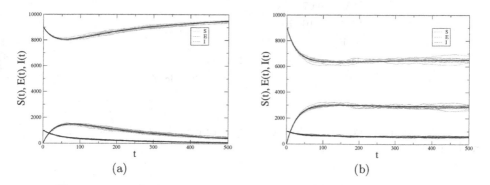

(a)   (b)

Fig. 1. Number of susceptible, exposed and infected individuals for the SEI model (black lines) and average number of susceptibles, exposed and infected individuals for the IBM with $t_f = 500$ in (a) an epidemic ($\mathcal{R}_0 = 1.48$) and (b) non-epidemic ($\mathcal{R}_0 = 0.82$) states, respectively.

In the SEI model and in the original IBM formulation, the relationships between individuals are represented by a complete graph, i.e. all individuals are equally connected to each other. However, in real contact networks this behaviors is not observed. Thus, in this work the IBM for the SEI model was modified in order to incorporate more realistic models of contact networks for the tuberculosis propagation. Unlike the IBM without complex networks, in the IBM with complex networks an infected individual can infect another individual only if they are connected. The complex networks used in this work were generated using a set of parameters, as shown in Table 1, where p is the probability of connection (RAN e MOD) and re-connection (SMW), respectively. k is the number of neighbors of a given node, n_0 is the initial number of vertices, m is the number of modules, r is the ratio between connections inside and outside a given module, h is the hierarchical factor and b is number of additional edges [13].

Figure 2 shows an example of the IBM in combination with the random, small world, scale-free, modular and hierarchical networks with $N = 15$ vertices for $0 \le t \le 4$. In all cases, vertices in blue, red and green represent suscep-tible, exposed and infected individuals, respectively. In the random network, the long-range connections make a given vertex to infect, preferably, its more distant neighbors. In a small world network, the infection propagates, prefer-ably, between the closest neighbors of a given vertex. In a scale-free network, the disease propagation occurs from the center to the periphery of the network, since the central vertices have the largest connectivity degrees. In a modular network, the disease propagates, preferably, between vertices belonging to the same module. Finally, in a hierarchical network, the disease propagates from the

Table 1. Parameters for the random (RAN), small world (SMW), scale-free (SCF), modular (MOD) and hierarchical (HIE) networks models.

	p	k	n_0	m	r	h	b
RAN	0.07	–	–	–	–	–	–
SMW	0.10	70	–	–	–	–	–
SCF	–	–	73	–	–	–	–
MOD	0.07	–	–	14	0.95	–	–
HIE	–	–	–	–	–	2	138,001

top (vertices with larger hierarchy) to the bottom (vertices with lower hierarchy) of the network [13].

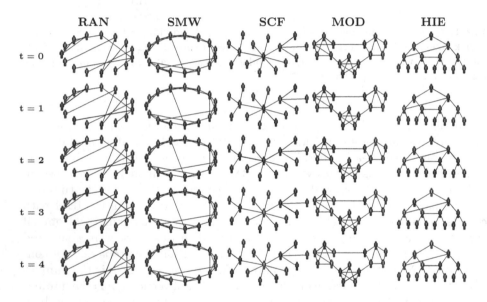

Fig. 2. Example of the IBM with complex network for the tuberculosis spread using $N = 15$ vertices and $t = 0, 1, 2, 3$ and 4. Vertices in blue, green and red correspond to susceptible, exposed and infected individuals, respectively. (Color figure online)

Figure 3 presents the solution of the IBM with complex networks, i.e. the mean number of infected individuals at time $t_f = 20,000$ as a function of β_{ibm} for the five networks models under study, over 200 realizations. The parameters used were $N = 2,000, S(0) = 1,500, E(0) = 0, I(0) = 500, \gamma_{ibm} = 1/0.0027, \mu_{ibm} = 70, \rho_{ibm} = 1/0.0083$ and $\delta_{ibm} = 0.0026$ with $0.05 \leq \beta_{ibm} \leq 0.25$ and $\Delta\beta_{ibm} = 0.008$. In general, complex networks with different topologies result in different epidemic thresholds (β^*). More specifically, the larger the heterogeneity of connections the smaller the epidemic threshold. Moreover, for given values of β_{ibm} and for some network models the disease is epidemic (for example, $\beta_{ibm} = 0.125$ in the hierarchical and scale-free networks). Finally, it is observed that at $\beta_{ibm} \approx 0.25$ the number of infected individuals in all networks are similar.

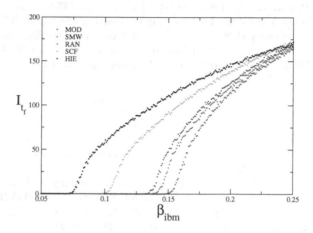

Fig. 3. Number of infected individuals for the IBM with complex network at time $t_f = 20,000$ as a function of $0.05 \leq \beta_{ibm} \leq 0.25$, over 200 realizations.

4   Conclusions

In this study, we used the IBM with several complex networks models for the tuberculosis spreading modeling. Analysis regarding the effect of such networks topologies were performed. We concluded that the propagation of a given disease is highly sensitive to the network topology. More specifically, the hierarchical and the scale-free networks, due to their large heterogeneity of connections, have a smaller epidemic threshold. At $\beta_{ibm} = 0.25$ the number of infected individuals at $t_f = 20,000$ are the same, regardless the network topology. Therefore, with the knowledge of the infection rate value (β_{ibm}) and the structure of the network, it might be possible to predict whether the tuberculosis is epidemic or not, and to elaborate interventions in order to reduce or eradicate this disease, such as immunization strategies or personal distancing.

The IBM in combination with the complex networks theory can be used to further study different compartmental models such as SIRV and SEIR and to investigate epidemics such as influenza, measles and others. In the future, we intend to validate the proposed model by verifying whether the numerical solutions produced by it will match the real dynamics of tuberculosis. This will be done by comparing the data produced by the proposed model with the real data freely available in the literature [11].

It is worthy mentioning that the IBM has a computational complexity proportional to the product among n_{real}, N and t_f, where n_{real} is the number of realizations. In cases which those parameters are large, parallel simulation is recommended.

Acknowledgments. E. R. Pinto acknowledges the support of Coordenação de Aperfeiçoamento de Pessoal de Nível Superior (CAPES), grant 1770124 and supported by resources supplied by the Center for Scientific Computing (NCC/GridUNESP) of the São Paulo State University (UNESP). A. S. L. O. Campanharo acknowledges the support of Fundação de Amparo à Pesquisa do Estado de São Paulo (FAPESP), grant 2018/25358-9. All codes were written in C language and all figures were generated with XmGrace and Pajek.

References

1. Barabási, A.L., Albert, R.: Emergence of scaling in random networks. Science **286**(5439), 509–512 (1999)
2. Dodds, P.S., Watts, D.J., Sabel, C.F.: Information exchange and the robustness of organizational networks. Proc. Nat. Acad. Sci. **100**(21), 12516–12521 (2003)
3. Edling, C.R., Åberg, Y., Liljeros, F., Amaral, L.A.N., Stanley, H.E.: The web of human sexual contacts. Nature **411**(6840), 907–908 (2002)
4. Erdös, P., Rényi, A.: On random graphs. Publ. Math. Debrecen **6**, 290–297 (1959)
5. Keeling, M.J., Grenfell, B.T.: Individual-based perspectives on R0. J. Theor. Biol. **203**(1), 51–61 (2000)
6. Moreno, V., et al.: The role of mobility and health disparities on the transmission dynamics of tuberculosis. Theor. Biol. Med. Modell. **14**(1), 1–17 (2017)
7. Nepomuceno, E.G., Takahashi, R.H.C., Aguirre, L.A.: Individual based-model (IBM): an alternative framework for epidemiological compartment models. Biometric Braz. J./Revista Brasileira de Biometria **34**(1), 133–162 (2016)
8. Nepomuceno, E.G., Barbosa, A.M., Silva, M.X., Perc, M.: Individual-based modelling and control of bovine brucellosis. Roy. Soc. Open Sci. **5**(5), 180200 (2018)
9. Newman, M.E.J.: Spread of epidemic disease on networks. Phys. Rev. E **66**(1), 016128 (2002)
10. Newman, M.E.J.: Networks: An Introduction. Oxford University Press, New York (2010)
11. World Health Organization, et al.: Global tuberculosis report 2016. World Health Organization (2016)
12. Pastor-Satorras, R., Castellano, C., Van Mieghem, P., Vespignani, A.: Epidemic processes in complex networks. Revi. Mod. Phys. **87**(3), 925–979 (2015)
13. Pinto, E.R., Campanharo, A.S.L.O.: Estudo do efeito topológico das redes contato na propagação de doenças infecciosas. Proc. Ser. Braz. Soc. Comput. Appl. Math. **6**(2), 1–7 (2018)
14. Solé, R.V., Gamarra, J.G., Ginovart, M., López, D.: Controlling chaos in ecology: from deterministic to individual-based models. Bull. Math. Biol. **61**(6), 1187–1207 (1999)
15. Watts, D.J., Strogatz, S.H.: Collective dynamics of "small-world" networks. Nature **393**(6684), 440 (1998)

Computational Neuroscience of
Learning and Memory

Association Between Fast and Slow Learning and Molecular Processes in Repetitive Practice: A Post Hoc Analysis

Tércio Apolinário-Souza[1,2,4(✉)], Ana Flavia Santos-Almeida[3],
Natália Lelis Torres[1], Juliana Otoni Parma[1],
Lidiane Aparecida Fernandes[1], Grace Schenatto Pereira[3],
and Guilherme Menezes Lage[1]

[1] School of Physical Education, Physiotherapy and Occupational Therapy,
NNeuroM, Universidade Federal de Minas Gerais, Belo Horizonte, Brazil
edf.tercio@hotmail.com
[2] Department of Human Movement Sciences, GEPECOM, Universidade
do Estado de Minas Gerais, Ibirité, Brazil
[3] Institute of Biological Sciences, NNC, Universidade Federal de Minas Gerais,
Belo Horizonte, Brazil
[4] Rua Desembargador Paula Mota, 30, ap.201. Ouro Preto, Belo Horizonte CEP
31310-340, Brazil

Abstract. The explanations for the positive effects of less repetitive practice in learning, compared to more repetitive practice, converge towards an idea of a greater memory strengthening in less repetitive practice. These benefits are associated with the AMPA glutamate receptor. However, there are no studies in the literature that explain, in molecular terms, how memory processes during practice (or acquisition) are associated with these benefits. Overall, the process of memory strengthening in the acquisition of a motor skill has two distinct stages: a fast initial performance improvement followed by a gradual change associated with the memory state termed slow learning. Computational models, like the multi-rate learning model, help to identify these two distinct stages (fast and slow learning). This study aimed to investigate if the AMPA receptors are associated with the memory's fast state (fast learning) and slow state (slow learning). Mice (n = 30) practiced the rotarod in two days of constant (one rotation frequency) or varied (three different rotation frequencies) practice. Animals were tested both 24 h and 10 days after acquisition. Two analyses were conducted, stepwise discriminant analysis and analysis of the difference between the predicted and observed values. Varied practice was more associated with the slow state. The findings of the present study advance in the explanations of the molecular mechanisms underpinning the greater memory strengthening proposed by behavioral hypotheses. Furthermore, we propose an alternative explanation for the explanations formulated at behavioral level, highlighting the role of the reference of the error that is produced trial-to-trial.

Keywords: Motor learning · Practice schedule · AMPA receptor · Fast learning · Slow learning

© Springer Nature Switzerland AG 2019
V. R. Cota et al. (Eds.): LAWCN 2019, CCIS 1068, pp. 91–103, 2019.
https://doi.org/10.1007/978-3-030-36636-0_7

1   Introduction

The degree of repetition within a practice session affects the learning levels in distinct ways [1]. Generally, less repetitive practice (e.g., variable practice) leads to increased learning levels than more repetitive practice (e.g., constant practice) [2]. Traditionally, the explanations regarding the differences in learning levels produced by the degree of repetition during a practice session have one convergence point, the process of memory strengthening [3–5]. Despite this convergence point, the molecular process of the mechanisms of memory strengthening still lacks explanation.

Recently, Apolinário-Souza et al. [6] showed that less repetitive practice produced a greater expression of the α-amino-3-hydroxy-5-methyl-4-isoxazolepropionic receptor (AMPA) in the motor cortex than more repetitive practices. AMPA is an ionotropic glutamate receptor associated with long-term potentiation (LTP). LTP typically occurs in glutamatergic synapses and it is established by the coincident activity of pre- and postsynaptic neurons [7]. LTP can be elicited by the activation of the N-methyl d-aspartate (NMDA) glutamate receptor [8]. The influx of Ca2+ through the NMDA receptor acts as an important postsynaptic second messenger, activating many intracellular signaling [9]. For instance, Ca2+ binds to the calmodulin, activating kinase proteins such as the calcium/calmodulin-dependent protein kinase II (CaMKII) [10]. One of the roles of the CAMKII is to promote the insertion of AMPA receptors in the postsynaptic membrane [11].

Although Apolinário-Souza et al. [6] showed an important molecular process of memory strengthening mechanism associated with the degree of repetition within a practice session, it is not known how the memory processes occurring during practice (or acquisition) are associated with these benefits. The process of memory strengthening during the acquisition of a motor skill has two distinct stages [12] that are associated with the contribution of two different memory states [13]. A fast initial performance improvement associated with the memory state termed fast learning is observed at the beginning of practice. Following this, there is a gradual change associated with the memory state termed slow learning. While fast learning has a small contribution to memory consolidation, slow learning is associated with persistent and resistant to interferences skill acquisition [14]. This time course reflects changes in the basic mechanisms of neural plasticity [12].

In the last years, computational modeling methods have been applied to help to produce an increasingly quantitative understanding of the two distinct memory states [13, 15, 16]. A multi-rate learning model, one of these computational models, starts from the premise that the process of motor learning occurs by a simultaneous and competitive update of both memory states: the fast state (fast learning) and the slow state (slow learning) [13]. Each state maintains an estimate (x_f and x_s for the fast and slow states, respectively), and the sum of these states ($y = x_f + x_s$) forms an estimate of the adjustments used to reach the goal. Each state is updated based on two process, the retention factor (A) and the error sensitivity (B), bringing forth four parameters: As, the retention factor of the slow state; Bs, the error sensitivity of the slow state; Af, the retention factor of the fast state and; Bf, the error sensitivity of the fast state. Every parameter must be positive, the Bf must have a bigger value than the Bs, and the Af

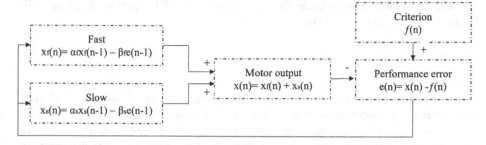

Fig. 1. Computational model - Multi-rate learning. Both the fast state (xf) and the slow state (xs) change in function of the trials and incorporate part of the performance error (e) to themselves. If compared to the slow state, the fast state is responsible for the fast performance improvement in the first trials (indicated by the bigger error sensitivity value, $\beta f > \beta s$), but has a weak contribution to long-term retention (indicated in the model by the lower retention factor value $\alpha f < \alpha s$). The motor output, x(n), represents the combining of both states, fast and slow. The performance error, e(n), is the difference between the motor output and the goal of the task, f(n).

must have a bigger value than the As. The retention factor (A) encodes the rate to which each state decreases in the absence of error, and its value is inversely proportional to the rate of decay. The error sensitivity (B) encodes the rate by which each state, fast and slow, improves the performance in function of the error [17]. Therefore, the retention factor (A) is more associated with the slow state, while the processes related to error sensitivity (B) are better associated with the fast state [13, 17] (Fig. 1).

Schweighofer et al. (2011) used a multi-rate learning model and found a greater association of less repetitive practice with the update of the slow state rather than of the fast state. We aim to replicate these findings adding the association between the AMPA receptor and less repetitive practice. This study's objective was to investigate if the AMPA receptors are associated with the memory's fast state (fast learning) and slow state (slow learning). The hypothesis is that the AMPA receptor expression will be more associated with slow learning than to fast learning in less repetitive practice. This manuscript is additional analyses after completing the experiment in Apolinário-Souza et al. [6].

2 Method

2.1 Animals

This study included 30 male C57/BL6 mice (weighting 25–30 g, aged 8–12 weeks), acquired in the University Vivarium (CEBIO). The animals were housed in groups of three to five per cage in a temperature-controlled environment (22 ± 1 °C) under a 12 h light/12 h dark cycle, and free access to water and feed. All experimental procedures were approved by The Animal Use Ethics Committee of Universidade Federal de Minas Gerais (156/2015 and 273/2016) and carried out in accordance with the

National Institute of Health guide for the care and use of Laboratory Animals (NIH Publication 8023, revised 1978).

2.2 Motor Task

A balance task performed on a rotating rod was used to assess motor learning. The plastic apparatus (rotarod) had a diameter of 5 cm and an 8 cm width per stall (Insight Equipamentos, Ribeirão Preto, Brasil). In this task, the mouse must balance itself on the rotating rod to prevent falling. Thus, the lower the number of falls, the better the performance. The time in balance was measured by a mechanic sensor in the apparatus floor. By changing the rotating speed of the rod along the sessions, we applied the two distinct practice schedules, variable and constant.

2.3 Experimental Design and Procedures

We allocated the animals in two groups: constant practice group (CG, n = 15) and variable practice group (VG, n = 15). The experiment was divided in four phases: acquisition, retention test, transfer test 1 and transfer test 2. The acquisition phase consisted of two sessions of six trials each, performed 24 h apart from each other. In this phase, the CG animals practiced only under the rotation frequency of 24 rpm, while the VG animals practiced under three different rotation frequencies, 16, 24 and 32 rpm, randomly assigned along the acquisition phase trials. The retention test and the transfer test 1 were performed approximately 24 h after the end of the acquisition phase, under a rotation frequency of 24 rpm and 40 rpm, respectively. The transfer test 2 was performed 10 days after the end of the acquisition phase, under a rotation frequency of 42 rpm. In each of the three tests, the animals performed one trial. Each trial lasted one minute, and the clock was interrupted at each fall. No interval was provided after a fall. The inter-trial rest interval lasted 2 min, when we placed the animal in a box apart from the other animals.

At the end of the experiment, which lasted for 13 days, the animals were euthanized by cervical dislocation followed by decapitation without anesthesia, to prevent interferences in the biochemical analyses. Afterward, the brains were dissected for removal of the motor cortex. Tissues of 10 animals (5 CG and 5 VG) were used to the AMPA receptors expression Western Blot analysis.

2.4 Western Blot

The motor cortex of the animals that were part of the experimental paradigm definition was promptly removed after the end of the experiment, frozen in liquid nitrogen and stored at a temperature of −80 °C until their use. The samples were homogenized in RIPA buffer (150 mM NaCl, 50 mM Tris, pH = 7.4, 1 mM EDTA, 1% Nonidet P40, 1 mM phenylmethylsulfonyl fluoride, 0.5% sodium deoxycholate) and centrifuged at 2040.35 G (Centrifuge Eppendorf 5415R, Germany) at 4 °C for 15 min. The protein concentration of the supernatant was determined by the Bradford method [18]. Proteins (50 μg) were denatured in sample buffer (100 mM Tris-HCl, pH = 6.8, 4% SDS, 0.2% bromophenol blue, 20% glycerol, 20% H2O, 0.5% β-mercaptoethanol) at a temperature of 100 °C for 4 min. The samples were separated on 10% SDS polyacrylamide gels and transferred to a polyvinylidene difluoride (PVDF Immobilon-P, Millipore, MA) in a Bio-Rad electrophoresis system (Bio-Rad, Hercules).

After the 2 h blocking with TBS-T (Tris-buffered saline with 0.1% Tween) containing 5% BSA, the membranes were incubated overnight at 4°C with primary antibodies against specific proteins [anti-GluA1 (106 kDa, Anti-Glutamate receptor 1 Polyclonal Antibody, rabbit, Millipore®, 1:1000) and anti-GluA2 (98 kDa, Anti-Ionotropic Glutamate receptor 2 Antibody, rabbit, Abcam®, 1:1000) diluted in TBS-T and BSA (3%). Afterward, membranes were washed 3 times, 5 min each, with TBS and were incubated with anti-rabbit antibody (1: 5000) diluted in TBS-T and BSA (3%) for 1 h. The normalization protein used was the antibody β-actin (42 kDa, Bio Rad®, mouse, 1:1000) diluted in TBS-T and BSA (3%), and membranes were incubated for 24 h. Afterward, membranes were incubated with anti-mouse antibody (1: 5000) diluted in TBS-T 1x and BSA (3%) for 1 h. Target protein bands were detected using ECL western blotting detection system (Millipore®). Proteins were detected by chemiluminescent scanning system using Image Quant LAS-4000 (GE Healthcare®). Blotting band densities were quantified by ImageJ software (Versão 1.44p). The GluA1 and GluA2 subunits were analyzed in this study due to the greater association of these subunits with learning [19].

2.5 Computational Model

For each animal, we fit a multi-rate learning model. In this model, as mentioned, the process of motor learning occurs by a simultaneous and competitive two-states update: a fast state (fast learning) and a slow state (slow learning). Each state is updated based on two processes, the retention factor (A) and the error sensitivity (B), bringing forth four parameters (As, Bs, Af, and Bf). Every parameter must be positive, the Bf must have a bigger value than the Bs, and the Af must have a bigger value than the As. In this study, the values were simulated separately in each day (6 trials per day).

2.6 Data Analysis

To compare the fast and slow states of the computational model between groups, two analyses were conducted, (a) stepwise discriminant analysis and (b) analysis of the difference between the predicted and observed values. In stepwise discriminant analysis groups were defined as the dependent variable and the four parameters (Af, As, Bf, and Af) of each day plus all possible interactions among these parameters as independent variables. In this analysis, independent variables are inserted in the model in order of significance, as long as they meet the entry criteria (defined as $p < 0.05$) and are removed from the model if they meet the removal criteria (defined as $p > 0.10$). A separate independent t-test was performed for each parameter (Af, As, Bf, and Af) comparing the GC and GV groups.

In the analysis of the difference between the predicted and observed values the values of the fast and slow states were simulated in the learning tests situations (retention, transfer 1 and transfer 2), and the absolute value of the difference between these predicted values and the observed values was established. Thus, the smaller the

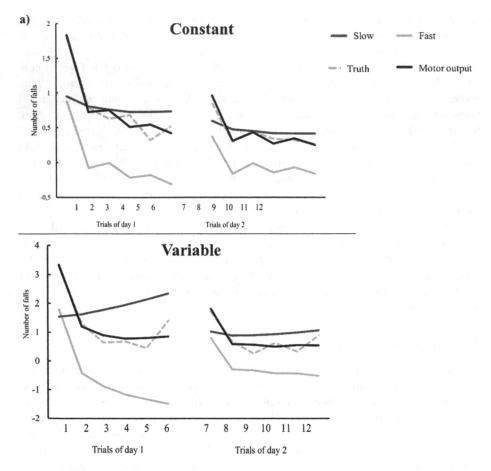

Fig. 2. Simulation of the computational model. In both practice schedules (a – constant and b – variable). Initially, the fast state (shown in green) contributes better to the performance improvement than the slow state (shown in lilac), but this contribution decays in function of the trials. The real values (Truth – shown in grey) is similar to the simulated values (shown in black). (Color figure online)

difference, the closest is the prediction of the state to the performance in the learning tests. The discriminant analysis assists the identification of the main parameters within each state that differ the practice schedules during the acquisition phase [20]. On the contrary, the analysis of the difference between the predicted and observed values assists the explanation of how much each state contributed to the performance in the learning tests. A Pearson correlation between the four parameters (Af, As, Bf and Af) and the AMPA receptors GluA1 and GluA2 was conducted based on the differences previously indicated (i.e., only the analyses in which significant differences were found).

We set the level of statistical significance at 5%. The effect size was calculated using the eta-squared (η^2) for the ANOVAs, and Cohen (d) for the Student t tests.

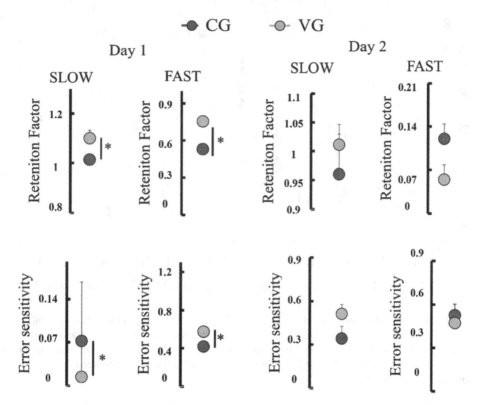

Fig. 3. Model parameters. Mean and standard deviation values. The groups differed only in the first day when the variable practice group (VG) was superior in all parameters if compared to the constant practice group (CG), except for the error sensitivity of the slow state. * = p < 0.05.

3 Results

Figure 2 presents the data of the practice schedules and the fast and slow states in the 12 trials. The fast and slow states behaved such as proposed by the model, with greater participation of the fast state at the beginning of practice and a quick decay of its participation, and gradual and slow participation of the slow state [13].

The discriminant analysis indicated that the only variable inserted into the model was the As in the first day, the retention factor of the slow state (p = 0.01). In other words, the only factor that better distinguished groups was the retention factor of the slow state (As). In Fig. 3, it is possible to observe that the retention factor of the slow state was higher for variable practice than for constant practice. To complement our analyses, we conducted t-tests to compare variable and constant practices for each of the four parameters in both practice days. Differences between groups were detected for all parameters in the first day, As [t(df = 28) = −2.70, p = 0.01], Af [t(df = 28) = −2.10, p = 0.04], Bs [t(df = 28) = 2.48, p = 0.01] and Bf [t(df = 28) = −2.10, p = 0.01]. As shown in Fig. 3, variable practice resulted in greater parameters values than constant practice, except for the Bs parameter, the error sensitivity of the slow

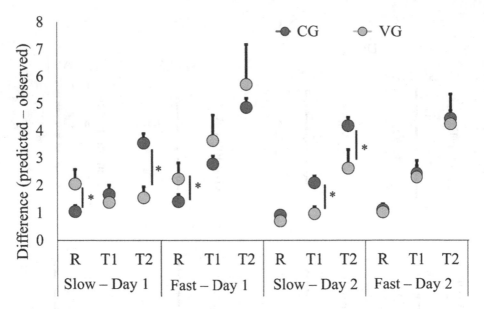

Fig. 4. Differences between predicted and observed values. Mean and standard deviation values. The constant practice group (CG) showed smaller differences between predicted and observed values than the variable practice group on retention test (R) in both states on the first day. On transfer test 1 (T1) and transfer test 2 (T), in the second day in the slow state, the effect was the opposite. * = p < 0.05.

state. In the second day, no differences between groups were found, As [t(df = 28) = −1.02, p = 0.31], Af [t(df = 28) = −1.60, p = 0.11], Bs [t(df = 28) = 1.95, p = 0.06] and Bf [t(df = 28) = 0.70, p = 0.48].

Regarding the analyses of the differences between the predicted and observed values, t tests indicated that variable practice resulted in smaller differences between the predicted and observed values than constant practice on transfer test 2 [t (df = 28) = 4.13, p = 0.00] in the slow state of the first day, and on transfer test 1 [t (df = 28) = 3.53, p = 0.00] and transfer test 2 [t (df = 28) = 3.72, p = 0.00] in the slow state of the second day (Fig. 4). Moreover, t-tests indicated that for the retention test, in the first day, differences between the slow state [t (df = 28) = −2.18, p = 0.04] and fast state [t (df = 28) = −2.04, p = 0.04] were higher in variable practice than in constant practice. For the other learning tests, no differences were found. Regarding transfer test 1, in the first day, the slow state [t (df = 28) = 0.64, p = 052] and fast state [t (df = 28) = −1.77, p = 0.08]. Regarding transfer test 2, in the first day, the fast state [t (df = 28) = −1.94, p = 0.06]. Regarding retention test, in the second day, the slow state [t (df = 28) = 0.78, p = 0.44] and fast state [t (df = 28) = 0.24, p = 0.80]. No difference was also found in the second day, in the fast state, neither for transfer test 1 [t (df = 28) = 0.31, p = 0.75] nor for transfer test 2 [t (df = 28) = 0.23, p = 0.56] (Fig. 4).

After identifying the main parameters of the states that discriminate the practice schedules during the acquisition phase and the main associations of the states with the

Table 1. Correlations between the four parameters and the AMPA receptor subunits, GluA1 e GluA2. Pearson coefficient (R) and significance values (p-value). For variable practice, significant correlations regarding the error sensitivity parameter in the slow state (Bs) and in the fast state (Bf) were found. * = p < 0.05.

			Day 1			
			As	Bs	Af	Bf
Constant	GLUA1	R	-0.45	0.53	-0.29	-0.45
		p-value	0.44	0.35	0.64	0.45
	GLUA2	R	-0.14	-0.35	-0.47	0.17
		p-value	0.82	0.57	0.42	0.8
Variable	GLUA1	R	0.09	-0.88	0.30	-0.28
		p-value	0.89	0.04*	0.62	0.65
	GLUA2	R	0.22	0.12	-0.71	-0.98*
		p-value	0.72	0.84	0.18	0.00

learning tests, a Pearson correlation was conducted between the four parameters and the AMPA receptor subunits, GluA1 and GluA2. The correlations were based on the differences previously presented. In other words, only performed for the analyses that detected significant differences. In Table 1, it is possible to observe the significance values (p) and the correlation coefficient (R) of the correlations between the parameters and the receptors. The only analyses with significant correlations were between Bs, error sensitivity in the slow state, and the GluA1 in variable practice (R = −0.88, p = 0.04), and between Bf, error sensitivity in the fast state, and the GluA2 in variable practice (R = −0.98, p = 0.04). In both situations, a strong inverse correlation was found. In other words, the higher the Bs and Bf values, the lower the expression of the receptors.

4 Discussion

This study aimed to investigate if the AMPA receptors are associated with the memory's fast state (fast learning) and slow state (slow learning). Overall, the results confirm the study's hypotheses. The greater AMPA receptor expression is associated with the slow state of learning.

We found that variable practice resulted in higher values of the retention factor in both memory states, fast and slow, when compared to constant practice. For the error sensitivity, however, variable practice resulted in lower values in the slow state and higher values in the fast state than constant practice. The retention factor encodes the rate by which each state, fast and slow, improves the performance in function of the error. The model predicts that the processes related to the retention factor are more associated with the slow state, while the processes related to the error sensitivity are better associated with the fast state [13]. The smaller error sensitivity value in the slow state, associated with the higher retention factor value in the slow state indicates that variable practice relies more on the slow state to better estimate the trials. It is a result of the variable practice reduced weight of the processes better associated with the fast state, the error sensitivity, and the increased weight of the processes better associated with the slow state, the retention factor. These results are supported by the literature [21]. One possible explanation for these results comes from the lower levels of performance improvement of less repetitive practice compared to more repetitive practice throughout the acquisition phase, especially in the first trials. Considering that the fast state contributes to the fast and initial performance improvement, it is possible to assume that the less pronounced performance improvements in less repetitive practice negatively affects the fast state and positively affects the slow state [21]. The hypothesis of interferences in the states was raised by Schweighofer et al. (2011), who assumed that the intermixing of skills in less repetitive practice promotes greater intertrial forgetting than more repetitive practice, updating the slow state rather than the fast state. Thus, a greater dependency on the slow state to response production is created [21].

The correlation results for variable practice indicated that the lower the error sensitivity values in both states, the higher the AMPA receptors expression values. The inverse correlation between the error sensitivity values and the AMPA receptors expression suggests that the lower the rate by which each state improves performance in function of the errors during acquisition, the greater the AMPA receptors expression. A smaller rate of improvement in function of the errors is the behavior better associated with slow changes, with a greater contribution to long-term changes than fast changes [13]. These results indicate that the processes associated with the slow state in less repetitive practice result in greater AMPA receptor expression.

The results of the differences between the predicted and observed values showed that variable practice had smaller differences on transfer test 2 in the 1st day, and transfer test 1 and 2 in the 2nd day, all for the slow state. These results suggest that variable practice is more associated with the slow state than to the fast state to estimate its performance on the learning tests with changes in the environment (transfer tests). Many studies in the literature suggest that the benefits of less repetitive practice are more evident with changes in the context of execution [3, 22, 23]. The variability of motor experiences due to less repetition provides a higher number of relationships between the information processed. These pieces of information (initial conditions, response specifications, sensory consequences of the produced response, and effects of the movement in the environment) are stored in memory as schemes [24]. The stronger the schemes in memory, the better the reorganization of information, allowing a better transfer for new variations of the same skill [3, 24].

The results of our study, together with others in the literature, enable the formulation of an alternative explanation, illustrated in Fig. 5. The intermixing of different goals during variable practice reduces the reference and increases the ambiguity generated trial-to-trial when compared to constant practice. This diminished reference and increased ambiguity induces the system to increase the transmission of signals between

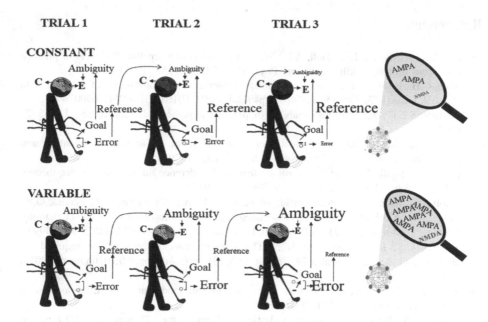

Fig. 5. Explanation in molecular level to the benefits of less repetitive practice. E = expectation; C = sensory consequences. The blue color indicates the posterior regions and the red color the frontal regions. (Color figure online)

cerebral regions (illustrated in the figure by the maintenance of the shining brain in variable practice across trials), increasing the NMDA receptor activity and AMPA expression (illustrated by the increase of the font of the "NMDA" letters, by the increase in the number of AMPA written, and by the red color in the magnifying glass in variable practice).

5 Conclusion

The results found in this study suggest an association between the slow state in less repetitive practice and increased AMPA receptor expression. It is possible that less repetitive practice produces higher levels of LTP and, consequently, increased insertion of novel AMPA receptors. These findings make progress in the explanations of the molecular mechanisms underlying the greater memory strengthening produced by less repetitive practiced proposed by behavioral hypotheses [3, 4, 25].

The experimental paradigm defined in the present study could help future studies using animal models aiming to investigate different types of practice organization.

Acknowledgments. This study was supported by Fundação de Amparo à Pesquisa do Estado de Minas Gerais (FAPEMIG) (grant APQ-03305-15) and Coordenação de Aperfeiçoamento de Pessoal de Nível Superior - Brasil (CAPES), finance Code 001.

References

1. Lee, T.D., Swanson, L.R., Hall, A.L.: What is repeated in a repetition? Effects of practice conditions on motor skill acquisition. Phys. Ther. **71**, 150–156 (1991)
2. Shea, C.H., Kohl, R., Indermill, C.: Contextual interference: contributions of practice. Acta Psychol. (Amst) **73**, 145–157 (1990). https://doi.org/10.1016/0001-6918(90)90076-R
3. Moxley, S.E.E.: Schema: the variability of practice hypothesis. J. Mot. Behav. **11**, 65–70 (1979)
4. Shea, J.B., Morgan, R.L.: Contextual interference effects on the acquisition, retention, and transfer of a motor skill. J. Exp. Psychol. **5**, 179–187 (1979)
5. Lee, T., Magill, R.: The locus of contextual interference in motor-skill acquisition. J. Exp. Psychol. Learn. Mem. Cogn. **9**, 730–746 (1983)
6. Apolinário-Souza, T., Santos Almeida, A.F., Lelis-Torres, N., Parma, J.O., Pereira, G.S., Lage, G.M.: Molecular mechanisms associated with the benefits of variable practice in motor learning. J. Mot. Behav. **51**, 1–12 (2019). https://doi.org/10.1080/00222895.2019.1649997
7. Tabone, C.J., Ramaswami, M.: Is NMDA receptor-coincidence detection required for learning and memory? Neuron **74**, 767–769 (2012). https://doi.org/10.1016/j.neuron.2012.05.008
8. Zito, K.: NMDA receptor function and physiological modulation. In: Encyclopedia of Neuroscience, pp. 1157–1164 (2009)
9. Lisman, J.E.: Three Ca^{2+} levels affect plasticity differently: the LTP zone, the LTD zone and no man's land. J. Physiol. **532**, 285 (2001)
10. Lisman, J., Yasuda, R., Raghavachari, S.: Mechanisms of CaMKII action in long-term potentiation. Nat. Rev. Neurosci. **6**, 2166–2171 (2008). https://doi.org/10.1038/nrn3192
11. Rumpel, S., Ledoux, J., Zador, A., Malinow, R.: Postsynaptic receptor trafficking underlying a form of associative learning. Science **308**, 83–88 (2005). https://doi.org/10.1126/science.1103944
12. Karni, A., et al.: The acquisition of skilled motor performance: fast and slow experience-driven changes in primary motor cortex. Proc. Natl. Acad. Sci. **95**, 861–868 (1998). https://doi.org/10.1073/pnas.95.3.861
13. Smith, M.A., Ghazizadeh, A., Shadmehr, R.: Interacting adaptive processes with different timescales underlie short-term motor learning. PLoS Biol. **4**, 1035–1043 (2006). https://doi.org/10.1371/journal.pbio.0040179
14. Ungerleider, L., Doyon, J., Karni, A.: Imaging brain plasticity during motor skill learning. Neurobiol. Learn. Mem. **78**, 553–564 (2002). https://doi.org/10.1006/nlme.2002.4091
15. Thoroughman, K.A., Shadmehr, R.: Learning of action trough adaptative combination of motor primitives. Nature **407**, 742–747 (2000). https://doi.org/10.1038/35037588.Learning
16. Scheidt, R.A., Dingwell, J.B., Mussa-ivaldi, F.A., Robert, A., Dingwell, J.B., Ferdinando, A.: Learning to Move Amid Uncertainty. J. Neurophysiol. **86**, 971–985 (2001). citeulike-article-id:406856
17. Albert, S.T., Shadmehr, R.: Estimating properties of the fast and slow adaptive processes during sensorimotor adaptation. J. Neurophysiol. **119**, 1367–1393 (2017). https://doi.org/10.1152/jn.00197.2017
18. Bradford, M.M.: A rapid and sensitive method for the quantitation of microgram quantities of protein utilizing the principle of protein-dye binding. Anal. Biochem. **72**, 248–254 (1976). https://doi.org/10.1016/0003-2697(76)90527-3
19. Grosshans, D.R., Clayton, D.A., Coultrap, S.J., Browning, M.D.: LTP leads to rapid surface expression of NMDA but not AMPA receptors in adult rat CA1. Nat. Neurosci. **5**, 27–33 (2002). https://doi.org/10.1038/nn779

20. Trewartha, K.M., Garcia, A., Wolpert, D.M., Flanagan, J.R.: Fast but fleeting: adaptive motor learning processes associated with aging and cognitive decline. J. Neurosci. **34**, 13411–13421 (2014). https://doi.org/10.1523/JNEUROSCI.1489-14.2014
21. Schweighofer, N., et al.: Mechanisms of the contextual interference effect in individuals poststroke. J. Neurophysiol. **106**, 2632–2641 (2011). https://doi.org/10.1152/jn.00399.2011
22. Lage, G.M., Vieira, M.M., Palhares, L., Ugrinowitsch, H., Benda, R.: Practice schedules and number of skills as contextual interference factors in the learning of positioning timing tasks. J. Hum. Mov. Stud. **50**, 185–200 (2006)
23. Silva, A.B., Lage, G.M., Gonçalves, W., Palhares, L.R., Ugrinowitsch, R., Benda, H.: Contextual interference and manipulation of generalized motor programs and parameters in timing tasks. J. Sport Exerc. Psychol. **26**, 173 (2004)
24. Schmidt, R.A.: A schema theory of discrete motor skill learning. Psychol. Rev. **82**, 225–260 (1975)
25. Shea, J.B., Zimny, S.T.: Context effects in memory and learning movement information. Mem. Control Action. **12**, 345–365 (1983)

Reading Span Test for Brazilian Portuguese: An Eye-Tracking Implementation

Jaime A. Riascos[1,4,5](✉) [ID], Arthur M. Brugger[1], Priscila Borges[2] [ID],
Ana B. Arêas da Luz Fontes[3], and Dante C. Barone[1]

[1] CONCYS, Institute of Informatics,
Federal University Rio Grande do Sul (UFRGS), Porto Alegre, RS, Brazil
jarsalas@inf.ufrgs.br
[2] University of Groningen, Groningen, The Netherlands
p.borba.borges@student.rug.nl
[3] LABICO, School of Languages and Literature,
Federal University Rio Grande do Sul (UFRGS), Porto Alegre, RS, Brazil
ana.fontes@ufrgs.br
[4] SDAS Research Group, Ibarra, Ecuador
contact@sdas-group.com
[5] Corporación Universitaria Autnoma de Nariño, Pasto, Colombia
http://www.inf.ufrgs.br/~concys

Abstract. The Reading Span Test (RST) is an instrument created for assessing verbal working memory capacity. Since its first version, the RST has undergone several modifications, including translations to different languages. This work aims to create a version of a standardized RST in Brazilian Portuguese. In addition, an implementation for eye-tracking devices on the RST is presented. Two reading conditions, aloud and silent, were compared to ensure optimal methodology for future studies. Significant differences were found between the two reading conditions, and distinct reading strategies were revealed by the eye-tracker.

Keywords: Reading Span Test · Eye-tracking · Working Memory · Brazilian Portuguese

1 Introduction

Working Memory (WM) is responsible for briefly maintaining information and manipulating it in order to perform tasks such as making decisions, reading, and performing logical operations (Cowan 2008); in reading, its job is to temporarily hold words or sentences in memory and compare them with information retrieved from the mental lexicon to create a logical discourse that makes sense for the reader (Baddeley 1979).

In the eighties, the Reading Span Test (RST) was introduced in an effort to measure both processing and storage functions of working memory. In this initial test, participants were asked to read aloud a series of unrelated sentences

© Springer Nature Switzerland AG 2019
V. R. Cota et al. (Eds.): LAWCN 2019, CCIS 1068, pp. 104–118, 2019.
https://doi.org/10.1007/978-3-030-36636-0_8

presented in cards with 13–15 words in length, and to recall the last word of each sentence in order at the end of each series. The number of sentences was progressively increased from two to six. The maximum number of final words remembered correctly on at least two sets was the participant's reading span.

Thus, RST was the first attempt to use a reading task to assess working memory capacity (WMC) (Conway et al. 2005); moreover, following the WM model proposed by Baddeley and Hitch (1974), the RST has been used for studying the relationship between reading comprehension and WMC (Friedman and Miyake 2004; Carretti et al. 2009), as both depend on domain-specific factors, namely those related to verbal memory (Cornoldi and Vecchi 2003; Carretti et al. 2009).

The implementation of the RST has changed over the last few decades due to a variety of factors (see next section), leading to a need for a computerized and standardized version of the test. Van den Noort and colleagues (2008) proposed a standardized test that sought to reduce the variability across versions. Likewise, implementing the RST in different languages is paramount and involves the consideration of both structural and lexical aspects that might differ between the languages, allowing for variation while controlling for a minimum number of factors to warrant comparisons between studies in different languages. Previous works have translated the original Daneman and Carpenter (1980) RST into other languages (Tomitch 1999; Bailer 2011), and recently also into Portuguese (Cassol Rigatti et al. 2018), but none of them have translated or implemented the standardized version proposed by Van den Noort.

In addition to a standardized version, the inclusion of new technologies on WM tests is of great interest both for research purposes and for clinical purposes (Charchat Fichman et al. 2014). Indeed, rapid advances in technology have made it possible to assess individuals' cognitive states during tasks such as the RST, including those related to eye-tracking (ET), but also those related to electroencephalography (EEG) and electrodermal activity (EDA), among others (Parsey and Schmitter-Edgecombe 2013).

The primary purpose of this work is to create a standardized RST in Brazilian Portuguese, and as a further contribution, to outline an eye-tracking implementation to verify eye-movement patterns during the reading task. Therefore, this study is divided in two stages: first, the implementation and validation of the standardized RST proposed by van den Noort et al. (2008) in Brazilian Portuguese; and second, the inclusion of eye-tracking technology for assessing reading patterns in two reading conditions: aloud and silently.

ET has successfully been used for monitoring ongoing activity of the eyes during reading (Clifton et al. 2015). However, in working memory tasks that are based on reading, eye-tracking data can reveal information about information processing and memory (Alptekin and Ercetin 2015). Thus, the idea behind the use of eye-tracking is to reveal similarities and differences in cognitive processes in two different reading conditions. Such effort leads to the following hypothesis:

(a) There is a difference between reading patterns as indexed by eye-tracking data between silent and aloud conditions. This in turn could lead to different scores on the RST.

(*b*) Users who adopt reading strategies can be identified by the eye-tracker. These users may have higher scores on the RST.

(*c*) Reading conditions could be associated with different cognitive load.

The article is organized as follows: The first section discusses similar works and the evolution of the RST since its beginnings; next, the materials and methods used in this study are described; finally, the results with their respective discussion and conclusions are presented.

2   Related Works

2.1   RST Through Time

RST has been a subject of discussion in the past decades; initially, Engle and colleagues (Engle et al. 1999; Turner and Engle 1989) asked WMC depended on task modality, that is, if WMC during reading comprehension, for example, relied on components specific to the task (Carretti et al. 2009). To clarify this matter, they proposed the Operation Span Task, where participants have to verify arithmetic operations while trying to remember words presented after each equation. As a result, it was demonstrated that tasks in which subjects have to actively process and store incoming information can be successfully used for assessing WMC, regardless of whether they contain verbal components or not (Carretti et al. 2009).

In their turn, Waters and Caplan (1996a) disagreed with the theory of Just and Carpenter Daneman and Carpenter (1980) that posited that the RST could effectively measure sentence comprehension, depending only on how information was processed (performance) (Just and Carpenter 1992). They demonstrated that even people with verbal disorders (and low WMC) were able to determinate the meaning of sentences using syntactic structures. Therefore, they proposed a new version of the RST (Waters and Caplan 1996b) incorporating two main changes: (i) Subjects were asked to read the sentences silently; (ii) in addition to reading and remembering the last words of each sentence, participants should evaluate the acceptability of each sentence semantically.

Besides these theoretical issues, the scoring method of the reading span test has also been debated (for a review, see Conway et al. (2005)). The scoring in the original study of Daneman and Carpenter (1980) was assessed through the maximum level at which the participant was able to recall two of three items correctly. This quasi-absolute measure does not differentiate the data from trials which the subject currently finds him or herself (his or her reading span). Moreover, in such evaluation, the score ranges from two to six, affecting the sensitivity of the measure (Oberauer and Süß 2000). Likewise, the variability of the test represents an issue, insofar as the length of the sentences (Towse et al. 2002), the time of exposure and the similarity of the stimuli (Conway et al. 2005; Copeland and Radvansky 2001) can all influence participants' performance. These limitations demonstrated a need for a standardized version of the RST.

With this in mind, Van den Noort and colleagues (van den Noort et al. 2008) proposed a standardized test that aimed to overcome the above-mentioned limitations. In this version, the authors identified the issues of the original Daneman and Carpenter (1980) RST and created an RST that takes into consideration the following factors: (i) length of sentences and sentence-final words; (ii) time of stimuli exposure; (iii) frequency of sentence-final words; (iv) abstractness/concreteness of sentence-final words; (v) scoring; and (vi) variability in adaptations to other languages. With this version, it is argued that the assessment of WMC can be more objective and open to the possibility of obtaining comparable measures between languages.

2.2 Current Study

The present work is divided into two separable, yet complementary parts. The first section aims to validate the standardized RST into Portuguese (Brazilian) language. Previous works have only translated the original Daneman and Carpenter (1980) RST (Tomitch 1999; Bailer 2011) and the Waters and Caplan (1996b) RST (Cassol Rigatti et al. 2018) from English into Portuguese, accounting for lexical and syntactic differences between the languages, as well as cultural factors. However, rather than translating the RST, this work creates a RST following as closely as possible the guidelines proposed by van den Noort et al. (2008). The complementary section explores the inclusion of eye-tracking measures on the RST, emphasizing its importance, replicability and impact on future works. This implementation also allowed the analysis of possible differences in performance on the RST when reading silently or aloud. Moreover, a measure of the cognitive load of each reading condition was obtained using the NASA-TLX (Hart and Stavenland 1988). This study includes three major sections:

(a) Performance and reaction times on the RST;
(b) Eye-movement patterns;
(c) Subjective assessment of the cognitive load for each reading condition using NASA-TLX (Hart and Stavenland 1988).

3   Materials and Methods

3.1   Construction of the Sentences

Following van den Noort et al. (2008), we sought to improve the reliability of the RST by adopting the following methodological criteria:

Condition	Words	Syllables	Letters	Syllables FW	Letters FW	Log frequency FW
Silently	11.6(1.3)	21.1(1.0)	49.4(3.8)	2.4(0.8)	5.8(1.9)	4.5(0.8)
Aloud	11.6(1.3)	21.1(1.0)	49.3(3.7)	2.5(0.9)	5.8(1.9)	4.5(0.8)

(a) The length of the sentences was controlled, ranging from 9 to 16 words, 17 to 25 syllables, and 42 to 61 letters. As a result, the sentences of the RST (see Table 1) had similar length to those employed by van den Noort et al. (2008). Likewise, there are no statistically significant difference between conditions, making the sentences syntactically comparable.

(b) The number of syllables and the number of letters were controlled for over four series.

(c) The frequency of the sentence-final words was controlled for over the four series. The Corpus *Brasileiro* lexical database (Estivalet and Meunier 2015) was used to determine the frequency of sentence-final words. The Fig. 1 shows the log frequency of final words ($u = 4.54$, $SD = 0.82$) as a function of sentence-final word length ($u = 5.88$, $SD = 1.92$) as well as an histogram that shows the distribution of the number of letters used for constructing the sentence-final words.

(d) All sentences had a maximum presentation time of 8 seconds. This time was determined following a pilot study to assess Brazilian individuals reading time.

(e) Within the sets, sentences and sentence-final words were controlled for semantic relations to avoid semantic influences on the RST. In order to do that, the sentences were randomly presented, and repetition of final words was avoided.

Contrary to van den Noort et al. (2008), sentences were not controlled for plausibility or level of abstraction due to time constraints. This, however, will be done in a future study. It is worth noting that even though sentence length and number of syllables and letters were similar to those in van den Noort et al. (2008), morphosyntactic idiosyncrasies of the Portuguese language did not allow for the same numeric constraints. These include the fact that one-syllable words abound in English whereas in Portuguese those are much rarer, leading to a higher number of syllables and a lower number of words overall.

3.2   Implementation of the RST

We created 160 unrelated sentences in total, 80 for each condition (reading aloud and silently). These sentences were pseudo-randomized for each user. We built randomized blocks containing two to six sentences each, representing different difficulty levels. Each block was tested four times. We set 8000 ms as the maximum time of presentation for each sentence. The blocks were separated by fixation screens (with a cross at the center) signaling moments where the participant should recall the words. Subjects had unlimited amount of time for recall. Participants were instructed to say out loud the sentence's final words that they could remember, regardless of the reading condition (aloud or silently). Likewise, the user was free to choose the order of the remembered words. A possible carry-over effect was avoided by alternating the order of the reading condition for each user. Each subject's score (their reading span) corresponded to the total number of correctly recalled items (i.e., x% of 80 sentences). At the end, after of

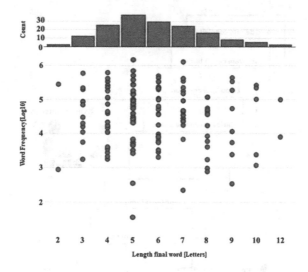

Fig. 1. Log frequency and length of the sentence-final word.

the 80 sentences were read, participants had to answer ten questions related to the content of the sentences and complete the NASA-TLX questionnaire. The motivation for applying the questions was to ensure the participant' attention while reading. This way, we attempted to simulate study-like reading patterns during the RST, which are arguably the most naturalistic in the population under scrutiny; however, the answers to the questions were not relevant for the current study. In its turn, the NASA-TLX was used to subjectively assess the workload in each condition. This instrument contains questions related to how demanding the subject perceives a task to be, both in terms of mental effort as well as physical effort, besides gathering subjective data regarding participant's performance, frustration levels and temporal demands. Figure 2 summarizes the RST procedure.

3.3 Participants

The study was approved by the institutional ethics committee of the Federal University of Rio Grande do Sul under reference number 2.825.143. All participants read and signed a written consent form before the experiment. Recruitment was conducted via Internet. In total, 30 university students and technicians participated in the study (M = 22, F = 8). Participant's average age was 23.1 years (SD = 4.4). Half of them reported having visual problems, and 93.3% of them wore glasses for correcting their visual impairment. The experiment was carried out in a noise-reduced room. The participants were seated on a comfortable chair 70 cm away from the screen.

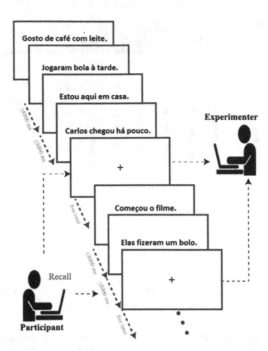

Fig. 2. RST procedure and experimental setup. Participants' responses were recorded by the experimenter on a computer.

3.4   Apparatus

The Portuguese RST was presented on am AlienWare 17 laptop, which has an embedded eye-tracker Tobii 4C. This eye-tracker has an accuracy of 0.34° and frequency sample of 60 Hz. A seven-point calibration was done twice before each stage of the RST (silently and aloud); subsequently, the experimenter verified the precision with a nine-point grid. The RST software was implemented in C# in order to use the raw data directly from the Tobii SDK, assuring high temporal precision for the stimuli.

The eye-tracking data collected was processed and analyzed using the Python toolbox PyGaze (Dalmaijer et al. 2014); For saccades detection, the toolbox uses an online saccade detection algorithm proposed by Engbert and Kliegl (2003) which calculates eye movement speed based on multiples samples. For fixations, it uses a geometrical approach based on inter-sample distance set up by a number of pixels. Three filters were applied:

(a) Fixations with duration of more than three times the standard deviation were removed (van der Lans et al. 2011);
(b) Saccades with amplitudes smaller than 0.5° were discarded (Over et al. 2007);
(c) Saccades with amplitudes bigger than 20° were discarded (maximum length of the reading lines).

For fixations, 80 ms was set up as the minimum duration and 50 px as the maximal inter-sample distance; for saccades, the velocity and acceleration threshold was set at $30°/s$, and $8000°/s^2$ (van der Lans et al. 2011); and the minimal duration was 20 ms (based on our equipment sampling frequency). All software and codes used for this research can be found at[1].

3.5   Cognitive Load Measure

The most typical subjective technique to measure perceived workload is the NASA-TLX (Task Load Index) (Hart and Stavenland 1988), which provides a six-dimensional rating of workload that yield a final workload score. These dimensions are related to different aspects involved in completing a task:

- Mental demands.
- Physical demands.
- Temporal demands.
- Performance.
- Effort.
- Frustration level.

Each dimension is assessed on a 10-point scale ranging from "low" to "high" or "good to poor" (with regard to performance). An example is the question "How mentally demanding was the task?", which corresponds to the first dimension, Mental demands. In addition, there is a binary selection among demands (which demand was more important?). The questionnaire was filled up by the participants after each reading condition (either aloud or silently).

4   Results

4.1   Reading Span Test

We analyzed the outcomes of the RST in terms of performance, that is, the number of correctly remembered items over the maximum number of items and reaction times (RT), and compared them for the two reading conditions. The results as a function of the number of words recalled (the number of sentences read) are presented in Figs. 3 and 4 for performance and RT respectively.

A paired Wilcoxon signed-rank test revealed a significant difference for six words ($V = 80.5, p \leq 0.02$), showing better performance for silent reading. Likewise, there are significant differences for six ($V = 142245, p \leq 0.0001$) and three ($V = 36637, p \leq 0.001$) words in RT, with reading aloud presenting longer time than silent reading. Meanwhile, a Pearson product-moment correlation coefficient was computed to assess the relationship between performance and RT, finding only a significant negative correlation between the two variables for three words in the reading aloud condition ($r = -0.40, p \leq 0.02$).

---

[1] https://github.com/JARS29/experiment_eye.

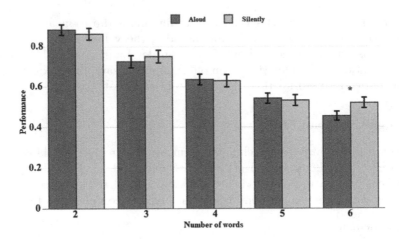

Fig. 3. Normalized performance for each level of difficulty (Numbers of words to be recalled). Significant difference found for six words where Silently reading has the best performance.

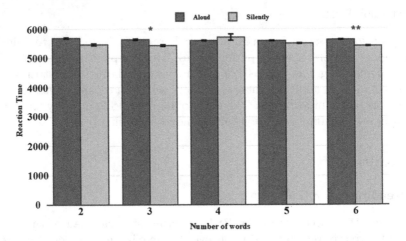

Fig. 4. Reaction times for each level of difficulty (Numbers of words to be recalled). Significant differences found for three and six words where Aloud reading has longer reaction times.

Next, the same variables are presented as a function of the series, i.e. with all levels of difficulty (20 sentences, randomized order). The Table 1 shows the values per series and the overall picture for the experiment. No significant differences were found for performance in either reading conditions or series. However, a paired Wilcoxon signed-rank test showed significant differences in RT for series two ($V = 1.09e5, p \leq 3.03e-6$) and four ($V = 9.89e4, p \leq 3.93e-2$). Similarly, a Dunn's Kruskal-Wallis Multiple Comparisons with Bonferroni correction showed a significant difference in RT in the silent condition between series 1–2 ($z =$

Table 1. Mean and standard error for performance and reaction time per series for the two conditions.

	Performance	RT
Aloud		
Serie 1	12.0(0.5)	5892.3(189.6)
Serie 2	11.4(0.3)	5665.9(167.8)***
Serie 3	12.1(0.5)	5468.0(169.1)
Serie 4	11.9(0.4)	5490.8(181.8)*
Overall	47.6(1.6)	5626.1(25.7)
Silently		
Serie 1	12.0(0.6)	5811.3(214.1)
Serie 2	12.2(0.5)	5382.3(223.0)***
Serie 3	12.3(0.4)	5567.5(303.1)
Serie 4	12.4(0.5)	5301.0(249.7)*
Overall	49.0(1.6)	5503.5(41.7)

$4.78, p \leq 1e-5$); series 1–3 ($z = 4.07, p \leq 1e-4$); and series 1–4 ($z = 5.50, p \leq 1e-5$); and in the aloud condition, series 1–2 ($z = 2.83, p \leq 0.01$); series 1–3 ($z = 5.56, p \leq 1e-5$); series 1–4 ($z = 25.90, p \leq 1e-6$); series 2–3 ($z = 25.90, p \leq 1e-6$); series 2–4 ($z = 25.90, p \leq 1e-6$). No correlations were found between the variables per series.

4.2 Eye-Tracking

After visual inspection of the data, six participants were discarded from the eye-movement analysis due to technical issues. With data from the 24 remaining participants, the following eye movements were studied:

(*a*) Total number of fixations;
(*b*) Duration of fixations;
(*c*) First and last fixation duration;
(*d*) Gaze duration;
(*e*) Size of saccades;
(*f*) Regression probability;
(*g*) Size of regressive and progressive saccades.

Table 2 shows the data of these variables. Significant differences were found with a paired Wilcoxon signed-rank test between reading condition for the number of fixations ($tau = -0.44, p \leq 0.0024$); duration of first fixation ($tau = -0.44, p \leq 0.0024$); gaze duration ($tau = -0.44, p \leq 0.0024$); size of saccades ($tau = -0.44, p \leq 0.0024$); probability of regression ($tau = -0.44, p \leq 0.0024$), and size of progressives saccades ($tau = -0.44, p \leq 0.0024$). Furthermore, several correlations (Kendall) were found between eye measures, the NASA-TLX factors and RT. Due to space limitations, we will only describe the most relevant for our discussion.

Table 2. Mean and standard error of the eye-tracking data

	Aloud	Silently
Number of fixations**	15.7(0.5)	15.9(0.7)
Duration of fixations (ms)	176.9(4.9)	177.9(5.5)
Duration first fixation (ms)*	248.3(9.0)	253.6(7.6)
Duration last fixation (ms)	256.1(24.3)	253.0(18.8)
Gaze duration (ms)***	2620.4(118.1)	2662.0(163.8)
Size saccades (°)***	3.3 (0.0)	3.6(0.1)
Regression probability***	0.3(0.0)	0.36(0.0)
Size progressive (°)***	2.8(0.0)	3.0 (0.1)
Size regressive (°)	4.8(0.1)	5.0(0.1)

In the reading aloud condition, performance on the NASA test correlated with the size of saccades ($tau = -0.42, p \leq 0.005$), the number of fixations ($tau = 0.37, p \leq 0.01$) and gaze duration ($tau = 0.33, p \leq 0.02$). Also, the duration of the last fixation shows a relationship with RT ($tau = 0.32, p \leq 0.02$) and mental demand ($tau = -0.46, p \leq 0.002$). On the other hand, the reading silently condition presented correlations between the duration of the last fixation, RT ($tau = 0.33, p \leq 0.024$) and effort ($tau = 0.36, p \leq 0.01$). Moreover, the regression probability correlates with the level of frustration ($tau = -0.31, p \leq 0.03$)m and the size of regressive saccades with RT ($tau = 0.31, p \leq 0.03$). As is expected, the number of fixations strongly correlated with RT in both conditions (Silently: $tau = 0.66, p \leq 8.06e - 6$; Aloud: $tau = 0.66, p \leq 9.05e - 6$), but interestingly, the size of progressives saccades was correlated with performance on the NASA test both conditions too (Silently: $tau = -0.33, p \leq 0.03$; Aloud: $tau = -0.42, p \leq 0.004$).

4.3 Cognitive Load

Figure 5 shows the scores measured by the NASA-TLX. This questionnaire gives a multi-dimensional rate of the workload that a task exerts on the participant (Hart and Stavenland 1988). Such dimensions referrer to mental, physical and temporal demands as well as the performance, effort and frustration level that the user experimented while performing a task. The load in all the dimensions of the NASA-TLX did not differ significantly between reading conditions. In fact, it was similar on several factors as well as on general workload. Only the mental demands dimension Was higher in the reading silently condition. Besides, reading aloud had more load in the dimensions related to performance, and physical and temporal demands.

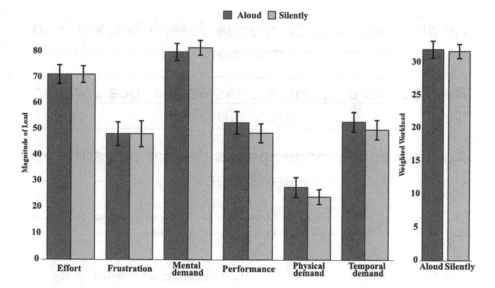

Fig. 5. NASA-TLX scores for each factor and for workload per reading condition.

Intriguingly, correlations were found between overall RST performance and temporal demands in reading silently ($tau = 0.28, p \leq 0.03$), and between overall RT and physical demands in reading aloud ($tau = -0.44, p \leq 0.0024$). Due to limitations of the NASA-TLX in measuring the cognitive load during the execution of the task, we could not analyze correlations between the series.

5 Discussion

We implemented a Portuguese (Brazilian) version of the Reading Span Test proposed by van den Noort et al. (2008). The outcomes of interest in this study were performance and reaction times on the RST. There where significant differences in performance in task exclude; however, RT tended to decrease for each series. This result indicates that there might be training effects in the RST. Test scores are comparable to those in (van den Noort et al. 2008) and showed similar results, suggesting good reliability of the version produced, despite a few methodological divergences due to the implementation of eye-tracking technology.

Adding the eye-tracking apparatus to the test allowed us to observe different reading patterns and strategies adopted by participants during the test. This decision led us to compare two reading conditions, silent and aloud. Initially, performance on the six sentence-final words (maximal difficulty) presented significant difference between conditions, suggesting silent reading outperforms aloud reading with shorter reaction times for greater number of sentences. This result might be interpreted by considering the effects of subvocalization (internal speech) during silent reading, which could help hold the items to be recalled in memory for longer (Slowiaczek and Clifton Jr. 1980).

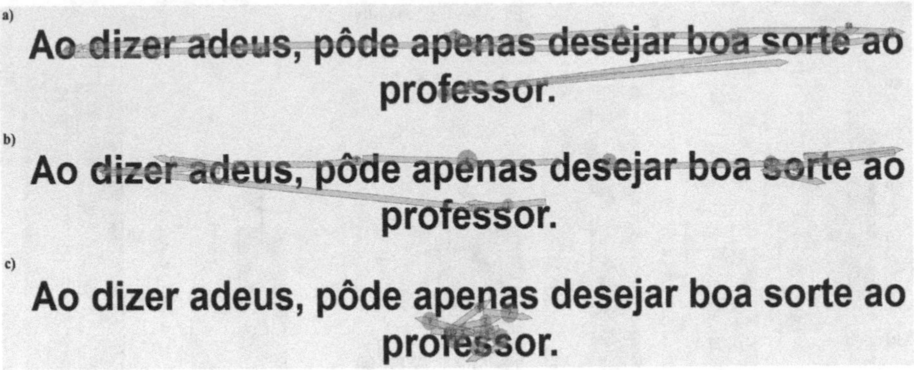

a)

Ao dizer adeus, pôde apenas desejar boa sorte ao professor.

b)

Ao dizer adeus, pôde apenas desejar boa sorte ao professor.

c)

Ao dizer adeus, pôde apenas desejar boa sorte ao professor.

Fig. 6. Patterns of reading for different subjects on (a) reading aloud; (b) reading silently; (c) reading silently with fixation only on the last word.

Eye-tracking data was successful in revealing strategies adopted by the participants. Figure 6 shows how different the reading patterns were in the reading conditions. In the silent reading condition, participants promptly fixated on the last word during the time of exhibition (see c) in the figure). The participants who chose to fixate only on the last word of sentences were clearly trying to reach a higher score on the test by not following the instructions. Initially fixating the gaze on the last word and then starting to read the sentence as instructed (see b) in the figure) was a common behavior. Similarly, the data show that participants took more time looking at the final word. Despite such intriguing differences between reading patterns and strategies, no influence on the RST performance was found.

NASA-TLX did not show significant differences between reading conditions, although several factors were correlated with the eye-tracking data, especially the perception of how successful participants considered themselves to have been in accomplishing the goal of the task (performance and levels of frustration) and the size of the saccades, the probability of regression and the number of fixations. Overall, the exploratory methodology of integrating eye-tracking on the RST motivates future studies that seek to incorporate new technologies to improve the assessment of WMC.

Acknowledgement. Special thanks to FAURGS - Petrobras by the support through the Annelida research project (8147-7). The first author would like to thank to the SDAS Research Group (www.sdas-group.com) for its valuable support and the International Brain Research Organization (IBRO) for the support through the travel grant.

References

Alptekin, C., Ercetin, G.: Eye movements in reading span tasks to working memory functions and second language reading. Eurasian J. Appl. Linguist. **1**, 35–56 (2015). https://doi.org/10.32601/ejal.460617

Baddeley, A.: Working memory and reading. In: Kolers, P.A., Wrolstad, M.E., Bouma, H. (eds.) Processing of Visible Language. NATOCS, vol. 13, pp. 355–370. Springer, Boston (1979). https://doi.org/10.1007/978-1-4684-0994-9_21

Baddeley, A., Hitch, G.: Working memory. In: Bower, G.H. (ed.), vol. 8, pp. 47–89. Academic Press (1974). https://doi.org/10.1016/S0079-7421(08)60452-1

Bailer, C.: Working memory capacity and attention to form and meaning in EFL reading. Masters thesis, Universidade Federal de Santa Catarina (2011)

Carretti, B., Borella, E., Cornoldi, C., Beni, R.D.: Role of working memory in explaining the performance of individuals with specific reading comprehension difficulties: a meta-analysis. Learn. Ind. Differ. **19**(2), 246–251 (2009). https://doi.org/10.1016/j.lindif.2008.10.002

Cassol Rigatti, P., Aras da Luz Fontes, A., Pereira Magagnin, K., Finger, I.: Traduo de teste de capacidade de memria de trabalho do ingls para o portugus brasileiro. Letrnica **10**, 743 (2018). https://doi.org/10.15448/1984-4301.2017.2.26434

Charchat Fichman, H., Uehara, E., Fernandes dos Santos, C.: New technologies in assessment and neuropsychological rehabilitation. Trends Psychol. **22**(3), 539–553 (2014). https://doi.org/10.9788/TP2014.3-01

Clifton, C., et al.: Eye movements in reading and information processing: Keith Rayner's 40 year legacy. J. Mem. Lang. **86**, 1–19 (2015). https://doi.org/10.1016/j.jml.2015.07.004

Conway, A.R.A., Kane, M.J., Bunting, M.F., Hambrick, D.Z., Wilhelm, O., Engle, R.W.: Working memory span tasks: a methodological review and user's guide. Psychon. Bull. Rev. **12**(5), 769–786 (2005). https://doi.org/10.3758/BF03196772

Copeland, D.E., Radvansky, G.A.: Phonological similarity in working memory. Mem. Cogn. **29**(5), 774–776 (2001). https://doi.org/10.3758/BF03200480

Cornoldi, C., Vecchi, T.: Visuo-spatial working memory and individual differences. Visuo-spatial Working Memory and Individual Differences, pp. 1–169 (2003). https://doi.org/10.4324/9780203641583

Cowan, N.: What are the differences between long-term, short-term, and working memory? Prog. Brain Res. **169**, 323–338 (2008)

Dalmaijer, E.S., Mathôt, S., Van der Stigchel, S.: PyGaze: an open-source, cross-platform toolbox for minimal-effort programming of eyetracking experiments. Behav. Res. Methods **46**(4), 913–921 (2014). https://doi.org/10.3758/s13428-013-0422-2

Daneman, M., Carpenter, P.A.: Individual differences in working memory and reading. J. Verbal Learn. Verbal Behav. **19**(4), 450–466 (1980)

Engbert, R., Kliegl, R.: Microsaccades uncover the orientation of covert attention. Vision. Res. **43**(9), 1035–1045 (2003). https://doi.org/10.1016/S0042-6989(03)00084-1

Engle, R., Kane, M., Tuholski, S.W.: Individual differences in working memory capacity and what they tell us about controlled attention, general fluid intelligence, and functions of the prefrontal cortex, pp. 102–134 (1999)

Estivalet, G.L., Meunier, F.: The Brazilian Portuguese Lexicon: an instrument for psycholinguistic research. PLoS ONE **10**(12), e0144016 (2015). https://doi.org/10.1371/journal.pone.0144016

Friedman, N.P., Miyake, A.: The reading span test and its predictive power for reading comprehension ability. J. Mem. Lang. **51**(1), 136–158 (2004). https://doi.org/10.1016/j.jml.2004.03.008

Hart, S.G., Stavenland, L.E.: Development of NASA-TLX (Task Load Index): results of empirical and theoretical research. In: Hancock, P.A., Meshkati, N. (eds.) Human Mental Workload, pp. 139–183. Elsevier (1988)

Just, M.A., Carpenter, P.: A capacity theory of comprehension: individual differences in working memory. Psychol. Rev. **99**(1), 122–149 (1992)

Oberauer, K., Süß, H.-M.: Working memory and interference: a comment on Jenkins, Myerson, Hale, and Fry (1999). Psychon. Bull. Rev. **7**(4), 727–733 (2000). https://doi.org/10.3758/BF03213013

Over, E., Hooge, I., Vlaskamp, B., Erkelens, C.: Coarse-to-fine eye movement strategy in visual search. Vis. Res. **47**(17), 2272–2280 (2007). https://doi.org/10.1016/j.visres.2007.05.002

Parsey, C.M., Schmitter-Edgecombe, M.: Applications of technology in neuropsychological assessment. Clin. Neuropsychol. **27**(8), 1328–1361 (2013). https://doi.org/10.1080/13854046.2013.834971

Slowiaczek, M.L., Clifton Jr., C.: Subvocalization and reading for meaning. J. Verbal Learn. Verbal Behav. **19**(5), 573–582 (1980)

Tomitch, L.: Individual differences in working memory capacity and the recall of predicted elements in the text (1999)

Towse, J., Hitch, G., Hutton, U.: On the nature of the relationship between processing activity and item retention in children. J. Exp. Child Psychol. **82**(2), 156–184 (2002). https://doi.org/10.1016/S0022-0965(02)00003-6

Turner, M.L., Engle, R.W.: Is working memory capacity task dependent? J. Mem. Lang. **28**(2), 127–154 (1989). https://doi.org/10.1016/0749-596X(89)90040-5

van den Noort, M., Bosch, P., Haverkort, M., Hugdahl, K.: A standard computerized version of the reading span test in different languages. Eur. J. Psychol. Assess. **24**(1), 35–42 (2008). https://doi.org/10.1027/1015-5759.24.1.35

van der Lans, R., Wedel, M., Pieters, R.: Defining eye-fixation sequences across individuals and tasks: the Binocular-Individual Threshold (BIT) algorithm. Behav. Res. Methods **43**(1), 239–257 (2011)

Waters, G., Caplan, D.: The capacity theory of sentence comprehension: critique of Just and Carpenter. Psychol. Rev. **103**, 761–772 (1996a)

Waters, G., Caplan, D.: The measurement of verbal working memory capacity and its relation to reading comprehension. Q. J. Exp. Psychol. A Hum. Exp. Psychol. **49**(1), 51–75 (1996b)

Neural Signal Processing

Multi-harmonic Analysis Using Magnitude-Squared Coherence and Its Application to Detection of Auditory Steady-State Responses

Abdon Francisco Aureliano Netto[1]($\boxtimes$) , Tiago Zanotelli[3,4] ,
and Leonardo Bonato Felix[1,2]

[1] Graduate Program in Electrical Engineering, Federal University of Sao Joao
del-Rei, Sao Joao del-Rei, MG, Brazil
abdonfan@hotmail.com
[2] NIAS, Department of Electrical Engineering, Federal University of Vicosa, Vicosa,
MG, Brazil
[3] Graduate Program in Electrical Engineering, Federal University of Minas Gerais,
Belo Horizonte, MG, Brazil
[4] Department of Electrical Engineering, Federal Institute of Espirito Santo,
Sao Mateus, ES, Brazil

Abstract. The detection of auditory evoked brain responses is an important task in hearing science, especially in the role of investigation of hearing thresholds. Objective Response Detection (ORD) techniques aim to identify the presence of evoked potentials based purely on statistical principles that perform an automatic hypothesis test in the frequency domain and the Magnitude-Squared Coherence (MSC) is a well-known and very efficient uni-variate ORD technique. The use of q-sample tests, which, in addition to the fundamental frequency, also includes higher harmonics in the detection has shown trends to better detection of ASSRs performance. The database used in this work contains ASSRs that were collected when evoked by amplitude modulation of pure tones delivered binaurally at 70 dB SPL to 24 volunteers with normal hearing thresholds. This paper analyses the detection of response using a multi-harmonic approach combining the fundamental frequencies, 84 and 88 Hz, and its six next harmonic frequencies. A detection threshold was estimated using a Monte Carlo simulation. Both the detection rate and area bellow the detection curve increased using q-MSC techniques when compared to the one-channel and one-harmonic technique. The best results trends to be using a mean value (mean q-MSC) up to the third harmonic frequency, with an increase of 7.4% of detection rate mean, statistically proven with McNemar test, and the mean area bellows the detection curve increased 24.37%, statistically proven with t paired test, for the 14 channels compared.

Supported by Federal University of Sao Joao del-Rei and CAPES.

V. R. Cota et al. (Eds.): LAWCN 2019, CCIS 1068, pp. 121–129, 2019.
https://doi.org/10.1007/978-3-030-36636-0_9

Keywords: Magnitude-Squared Coherence · q-Sample ·
Multi-harmonic · Objective Response Detection

1   Introduction

The auditory evoked potential (AEP) is a type of signal, that can be measured through Electroencephalography (EEG), considered as a brain response due to an acoustical stimulus. EEG is a very useful non-invasive clinical tool to measure and monitor vital brain activities from newborns to adults, and it can be used for both medical and research application to an investigation of hearing thresholds [2,17]. The evoked potentials with constant both, phase and amplitude, during a long period of time it is considered as steady-state responses (SSRs) [20].

The auditory steady-state responses (ASSRs) have shown that it can provide a demonstration that sounds have been processed by the brain and it is important in objective audiometry studies [18]. Some parameters of human hearing sensitivity can be estimated by audiological tests based on ASSRs data, principally due to the fact that multiple stimulus responses can be simultaneously assessed, and so the ASSRs can be objectively detected using statistical tests using objective response detection (ORD) techniques to achieve them [21]. According to [5], ORD has several potential goals: It can be useful to remove an observer from a neonatal intensive care screening; an automatic controlled false positive rate can be set; it is proved to have performance superior to human observers in some cases; and can provide hidden useful information that can be used in training needed human observers.

In 1984, [13] introduced the ORD technique known as Phase Coherence (PC) in the analysis of ASSRs. [27] applied the PC as a way to predict auditory threshold in adults with normal hearing. In 1987, [19] applied the T^2 Hotelling test [14] and the PC to ASSRs. In 1989, [3] introduced the use of the Magnitude-Squared Coherence (MSC), an ORD technique that uses the phase and magnitude components of the response and stimulus in order to identify the frequencies that contribute to the AEP. In a later work in 1990, [4] applied the MSC to a filtered AEP with the called Optimal 'Wiener' Filter considered to be an auspicious process when compared to a low signal-to-noise ratio (SNR) non-filtered version. Similar work papers comparing ORDs techniques came up later [5–7,11,12]. Recently, [8,26] compared the univariate (MSC) and multivariate magnitude-squared coherence (MMSC) in the detection of ASSRs.

Detection rate is the rate achieved based on statistical comparison between signal and noise powers in the evoked potential measured, and is an rate highly used in several papers [1,7,9,10,26] in order to measure responses.

According to [1], the ASSR is also represented by several relevant higher harmonics in the frequency domain and the use of the fundamental frequency and its first harmonic in a q-sample test leads to significantly higher detection rates and shorter detection times in comparison to a one-sample test, which uses the information of the fundamental frequency only. [15] shown that weighted averaging is a useful technique to gave the best signal-to-noise ratios.

This paper investigates the use of a q-MSC, which is a technique that combines higher levels of harmonics in order to increase detection rates from ASSRs collected and compare the results to the regular MSC test.

2 Methodology

2.1 Database

The database used in this work was collected at *Nucleo Interdisciplinar de Analise de Sinais* located at the Department of Electrical Engineering in Federal University of Vicosa (NIAS-UFV). This dataset contains EEG signal data from 24 volunteers (8 females and 16 males) with normal hearing and ages ranging from 20 to 43 years old. For each volunteer, the stimuli were presented binaurally and the carriers always the same for both ears with carrier frequencies of 500, 1000, 2000, 4000 Hz, with modulation frequencies of 84 Hz for the left ear and 88 Hz for the right one [26]. The EEG signal collected contains data of 14 electrodes (C_z; P_z; F_z; O_z; F3; F4; C3; C4; T3; T4; P3; P4; T5 and T6) arranged on the scalp of each volunteer according to the 10–20 International System [24]. The signals were sampled in a sampling frequency of $f_s = 1250$ Hz and windowed in a 1024 windowing points for an offline analyze (0.8192 s each window) and processed up to 600 windows (total time of 491.52 s).

2.2 Magnitude-Squared Coherence (MSC)

The MSC technique, introduced in 1989 by [3], appeared promising for purposes of objectively identify stimulus-response relationships in the frequency domain. The MSC indicates the linearity involving the component of the harmonic stimulus and the response obtained by the EEG, and can be estimated by using the following equation [3]:

$$\widehat{MSC}(f) = \frac{|\sum_{i=1}^{M} Y_i(f)|^2}{M|\sum_{i=1}^{M} Y_i(f)|^2} \tag{1}$$

Where M is the number of windows, Y_i is the Discrete Fourier Transform (DFT) of the i-th window and $\widehat{\ }$ refers to estimate value. The $\widehat{MSC}$ value ranges from 0 to 1. For the null hypothesis (H_0) and in order to check whether or not you have a detected response, the MSC value must be compared to a threshold, called critical value, and it is calculated by [23]:

$$MSC_{crit} = 1 - \alpha^{\frac{1}{M-1}} \tag{2}$$

where α is the significance level. To reject the (H_0), the $\widehat{MSC}$ value must be greater than MSC_{crit}, indicating detection of response.

2.3   The q-MSC

The data analysis for the q-Samples cases, averaged and product of the MSC, proposed in this paper is related to the fact of the ASSR present an energy in the fundamental frequency and its harmonics [1]. So this paper introduces the use of an averaged MSC (aMSC) and product MSC (pMSC) q-Sample test, and are calculated by the following equations:

$$aMSC_k = \frac{\sum_{h=1}^{H} MSC_i(f_h)}{H} \tag{3}$$

$$pMSC_k = \prod_{h=1}^{H} MSC_i(f_h) \tag{4}$$

where k is k-th averaged MSC calculated, H is the number of harmonics tested, i, h is h-th frequency harmonic with h = 1 being the fundamental. Both, aMSC and pMSC values, range from 0 to 1.

The result of aMSC in Eq. 3 is given by the sum of combined MSC divided by number of harmonics involved, and the result of pMSC in Eq. 4 is given by the product of MSC into number of harmonics involved.

2.4   Critical Value

The values of $aMSC_{crit}$ and $pMSC_{crit}$ were estimated by using 100,000 iterations of Monte Carlo simulation, with a significance level of $\alpha = 5\%$, generating signals to be applied on both, aMSC and pMSC techniques. The corresponding critical value is the result of the quantile of 5% lower values $(1 - \alpha)$, as a function of values of windows and number of signals [9,10,22].

2.5   Performance of the Detectors

The techniques were done in the frequency domain, with a fixed significance level (α) of 5% for the Monte Carlo simulation, then the aMSC and pMSC were estimated in the fundamental frequencies of 84 Hz and 88 Hz and its next 5 harmonics, according to Eqs. 3 and 4, and compared to the value of the calculated threshold, $aMSC_{crit}$ and $pMSC_{crit}$, for each sweep.

For the detection rate estimation, values of 1 or 0, were assigned to values of each of the methods when the Eqs. 1, 3 and 4 value was, respectively, greater or smaller than the corresponding MSC_{crit} value for each window [15].

The criterion for deciding whether or not to have a false positive was, for detection of response at defined rejection frequencies. In both cases, the rejection fundamental frequency is 79 Hz and 85 Hz and its next 5 harmonics, these values were defined based on criteria during data acquisition [26].

In order to evaluate the performance of the detectors, the detection and false positive rate on the M = 600 windows, and the area below the detection curve were estimated. The value of the area takes into account the size of the analyzed signal, giving an indication of how fast the detector improves with the increase of the window size.

3   Results

In this section, we present the results of the multi-harmonic detection rate and area bellow the detection curve in comparison with one-channel and one-harmonic detection rate, up to a window M = 600.

As the data used were real EEG signals, only the results with a false positive rate less than or equal to 5.73% were analyzed, instead of the false-positive rate of less than or equal to 5%, usually used in similar studies. So, the only criterion chosen to determine whether a result will be analyzed is whether it has a false positive rate of less than or equal to 5.73%.

Figures 1 and 2 shows, respectively, the results of the mean detection rate and mean area bellow the detection curve for each h number of harmonics utilized.

Figures 3 and 4 shows, respectively, the detection rate graphs for the electrode with the best responses analysed (F_z) found utilizing the mean (aMSC) and product (pMSC) techniques, for up the six first harmonics. From these results, the areas below the detection curves were calculated. These areas are dimensionless values directly correlated with detection time, and are better explained in Sect. 4.

For the significance testing of the differences between the detection rates found for the best q-sample case (three-sample) and one-sample within and between the subsamples, McNemar's test [25] was applied. For significance testing of differences between areas bellow the detection curve, the t-paired test was applied [16].

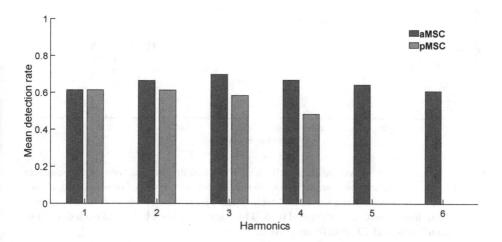

Fig. 1. Average detection rates for one-channel and multi-harmonic tests for each of the first six harmonics of the spectrum of the modulation frequencies. Mean detection rate is the simple average of the channels used, with false positive rate lower than 5.73%.

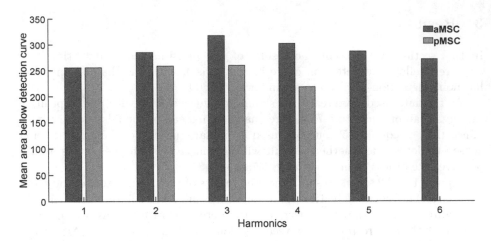

Fig. 2. Average area bellow the detection curve for one-channel and multi-harmonic tests for each of the first six harmonics of the spectrum of the modulation frequencies. Mean area bellow the detection rate curve is the simple average of the channels used, with false positive rate lower than 5.73%.

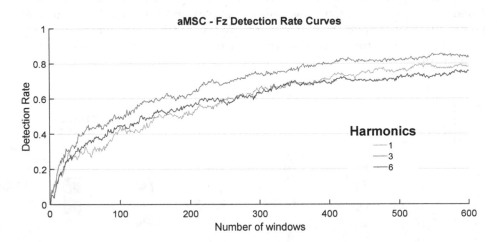

Fig. 3. F_z detection curves utilizing the aMSC technique in the case of a q-Sample test. The Figure shows the comparison between detection curves of one-Sample, three-Sample and six-Sample using the aMSC technique. The respective detection rate values, at M = 600, found were 0.78, 0.83 and 0.75. The respective area bellow of each detection curve found were 353.79, 406.18 and 351.95

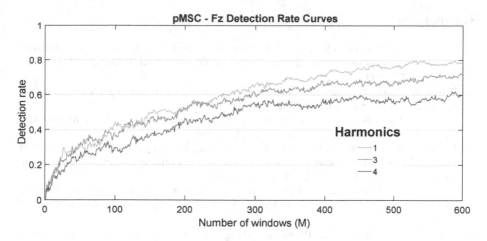

Fig. 4. F_z detection curves utilizing the pMSC technique in the case of a q-Sample test. The Figure shows the comparison between detection curves of one-Sample, three-Sample and four-Sample using the pMSC technique. The respective detection rate values, at M = 600, found were 0.78, 0.72 and 0.60. The respective area bellow of each detection curve found were 353.79, 327.42 and 275.76

4   Discussion and Conclusion

The F_z electrode, positioned in the sagittal plane of the frontal midline of the skull, is systematically present in all the best-analyzed cases. The detection rate increases with the course of the examination time. The results from aMSC three-Sample test led to better results when compared to the one-Sample MSC, with a 7.4% improvement in detection rate and up to a 24.37% increase in the area below the detection curve. A larger area below the detection curve can lead to a higher detection rate for window values than the analyzed one, that is, a better response for smaller windows. The use of the pMSC did not generate improvements in the detection rate, besides that it also led to an increase of the false positive rate, which even removed them from the analysis for a greater number of combined harmonics.

As a conclusion, the results from this study has shown that ASSRs is also present in several higher harmonics of the carrier frequency. However, it is important to note that the best results are not in the higher harmonic evaluated. As demonstrated in this work, the use of available information hidden in higher harmonics in a q-sample test leads to higher detection rates and shorter detection times in comparison to one-sample test.

Possible future works include the use of multiple channels combined with multiple frequencies utilizing the MSC.

References

1. Cebulla, M., Stürzebecher, E., Elberling, C.: Objective detection of auditory steady-state responses: comparison of one-sample and q-sample tests. J. Am. Acad. Audiol. **17**(2), 93–103 (2006)
2. Cummins, T.D., Finnigan, S.: Theta power is reduced in healthy cognitive aging. Int. J. Psychophysiol. **66**(1), 10–17 (2007)
3. Dobie, R.A., Wilson, M.J.: Analysis of auditory evoked potentials by magnitude-squared coherence. Ear Hear. **10**(1), 2–13 (1989)
4. Dobie, R.A., Wilson, M.J.: Optimal (wiener) digital filtering of auditory evoked potentials: use of coherence estimates. Electroencephalogr. Clin. Neurophysiol. Evoked Potentials Sect. **77**(3), 205–213 (1990)
5. Dobie, R.A., Wilson, M.J.: Objective response detection in the frequency domain. Electroencephalogr. Clin. Neurophysiol. Evoked Potentials Sect. **88**(6), 516–524 (1993)
6. Dobie, R.A., Wilson, M.J.: Phase weighting: a method to improve objective detection of steady-state evoked potentials. Hear. Res. **79**(1–2), 94–98 (1994)
7. Dobie, R.A., Wilson, M.J.: A comparison of t test, f test, and coherence methods of detecting steady-state auditory-evoked potentials, distortion-product otoacoustic emissions, or other sinusoids. J. Acoust. Soc. Am. **100**(4), 2236–2246 (1996)
8. Felix, L.B., Antunes, F., da Silva Carvalho, J.A., dos Santos Barroso, M.F., et al.: Comparison of univariate and multivariate magnitude-squared coherences in the detection of human 40-hz auditory steady-state evoked responses. Biomed. Signal Process. Control **40**, 234–239 (2018)
9. Felix, L.B., Infantosi, A.F.C., Yehia, H.C., et al.: Multivariate objective response detectors (mord): statistical tools for multichannel EEG analysis during rhythmic stimulation. Ann. Biomed. Eng. **35**(3), 443–452 (2007)
10. Felix, L.B., Rocha, P.F.F., Mendes, E.M.A.M., et al.: Multivariate approach for estimating the local spectral f-test and its application to the EEG during photic stimulation. Comput. Methods Programs Biomed. **162**, 87–91 (2018)
11. Felix, L.B., de Sa, A.M.F.M., Mendes, E.M.A.M., Moraes, M.F.D.: Statistical aspects concerning signal coherence applied to randomly modulated periodic signals. IEEE Signal Process. Lett. **13**(2), 104–107 (2006)
12. Felix, L.B., de Souza Ranaudo, F., Netto, A.D., et al.: A spatial approach of magnitude-squared coherence applied to selective attention detection. J. Neurosci. Methods **229**, 28–32 (2014)
13. Galambos, R., Makeig, S., Stapells, D.: The phase aggregation of steady state (40 hz) event related potentials: its use in estimating hearing thresholds. In: XVII International Congress of Audiology (1984)
14. Hotelling, H.: The generalization of student's ratio. Ann. Math. Statist. **2**(3), 360–378 (1931). https://doi.org/10.1214/aoms/1177732979
15. John, M.S., Dimitrijevic, A., Picton, T.W.: Weighted averaging of steady-state responses. Clin. Neurophysiol. **112**(3), 555–562 (2001)
16. Mee, R.W., Chua, T.C.: Regression toward the mean and the paired sample t test. Am. Stat. **45**(1), 39–42 (1991)
17. Paulraj, M., Subramaniam, K., Yaccob, S.B., Adom, A.H.B., Hema, C.: Auditory evoked potential response and hearing loss: a review. Open Biomed. Eng. J. **9**, 17 (2015)
18. Picton, T.W., John, M.S., Dimitrijevic, A., Purcell, D.: Human auditory steady-state responses: respuestas auditivas de estado estable en humanos. Int. J. Audiol. **42**(4), 177–219 (2003)

19. Picton, T.W., Vajsar, J., Rodriguez, R., Campbell, K.B.: Reliability estimates for steady-state evoked potentials. Electroencephalogr. Clin. Neurophysiol. Evoked Potentials Sect. **68**(2), 119–131 (1987)
20. Regan, D.: Human brain electrophysiology: evoked potentials and evoked magnetic fields in science and medicine (1989)
21. de Resende, L.M., et al.: Auditory steady-state responses in school-aged children: a pilot study. J. Neuroeng. Rehabil. **12**(1), 13 (2015)
22. de Sá, A.M.F.M., Felix, L.B.: Improving the detection of evoked responses to periodic stimulation by using multiple coherenceapplication to eeg during photic stimulation. Med. Eng. Phys. **24**(4), 245–252 (2002)
23. de Sá, A.M.F.M., Ferreira, D.D., Dias, E.W., Mendes, E.M., Felix, L.B.: Coherence estimate between a random and a periodic signal: bias, variance, analytical critical values, and normalizing transforms. J. Franklin Inst. **346**(9), 841–853 (2009)
24. Scharbrough, F., Chatrian, G., Lesser, R., Luders, H., Nuwer, M., Picton, T.: Guidelines for standard electrode position nomenclature. Am. EEG Soc. (1990)
25. Siegel, S.: Nonparametric statistics for the behavioral sciences (1956)
26. da Silva Eloi, B.F., Antunes, F., Felix, L.B.: Improving the detection of auditory steady-state responses near 80 hz using multiple magnitude-squared coherence and multichannel electroencephalogram. Biomed. Signal Process. Control **42**, 158–161 (2018)
27. Stapells, D.R., Makeig, S., Galambos, R.: Auditory steady-state responses: threshold prediction using phase coherence. Electroencephalogr. Clin. Neurophysiol. **67**(3), 260–270 (1987)

EEG Classification of Epileptic Patients Based on Signal Morphology

Davi Nascimento[1]([⊠]), Jonathan Queiroz[2], Luis Claudio Silva[2],
Gean Carlos de Sousa[2], and Allan Kardec Barros[2]

[1] Bachelor of Science and Technology, Federal University of Maranhão,
São Luís, MA, Brazil
davi.nascimento777@gmail.com

[2] Department of Electrical Engineering, Federal University of Maranhão,
São Luís, MA, Brazil

Abstract. Epilepsy is a chronic neurological disorder, which potentiates the occurrence of seizures in its victims. This clinical picture significantly affects the daily lives of patients, which in some cases, the occurrence of seizures can promote injury, trauma or even sudden death. People who suffer from epilepsy could live free of seizures, if they were previously diagnosed or given appropriate treatment. Therefore methodologies that simplify and expedite the diagnosis and treatment of these individuals are valid and necessary. This study aims to develop a classification model of electroencephalograms (EEG) with presence or absence of epileptic seizures. It was adapted a methodology of extraction of characteristics used for classification of electrocardiograms (ECG) with or without cardiac arrhythmias, which is based on the calculation of statistical moments in time windows. After defining the statistical characteristic that promotes greater separation between the two groups, this characteristic was calculated from a set of 119 electroencephalograms from the CHB-MIT database. The acquired characteristic vectors were classified using linear classifiers, reaching 97% accuracy. The results suggest that the proposed classification methodology can be used to aid in the diagnosis of patients with suspected epilepsy.

Keywords: Epilepsy · Electroencephalogram · Machine learning · Statistics

1 Introduction

Epileptic seizures are the transient occurrence of signs due to a synchronous or excessive neuronal activity of the brain. This abnormal signal activity causes changes in consciousness, involuntary muscular, psychic, sensory and autonomic events [1]. Epilepsy is the persistent predisposition of the brain to generate recurrent epileptic seizures [2,3].

Supported by Federal University of Maranhão.

Several authors have proposed the identification of epileptic seizures in electroencephalogram (EEG) analysis, providing several options to aid in the diagnosis of individuals with suspected epilepsy and also to follow up the treatment of patients suffering from epilepsy. It is noteworthy that most of the methods for EEG's classification are individual character, that is, specific binders for a single patient, with little or no generalization.

The database CHB-MIT [4] is the object of study of several researchers who have already developed solutions to the problem.

We also highlight the contribution of Khan [5], who performed the extraction of features like coefficient variation, standardized coefficient of variation and relative variation coefficient, and using LDA obtained 91.8% of accuracy. In his contribution, Fergus [6] developed a model based on supervised machine learning, in order to classify records with and without seizures. Using the k-NN classifier, it was obtained values of 93% sensitivity, 94% specificity and 98% accuracy. Nandy [7] used various features of the domains of time and frequency for 97.05% accuracy with the RBF kernel of SVM classifier.

In this context, the development of technologies that facilitate the diagnosis of epilepsy and its treatment become valid and necessary. This work aims to develop a new binary model of classification of electroencephalograms with presence or absence of seizures. Making an adaptation of the features extraction made to classify electrocardiograms with and without cardiac arrhythmias [8]. This methodology is based on identifying which statistical feature promotes the greatest distance between groups of windows with or without seizures. Then the feature vectors acquired by better statistics will be classified by linear classifiers. This methodology is based on the identification of which statistical resource promotes the largest distance between groups of windows with or without convulsions. Next, the feature vectors acquired by better statistics will be classified by linear classifiers. Thus it will be possible to propose a classification model with results similar to those of other authors. And with a lower computational and mathematical cost and its use of acquired characteristics in the frequency domain. This methodology is based on the identification of which statistical resource promotes the largest distance between groups of windows with or without convulsions. Next, the feature vectors acquired by better statistics will be classified by linear classifiers. Thus it will be possible to propose a classification model with results similar to those of other authors. And with a lower computational and mathematical cost and without using features acquired in the frequency domain.

2   Data Base

The database CHB-MIT [4] consists of recordings of 23 patients, men and women, from 1.5 to 22 years of age, with each patient having between 9 and 42 EEG collections. The base contains 664 EEG's, of which 129 are labeled with seizures. All with sample frequency of 256 Hz. The Table 1 provides information on each case, such as gender, age and number of seizures.

Table 1. Database information.

Case	Gender	Age (years)	Number of seizures
chb01	F	11	7
chb02	M	11	3
chb03	F	14	7
chb04	M	22	4
chb05	F	7	5
chb06	F	1.5	10
chb07	F	14.5	3
chb08	M	3.5	5
chb09	F	10	4
chb10	M	3	7
chb11	F	12	3
chb12	F	2	27
chb13	F	3	10
chb14	F	9	8
chb15	M	16	20
chb16	F	7	8
chb17	F	12	3
chb18	F	18	6
chb19	F	19	3
chb20	F	6	8
chb21	F	13	4
chb22	F	9	3
chb23	F	6	7
chb24	Unknown	Unknown	16

2.1   Pre-processing

In the initial exploration of the data we observed that some EEG's have channels with distinct characteristics, such as repeated signals, generated artificially and also other biological signs, such as electrocardiogram and vagus nerve stimulus. And yet been identified EEG different montages within the database were sometimes taken over a montage for the same patient. Initially, duplicate channels were removed as well as those containing other biological signals, and the EEG montage with the highest occurrence within the base (FP1-F7, F7-T7, T7-P7, P7-O1, FP1-F3, F3-C3, C3-P3, P3-O1, FP2-F4, F4-C4, C4-P4, P4-O2, FP2-F8, F8-T8, T8-P8, P8-O2, FZ-CZ, CZ-PZ, P7-T7, T7-FT9, FT9-FT10 e FT10-T8). EEG with different montage of the Fig. 1 were not used in the other stages of this work.

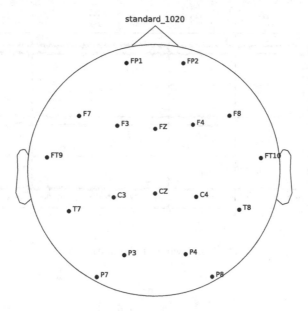

Fig. 1. EEG montage adopted.

This montage follows the international standard 10–20 [3]. The names of the electrodes are given based on brain regions that cover. The abbreviations Fp, F, C, P, O and T correspond respectively to the frontal polar, frontal, central, parental, occipital and temporal regions. The numbering corresponds to the cerebral hemisphere in which the electrode is located, odd numbers to the left hemisphere, and even numbers to the right hemiphysis. Electrodes with the "z" termination are located in the central region of the brain.

2.2   Windowing the EEG Signal

From EEGs labeled as positive for epilepsy, their seizure periods were withdrawn, based on information provided by the database. A matrix **A** was generated by the concatenation of the episodes with seizures. Similarly, periods with no seizures were withdrawn from the remaining EEGs and concatenated to generate matrix **B**, with the same order as matrix **A**. In each row of matrices **A** and **B** the windowing was applied, which consists of the product of the period in seconds by the sampling frequency of the signals, 1 s and 256 Hz, respectively, as described in Fig. 2.

$$\mathbf{A}_{m,n} = \begin{bmatrix} a_{11} & \cdots & a_{1n} \\ \vdots & \ddots & \vdots \\ a_{m1} & \cdots & a_{mn} \end{bmatrix} \tag{1}$$

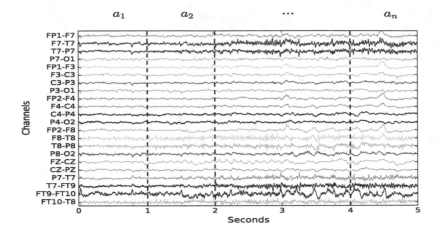

Fig. 2. Windowing of the matrix **A**.

$$\mathbf{B}_{m,n} = \begin{bmatrix} b_{11} & \cdots & b_{1n} \\ \vdots & \ddots & \vdots \\ b_{m1} & \cdots & b_{mn} \end{bmatrix} \tag{2}$$

Where m corresponds to the number of EEG channels and n the number of windows.

3 Methods

The proposed methodology for feature extraction is based on calculating statistical features in EEG windows, and determining which of these features promotes the greatest distance between groups of windows. The sequence of steps for the described methodology is illustrated by Fig. 3.

3.1 Feature Extraction

To feature extraction of this work we used the statistics second, third and fourth order, which are respectively variance, skewness and kurtosis.

$$\sigma^2 = E((X - \mu)^2), \tag{3}$$

$$\gamma = \frac{E(X - \mu)^3}{\sigma^3}, \tag{4}$$

$$\kappa = \frac{E(X - \mu)^4}{\sigma^4}. \tag{5}$$

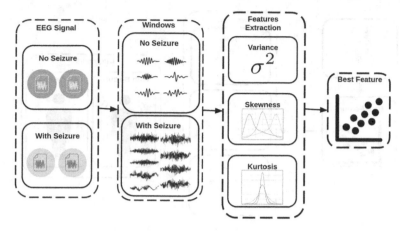

Fig. 3. Flowchart for feature definition that promotes bigger grouping of windows with and without seizures.

Subsequently, (3), (4) and (5) were calculated in (1) and (2), generating new matrices. And the feature vectors were formed by the average of the columns of the matrices obtained by the statistical characteristics

$$C(\mathbf{A}) = \left[\frac{\sum_{i=1}^{m} C(\mathbf{A}_{i,1})}{m}, \cdots, \frac{\sum_{i=1}^{m} C(\mathbf{A}_{i,n})}{m} \right], \tag{6}$$

Where C are the feature vectors resulting from the whole windowing process and the calculation of the statistical measures.

3.2 Classifiers

The proposed classification of the feature vectors obtained from the EEG's uses three linear classifiers: K-neighbor neighbors (k-NN), support vector machine (SVM) and linear discriminant analysis (LDA). The k-NN classifier memorizes its training base and predicts the label of a new instance based on the labels of its closest neighbors in the training set, using euclidean distance [9]. The SVM encounters linear boundaries in the input resource space in order to classify two classes [10]. The LDA seeks to establish a linear transformation through maximizing the inter-class distance and minimizing intra-class distance [10]. The classification model is described by Fig. 4.

3.3 Evaluation Metrics

Subsequently, the accuracy percentages were obtained from each of the classifiers

$$Accuracy = \frac{TP + TN}{TP + TN + FN + FP} \times 100. \tag{7}$$

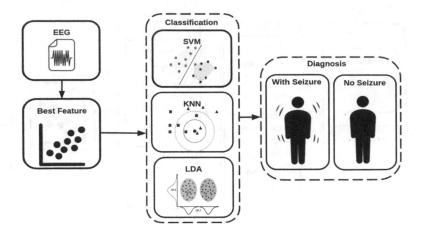

Fig. 4. EEG classification flowchart with or without seizures.

Where TP corresponds to the number of true positives for the presence of epileptic seizures, TN the real negatives for absence of crisis, FP for records with seizures classified as absent and FN for positive classifications in records with absence.

4   Results

4.1   Statistical Analysis

In the Fig. 5, there are the scatter plot and the boxplot of the features obtained from (1) and (2).

We used as a metric to choose the characteristic the difference of the medians [8]. The bigger the difference, bigger will be the distance between the groups.

Table 2 shows the maximum, minimum and median values of the feature vectors of each of the groups. Where Δ corresponds to the difference between the medians of the feature vectors.

We observed that the difference of the variances between the two groups of windows is $\Delta = 10487.944$, much bigger value in relation to the difference between medians of the other features.

A statistical test was performed with the obtained characteristic vectors. Initially the test had the null hypothesis that the samples came from a normal distribution [11], This hypothesis was rejected. Knowing that the distributions are not normal, we used the nonparametric test Mann-Whitney U-test [12]. The null hypothesis is that data with crisis and without crisis comes from continuous distributions and equal medians. The test was performed with pairs of variance, asymmetric and kurtosis values, with and without crisis. The null hypothesis is rejected for all three characteristics. We obtained p-values of 0, 2.6^{-33} and 2.4^{-11}, respectively for variance, skewness and kurtosis.

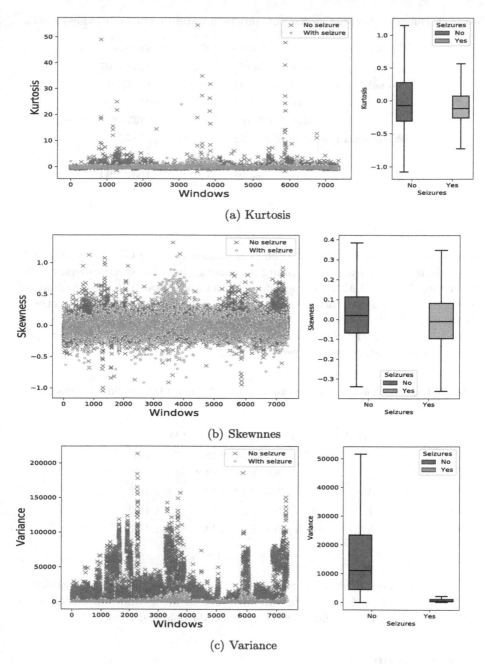

(a) Kurtosis

(b) Skewnnes

(c) Variance

Fig. 5. Scatterplot and boxplot features of windows with and without seizures.

The largest grouping of EEG windows is based on variance. Therefore based on the results of Table 2, stastiscal test and the Fig. 5c, the variance was adopted as a feature to be extracted from the EEG's.

Table 2. Difference between medians of statistical feature vectors of windows EEG's.

Groups		Kurtosis	Skewness	Variance
No seizures	Max	54.67	1.32	213910.07
	Median	−0.07	0.02	11143.51
	Min	−1.73	−1.04	0.22
With seizures	Max	24.02	1.1	28955.8
	Median	−0.12	−0.01	655.57
	Min	−0.73	−0.91	154.45
	Δ	−0.05	0.01	**10487.94**

4.2   Classification

The classification of the feature vectors obtained from EEG's was performed, establishing 80% of them for training and using three linear classifiers: the k-NN having $k = 5$, SVM using the linear kernel and LDA. The cross-validation technique was applied to each of the classifiers, specifically the Kfold [10] method, with $k = 10$. In the Table 3 are shown the mean and standard deviation values of the accuracies of the classifiers obtained by the k-Fold, and in different time windows where feature vectors were obtained.

Table 3. Classification accuracy indexes (SVM, k-NN and LDA) in different windowing using variance vectors.

Windows	SVM	k-NN	LDA
1	97.3 ± 8.6	89.6 ± 18.0	87.9 ± 14.3
2	96.4 ± 8.8	92.4 ± 14.3	84.1 ± 17.7
3	96.4 ± 8.8	92.4 ± 14.3	86.9 ± 15.9
4	95.5 ± 9.8	92.4 ± 14.3	79.5 ± 19.4
5	95.5 ± 9.8	92.4 ± 14.3	83.4 ± 17.6

The same Mann-Whitney U-test was performed with the accuracy values of the SVM and k-NN classifiers, in windows of 1 to 5 s. P-values of 0.2413 were obtained for 1 s windows and 0.5205 for all windows longer than 1 s.

5   Discussion

All classifiers obtained maximum accuracy at some point in all time windows. However, the SVM stands out with an average accuracy of 97.3% in the 1 s window and the standard deviation of ±8.6, which indicates the lower variability of these results. It is possible to observe the performance drop of the SVM with the increase of the time window. The k-NN begins to show steady performance from the 2 s window with average accuracy of 92.4% ± 14.29.

Knowing that the accuracy of the SVM is inversely proportional to the size of the window of time, the hypothesis arises that the classification with windows smaller than 1 s can allow the average accuracy to reach its maximum value. The good performance of the SVM in smaller time windows may favor the development of a future methodology for identifying the beginning and ending of seizures, with possibly better performance than [13], which detected the onset of 96% of 173 seizures with an average delay of 3 s, and [14], which detected the end of 132 seizures with a margin of error of 10.3 ± 5.5 s. We emphasize that a future methodology for identifying the beginning and end of seizures would be generalist, not individual classifiers, similar to the methodologies cited above.

Another hypothesis is to verify if the accuracy of the k-NN remains constant in windows longer than 5 s. Thus it would be possible to develop a classification model of EEG's with an even lower computational cost.

The LDA performs less than the classifiers mentioned above, in addition to inconstant values for accuracy. In Fig. 5c there is greater dispersion of the windows without seizures. However, where there is concentration of windows with seizures there are also windows without seizures. A proposal for future work is to use the LDA to establish a threshold decision, and maintain the set of classification only windows that are within the concentration windows seizures. So, a classifier could more accurately separate all windows below the threshold set by the LDA.

Table 4 summarizes the information on previously proposed methodologies in order to make a comparison with the best results of the present study.

Table 4. Comparative performance of previous methodologies with the performance obtained in this work.

Author	Year	Features	Classifiers	Acurracy
This work	2019	Variance of EEG morphology	SVM-Linear	97.3%
			k-NN	92.4%
			LDA	87.9%
Nandy	2019	Time, frequency and entropy	LDA	76.41%
			SVM-RBF	97.05%
			QLDA	80.79%
Fergus	2014	Median frequency	k-NN	98%
		Peak frequency	LOGLC	94%
		Median frequency	TREEC	94%
Khan	2012	COV, RCOV and NCOV	LDA	91.8%

Coefficient of Variation (COV); Relative Coefficient of Variation (RCOV); Normalized Coefficient of Variation (NCOV); Radial Base Function (RBF); Logistic Classifier (LOGLC); Decision Tree Classifier (TREEC); Quadratic Linear Disciminant Analysis (QLDA).

The values of accuracy obtained previously are quite similar to each other and to those obtained in this work, especially th SVM and k-NN. The classifiers used are the same, except for Nandy [7], which used the SVM with a radial base function kernel (RBF).

The 97.3% accuracy of SVM-Linear is similar to 97.05% of Nandy's SVM-RBF. It is noteworthy that the application of SVM-RBF includes a linear transformation and the search for the optimal value of the radial base function γ parameter. Which demands higher computational cost.

There is a difference of about 5% between the best accuracy value of k-NN obtained in this study and the accuracy obtained by Fergus. But the feature vectors used in the Fergus classification are from the frequency domain. Which requires more sophisticated techniques to obtain.

So, the differential of the methodology presented here in relation to the previous ones occurs in the feature extraction stage. In these methodologies were extracted features of the frequency domain, so the techniques with the Fourier transform and Wavelet transform were necessary, and such tools are of bigger mathematical complexity. The feature extraction proposed in this work uses only features related to the amplitude of EEG signals in the time domain.

6   Conclusion

In this work, a new model was proposed for the classification of electroencephalograms with and without seizures, made by the adaptation of a characteristic extraction methodology for the classification of electrocardiograms with and without cardiac arrhythmias. Two of the classifiers used obtained good results, with accuracy values of 97.3% for SVM in 1 s windows and 92.4% for k-NN in windows longer than 1 s. Values similar to the percentages of accuracy obtained by the previously proposed solutions. Do to the fact that the developed model presents lower computational and mathematical complexity, we believe that it can be used in the screening of patients with suspected epilepsy. Its lower complexity and the obtained results form a basis for future methodologies for identification of electroencephalographic patterns in real time. One of them is the development of a device to identify such pattern, which can become a tool to aid the treatment and monitoring of patients with epilepsy.

References

1. Thurman, D.J., et al.: Standards for epidemiologic studies and surveillance of epilepsy. Epilepsia **52**, 2–26 (2011)
2. Fisher, R.S., et al.: Epileptic seizures and epilepsy: definitions proposed by the international league against epilepsy (ILAE) and the international bureau for epilepsy (IBE). Epilepsia **46**(4), 470–472 (2005)
3. Yacubian, E.M.T., Kochen, S.: Crises epilépticas. Ed. Casa Leitura Médica, São Paulo, 6 (2014)
4. Physionet CHB-MIT scalp EEG database. https://www.physionet.org/physiobank/database/chbmit/. Accessed 25 Mar 2019

5. Khan, Y.U., Rafiuddin, N., Farooq, O.: Automated seizure detection in scalp EEG using multiple wavelet scales. In: 2012 IEEE International Conference on Signal Processing, Computing and Control, pp. 1–5. IEEE (2012)

6. Fergus, P., Hignett, D., Hussain, A., Al-Jumeily, D., Abdel-Aziz, K.: Automatic epileptic seizure detection using scalp EEG and advanced artificial intelligence techniques. BioMed Research International (2015)

7. Nandy, A., Alahe, M.A., Uddin, S.M.N., Alam, S., Nahid, A.-A., Awal, M.A.: Feature extraction and classification of EEG signals for seizure detection. In: 2019 International Conference on Robotics, Electrical and Signal Processing Techniques (ICREST), pp. 480–485. IEEE (2019)

8. Queiroz, J.A., Junior, A., Lucena, F., Barros, A.K.: Diagnostic decision support systems for atrial fibrillation based on a novel electrocardiogram approach. J. Electrocardiol. 51(2), 252–259 (2018)

9. Shalev-Shwartz, S., Ben-David, S.: Understanding Machine Learning: From Theory to Algorithms. Cambridge University Press, Cambridge (2014)

10. Hastie, T., Tibshirani, R., Friedman, J., Franklin, J.: The elements of statistical learning: data mining, inference and prediction. Math. Intell. 27(2), 83–85 (2005)

11. D'Agostino, R., Pearson, E.S.: Tests for departure from normality. Empirical results for the distributions of b2 and b. Biometrika 60(3), 613–622 (1973)

12. Gibbons, J.D., Chakraborti, S.: Nonparametric Statistical Inference. Springer, Heidelberg (2011). https://doi.org/10.1007/978-3-642-04898-2_420

13. Shoeb, A.H., Guttag, J.V.: Application of machine learning to epileptic seizure detection. In: Proceedings of the 27th International Conference on Machine Learning (ICML 2010), pp. 975–982 (2010)

14. Shoeb, A., Kharbouch, A., Soegaard, J., Schachter, S., Guttag, J.: A machine-learning algorithm for detecting seizure termination in scalp EEG. Epilepsy Behav. 22, S36–S43 (2011)

Epileptiform Spike Detection in Electroencephalographic Recordings of Epilepsy Animal Models Using Variable Threshold

Sofia M. A. F. Rodrigues, Jasiara C. de Oliveira,
and Vinícius Rosa Cota$^{(\boxtimes)}$

Laboratório Interdisciplinar de Neuroengenharia e Neurociências,
Universidade Federal de São João del-Rei, São João del-Rei,
Minas Gerais, Brazil
vrcota@ufsj.edu.br

Abstract. Epilepsy is a public health issue worldwide, given its biological, social, and economic impacts. Moreover, and particularly important, a significant portion of patients is refractory to conventional treatments and novel treatments are in need. By this token, the use and development of computational tools for the detection of epileptiform spikes, together with its feature extraction, have central significance, since these are recognized electrographic signatures of the disorder. In the present work, a detection method of such paroxysms in electroencephalographic recordings is proposed. With low mathematical complexity, the algorithm was developed for fast spike detection by using amplitude and time thresholds - both of them adjustable by the user - and applying a moving and variable amplitude threshold, calculated in each temporal window of analysis. This was done in order to provide greater adaptability to the algorithm and cope with the variable nature of epileptiform spikes. The algorithm was applied to recordings of animals submitted to acute seizures induced by a chemoconvulsant and results were compared to the visual detection of a specialist. Results showed the proposed algorithm can perform at the same level of other previously described approaches, considering the highly variable amplitude of spikes.

Keywords: Epileptiform spike · Ictal detection · Electroencephalographic recordings · Animal models · Epilepsy · ROC curve

1 Introduction

Epilepsy is a serious disease with large prevalence in developing countries and it is considered a public world health issue, due to biological, social and economic impacts [1, 2]. This disorder is characterized by recurrent and spontaneous occurrence of epileptic seizures - its main clinic manifestations - marked by intense and aberrant neural activity originating from a condition of hyperexcitability [3]. In addition, from

V. R. Cota et al. (Eds.): LAWCN 2019, CCIS 1068, pp. 142–156, 2019.
https://doi.org/10.1007/978-3-030-36636-0_11

the neural network perspective, hypersynchronism is frequently associated as a property of a hyperexcitable tissue in such condition [4, 5].

Extracellular recording of neuronal populations as local field potentials (LFP) has become an interesting approach for the assessment of neural synchronism in epilepsy. In fact, the synchronous firing of neuronal populations, associated to pathological scenarios, generates distinguishable electrographic patterns, such as epileptiform spikes. This signature, a recognized hallmark of epilepsy [6] and a type of epileptiform paroxysm frequently studied in this pathology, is generated from the neurophysical enveloping of bursts of highly synchronous potentials [7].

The development of epileptiform spike detection methods has been carried out since 1970 [8–14], mainly by applying different computational algorithms. In 2002, Wilson and Emerson reviewed and compared several methods, showing a common trend where the algorithms generally use a combination of techniques. Recently, in 2018, El-Samie and collaborators made similar considerations and also showed that such algorithms usually have a pre-processing stage, highlighting the signal-noise ratio and other aspects, plus a feature extraction phase followed by a final classification. In addition, the usage of methods based in neural networks, aleatory tree and wavelet analysis are most frequent, but although less common amplitude thresholds in computational detection is also seen [10]. Finally, *findpeaks*, a *MATLAB*® function, has also been used in similar contexts [15–17].

An important aspect of epilepsy is the fact that a considerable number of patients suffers from pharmacological refractoriness [20], without surgical medical referral [21], requiring the investigation of alternative treatments such as electrical stimulation. With this goal, and considering the hypersynchronism aspect of the disease, Cota and collaborators developed a non-standard form of electrical stimulation to epilepsy treatment [22], termed non-periodic stimulation (NPS). This new approach was designed to deliver 4 pulses per second (on average) to the neural target, but with intervals between pulses randomized by a specific algorithm. Being low-energy, some possible benefits of this protocol can be highlighted: lower possibility of a lesion to the tissue and better performance of batteries for a prospective implantable device, for instance. Besides this, choosing the amygdala as neural target promising results were obtained with NPS used unilaterally against acute [22] or chronic seizures [23] and also, most recently, when applied in bilateral and asynchronous form between brain hemispheres [24, 25].

So, given the current interest of our group in the investigation of NPS therapeutic mechanisms by means of studying neural synchronism as revealed in LFP recordings, a technique for spike detection was in need. The present work offers a simple but powerful solution to epileptiform spike detection in electrographic recordings, by a method where false positives are avoided and with the use of simple and relatively adaptable mathematical development. Here we present the validation of the tool and the comparison of its results obtained in experimental recordings to those of other algorithms, including the *MATLAB*® function *findpeaks*.

2 Methodology

2.1 Proposed Method – Computational Detection of Epileptiform Spikes

The proposed method was developed in the MATLAB® platform. For best performance, recordings should be previously filtered at 10 to 100 Hz, which provides a better highlight to the spike content of interest, while cutting out slow oscillations that may induce an increase of false positives. Spikes are detected based in its established description in the literature. Thus, for this work, these paroxysms are defined as voltage transients in LFP recordings which are significantly above baseline, with a distinguishable peak, and a total duration between 20 and 80 ms [6].

In this semi-automated algorithm, users must define both the analysis period and the levels of three different thresholds. First, a threshold between 0 and 1 (corresponding to 0 and 100% respectively), named moving threshold is defined. Thus, for each sliding window of analysis with duration of 1 s, the algorithm finds the maximum voltage value and calculates the moving threshold level as a percentage result of this maximum amplitude seen in the window. Thereby, if the user chooses 0.6 (60%) and the maximum amplitude in the window is 1 mV, the threshold will be 0.6 mV. Then, if an oscillation crosses the moving threshold in a rising border quickly followed by a falling border, the algorithm detects a spike and the calculation of the maximum value between the two crossing (up and down) define the spike peak. By doing this, the algorithm may be able to cope with the highly variable nature of epileptiform spike amplitudes in a way a fixed threshold is not. The other two thresholds configured by the user determine: (1) the minimum distance between spikes (temporal threshold) – and thus the maximum temporal distance between up and down crossing – and; (2) the minimum admissible amplitude for a spike peak (minimum threshold). So, with these thresholds, it is expected that a polyphasic spike should be counted just once, like a unique spike, and spurious oscillations should be not considered as spikes, even with an amplitude distinguishable from the background activity. Figure 1 illustrates the proposed algorithm with an example.

The detection occurs according to the following steps, at each 1 sec-analysis window sliding along the analyzed period. Initially the peaks are detected from the moving threshold and in comparison with the adjacencies; next, the minimum temporal distance between spikes (temporal threshold) is verified, and lastly, it is checked if the peaks are in fact within the minimum amplitude (minimum threshold).

The developed computational tool automatically provides a set of measures and results, useful to posteriori research regarding, for instance, local microcircuits analyses or even to investigate neural network implications. These results are: spike firing rate; spike count; maximum, minimum and average amplitude values of the detected spike peaks; maximum, minimum and average distance between the spikes; a vector with time and peak values and a matrix of clippings, correspondent to the periods of the detected spikes (duration of 80 ms). Furthermore, it is also possible to obtain three types of graphs from these results, with the marked ictal activity in the analyzed recording, an overlapping of detected spikes, and a figure of the average of these spikes with the corresponding standard deviation. Scripts of the proposed method can be obtained free of charge by contacting the corresponding author.

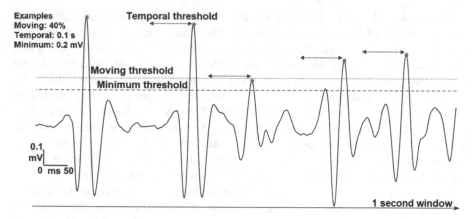

Fig. 1. Running the detection method in chosen examples of thresholds.

2.2   Validation

Similarly to other classifiers in the literature, the proposed method was validated using the Receiver Operating Characteristic curve (ROC curve), represented by the scalar calculation of the area under the curve (AUC) [18]. Besides this, validation of these methods is frequently made to compare the developed algorithm with the detection obtained by expert visual inspection, the gold-standard for spike detection algorithms. So, in this work, recordings from eight animal obtained from the same substrate (cortex) and experimental group were used. The ictal period corresponding to the forelimb clonus, the myoclonic phase of the epileptic seizure, where spikes were identified as a series of sustained activities, with 1 s of maximum temporal distance between them, was used.

The choice of visual inspection as a reference is also based in the fact that the detection is frequently carried out in this way on the expert analysis routine, although it is oftentimes impracticable in many recurrent situations such as longer recordings or for numerous experiments, for instance. On the other hand, visual detection may be less susceptible to error compared to computational algorithms, if common occurrences are considered, such as: recurrent variations in the spike morphology, even in the actual recording; including some possible inconsistencies in spike definitions. Thus, visual inspection provided here both the marking of spikes and the classification of non-spikes.

Throughout the validation process the algorithm had the temporal and minimum thresholds configured as presented in Table 1.

Table 1.   Standard configuration of the algorithm in the proposed method

Threshold	Adopted value
Temporal	0.1 s
Minimum	0.2 mV

The threshold for spike detection was initially set at 60% of the peak value in the analysis window of the proposed algorithm. The same value of 60% and those of Table 1 were used to obtain the results using *MATLAB*® function *findpeaks*. Thus, single threshold results of Figs. 4 and 5, and Tables 2 and 3 were obtained with this set of parameters. In order to better understand the benefits of the moving threshold, adjustable to each 1-second window as proposed here, we compared ROC results of our detector to those obtained with a fixed value of threshold, calculated as percentage of the maximum value of the recording across the whole analysis period (forelimb clonus), such as it is conventionally done. To obtain the ROC, different values of the threshold must be applied, one for each analysis. Thus, this has been carried out by varying the threshold value between 0 and 100%, as it is shown in Figs. 7, 8, and 9.

The measures and indicators used in ROC assessment are obtained by the count of positive and negative events and by the confusion matrix, that correlates true positives (TP), true negatives (TN), false positives (FP), and false negatives (FN) (Fig. 2):

True positives (TP)	False positives (FP)
False negatives (FN)	True negatives (TN)

Fig. 2. Confusion matrix [18].

In this kind of validation, the number of positives (P) is the count of the spikes and the negative (N) is the number of oscillations that are not considered as spikes, both provided from the reference visual inspection. The false positives are oscillations that the algorithm eventually considered as spikes but the reference classified as negatives. The false negatives, in their turn, are given by oscillations that are spikes for the visual reference but the algorithm did not detect. As expected, true positives parameter indicates the correct spike number, the true negatives measure is the correct classification as non-spikes. Lastly, NS is defined as the total number of spikes provided by the method.

The number of false positives, for instance, is calculated by the difference between NS and the correspondences (NS − TP). For false negatives, the difference between the reference and the correspondences (P − TP) is calculated. Besides this, it is possible to define a false positives rate (false alarm rate) as a function of the number of negatives by the reference, as expressed in Eq. 1 [18]:

$$FP\,rate = \frac{FP}{N} \tag{1}$$

From the confusion matrix, it is also obtained the true positives rate (hit rate), the ratio between TP and number of positives, translating the algorithm sensitivity:

$$TP\,rate = sensitivity = \frac{TP}{P} \tag{2}$$

Other widely used indicators, correlating measurements of true positives, true negatives, and the number of positives and negatives, are presented in Eqs. 3, 4, and 5 [19]. These equations express specificity, positive predictive value (precision), and the algorithm accuracy, respectively:

$$specificity = 1 - FP\,rate = \frac{TN}{TN + FP} \tag{3}$$

$$positive\,predictive\,value = precision = \frac{TP}{TP + FP} \tag{4}$$

$$accuracy = \frac{TP + TN}{P + N} \tag{5}$$

Assuming that the number of correctly identified spikes is the correct information to the algorithm and FP and FN are random noises in the detection process, it is defined η as an expression parameter of the signal/noise ratio [19]:

$$\eta = \frac{TP}{FP + FN} = \frac{TP}{(P - TP) + (NS - TP)} \tag{6}$$

In doing so, η is approaching zero when there are no correspondences between the algorithm and the reference (worst case) and approaching infinity when NS = P = TP (best case). This parameter is also used for the computation of efficiency, whose values variate between 0 (0%) to 1 (100%), as a global evaluation of its hit capacity:

$$efficiency = \frac{\eta}{\eta + 1} \rightarrow \eta = \frac{TP}{P + FP} \tag{7}$$

During the validation, the ROC curve was used [18], obtained in the ROC space (Fig. 3) by the false positives rate in the x-axis and the true positives rate in the y-axis. So, it is desirable that the classifier curve to be above the diagonal in the ROC space (the curve of a random classifier, with 50% of hit chance). Besides this, the area under the curve (AUC) should be higher than 0.5, the area of the random classifier.

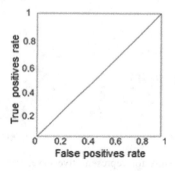

Fig. 3. ROC space to the characteristic curve of a random classifier [18].

2.3   Animal Model and Electrophysiological Recordings

Seizures were acutely induced in male Wistar rats by the controlled intravenous infusion of Pentylenetetrazole (PTZ), a chemoconvulsant with GABAergic antagonistic effects widely used for the screening of new antiepileptic drugs and the development of novel treatments. In this model, animals usually display a sequence of stereotypical behaviors that include forelimb clonus followed by generalized tonic-clonic seizures, which, by its turn is related to the gradual recruitment of neural substrates into aberrant epileptiform activity. Microsurgical screws chronically inserted into the animals' skull served as electrodes for cortical recordings. Using A-M Systems (Washington, USA) pre-amplifier model 3500, tracings were amplified with a gain of 2000 V/V, band-pass filtered analogically at 0.3 to 300 Hz, digitized with a sampling rate of 1000 Hz, and digitally band-pass filtered at 10 to 100 Hz to highlight spikes, as it has been already mentioned.

3   Results

3.1   Proposed Method Operation

The algorithm was configured at this point as follows: moving threshold in 60%; 0.1 s of temporal threshold and 0.225 mV for the minimum threshold. So, the following figures exhibit the detected ictal activity, the result of the detected spike superposition,

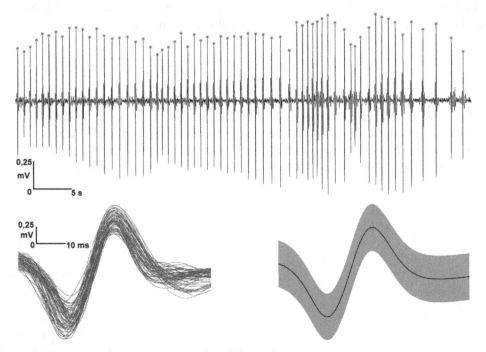

Fig. 4. Algorithm detection results for representative case, for analysis during the forelimb clonus phase.

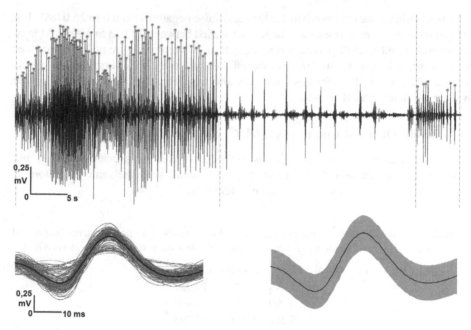

Fig. 5. Algorithm detection results for representative cases, for analysis during afterdischarges (see reference 23 for further details).

and the average of these signatures with the corresponding standard deviation, for Animal 1 (Fig. 4 – forelimb clonus) and for Animal 2 (Fig. 5, with onset and termination of the afterdischarges marked by vertical dashed lines):

3.2   Results Obtained Using the Moving Threshold at 60% of Local Maximum

Table 2 presents results and averages during the forelimb clonus for false positives and false negatives, both expressed in relation to NS and efficiency for the eight recordings:

Table 2. Individual results and the averages for false positives and false negatives (expressed with respect to NS), and efficiency, for recordings in the test set with 60% of moving threshold.

Animal	FP (%)	FN (%)	Efficiency (%)
1	1.667	24.359	74.683
2	0.000	0.000	100.000
3	0.000	18.182	81.818
4	0.000	16.327	83.673
5	0.000	26.078	73.913
6	7.143	4.878	88.636
7	0.000	11.765	88.235
8	1.429	13.75	85.185
Average	1.279	14.418	84.518

False positives varied from 0 to 7.143% and false negatives from 0 to 26.078%. For the efficiency parameter, results for the test set varied between 73.913 to 100%. At least one animal (number 2) displayed perfect detection, where there were no false positives nor false negatives, thus with 100% of the efficiency. Lastly, the average of the results was 1.279% and 14.418% for false positives and false negatives, respectively, and the average efficiency was 84.518%.

3.3   Results Obtained with the *MATLAB*® Function *Findpeaks*

The results seen below were obtained with *findpeaks*, for the previous data set and same ictal phase. Table 3 shows results for all animals, with the same indicators as before, and Fig. 6 presents a representative detection.

Table 3. Individual results and the averages for false positives and false negatives (expressed with respect to NS), and efficiency, for recordings in the test set with *findpeaks* (*MATLAB*®).

Animal	FP (%)	FN (%)	Efficiency (%)
1	12.048	0.000	87.952
2	0.000	0.000	100.000
3	28.261	0.000	71.793
4	37.984	0.000	62.015
5	38.462	0.000	61.538
6	25.581	0.000	74.418
7	31.818	0.000	68.181
8	23.077	0.000	76.923
Average	24.654	0.000	75.346

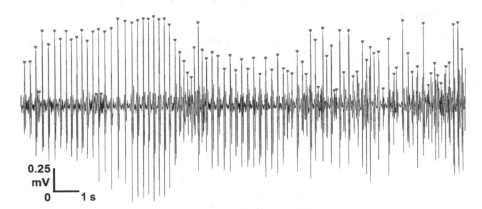

Fig. 6. Spike detection results for example, using the *findpeaks* function for analysis during the forelimb clonus phase.

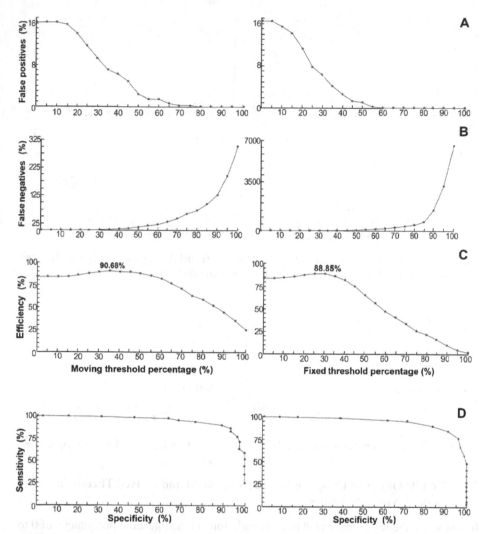

Fig. 7. Average curves showing the results of false positives (panel A), false negatives (panel B), efficiency (panel C), and specificity versus sensitivity (panel D), using the moving threshold (left side) and the fixated configuration (right side).

False positives varied from 0 to 38.462% and the false negatives were always in 0%. For the efficiency parameter, results for the test set varied between 61.538 to 100%. At least one animal (number 2) displayed again perfect detection, where there were no false positives nor false negatives, thus with 100% of the efficiency. Lastly, the average of the results was 24.654% and 0% for false positives and false negatives, respectively, and the average efficiency was 75.346%.

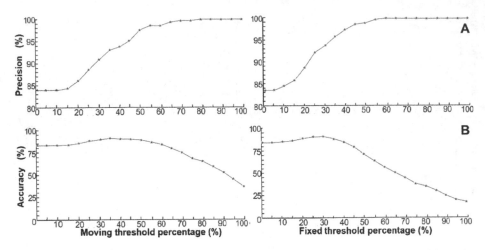

Fig. 8. Average curves showing the results of precision (panel A) and accuracy (panel B), using the moving threshold (left side) and the fixated configuration (right side).

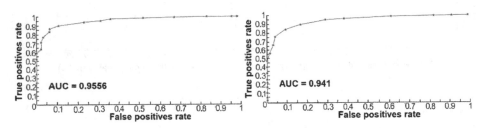

Fig. 9. ROC curves for the moving threshold (left side) and for the fixed threshold (right side).

3.4   Results Obtained Using the Moving Threshold and a Fixed Threshold Both at Variable Values

In this stage, the results presented refer to variations in the threshold percentage, of 0 to 100% (Tables 1 and 2), assessing the method capacity for the moving threshold configuration and for an alternative, fixating the previous moving threshold (for comparison). For these figures, the moving threshold results were always plotted in left side, while the fixed configuration results were plotted in right side. Figure 7 presents false positives (panel A) and false negatives (panel B), expressed with respect to NS, efficiency (panel C) and specificity versus sensitivity (panel D). Figure 8 presents precision (panel A), and accuracy (panel B).

Finally, the last figure shows the ROC curves (Fig. 9) obtained from the variation in the percentage to both previously configurations (moving threshold and the fixed configuration for comparison), with the corresponding AUCs.

Variations of false positives for both configurations have similar results, but with a faster decay for the fixed threshold (Fig. 7 - panel A). An increase in the false negative measurements, according to the increment in the threshold is also perceptible

(Fig. 7 - panel B). This is most prominent for the fixed configuration, where the rise in the final percentages was larger compared to the moving threshold.

Regarding efficiency (Fig. 7 - panel C), the moving threshold configuration presented a maximum average value of 90.68%, while the fixed option obtained a maximum of 88.85%. For the relation between specificity and sensitivity (Fig. 7 - panel D), curves display similar values until a certain percentage. Yet, a larger decrement for the fixed configuration, as the percentage increases, is present. In addition, the average results of precision (Fig. 8 - panel A) demonstrate similar relations between the configurations, including the accuracy results (Fig. 8 - panel B), although lower values of accuracy, in higher percentage values of the threshold observable for the fixed option.

In the end, for the ROC analysis (Fig. 9) it was obtained an area of 0.9556 for the moving threshold configuration, while the same scalar for the fixed configuration was 0.941.

4 Discussion

The presented detection method was developed, at first, as a method to provide the computational detection of epileptiform spikes, a tool to be used in the investigation carried out by our group, regarding the development of and mechanisms underlying non-periodic electrical stimulation. Thus, the main proposal for the method was the development of a mathematically simple algorithm, capable of avoiding false positives identification and, at the same time, yielding a good classification/detection of spikes according to AUC analysis of the ROC curve.

The results showed in the Subsect. 3.1 demonstrate the operation of the proposed tool and its possible contribution capacity, using two examples for epileptiform spike identification during forelimb clonus of an epileptic seizure (Fig. 4) and other typical activities like late after discharges (Fig. 5). Detected activity and its feature extraction, with the set of measures provided by the algorithm, allowed for several analyses being carried out by our group, regarding mostly the viewpoint of local microcircuits and neural networks [6, 13, 14, 26, 27]. One other possibility is assessing the action mechanisms of the non-periodic stimulation in a certain experimental context, also using non-stimulated groups, for instance (see Ref. [25]).

Initially, evaluating specific aspects of the proposed method configuration, it seems an optimal operation region for the percentage values of the moving threshold and for the fixed alternative, between 30 to 60%, may exist, as can be seen for all measures and indicators results. Consequently, it is suggestive that the method is configured on this operation region, beyond preference to the moving threshold.

Moreover, results pointed by the validation process bring promising perspectives, mainly when comparing the usage of moving threshold with a fixed option and also in comparison with a *MATLAB®* function like the *findpeaks*. So, first comparing to the alternative configuration where the amplitude threshold was fixed as a percentage of the maximum across the whole analysis window, results demonstrate that the moving threshold configuration is superior for all measurements and indicators analyzed. Besides this, it was also showed in Subsect. 3.2 that the proposed algorithm seems to have a superior performance for spike detection, at least in this type of activity, compared to *findpeaks* function.

Still regarding comparisons for the proposed method, the ROC curve analysis is a great option for direct comparison and for additional confirmations in relation to the literature. So, in the present work an AUC value of 0.9556 for the configuration with the best result (moving threshold) was obtained, meaning a satisfactory result for a classifier method. As direct comparison examples, the method elaborated by Anh-Dao and collaborators can be cited, with AUC of 0.972. Other options, like the work of Maccione and colleagues for the spikes in neuronal activity, have an AUC of 0.945.

Some of the possible errors in spike detection, such as false positives and false negatives, may be related to known reasons. The recurrent presence of polyphasic spikes in a recording or even abrupt changes in amplitude, with similar duration of the spikes, may hinder the computational detection generating false positives. In addition, recurrent differences in the spike morphology can generate false negatives, like a large variability in peak amplitudes, even within the same recording. Furthermore, negative spikes may be less visible and often disregarded in computational detection.

However, it is primordial keep in mind that factors such as noises and other adversities in the recording and the relation between spikes and the recording background activity carry the potential to interfere in the spike detection quality provided by computational algorithms, including the proposed method. Thus, it is essential for a full validation process to study the effects of signal-noise and spikes-background ratios on the algorithm robustness. On the other hand, although these effects have been not directly assessed yet, it is known that certain actions during the preprocessing can highlight the spikes in the recording, modifying the spikes-background relation and contributing for the computational detection. An example is the digital filtering implemented for this method, once recordings were band-pass filtered from 10 to 100 Hz.

Finally, it is important to highlight the apparent existing gap of methods and computational tools developed to animal experimentation, where the proposed method may contribute to the investigations in this context. On the other hand, we believe that the detection by this algorithm could be performed in similar electrographic recordings, for the human brain.

References

1. Epidemiology, S.N.: The complexities of epilepsy. Nature **511**, S2–S3 (2014)
2. Birbeck, G.L.: Epilepsy care in developing countries: part I of II. Epilepsy Curr. **10**(4), 75–79 (2010)
3. Fisher, R.S., van Emde Boas, W., Blume, W., Elger, C., Genton, P., Lee, P.: Epileptic seizures and epilepsy: definitions proposed by the International League Against Epilepsy (ILAE) and the International Bureau for Epilepsy (IBE). Epilepsia **46**, 470–472 (2005)
4. Penfield, W., Jasper, H.: Epilepsy and the functional anatomy of the human brain. Little Brown, Boston (1954)

5. Cota, V.R., Drabowski, B.M.B., de Oliveira, J.C., Moraes, M.F.D.: The epileptic amygdala: toward the development of a neural prosthesis by temporally coded electrical stimulation. J. Neurosci. Res. **94**(6), 463–485 (2016)
6. Niedermeyer, E.: Epileptic seizure disorders. In: Niedermeyer, E., Lopes Da Silva, F. (eds.) Electroencephalography: Basic Principles, Clinical Applications, and Related Fields, 5th Edn. Lippincott Williams and Wilkins, Philadelphia (2005)
7. Bromfield, E.B., Cavazos, J.E., Sirven, J.I.: An Introduction to Epilepsy (2006)
8. Wilson, S.B., Emerson, R.: Spike detection: a review and comparison of algorithms. Clin. Neurophysiol. **113**(12), 1873–1881 (2002)
9. Gotman, J., Gloor, P.: Automatic recognition and quantification of interictal epileptic activity in the human scalp EEG. Electroencephalogr. Clin. Neurophysiol. **41**(5), 513–529 (1976)
10. Medeiros, D.C., et al.: Temporal rearrangement of pre-ictal PTZ Induced spike discharges by low frequency electrical stimulation to the amygdaloid complex. Brain Stimul. **7**(2), 170–178 (2014)
11. Le Douget, J.E., Fouad, A., Filali, M.M., Pyrzowski, J., Le Van Quyen, M.: Surface and intracranial EEG spike detection based on discrete wavelet decomposition and random forest classification. In: 2017 39th Annual International Conference of the IEEE Engineering in Medicine and Biology Society (EMBC), pp. 475–478 (2017)
12. Scheuer, M.L., Bagic, A., Wilson, S.B.: Spike detection: inter-reader agreement and a statistical Turing test on a large data set. Clin. Neurophysiol. **128**(1), 243–250 (2017)
13. Anh-Dao, N.T., Linh-Trung, N., Van Nguyen, L., Tran-Duc, T., Boashash, B.: A multistage system for automatic detection of epileptic spikes. REV J. Electron. Commun. **8**(1–2), 1–13 (2018)
14. El-Samie, F.E.A., Alotaiby, T.N., Khalid, M.I., Alshebeili, S.A., Aldosari, S.A.: A review of EEG and MEG epileptic spike detection algorithms. IEEE Access **6**, 60673–60688 (2018)
15. Gersner, R., Ekstein, D., Dhamne, S.C., Schachter, S.C., Rotenberg, A.: Huperzine A prophylaxis against pentylenetetrazole-induced seizures in rats is associated with increased cortical inhibition. Epilepsy Res. **117**, 97–103 (2015)
16. Jiao, J., Harreby, K.R., Sevcencu, C., Jensen, W.: Optimal vagus nerve stimulation frequency for suppression of spike-and-wave seizures in rats. Artif. Organs **40**(6), E120–E127 (2016)
17. Santos-Valencia, F., Almazán-Alvarado, S., Rubio-Luviano, A., Valdés-Cruz, A., Magdaleno-Madrigal, V.M., Martinez-Vargas, D.: Temporally irregular electrical stimulation to the epileptogenic focus delays epileptogenesis in rats. Brain Stimulation (2019)
18. Fawcett, T.: An introduction to ROC analysis. Pattern Recognit. Lett. **27**(8), 861–874 (2006)
19. Maccione, A., Gandolfo, M., Massobrio, P., Novellino, A., Martinoia, S., Chiappalone, M.: A novel algorithm for precise identification of spikes in extracellularly recorded neuronal signals. J. Neurosci. Methods **177**(1), 241–249 (2009)
20. French, J.A.: Refractory epilepsy: clinical overview. Epilepsia **48**, 3–7 (2007)
21. Spencer, S.S.: When should temporal-lobe epilepsy be treated surgically? Lancet Neurol. **1**(6), 375–382 (2002)
22. Cota, V.R., Medeiros, D.C., Vilela, M.R.S.P., Doretto, M.C., Moraes, M.F.D.: Distinct patterns of electrical stimulation of the basolateral amygdala influence pentylenetetrazole seizure outcome. Epilepsy Behav. **14**, 26–31 (2009)
23. de Oliveira, J.C., de Castro Medeiros, D., e Rezende, G.H.D.S., Moraes, M.F.D., Cota, V.R.: Temporally unstructured electrical stimulation to the amygdala suppresses behavioral chronic seizures of the pilocarpine animal model. Epilepsy Behav. **36**, 159–164 (2014)
24. de Oliveira, J.C., Maciel, R.M., Moraes, M.F.D., Cota, V.R.: Asynchronous, bilateral, and biphasic temporally unstructured electrical stimulation of amygdalae enhances the suppression of pentylenetetrazoleinduced seizures in rats. Epilepsy Res. **146**, 1–8 (2018)

25. de Oliveira, J.C., Drabowski, B.M.B., Rodrigues, S.M.A.F., Maciel, R.M., Moraes, M.F.D., Cota, V.R.: Seizure suppression by asynchronous non-periodic electrical stimulation of the amygdala is partially mediated by indirect desynchronization from nucleus accumbens. Epilepsy Res. **154**, 107–115 (2019)
26. Steriade, M.: Neuronal Substrates of Sleep and Epilepsy. Cambridge University Press, Cambridge (2003)
27. Wu, J., Yang, H., Peng, Y., Fang, L., Zheng, W., Song, Z.: The role of local field potential coupling in epileptic synchronization. Neural Regen. Res. **8**, 745 (2013)

Graph Model Evolution During Epileptic Seizures: Linear Model Approach

Talysson M. O. Santos[1], Victor H. B. Tsukahara[1], Jasiara C. de Oliveira[2], Vinicius Rosa Cota[2] (ID), and Carlos D. Maciel[1(✉)]

[1] Signal Processing Laboratory, Department of Electrical Engineering, University of São Paulo, São Carlos, Brazil
talyssonsantos@usp.br, maciel@sc.usp.br
[2] Laboratory of Neuroengineering and Neuroscience, Department of Electrical Engineering, Federal University of São João Del-Rei, São João del-Rei, Brazil

Abstract. Epilepsy is a brain disorder characterized by sustained predisposition to generate epileptic seizures. According to the World Health Organization, it is one of the most common neurological disorders, affecting approximately 50 million people worldwide. A modern approach for brain study is to model it as a complex system composed of a network of oscillators in which the emergent property of synchronization arises. By this token, epileptic seizures can be understood as a process of hyper-synchronization between brain areas. To assess such property, Partial Directed Coherence (PDC) method represents a suitable technique, once it allows a more precise investigation of interactions that may reveal direct influences from one brain area on another. During connectivity analysis, there may be a need to assess the statistical significance of the communication threshold and Surrogate Data, a method already applied for that purpose, can be used. Hence, the objective in this work was to carry out PDC connectivity analysis in combination with Surrogate Data to evaluate the communication threshold between brain areas and develop a graph model evolution during epileptic seizure, according to the classical EEG frequency bands. The main contribution is the threshold analysis adding statistical significance for connectivity investigation. A case study performed using EEG signals from rats showed that the applied methodology represents an appropriate alternative for functional analysis, providing insights on brain communication.

Keywords: Epilepsy · Seizures · Connectivity analysis · Partial directed coherence · Surrogate

1 Introduction

Neurological disorders represent a global burden issue for the healthcare area due to their increasingly important role in death and disability causation [1]. Among them, epilepsy is a highly and prevalent disease, characterized by a sustainable

V. R. Cota et al. (Eds.): LAWCN 2019, CCIS 1068, pp. 157–170, 2019.
https://doi.org/10.1007/978-3-030-36636-0_12

predisposition to generate epileptic seizures which result in social, psychological, cognitive, and neurobiological deficits [2]. Approximately 50 million people worldwide suffer from this condition [3].

There are many mechanisms to explain this disease [4]. A well-accepted theory has to do with multifaceted unbalance between excitatory and inhibitory neural tonus [4–6]. Another important aspect discussed in the literature is synchronization. This perspective models the brain as a system of systems in which the understanding of the organ as a set of subsystems (brain areas) interacting among themselves is implied. As a consequence, there is synchronization from a particular brain region with other areas giving rise to emergent properties [7,8]. Therefore epileptic seizures under this scope is interpreted as hypersynchronization phenomena [4,8–10].

Following this rationale, epileptic seizures are a neural synchronization expression and usually its epileptiform activity is evidenced into electrographic (EEG) recording through high-amplitude spikes and other disturbances resulting in its prevalence to develop epilepsy-based studies [11]. EEG signals can be collected using invasive or non-invasive techniques [12]. However, using electrodes directly in brain tissue to perform acquisition could be an essential option to map measurable indicators of epileptogenicity with good enough resolution [13].

Specifically, to develop a brain functional analysis, there are many methods to be applied. On the other hand, technique selection depends on signal features and study objectives. A multivariate autoregressive (MVAR) modelling to perform connectivity analysis of electroencephalographic signals represents a suitable technique, and Partial Directed Coherence (PDC) fits in this situation [14]. It is a well-established method used in Neuroscience [15–19] proposed by [20] and allows a more precise study of the interactions [21] because of its main advantage: its capability to denote active connections exhibiting the direct influences from a given brain area to other regions [22].

Once the PDC method is carried out, there may be a need to assess the statistical significance of connectivity measures, and Surrogate Data can be used [23]. The method basically creates data based on original signals, maintaining the power spectrum and randomizing Fourier phases. Then, they are compared with original signals through a hypothesis test to check the strength of connectivities discovered during functional analysis. It was used in combination with Information Theoretical methods in [24,25], with Granger Causality in [23], and with Directed Coherence and Partial Directed Coherence in [21,26–28] for that aim.

Hence, the paper presents the use of the PDC method combined with Surrogate Data to develop a functional connectivity analysis of EEG epileptic signals and with monitoring of its graph model evolution. Section 2 is going to present the theory related to Partial Directed Coherence, Surrogate Data Analysis. Section 3 presents the EEG data used and the applied methodology. Section 4 reports the results achieved, and Sect. 5 discusses the results. To close the paper, the Sect. 6 presents a conclusion.

2   Theory

The section presents a brief review of the required theory to comprehend the methodology application of this paper. Partial Directed Coherence and Surrogate Data are defined. Some equations are established to uniform mathematical notation of this paper.

2.1   Partial Directed Coherence (PDC)

Partial Directed Coherence is a frequency-domain approach of Granger Causality [29]. The method is grounded on a multivariate autoregressive model, aiming the study of direct connection among time series [20].

Initially, the time series matrix can be drafted as:

$$X(t) = \sum_{r=1}^{p} A_r(r)X(t-r) + E(t) \tag{1}$$

being p the order of autoregressive equation, $A_r(r)$ representing the coefficients matrix - whereby contains a_{ij} items and E(t) the noise matrix - for each time series. It is important to note a_{ij} elements, which depict the effect of $x_j(n-r)$ towards $x_i(t)$. Another issue is the equation in time domain, and PDC is performed in frequency domain. In this regard, Discrete Time Fourier Transform (DTFT) is applied [30]. Therefore, the coefficient matrix $A_r(r)$ is transformed into $A_r(f)$:

$$A_r(f) = \sum_{r=1}^{p} A_r e^{-ir2\pi f} \tag{2}$$

in Eq. 2, p is still the autoregressive model order. The i variable inside squared root represents the complex number unit - $i = \sqrt{-1}$. Thus, the PDC equation which expresses the effect of $x_j(n-r)$ towards $x_i(t)$ can be written as follows:

$$PDC = \pi_{ij}(f) = \frac{A'_{ij}(f)}{\sqrt{a'^H_j(f)a'_j(f)}} \tag{3}$$

the variable H represents the Hermitian matrix, a_j denotes the jth item from matrix A', being calculated as:

$$A'(f) = I - A(f) \tag{4}$$

variable I denotes identity matrix.

2.2   Surrogate Data for Hypothesis Test

The investigation of connectivity between brain regions when using the PDC method may reveal issues to handle and one of the questions that may appear is the connectivity threshold. In that case, statistical methods may be helpful. In particular, when there is a lack of data, Surrogate Data can be useful [31]. Another important issue is the conclusions provided: they are sufficiently robust to provide new information on the subject under investigation [21].

For method application, there are quite a few techniques like Random Permutation (RP) Surrogates, Fourier Transform (FT), Amplitude Adjusted Fourier Transform (AAFT), and Iterative Amplitude Adjusted Fourier Transform (IAAFT). With regard to the IAAFT technique, it was proposed by Schreiber & Schmitz [32], and had the aim to overcome the AAFT technique bias [21]. It consists of generating a Surrogate Data from the original signal, keeping the same power spectrum and randomizing Fourier phases. Therefore, when comparing the statistics from original signals and Surrogate Data statistics, the null hypothesis can be accepted or rejected. Some literature can be reviewed in neuroscience related to the use of Surrogate Data to assist the strength as well as the type of interdependency among electroencephalographic signals [21, 26, 33, 34].

Related with the number of Surrogate Data to be created, there is a well established rank-order test proposed by [35] that can be used [36]. Assume Ψ is the probability of false rejection - defining the level of significance(S) as:

$$S = (1 - \Psi) \cdot 100\% \tag{5}$$

The number of Surrogate Data to be created(M) is defined as follows:

$$M = \frac{K}{\Psi} - 1 \tag{6}$$

where K is an integer number defined by the type of test - 1 if it is one-sided and 2 in the case of a two-sided test- and Ψ is the probability of false rejection. Usually, K=1 is adopted due to computational effort to generate surrogates [36].

Therefore, to evaluate the connectivity threshold between EEG signals, Surrogate Data can be created using the IAAFT algorithm. Then original signals can be compared with built data, using a hypothesis test to evaluate the hypothesis of presence or absence of connectivity.

3   Materials and Methods

In this section information about the EEG signals used to perform the study is reported, as well as the applied methodology, including algorithms and the computational environment.

3.1   Applied Methodology

The summary of the applied methodology can be observed in Fig. 1. The first step was the application of PDC method on the original EEG time series. The second step was the creation of Surrogate Data by reference to three brain areas signal recordings: cortex (CX), thalamus (TH) and hippocampus (HP). It was defined $\Psi = 3\%$ and K $= 1$, resulting on M number of 35 for rounding purpose. Each

Surrogate Data was used with the other original signals to perform PDC method. Finally, the connectivity analysis was performed, comparing the Surrogate Data PDC with original time series PDC. Details of Surrogate analysis can be observed in Fig. 2.

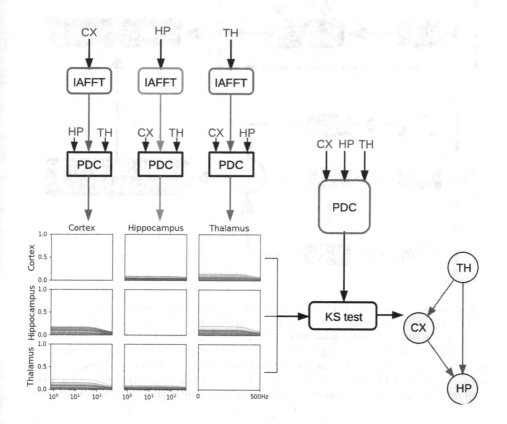

Fig. 1. Methodology diagram: Using Surrogate Data, 35 signals from each area are generated to determine the connectivity threshold. Kolmogorov-Smirnov test is used for null hypothesis test comparing the PDC of the real signal with PDC obtained with the Surrogate Data.

To perform the connectivity analysis, classical EEG frequency bands were observed. For each frequency interval, Kolgomorov-Smirnov statistical test was applied, defining p-value = 5%, to validate the communication between brain areas. The acceptance of the null hypothesis represents that there is no connection.

The applied methodology described and represented in Fig. 1 was used to investigate two periods of EEG signals: the basal and PTZ infusion - until generalized tonic-clonic (GTCS) behaviour. The analysis was performed in the recordings of six rats.

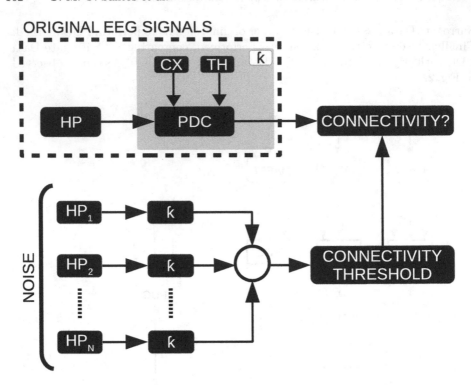

Fig. 2. Surrogate analysis to check connectivity between hippocampus and other brain areas. PDC method is applied on original signals. Surrogate data for hippocampus (HP) EEG signals are built, mantaining the power spectrum. Then for each Surrogate signal PDC is performed using cortex (CX) and thalamus (TH) original signals to discover the connectivity threshold between hippocampus and cortex ($\pi_{HP->CX}$) and hippocampus and thalamus ($\pi_{HP->TH}$). Finally, threshold is compared with PDC from original signals to validate the connectivity values and strength through KS Test.

Simulations were developed in Python language, using the packages: Connectivipy, Graphviz, Matplotlib, Nolitsa, Numpy, Pandas, Scipy, Seaborn, and Time. The code was executed on a computer with an Intel i7 processor, 4 GB of RAM, running Linux Lite 4.0 operational system.

3.2   Simulated Data

To test the python package Connectivipy, examples of PDC application from [20, 37] were performed to reproduce their paper results. Nonlinear equations, a situation in which the method fails, were used to verify whether the python package is working properly. After all tests the case study was carried out.

3.3 Database to Perform Case Study

The study uses EEG signals database from the Laboratory of Neuroengineering and Neuroscience (LINNce), from Federal University of São João Del Rei. The laboratory uses male Wistar rats weighing between 250 and 350 grams - coming from the University Central Vivarium -, to collect data and test methods of electrical stimulation. All described procedures are in according to ethics committee under protocol 31/2014.

To collect the electroencephalographic signals, electrodes - monopolar type, stainless steel, covered by Teflon - were placed directly inside the rat brain through stereotactic surgery - inside right Thalamus and Hippocampus -[8]. Furthermore, two microsurgical screws (length 4.7 mm, diameter 1.17 mm, Fine Science Tools, Inc., North Vancouver, Canada) were implanted: the first aiming the cortical recording of right hemisphere, and the second to be used as the reference, positioned in frontal bone. Electrodes and screws were positioned with assistance of neuroanatomic atlas [38]. Pentylenetetrazole (PTZ; a proconvulsant drug) was used to induced acute epileptic seizures in the rats [8]. EEG signals from each rat were recorded and the rat was filmed at the same time to perform behavioural analysis (video-EEG technique) - observe classic seizure features such as facial automatisms, head myoclonus, forelimb and hindlimbs clonus, elevation and fall, generalized tonic-clonic seizure -, to enable correlation of them with the electrophysiological events verified during the brain activity recording.

EEG recording was performed using 1 KHz sampling rate. Signals were also amplified 2000 V/V, filtered (second-order Butterworth filter from 0.3 to 300 Hz band) using A-M Systems (model 3500) amplification system, and acquired on National Istruments (PCI 6023E) A/D converter controlled by LabView's Virtual Instrument developed at LINNce. Noise coming from power grid at 60 Hz frequency was avoided with employment of shielded cables and Faraday cage.

4 Results

An example of original EEG signals can be observed in Fig. 3. It is important to note the basal and infusion intervals: green vertical lines indicate the infusion interval, being the first line the end of the basal interval that starts in 0 mS. The blue vertical line represents the onset of epileptiform activity jointly with the beginning of convulsive behaviour, and the last green vertical line indicates the limit of infusion interval in which the rat did not present GTCS behaviour yet.

The PDC method was applied to EEG signals on basal and infusion intervals. After this step, Surrogate Data was created for each brain area and then used with other original signals to perform another PDC analysis. The computational time to run PDC on original signals was 32.33 s and to perform Surrogate Data and its PDC method was 2030.85 s, in a total of 2063.18 s - for each interval(basal and infusion). An example of PDC method, containing the original signals (blue

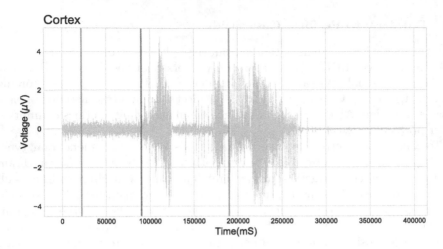

Fig. 3. Example of cortex signal - rat R070. The green vertical lines indicate the infusion interval - the first represent the end of basal interval which starts in 0 mS. The blue vertical line represents the limit of infusion interval in which the rat did not present GTCS behaviour yet. (Color figure online)

line) and Surrogate Data (red line), and an illustration of Surrogate Data power spectrum can be seen in Figs. 4-a and 4-b, respectively.

The result of the PDC method performed with Surrogate Data was used to discover the connectivity (π_{ij}) threshold between brain areas, for each standard EEG frequency - Fig. 4-a shows an example extracted from rat R070. Thus, the Kolgomorov-Smirnov Test was used to evaluate the PDC performed with original EEG signals, revealing the connectivity between brain regions, according to each threshold, and to compute the strength of each connection.

Figure 5 shows an example of a connectivity graph developed based on applied methodology. For each EEG frequency band, communication between cortex, hippocampus, and thalamus, during basal (blue edges), and infusion intervals (red edges) is shown.

The Table 1 reports the connectivity measures which remained among most rats used to build the EEG signals database. It is possible to check the connectivity threshold between each brain area, and the strength of its communication.

5   Discussion

It is possible to observe from recorded EEG signals, the basal and infusion intervals, including the epileptic seizure interval (not analysed in this paper). An important issue when applying MVAR modelling is stationarity, a requirement to perform linear models analysis such as PDC. The intervals used to apply methodology (basal interval and infusion interval only until GTCS behaviour) assured the conditions to apply PDC.

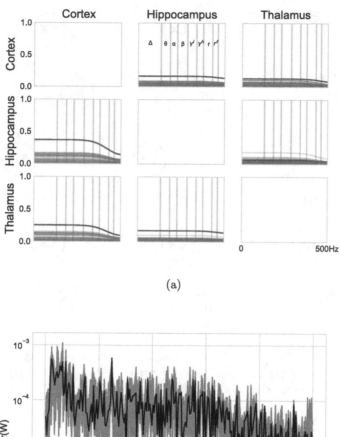

(a)

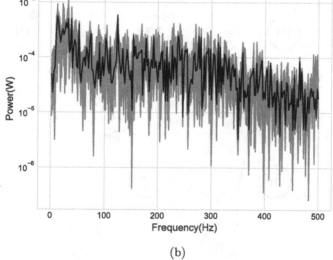

(b)

Fig. 4. (a) Example of connectivity threshold - extracted from rat R070, basal interval. The blue line represents the PDC for the real signal. Red lines represents the PDC for surrogate data. The x-axis is in logarithmic scale and vertical green lines represents frequency intervals. (b) Power spectrum of real data and Surrogate Data example - from cortex, rat R070. Black line represents the power spectrum for real EEG signal. Red blur represents the power spectrum for 35 surrogates data. (Color figure online)

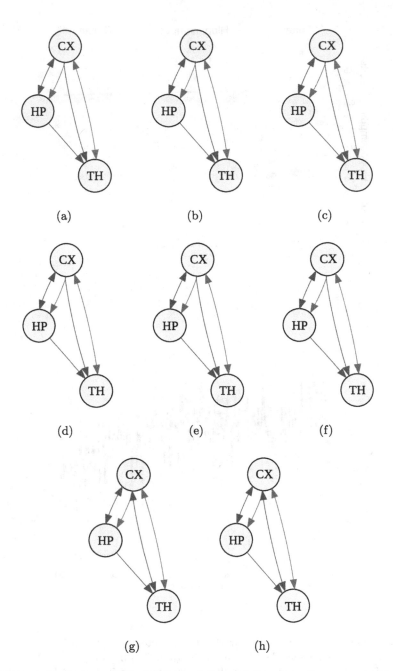

Fig. 5. Example of connectivity (π_{ij}) graph for each frequency range - extracted from rat R070. (a) Δ, (b) θ, (c) α, (d) β, (e) γ^l, (f) γ^h, (g) ripple and (h) fast ripple. Blue edges represents connectivity during basal interval and red edges represents connectivity during infusion interval. (Color figure online)

Table 1. Connectivity measures that remained for most rats. The table is organized according to classical EEG frequency intervals (Ω), time series interval - basal (B) or infusion (I) -, and connectivity (π_{ij}) between brain areas - cortex (CX), hippocampus (HP) and thalamus (TH). Arrows indicates the connectivity - e.g. C $\rightarrow$T represent the communication between cortex and thalamus. Threshold (λ) and strength (τ) - how much connectivity value surpassed threshold - and no connectivity (-) are pointed out.

Ω			Δ		θ		α		β		γ^l		γ^h		r		r^f	
Period			B	I	B	I	B	I	B	I	B	I	B	I	B	I	B	I
H → C	λ	Mean	0.33	-	0.33	-	0.32	-	0.30	-	0.24	-	0.18	-	0.13	-	0.09	-
		Max	0.69	-	0.68	-	0.65	-	0.56	-	0.39	-	0.24	-	0.18	-	0.14	-
		Min	0.09	-	0.09	-	0.09	-	0.09	-	0.09	-	0.09	-	0.09	-	0.06	-
	τ	Mean	0.11	-	0.11	-	0.11	-	0.11	-	0.09	-	0.07	-	0.05	-	0.04	-
		Max	0.38	-	0.38	-	0.38	-	0.36	-	0.32	-	0.24	-	0.14	-	0.08	-
T → C	λ	Mean	-	0.21	-	0.21	-	0.21	-	0.20	-	0.17	-	0.13	-	0.10	-	0.08
		Max	-	0.53	-	0.52	-	0.51	-	0.47	-	0.37	-	0.25	-	0.15	-	0.11
		Min	-	0.06	-	0.06	-	0.06	-	0.06	-	0.06	-	0.06	-	0.05	-	0.04
	τ	Mean	-	0.27	-	0.27	-	0.27	-	0.27	-	0.26	-	0.23	-	0.18	-	0.14
		Max	-	0.54	-	0.54	-	0.55	-	0.55	-	0.53	-	0.50	-	0.42	-	0.32
C → H	λ	Mean	0.25	0.11	0.25	0.11	0.24	0.11	0.22	0.11	0.18	0.11	0.15	0.09	0.11	0.07	0.08	0.06
		Max	0.45	0.16	0.44	0.16	0.40	0.16	0.30	0.16	0.23	0.16	0.19	0.14	0.16	0.11	0.12	0.08
		Min	0.14	0.07	0.14	0.07	0.14	0.07	0.14	0.07	0.14	0.07	0.10	0.06	0.06	0.05	0.04	0.04
	τ	Mean	0.10	0.29	0.10	0.29	0.10	0.29	0.10	0.29	0.11	0.28	0.11	0.27	0.10	0.26	0.09	0.24
		Max	0.15	0.38	0.15	0.38	0.15	0.38	0.15	0.38	0.16	0.37	0.18	0.37	0.17	0.39	0.15	0.42
T → H	λ	Mean	-	0.16	-	0.16	-	0.16	-	0.15	-	0.13	-	0.11	-	0.09	-	0.07
		Max	-	0.27	-	0.27	-	0.27	-	0.24	-	0.19	-	0.17	-	0.13	-	0.11
		Min	-	0.05	-	0.05	-	0.05	-	0.05	-	0.05	-	0.05	-	0.04	-	0.03
	τ	Mean	-	0.15	-	0.15	-	0.14	-	0.14	-	0.13	-	0.11	-	0.07	-	0.05
		Max	-	0.49	-	0.49	-	0.48	-	0.44	-	0.33	-	0.23	-	0.18	-	0.14
C → T	λ	Mean	-	0.12	-	0.12	-	0.12	-	0.12	-	0.12	-	0.10	-	0.09	-	0.07
		Max	-	0.19	-	0.19	-	0.19	-	0.18	-	0.18	-	0.16	-	0.13	-	0.10
		Min	-	0.08	-	0.08	-	0.08	-	0.08	-	0.08	-	0.07	-	0.06	-	0.04
	τ	Mean	-	0.17	-	0.17	-	0.17	-	0.17	-	0.17	-	0.18	-	0.19	-	0.19
		Max	-	0.35	-	0.35	-	0.35	-	0.36	-	0.36	-	0.38	-	0.42	-	0.46
H → T	λ	Mean	0.30	0.24	0.30	0.24	0.29	0.24	0.27	0.22	0.22	0.18	0.17	0.14	0.12	0.10	0.09	0.08
		Max	0.67	0.67	0.66	0.66	0.64	0.64	0.55	0.55	0.38	0.38	0.24	0.24	0.17	0.17	0.12	0.17
		Min	0.09	0.05	0.09	0.05	0.09	0.05	0.09	0.05	0.09	0.05	0.09	0.04	0.06	0.04	0.04	0.03
	τ	Mean	0.17	0.2	0.16	0.20	0.16	0.19	0.14	0.17	0.13	0.14	0.10	0.10	0.07	0.06	0.06	0.04
		Max	0.40	0.52	0.40	0.52	0.39	0.51	0.36	0.49	0.29	0.42	0.20	0.31	0.12	0.20	0.14	0.13

As it can be verified in Fig. 4-a, PDC was applied to original EEG signals and Surrogate Data. Sometimes visually it is not possible to check connectivity between brain areas, such as the link between thalamus and hippocampus. Kolgomorov-Smirnov Test was essential to identify where there is genuine communication and detect the strength and threshold for each case. Figure 4-b ascertain the maintenance of power spectrum for Surrogate Data, essential to evaluate threshold between brain areas - this is assuring the same information contained in EEG signals.

For most rats from EEG database, it is possible to verify connectivity between some areas (Table 1). For basal and infusion intervals, connectivity was identified between $\pi_{CX->HP}$ and $\pi_{HP->TH}$. It was identified only during infusion interval connectivity between $\pi_{TH->CX}$, $\pi_{TH->HP}$ and $\pi_{CX->TH}$. Only for the basal interval, it was observed connectivity between $\pi_{HP->CX}$.

Regarding hippocampus and cortex communication it was not possible to observe information flow between them during basal interval but appeared in the infusion interval. This result is not biologically plausible. Literature reveals bidirectional communication related with memory formation [39,40]. Probably the answer for the issue stems from communication strength between brain areas: EEG noise is affecting functional connectivity analysis resulting in no information flow identification.

A significant result is observed in the threshold values found for basal and infusion intervals. It is possible to check a smaller value for the infusion interval when compared with the basal period. It may represent that a slight value during infusion interval is cooperating to hypersynchronization between brain areas, aiding the maintenance of excitatory activity, a phenomenon studied in [41] and [42]. The connectivity difference observed between $\pi_{HP->TH}$ is supported by [43], in which it was identified that epileptic seizure starts in the limbic system (amygdala and hippocampus), recruiting thalamus that, thus, plays as a neural substrate synchronizer. As a consequence, the thalamus is responsible for propagating the epileptic activity to the cortex and other brain areas supporting the spread of the seizure.

Regarding threshold values, there is yet a critical behaviour. For low EEG frequencies (delta to approximately low gamma), it is possible to observe more difference between basal and infusion thresholds when compared with the difference in high frequency bands. It is consistent with the concept reported by [44] that low frequencies support the communication between brain substrates. Conversely, high EEG frequencies support the local hyper synchronism, and this is also consistent with the performed methodology.

6 Conclusions

The use of PDC method to perform functional connectivity analysis revealed to be a suitable option to investigate direct communications between brain areas, based on its MVAR model and linear approach. For EEG intervals where stationarity is ensured, the method works properly. The use of Surrogate Data and KS Test to implement the threshold analysis added more insights in connectivity analysis. Through this approach it was possible to discover differences between the threshold of EEG low and high frequencies, more about the communication dynamics between brain areas, consistent with neuroscience literature, allowing a thorough investigation. It demonstrates that the combination of methods proposed for this work is a suitable choice to perform functional analysis in electroencephalographic signals.

Acknowledgment. Laboratory of Neuroengineering and Neuroscience, Department of Electrical Engineering, Federal University of São João Del-Rei for partnership and EEG data used in this paper. Experimental procedures in animals were supported by the Fundação de Amparo à Pesquisa de Minas Gerais (FAPEMIG) [grant number APQ 02485-15].

References

1. Feigin, V.L., et al.: The Lancet Neurology (2019)
2. Fisher, R.S., et al.: Epilepsia **55**(4), 475 (2014). https://doi.org/10.1111/epi.12550.
3. Thijs, R.D., Surges, R., O'Brien, T.J., Sander, J.W.: The Lancet (2019)
4. Devinsky, O., Vezzani, A., O'Brien, T.J., Scheffer, I.E., Curtis, M., Perucca, P.: Nat. Rev. Dis. Primers **4** (2018). https://doi.org/10.1038/nrdp.2018.24. https://www.nature.com/articles/nrdp201824#supplementary-information
5. Mele, M., Costa, R.O., Duarte, C.B.: Front. Cell. Neurosci. **13**, 77 (2019). https://doi.org/10.3389/fncel.2019.00077
6. Oyarzabal, A., Marin-Valencia, I.: J. Inherit. Metab. Dis. **42**(2), 220 (2019). https://doi.org/10.1002/jimd.12071
7. Andrea Avena-Koenigsberger, O.S., Msic, B.: Nat. Rev. Neurosci. **19**, 17 (2017). https://doi.org/10.1038/nrn.2017.149
8. Cota, V., Drabowski, B.M.B., de Oliveira, J.C., Moraes, M.: J. Neurosci. Res. **94**, 463 (2016). https://doi.org/10.1002/jnr.23741
9. Weiss, S.A., et al.: Neurobiol. Dis. **124**, 183 (2019). https://doi.org/10.1016/j.nbd.2018.11.014. http://www.sciencedirect.com/science/article/pii/S0969996118 30682X
10. Olamat, A.E., Akan, A.: In: 2017 25th Signal Processing and Communications Applications Conference (SIU), pp. 1–4 (2017). https://doi.org/10.1109/SIU.2017.7960194
11. Ibrahim, F., et al.: Int. J. Speech Technol. **22**(1), 191 (2019). https://doi.org/10.1007/s10772-018-09565-7
12. St. Louis, E.K.M., Frey, L.C.M.: Electroencephalography (EEG): An Introductory Text and Atlas of Normal and Abnormal Findings in Adults, Children, and Infants. American Epilepsy Society (2016). https://www.ncbi.nlm.nih.gov/books/NBK390354/
13. Bartolomei, F., et al.: Epilepsia **58**(7), 1131 (2017). https://doi.org/10.1111/epi.13791
14. Pester, B., Lehmann, T., Leistritz, L., Witte, H., Ligges, C.: J. Neurosci. Methods **309**, 199 (2018)
15. Varotto, G., et al.: Clin. Neurophysiol. **129**(11), 2372 (2018). https://doi.org/10.1016/j.clinph.2018.09.008. http://www.sciencedirect.com/science/article/pii/S138 824571831229X
16. Schulz, S., Haueisen, J., Bär, K.J., Voss, A.: Physiol. Meas. **39**(7), 074004 (2018). https://doi.org/10.1088/1361-6579/aace9b
17. Ciaramidaro, A., Toppi, J., Casper, C., Freitag, C., Siniatchkin, M., Astolfi, L.: Sci. Rep. **8** (2018). https://doi.org/10.1038/s41598-018-24416-w
18. Gaxiola-Tirado, J.A., Salazar-Varas, R., Gutiérrez, D.: IEEE Trans. Cogn. Dev. Syst. **10**(3), 776 (2018). https://doi.org/10.1109/TCDS.2017.2777180
19. Ning, L., Rathi, Y.: IEEE Trans. Med. Imaging **37**(9), 1957 (2018). https://doi.org/10.1109/TMI.2017.2739740
20. Baccalá, L.A., Sameshima, K.: Biol. Cybern. **84**(6), 463 (2001). https://doi.org/10.1007/PL00007990
21. Adkinson, J.A., et al.: IEEE Trans. Neural Syst. Rehabil. Eng. **27**(1), 22 (2019). https://doi.org/10.1109/TNSRE.2018.2886211
22. Huang, D., et al.: Front. Hum. Neurosci. **10**, 235 (2016). https://doi.org/10.3389/fnhum.2016.00235

23. Rodrigues, P.L.C., Baccalá, L.A.: In: 2016 38th Annual International Conference of the IEEE Engineering in Medicine and Biology Society (EMBC), pp. 5493–5496 (2016). https://doi.org/10.1109/EMBC.2016.7591970
24. Endo, W., Santos, F.P., Simpson, D., Maciel, C.D., Newland, P.L.: J. Comput. Neurosci. **38**(2), 427 (2015)
25. Santos, F.P., Maciel, C.D., Newland, P.L.: J. Comput. Neurosci. **43**(2), 159 (2017)
26. Faes, L., Porta, A., Nollo, G.: IEEE Trans. Biomed. Eng. **57**(8), 1897 (2010). https://doi.org/10.1109/TBME.2010.2042715
27. Faes, L., Porta, A., Nollo, G.: In: 2009 Annual International Conference of the IEEE Engineering in Medicine and Biology society, pp. 6280–6283. IEEE (2009)
28. Faes, L., Pinna, G.D., Porta, A., Maestri, R., Nollo, G.: IEEE Trans. Biomed. Eng. **51**(7), 1156 (2004)
29. Chopra, R., Murthy, C.R., Rangarajan, G.: IEEE Trans. Signal Process. **66**(22), 5803 (2018). https://doi.org/10.1109/TSP.2018.2872004
30. Takahashi, D.Y., Baccalá, L.A., Sameshima, K.: J. Appl. Stat. **34**(10), 1259 (2007). https://doi.org/10.1080/02664760701593065
31. Lancaster, G., Iatsenko, D., Pidde, A., Ticcinelli, V., Stefanovska, A.: Phys. Rep. **748**, 1 (2018). https://doi.org/10.1016/j.physrep.2018.06.001. http://www.science direct.com/science/article/pii/S0370157318301340. Surrogate data for hypothesis testing of physical systems
32. Schreiber, T., Schmitz, A.: Phys. Rev. Lett. **77**, 635 (1996). https://doi.org/10.1103/PhysRevLett.77.635
33. Pereda, E., Quiroga, R.Q., Bhattacharya, J.: Prog. Neurobiol. **77**(1), 1 (2005). https://doi.org/10.1016/j.pneurobio.2005.10.003. http://www.sciencedirect.com/science/article/pii/S030100820500119X
34. Subramaniyam, N.P., Hyttinen, J.: Phys. Rev. E **91**, 022927 (2015). https://doi.org/10.1103/PhysRevE.91.022927
35. Theiler, J., Eubank, S., Longtin, A., Galdrikian, B., Farmer, J.D.: Phys. D: Nonlinear Phenom. **58**(1), 77 (1992). https://doi.org/10.1016/0167-2789(92)90102-S. http://www.sciencedirect.com/science/article/pii/016727899290102S
36. Schreiber, T., Schmitz, A.: Phys. D: Nonlinear Phenom. **142**(3–4), 346 (2000)
37. Chen, Y., Bressler, S.L., Ding, M.: J. Neurosci. Methods **150**(2), 228 (2006)
38. Paxinos, G., Watson, C.: The Rat Brain in Stereotaxic Coordinates, 7th edn. Elsevier (2013)
39. Preston, A.R., Eichenbaum, H.: Curr. Biol. **23**(17), R764 (2013)
40. Eichenbaum, H.: Nat. Rev. Neurosci. **1**(1), 41 (2000)
41. Uhlhaas, P.J., Singer, W.: Neuron **52**(1), 155 (2006)
42. Varela, F., Lachaux, J.P., Rodriguez, E., Martinerie, J.: Nat. Rev. Neurosci. **2**(4), 229 (2001)
43. Bertram, E.H., Mangan, P., Fountain, N., Rempe, D., et al.: Epilepsy Res. **32**(1–2), 194 (1998)
44. Schnitzler, A., Gross, J.: Nat. Rev. Neurosci. **6**(4), 285 (2005)

Software and Hardware
Implementations in Neuroscience

A Parallel RatSlam C++ Library Implementation

Mauro Enrique de Souza Muñoz[1], Matheus Chaves Menezes[1],
Edison Pignaton de Freitas[2], Sen Cheng[3], Areolino de Almeida Neto[1],
Alexandre César Muniz de Oliveira[1],
and Paulo Rogério de Almeida Ribeiro[1](✉) (iD)

[1] Federal University of Maranhão, Av. dos Portugueses, 1966 Bacanga, São Luís,
Maranhão, Brazil
mesmunoz@gmail.com,menezes.matheus@lacmor.ufma.br,
{areolino.neto,alexandre.cesar}@ufma.br,paulo.ribeiro@ecp.ufma.br
[2] Graduate Program on Computer Science, Federal University of Rio Grande do Sul,
Porto Alegre, Brazil
edison.pignaton@inf.ufrgs.br
[3] Computational Neuroscience, Institute for Neural Computation, Ruhr University
Bochum, Bochum, Germany
sen.cheng@rub.de

Abstract. RatSlam is a bio-inspired Simultaneous Location and Mapping (SLAM) algorithm used for autonomous mobile robots navigation tasks. This work presents a RatSlam algorithm implementation as a C++ library designed to take advantage of internal RatSlam modules parallelization. The RatSlam algorithm is presented with principal aspects of the library architecture design. Furthermore, its results using a well known RatSlam data set with a standard RatSlam implementation (OpenRatSLAM - Robot Operating System), and a Python implementation. The mapping found with the previous approaches and the proposed on this work were similar. Moreover, the execution times between the OpenRatSLAM and this C++ library was compared, with the proposed implementation having a lower execution time. Thus, the current implementation was validated and has some advantages against previous ones, which can be very relevant for real-time applications.

Keywords: RatSlam implementation · SLAM algorithm · C++
RatSlam library

1 Introduction

The manner a robot explores an unknown environment is a fundamental problem in mobile robotics. The problem is that the robot needs to know where it is with relation to a not currently known environment. Simultaneous Localization and Mapping (SLAM) algorithms address this problem simultaneously building a map of the environment while localizing itself in the map.

© Springer Nature Switzerland AG 2019
V. R. Cota et al. (Eds.): LAWCN 2019, CCIS 1068, pp. 173–183, 2019.
https://doi.org/10.1007/978-3-030-36636-0_13

Besides traditional approaches to solve the SLAM problem [9,11], it is worth mentioning that there are also bio-inspired strategies to solve it, e.g. [7,8,10]. One of them is called RatSLAM that is inspired by the neuroscience theories about the navigation system presented in the hippocampus of rodents brain that can be used in indoor as in outdoor environments [3,5–7].

RatSlam has its implementation publicly available in different programming languages such as MATLAB[1], robotC[2] and Python[3,4] [1]. Furthermore, there is also an implementation of RatSLAM supported by the Robot Operating System (ROS), which is a flexible framework for robot software development, called OpenRatSLAM [1]. The OpenRatSLAM has the advantage to make the processes parallel between the main modules of RatSLAM, which allows the algorithm to map large areas faster than traditional linear implementations.

This work presents a framework for RatSLAM algorithm implementation. The framework is intended to be used to research algorithms using the same base structure modules as RatSLAM. Additionally, is is written to be used as a standard C++ library.

The present work is organized as follows: Sect. 2 presents the RatSLAM algorithm; Sect. 3 details the proposed RatSlam implementation and shows how to use its code; Sect. 4 shows the results acquired with this proposed approach; and Sect. 5 presents the conclusion and the directions for further work.

2   RatSLAM

RatSLAM is a SLAM approach, i.e. mapping and localization system, inspired on computational models of the neural process underlying navigation in the hippocampus of rodents and the entorhinal cortex [7]. Over time, RatSLAM has been enhanced to work with general real-world examples of localization and mapping of mobile robots using vision system as its main input sensor [3,5, 6]. Figure 1 shows the RatSLAM architecture found in recent literature [1,2,6], where there are three of its main modules: Pose Cells, Local View Cells and Experience Map.

Additionally, on Fig. 1 there are a Robot Vision System and a Self Motion Cues modules. The Robot Vision System module is responsible for acquire the scenes of the environment whereas The Self Motion Cues provides the odometry information of the robot. The odometry information can be extracted by the scenes sent by the Robot Vision System module or others specific sensors such wheel encoders. The associations among Local View Cells, Pose Cells Network and Experience Map are depicted on Fig. 2 and explained as follow:

Pose Cells Network is a continuous attractor network (CAN) configured in a three-dimensional prism as shown in Fig. 2. CAN can be seen as a neural network

---

[1] https://wiki.qut.edu.au/display/cyphy/RatSLAM+MATLAB.
[2] https://github.com/mjs513/rsnxt08/tree/wiki.
[3] https://github.com/renatopp/ratslam-python.
[4] https://github.com/coxlab/ratslam-python.

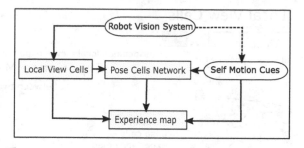

Fig. 1. Architecture of RatSLAM: The Local View Cells module is activated by the Robot Vision System. Self Motion Cues give suggestions for movement, which can be through visual odometry (dashed line). The Pose Cells Network is a three-dimensional continuous attractor network with each cell being the robot's pose. Local View Cells storage the different locations seen by the robot and injects energy into the Pose Cells Network. The Experience Map module, which is a graph, is a representation of the topological map of the environment [2].

of an array of cells equipped with weighted excitatory or inhibitory connections [4]. These connections cross the boundaries of the prism, allowing the network to function infinitely (with restrictions), but with a fixed dimensions sizes. Besides that, the CAN operates by varying the activity of the cells, rather than by changing the values of the weighted connections [6]. The attractor dynamics of CANs, in its stable state, usually creates a single cluster of activated cells, known as an *energy packet* or *activity packet* [1]. In addition, the cell array dimensions represent the three-dimensional information of x, y, and θ corresponding to the pose of a ground-based robot, and the centroid of the *activity packet* is the best estimate of the robot's current pose in the environment.

Local View Cells is an array of templates (squares on Fig. 2), which is a structure that stores the features of a distinct visual scene in the environment. When a new template is created, a link is formed between this template and the coordinates of the center of the most activity packet in pose cell network. Although, when a template is activated (robot "visit" the same place where it was created), it injects activity inside pose cell at the associated coordinates. This last mechanism supports robot re-localisation in the environment.

Experience Map is a two-dimensional graph map that combines Pose Cells, Local View Cells and odometry information to estimate the robot's pose. Each node in the graph is called *experience*, which has information of what template and activity packet were activated when this *experience* was created. If both the activity pack and the template associated with an exiting experience are activated, a loop closure and path correction process occurs on the Experiment Map. Between two experiences, a link is created containing information of distance and relative angle between them.

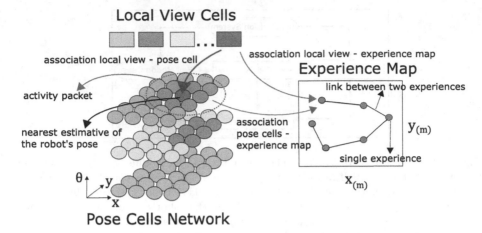

Pose Cells Network

Fig. 2. Associations among Pose Cells Network, Local View Cells and Experience Map. The Local View Cells (squares) inject energy (blue arrow) into Pose Cells Network (pink and purple circles) via activity packet. The closest estimate of robot's pose on the environment is the centroid of the activity packet represented by the pinkest circle on the Pose Cells Network. An experience is created or associated by linking both already existing Local View cell and Pose Cells activity packet (green arrow). The gray circles on the Experience Map, which are nodes of the graph, are experiences whereas its edges (graph) are links between two experiences and represented by straight lines [2] (Color figure onlne).

3   The RatSlam C++ Library Implementation

This section presents a RatSlam C++ library implementation to satisfy some issues that rose during researches related with the RatSlam algorithm. The library design prerequisites were:

1. The RatSlam implementation should be coded as a C++ library, so it can easily be used in other research projects;
2. It should use the same algorithm for each RatSlam module as those used by the OpenRatSLAM implementation;
3. The RatSlam library should take advantage of RatSlam modules parallelization;
4. It must be capable to read parameter configuration files used by the Open-RatSLAM implementation.

This section describes the computational design solutions used to satisfy the presented prerequisites.

3.1   Library Aspect

The OpenRatSLAM proposes a ROS embedded architecture where each Rat-Slam module is implemented as a ROS node [1]. This implementations has the advantage to use the inherent ROS node parallelization and the facility to be easily integrated using ROS architecture. The drawback of this approach is the impossibility to use OpenRatSLAM as part of systems not based in the ROS architecture, mainly because ROS nodes are implemented as different computational process. Another important point is that the RatSlam input data (odometries and images) should be feed into the system as ROS bags, which are controlled by the ROS system.

The adopted solution was to create a C++ class (*ratslam::RatSlam*) responsible to wrap all interactions between clients and the RatSlam algorithm implementation. Figure 3 shows the class diagram of the main RatSlam library classes.

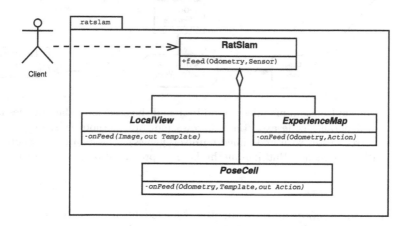

Fig. 3. The C++ RatSlam library main classes diagram.

3.2   Parallelization Aspect

The OpenRatSLAM implementation uses the inherently parallelization of ROS nodes. In ROS, each node runs as a different system process, synchronized by the ROS topic publishing mechanism.

As the proposed coding approach is meant to be a library, the module parallelization is implemented using *threads* rather than system processes. Figure 4 depicts how thread loops synchronize with each other using data queues.

Each RatSlam module (LocalView, PoseCell, ExperienceMap) has an associated thread loop. Each loop is responsible to read data from one or more synchronized queue, run its associated RatSlam module algorithm, and generate output data to be inserted in a queue that will be consumed by some other loop module. This implementation tries to reproduce the same data flow used by the OpenRatSLAM ROS implementation, but with threads rather than process.

For example, in Fig. 4, when *loopExperienceMap()* tries to read data from *QueueOdometry*, if the queue is empty the thread is blocked until some *Odometry* data is inserted in the queue. After that, the thread tries to read an *Action*

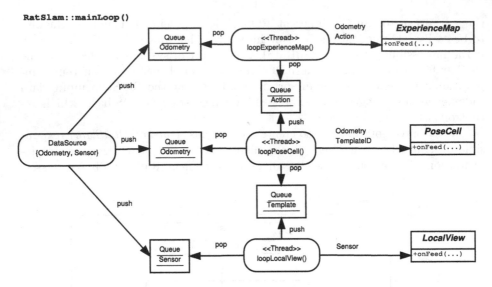

Fig. 4. Relations of RatSlam modules thread loop and the associated data queues used to synchronized parallel code execution. Arrows indicate method calls. Objects are represented by rectangles with underlined names (Queues). Classes are represented by rectangles with italic names. RatSlam methods are represented by rounded rectangles.

object from *QueueAction* and, again, it is blocked until there is some data to be read. After both Odometry and Action were read, the thread calls *ExperienceMap::onFeed()*. Then the loop continues and the thread blocks trying to read the next *QueueOdometry* data, and so on.

Note that all threads block when trying to read elements from empty queues and also block when trying to insert elements into full queues. Queue's push and pop blocking mechanisms ensure the synchronization between internal loop threads.

3.3 Usage

The library implements internal loop threads used to compute RatSlam modules. So, the library has an internal processing that must be started and stopped by clients. A basic library usage algorithm is shown on Fig. 5.

A ratslam::RatSlam object is instantiated, some settings are made, then the RatSlam threads are started running in different threads. The client loops reading data (Odometries and Images) from somewhere and feed them to the running "slam" object. It can be noted that the client is reading ExperienceMap data (slam::getDataEM()) and drawing it. After all data has been read, all threads are stopped (slam.stop()).

```
01.  ratslam::RatSlam slam( configurationFile )
02.  slam.setLogger( TimeLogger )               // Optional.
03.  slam.start()                               // Start all RatSlam threads.
04.  while ( readData( Odometry, Sensor ) )
04a.    slam.feed( Odometry, Sensor )
04b.    drawEM( slam.getDataEM() )              // Optional.
05.  slam.stop()                               // Stop all RatSlam threads.
```

Fig. 5. Simple algorithm to illustrate C++ RatSlam library usage.

4   Results

This section presents three experiments and their results. The first experiment is meant to validate the developed code using a standard data set, namely the iRat data set used by OpenRatSLAM [1]. The second and third experiment are related to a previous experiment that used a Python implementation of RatSlam [2].

The resulting experience maps, for the iRat scenario depicted on Fig. 6(a), of OpenRatSLAM (ROS Lunar version) and the current proposed implementation are shown on Fig. 6(b) and (c), respectively. It is worth mentioning, that each time the OpenRatSLAM is run, a similar, but different map is generated. Then, the maps are never equal even executing the same code, i.e. OpenRatSLAM (ROS). It can be seen that both approaches obtained a similar map (Fig. 6(b) and (c))

Additionally, the execution times were compared (Fig. 6): 960 s and 236 s for the for OpenRatSLAM (ROS) and proposed library, respectively. Then, even with the ROS parallelization of modules, it had a larger execution time when compared with the implementation in C++, which also has a parallel mechanism.

An investigation about the execution time of the proposed implementation was carried out and it is shown on Fig. 7, which indicates that LocalView module execution time grows linearly by iteration steps and is where the algorithm expends more time.

Similarly, as done for the first experiment, the second and third scenario and their experience maps are shown on Fig. 8(a), (b), and (c), respectively. This scenario is the same used on [2], which used the Robodeck robot and a Python implementation of RatSlam. As expected, the experience maps obtained on Fig. 8(b), and (c) are similar to Fig. 8 and Fig. 7 of [2].

The execution time of the proposed implementation for the second and third experiment, which are depicted on Fig. 8, are shown on for Fig. 9. As for the first experiment, the LocalView module execution time grows linearly by iteration steps and this part of the algorithm expends most of the execution time.

(a) The iRat scenario.

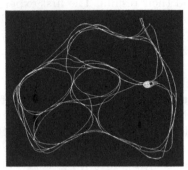

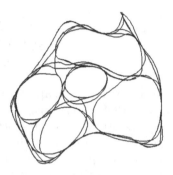

(b) The iRat scenario running under OpenRatSLAM (ROS). Execution time: 960s.

(c) The iRat scenario running under RatSlam implemented library. Execution time: 236s

Fig. 6. iRat scenario and the experience maps with OpenRatSLAM and the proposed implementation.

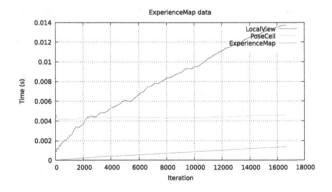

Fig. 7. The iRat scenario running under RatSlam implemented library. Modules execution time over iterations: LocalView (LV) average: 13.74 ms; PoseCell (PC) average: 4.56 ms; ExperienceMap (EM) average: 1.38 ms; Total time: 236.09 s.

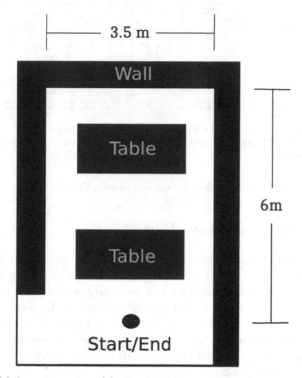

(a) Scenario used on [2]. The black boundary rectangles are walls whereas the black rectangles, on center, are tables. The robot starts and ends on the same point, it performs a counterclockwise turn on the lowest table, which is called a small loop, as well as a counterclockwise turn on the upper table that is called a large loop. Distance in meters (3.5m x 6m) For a further description of this environment see [2], where this scenario is depicted on Fig. 3 of [2].

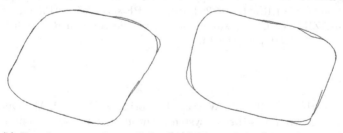

(b) Experience map in small loop (counterclockwise turn on the lowest black rectangle) obtained with the proposed library. It is, as expected, similar to Fig. 8 of [2].

(c) Experience map in large loop (counterclockwise turn on the upper black rectangle) obtained with the proposed library. It is, as expected, similar to Fig. 7 of [2].

Fig. 8. Scenario from [2] for Robodeck and the experience maps with the proposed implementation that must be similar to the ones on [2].

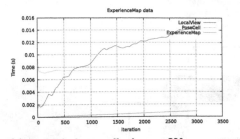
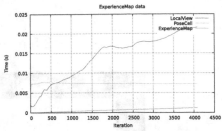

(a) Robodeck small loop: LV average: 14.48ms; PC average: 7.49ms; EM average: 0.87ms; Total time: 45.21s.

(b) Robodeck large loop: LV average: 21.62ms; PC average: 7.27mss; EM average: 1.22ms; Total time: 89.49s.

Fig. 9. Modules execution time over iterations for Fig. 8

5   Conclusions and Future Work

The proposed implementation has the basic infrastructure to put together the three RatSlam main modules. The framework is coded as a easy to use C++ library. Customized RatSlam modules can be easily added and tested keeping the same usage environment and the implementations of the other modules.

The proposed library was tested with three experiments and had similar results to previous literature. Additionally, its parallel mechanism allowed it to have a lower execution time when compared to a standard RatSlam algorithm, namely OpenRatSLAM (ROS).

The library described is meant to grow adding different RatSlam modules implementations. An other foresaw work is to insert the library as part of interesting robotic frameworks. For example, create a ROS node wrapper to for the library.

Acknowledgment. Our research group acknowledges financial support from FAPEMA (Proc. UNIVERSAL - 01294/16), CAPES/BRAZIL (Finance Code 001) and CNPq/BRAZIL. Sen Cheng was supported by the German Research Foundation (DFG) through SFB 1280, project B14.

References

1. Ball, D., Heath, S., Wiles, J., Wyeth, G., Corke, P., Milford, M.: Openratslam: an open source brain-based slam system. Auton. Robots **34**(3), 149–176 (2013). https://doi.org/10.1007/s10514-012-9317-9
2. Menezes, M.C., de Freitas, E.P., Cheng, S., de Oliveira, A.C.M., de Almeida Ribeiro, P.R.: A neuro-inspired approach to solve a simultaneous location and mapping task using shared information in multiple robots systems. In: 2018 15th International Conference on Control, Automation, Robotics and Vision (ICARCV), pp. 1753–1758, November 2018. https://doi.org/10.1109/ICARCV.2018.8581270
3. Milford, M.J., Wyeth, G.F.: Mapping a suburb with a single camera using a biologically inspired slam system. IEEE Trans. Robot. **24**(5), 1038–1053 (2008). https://doi.org/10.1109/TRO.2008.2004520

4. Milford, M., Wyeth, G.: Persistent navigation and mapping using a biologically inspired slam system. Int. J. Robot. Res. **29**(9), 1131–1153 (2010)
5. Milford, M., Wyeth, G., Prasser, D.: Ratslam on the edge: revealing a coherent representation from an overloaded rat brain. In: 2006 IEEE/RSJ International Conference on Intelligent Robots and Systems, pp. 4060–4065. IEEE (2006)
6. Milford, M.J., Wiles, J., Wyeth, G.F.: Solving navigational uncertainty using grid cells on robots. PLoS Comput. Biol. **6**(11), e1000995 (2010)
7. Milford, M.J., Wyeth, G.F., Prasser, D.: Ratslam: a hippocampal model for simultaneous localization and mapping. In: 2004 IEEE International Conference on Robotics and Automation, Proceedings, ICRA 2004, vol. 1, pp. 403–408. IEEE (2004)
8. Ni, J., Wang, C., Fan, X., Yang, S.X.: A bioinspired neural model based extended kalman filter for robot slam. Mathematical Problems in Engineering **2014** (2014)
9. Saeedi, S., Trentini, M., Seto, M., Li, H.: Multiple-robot simultaneous localization and mapping: a review. J. Field Robot. **33**(1), 3–46 (2016)
10. Silveira, L., et al.: An open-source bio-inspired solution to underwater slam*. IFAC-PapersOnLine **48**(2), 212–217 (2015)
11. Thrun, S., Burgard, W., Fox, D.: Probabilistic robotics In: Intelligent Robotics and Autonomous Agents. The MIT Press (2005)

Method for the Improvement of Knee Angle Accuracy Based on Kinect and IMU: Preliminary Results

D. Mayorca-Torres[1,2]([✉]), Julio C. Caicedo-Eraso[2],
and Diego H. Peluffo-Ordoñez[3,4]

[1] Facultad de Ingeniería, Universidad de la Mariana, Pasto, Colombia
dmayorca@umariana.edu.co
[2] Facultad de Ingeniería, Universidad de Caldas, Manizales, Colombia
[3] Escuela de Ciencias Matemáticas y Computacionales Yachay Tech,
San Miguel de Urcuquí, Ecuador
[4] Corporación Universitaria Autónoma de Nariño, Pasto, Colombia

Abstract. One way to identify musculoskeletal disorders in the lower limb is through the functional examination where the ranges of normality of the joints are evaluated. Currently, this test can be performed with technological support, with optical sensors and inertial measurement sensors (IMU) being the most used. Kinect has been widely used for the functional evaluation of the human body, however, there are some limits to the movements made in the depth plane and when there is occlusion of the limbs. Inertial measurement sensors (IMU) allow orientation and acceleration measurements to be obtained with a high sampling rate, with some restrictions associated with drift. This article proposes a methodology that combines the acceleration measures of the IMU and kinect sensors in two planes of movement (Frontal and sagittal). These measurements are filtered in the preprocessing stage according to a Kalman filter and are obtained from a mathematical equation that allows them to be merged. The fusion system data obtains acceptable RMS error values of 5.5° and an average consistency of 92.5% for the sagittal plane with respect to the goniometer technique. The data is shown through an interface that allows the visualization of knee joint kinematic data, as well as tools for the analysis of signals by the health professional.

Keywords: Multisensor fusion · Orientation estimation · Motion analysis · Knee flexion

1 Introduction

Currently, musculoskeletal disorders are becoming more frequent; every day we are exposed to new risks and accidents of work origin. According to the European Agency for Safety and Health at Work in 2010, this type of alterations accounted

V. R. Cota et al. (Eds.): LAWCN 2019, CCIS 1068, pp. 184–199, 2019.
https://doi.org/10.1007/978-3-030-36636-0_14

for more than 59% of all recognized occupational diseases in the world [1]. While in 2015 the World Health Organization indicated that around 40 million people in Europe had been diagnosed with some type of disorder [2]. Globally, musculoskeletal disorders due to cumulative trauma related to limb work have been studied extensively, but less attention has been paid to the epidemiology of musculoskeletal disorders and injuries in the lower extremities [3,4].

The health problems range from small discomforts and pains to more serious medical conditions that force them to request sick leave and even to receive medical treatment. One way to identify this type of disorder is through postural evaluation; characterized by the description of movement in relation to fundamental measures such as displacement and angular range of joints [5]. This evaluation is carried out by a specialized professional, who must examine that the movements of the joints are carried out within the range of normality [6]. Among the technologies used for the evaluation of joint movement are optical sensors, inertial measurement sensors and hybrids [7–9].

Currently, advances in sensors and computer technologies have provided new opportunities to optimize the capture processes, allowing the introduction of stimuli in the measurement processes to be minimized. Motion capture systems are the most used in clinical applications, since they allow the identification of three-dimensional patterns objectively and precisely [10,11]. The market offers high precision motion capture systems within which are Vicon (2017), OptiTrack (2017) and Qualisys (2017). Its disadvantage lies in the technological infrastructure that is required for its use, as well as the placement of markers in the joints in order to model the movement of the joints over time [12]. That is why much of the research is aimed at the search for low-cost and adaptable technological solutions for the conditions and laboratories in Colombia. In this sense the depth sensor of Kinect (2017) has been widely used for the functional evaluation of the movements of the human body. Its advantage lies in the fact that the placement of markers on the skin is not needed and its accuracy is comparable to that of some commercial equipment, providing the location of 20 points of articulations in an accurate manner [13]. Studies suggest that the Kinect sensor offers high repeatability compared to stereo vision devices based on markingres. In the same way, its measurements have been compared with systems such as Qualisys (2017), whose correlation for treading displacements is 78% and angles of 58% [14].

However, some authors suggest that Kinect may be viable for use in clinical settings, considering specific performance limits for the capture of some unconventional movements [15]. Nonconventional movements are those movements that are made in the plane of depth and with occlusion of the extremities. In the same way, other authors report certain disadvantages of Kinect against the use of other technologies, mainly due to its low sampling and sensibility with distance [16]. The inertial measurement sensors (IMU) allow obtaining measurements of speed, orientation and gravitational forces based on the use of precision triaxial gyroscopes, accelerometers and magnetometers. Studies such as that of Liu et al. [17] use the combination of biaxial accelerometers and 3D gyroscopes to obtain knee angle measurements with reliability using root mean square error (RMS).

Recent advances in the field of integrated circuits have led to these systems have merged with other technologies to solve much of the problems of the kinematics of the human body. That is to say, this combination allows us to take advantage of the advantages of the 3D positioning provided by optical sensors such as Kinect and the precision provided by IMU sensors for the measurement of angles [18,19].

This is how in this paper an exploratory study on signal acquisition and processing for the measurement of angles of the knee joint is presented from a system that combines kinect and IMU sensors. This work is structured as follows: Sect. 2 describes the methodological design where the stages of preprocessing and filtering the signals are described to obtain knee angle measurement. Section 3 describes the results and discussion and finally the conclusions and future work in Sect. 4. One of the great contributions of this study is the development of a methodology that allows the correction. This allows the correction and improvement of the measurements made by conventional methods.

2   Materials and Methods

This section describes the software architecture of the proposed system for the process of acquisition, calibration, calculation of joint kinematics, preprocessing and visualization of the data as can be seen in the block diagram explained in Fig. 1.

Fig. 1. Block diagram of the stages of preprocessing, filtering and visualization of data.

2.1   Data Acquisition

The Data was captured taking into account the population selection methods, protocols and functional evaluation guides of the lower limb. The database considered in this study was obtained from a register of knee flexion movements of 4 healthy subjects aged between [18–28] years, the register of sociodemographic variables and anthropometric variables. Knee flexion movements "squats" were performed due to the low level of joint overlap. Twenty-five repetitions of flexion of the frontal plane and 25 in the sagittal plane were performed with an angular velocity of movement within the range 250–400 $\frac{grad}{s}$. The movements were monitored and supervised by a professional specialist in the area. The technique used to contrast the measurements was through the goniometry technique, a protocol described in the clinical-functional evaluation of the human body [26].

Statistical analysis was carried out using the PSPP 4.0 statistical tool to determine the reliability and consistency of the system. The measurements obtained by Kinect, IMU and Kinect + IMU were evaluated. The statistical measures used for this comparison were the mean and the standard deviation of the mean square root (RMS) of the peak values. Consistency allows to determine the degree of stability of the results when the measurement is repeated with the same instrument under identical conditions. For the quantification of this parameter, two sessions were planned with a difference of 10 days. Since the primary objective is to guarantee the repeatability of the instrument, the optical system calibration and sensor positioning protocols were strictly followed. The statistical measures used were the average and the standard deviation of RMS and the intraclass correlation coefficient (ICC). The null hypothesis is rejected if the alpha value associated with the observed result is equal to or less than a significance level of 0.05. For the estimation of the significance parameters, the intra and intertester validation criteria were used as a reference for measures of maximum active knee flexion and extension with universal goniometers [25].

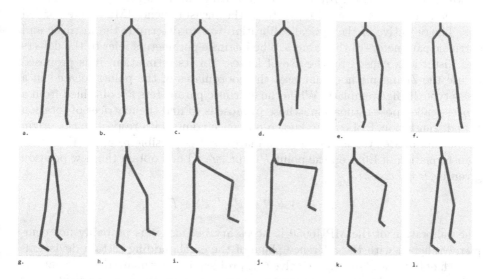

Fig. 2. The movements (a–f) correspond to the frontal plane. The movements (g–l) correspond to the sagittal plane.

For each subject, the registration of both the Kinect sensor skeleton data and the IMU angles was recorded. The configuration used to capture the Kinect sensor data was that of a fixed camera placed at a height of 1.5 m and at a distance of 2.1 m from the subject. This was connected via USB and connected to the computer was through the use of Kinect SDK. The measured data correspond to the coordinates (x, y, z) in meters of the hip, knee and ankle joints for the left leg in time. The sequence of knee flexion movement for the frontal plane can be seen in Fig. 2 in the images (a–f), while for the sagittal plane (g–h).

While the data corresponding to the IMU system corresponds to the angle measurement between body segments of hip-knee and knee-ankle. The device is made up of an Arduino processing unit, two MPU6050 sensors and an HC-06 bluetooth module. Each MPU6050 sensor incorporates an accelerometer and triaxial gyroscope, this information is sent by I2C communication protocol to the Arduino. The Arduino data is sent through the Bluetooth protocol at a frequency of 120 Hz to the PC where the software modules for filtering and processing the signals are located.

2.2   System Calibration

The kinect sensor establishes the origin of the coordinate system on itself defined by the axes (x', y', z'). The positive axis of the x extends to the left and the positive axis of the y extends upwards. The positive z axis extends through the depth plane of the sensor. The origin of the coordinate system was transferred to a fixed position, since the idea was that this would not change with the change of position of the sensor. After this, the optical calibration process (Kinect) and the determination of the initial state of the measurement (IMU) were carried out. The objective of the optical calibration was to determine the intrinsic and extrinsic parameters of the camera. The intrinsic parameters refer to the defects and distortions caused by the use of lenses. For its estimation, it is proposed to use the Zhang method that uses the coordinates of the points located in a chess type 2D flat template. While the extrinsic parameters are obtained from a process called pose estimation, whose purpose is to find the matrices of rotation R and translation T of certain known reference points with respect to the origin of the coordinate system. From these matrices it is possible to apply the linear transformation of Eq. 1 on the point $P = (x', y', z')$ and obtain the new position given by $P = (x, y, z)$.

$$(x, y, z) = R * (x', y', z') + T \qquad (1)$$

The calibration of the MPU6050 is necessary because it is probably not completely aligned with the reference plane of the earth, adding certain deviations to each of the axes. One way to solve this problem is to estimate these deviations (offsets) and in this way compensate for the errors on the measurements. The algorithm constantly modifies the offset trying to eliminate the error with the real measure and in the reference orientation by making $a_x = a_y = a_z = 0$ and $g_x = g_y = g_z = 0$. The offsets are calculated for a total of 200 measurements and then averaged in order to obtain the 6 adjustment parameters.

2.3   Measurement of Kinect Angles

The model for the measurement of angles for Kinect takes as input parameters the cartesian coordinates of the hip joints $P_h = (x_h, y_h, z_h)$, knee $P_k = (x_k, y_k, z_k)$ and ankle $P_a = (x_a, y_a, z_a)$ obtained from the skeleton. These points allow to define the model vectors as $\overrightarrow{v_{hk}}$ and as $\overrightarrow{v_{hk}}$ shown in Eqs. 2 and 3.

$$\overrightarrow{v_{hk}} = (x_h - x_k, y_h - y_k, z_h - z_k) \qquad (2)$$

$$\vec{v_{kt}} = (x_k - x_t, y_k - y_t, z_k - z_t) \tag{3}$$

Additionally it is possible to obtain the lengths of the segments of $S_1 = ||\vec{v_{hk}}||$ and $S_2 = ||\vec{v_{ka}}||$. From this data and the use of trigonometric properties, the orientations of each of the vectors along the orthogonal planes is possible. The convention used for the measurement of the angles was that of Tait-Bryan in which an arrangement is established (ρ, ϕ, θ). The angle ρ also called Pitch is defined as the relative angle on the x-axis with respect to the earth, the angle ϕ measures the angle of rotation of the axis and "Roll" and the angle θ measures the angle of rotation of the z-axis "Yaw" [20]. Finally, the angle formed by both segments in the sagittal plane at the time instant t can be calculated from the difference of the angle $\rho_{knee}(t)$ as follows Eq. 4,

$$\rho_{knee}(t) = \rho_{hk}(t) - \rho_{ka}(t) \tag{4}$$

Given the configuration of the system and placement of the device, the component $\rho_{knee}(t)$ is established as that which represents the angle of the knee in the sagittal plane. By applying the point product theorem on the vectors v_{hk} and v_{ka} it is possible to estimate the angle between the segments as shown in Eq. 5.

$$\rho_k = \frac{\vec{v_{hk}}\vec{v_{ka}}}{||v_{hk}||.||v_{ka}||} \tag{5}$$

2.4   Measurement of IMU Sensor Angles

The data captured from the MPU6050 sensor are the angular frequency (w_x, w_y, w_z) and the acceleration (a_x, a_y, a_z) in each of the orthogonal axes. By modifying the sensor registers it was possible to configure the sensitivity of both the gyroscope at $500 \frac{grad}{s}$ and the accelerometer $16\,g$. It should be noted that the origin of the system is unique for both devices, and for this it must be guaranteed that the orientation of the sensor in the initial position must coincide with that of the sensor described in Sect. 2.1. In the same way, consider a complementary filter that combines the information of the accelerometer and gyroscope from a proportionality constant k_1, whose purpose is to decrease the drift of the system (see Eq. 6).

$$\rho_{hk}(t) = k_1 * [\rho_{hk}(t-1) + \int_0^t w_x(t)\,dt] + (1-k_1) * atan(\frac{a_y}{\sqrt{a_x^2 + a_z^2}}) \tag{6}$$

Given that it is sought to obtain the existing orientation between two consecutive body segments, two MPU6050 sensors are used, placed as follows: The first sensor is fixed between the hip-knee joints and the second between the knee-ankle. From this configuration you can obtain the data ρ_{hk} and ρ_{ka} respectively. Like the kinect sensor, the angle formed by the hip-knee and knee-ankle segments can be calculated from the difference in angle ρ shown in Eq. 7 as long as the sensors are oriented on the plane in the that the movement is exercised.

$$\rho_k(t) = \rho_{hk}(t) - \rho_{ka}(t) \tag{7}$$

2.5   Preprocessing of Signals

This section describes the filtering process of the data obtained by the kinect sensor and those obtained through the gyroscopes system as shown in the Fig. 3.

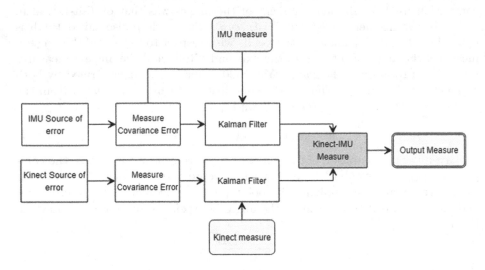

Fig. 3. Diagram of the preprocessing stages.

2.6   IMU and Kinect Controller Data Noise Correction

The first step to improve the data quality of the IMU component is the error compensation of the accelerometer due to different types of noise that may be present in the signal. The proposed filter is the Kalman Filter, this technique allows the filtering and prediction of the measurement in linear systems whose noise can be modeled as a Gaussian distribution. This filter contains a process model and a measurement model, where Eqs. 8 and 9 correspond to the equation of the process and the measurement.

$$x_k = Ax_{k-1} + Bu_k + w_{k-1} \tag{8}$$

$$z_k = Hx_k + v_k \tag{9}$$

Therefore, the Kalman filter estimates the state based on the time and measurement update equations, these are determined by Eqs. 10 and 11.

$$x_k^- = Ax_{k-1} + Bu_k \tag{10}$$

$$P_k^- = AP_{k-1}A^T + Q \tag{11}$$

In addition to the measured estimate of the state of the system, the Kalman filter also provides the uncertainty estimate. The process and measurement noise approximates a Gaussian distribution with mean equal to zero, $(0, Q)$ y $p(v) = N(0, R)$ i.e Q and R are the covariance matrices. Equation 12 calculates the Kalman gain, while Eqs. 13 and 14 update the state of the measure and the error covariance.

$$K_k^- = P_k^- H^T (H P_k^- H^T + R)^{-1} \tag{12}$$

$$\hat{x}_k = \hat{x}_k^- A K_k (z_k - H \hat{x}_k^-) \tag{13}$$

$$P_k = (I - K_k H) A P_k^- \tag{14}$$

Where K_k^- is the gain matrix, $\hat{x}_k^-$ is the estimation of the state priori at the instant k and $\hat{x}_k$ the subsequent state. While P_k^- is the prior error estimate of the covariance and P_k the posterior estimate of the error. From the Kalman state equations shown above we propose a model for the measure of the angle $\rho_{knee}(t)$ implemented and described by the Eq. 15.

$$\rho_k^- = A\rho_{k-1} + Bu_k \tag{15}$$

Taking the values of $u_k = 0$ y $A = 1$ it is possible to determine the process and measurement equations described by Eqs. 16 and 17 respectively for both the Kinect sensor and the IMU device.

$$\rho_k^- = A\rho_{k-1} \tag{16}$$

$$v_k = -Hx_k + z_k \tag{17}$$

Finally, for the merging of data from the two signals an alignment of the signal in the time domain is required, for the fulfillment of this objective the synchronization method proposed by Grzegorz [21] is applied. The aim of the synchronization of the IMU and Kinect signals is to find the time difference τ between two data streams. To synchronize both signals, the IMU signal is sub-sampling at the Kinect frequency. The average frequency of the study was 29.6 frames per second, taking into account that this sampling frequency is not constant and depends on both the resolution and the availability of the device. From this a window size of 4 s is determined, for the shifting of the IMU signal on the Kinect signal within a range of 0–4 s. For each displacement, the correlation between the signals is estimated, considering that the signals are synchronized when the maximum correlation value is detected. The value of τ_{max} is added to the timestamp of the IMU samples to align with the Kinect signal:

$$(\rho_{Imu} * \rho_{kinect})(\tau) = \int \rho_{Imu}(t) * \rho_{kinect}(t + \tau) dt \tag{18}$$

Where the synchronization parameter is obtained from the equation:

$$\tau_{max} = max[(\rho_{Imu} * \rho_{kinect})(\tau)] \tag{19}$$

Once the signals are synchronized, a method of merging the IMU and Kinect sensor data from the following algebraic operation is proposed:

$$\rho_{Fusion} = K_1 * \rho_{Imu} + K_2 * \rho_{kinect} \tag{20}$$

The values of K_1 and K_2 are selected from the orientation planes of 0° (Frontal) and 90° (Sagittal).

3 Results and Discussion

The first stage of this investigation refers to the acquisition of data by the IMU and Kinect sensor. A stage of temporal synchronization of the two signals is necessary, given the implications of the lack of this in relation to the error of the measurement. This variability has been estimated by authors such as [22, 23] within a range of 7.44 to 9.6° for synchronized and non-synchronized signals.

The synchronization algorithm used was that of maximum correlation since it proved to be effective for the estimation of the phase shift of the signals [24]. The displacement delta time was taken from the estimated IMU sensor signal $\delta t = 8.3$ ms. The maximum correlation was found iteratively and a maximum value was found for a time value of 24.15 ms. Given the high involvement of the RMS value with respect to the speed of movement, it was suggested to perform movements at an average speed of 400 °/s.

In the preprocessing stage, the Kalman filter was applied to the angle measurements for both the Kinect and the IMU sensors independently, as discussed in Sect. 2.4. For the application of this it was necessary to estimate the covariance matrices Q and R by means of the tuning method applying the model of Eqs. 16 and 17 for both signals. The R value of both signals was obtained by calculating the variance in the initial state of the system in static posture, i.e. for ρ. This procedure was performed for a time of 20 s, the calculated values were 0.028 for kinect and 0.44 for the IMU. These errors are associated to the angular velocity component given the model of estimation of angles given by Eqs. 4 and 5. The value of Q was estimated taking into account the behavior

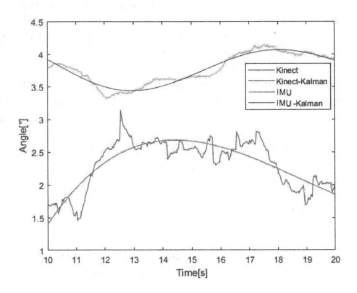

Fig. 4. Calculation of variance of the signal in initial condition.

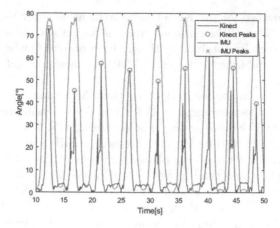

Fig. 5. Signals obtained from knee flexion of the frontal plane.

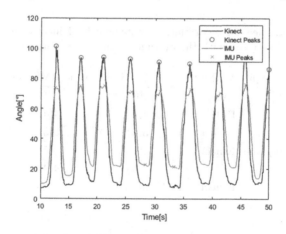

Fig. 6. Signals obtained from sagittal plane knee flexion.

of the signals as shown in Fig. 4, making variations on the signal with values between 0.01–0.05, finding no major differences between them.

Once the signals were filtered, the experimental test was carried out with the 4 subjects following the established protocols and the average RMS value measurements were compared with the value of the goniometer between both signals. The results obtained for the repetitions of the angles for hip-flexion in the frontal and sagittal plane for a total for a time of 50 s can be observed in Figs. 5 and 6.

The RMS was obtained using the three methods: capture from the Kinect sensor, IMU sensors and Kinect-IMU system for sessions 1 and 2 in the frontal and sagittal planes (See Table 1). In the frontal plane the RMS values for session 1 were estimated to be 19(12) for the Kinect measurement, 4(3) for the measurement of IMU and 3(3) for the proposed system IMU + Kinect. For session

2, 23(18) were obtained for the Kinect measurement, 4(4) for the measurement of IMU and 3(3). These data obtained from deviation with kinect [19–23°] are comparable to the results obtained by Bonneche et al. (2014) where deviations of measurement are established between [21–24°] for measurements in the frontal plane of knee flexion.

In the same way, in the sagittal plane the RMS values for session 1 were 10(5) for the Kinect measurement, 4(4) for the IMU measurement and 3 (2.3) for the proposed IMU Kinect system. For session 2, 9(5) were obtained for the measurement of Kinect, 4(4) for the measurement of IMU and 2(2.1). The results of deviation of Kinect for the case of measurement of knee flexion angle were lower in the sagittal plane than in the frontal plane. This could be interpreted in the following way, since the knee movement in the sagittal plane is done taking advantage of the field of vision of the camera on the plane (x, y), the measurement is obtained mainly by the information of the pixels and not of the depth plane.

Table 1. RMS and knee angle correlation coefficient for Kinect from session 1 and 2. The RMS value is expressed with the average (standard deviation).

Exercise type	Method	RMS Session 1	RMS Session 2
Frontal plane	Kinect	19(12)	23(18)
	IMU	4(3)	4(4)
	Kinect + IMU	3(3)	3(3)
Sagittal plane	Kinect	10(5)	9(5)
	IMU	4(4)	4(4)
	Kinect + IMU	3(2.3)	3(2.5)

Finally, the comparison between the measurements of both sessions is performed by ICC as observed in Table 2.

Table 2. The reliability of the test was estimated using the intraclass correlation coefficients. The peaks angles are expressed with the average (standard deviation).

Exercise type	Method	Peak Angle Session 1	Peak Angle Session 2	ICC
Frontal plane	Kinect	56(12)	52(18)	0,61
	IMU	76(4)	72(4)	0,78
	Kinect + IMU	70(3)	73(3)	0,90
Sagittal plane	Kinect	90(6)	89(5)	0,66
	IMU	75(4)	75(4)	0,75
	Kinect + IMU	71(3)	72(3)	0,93

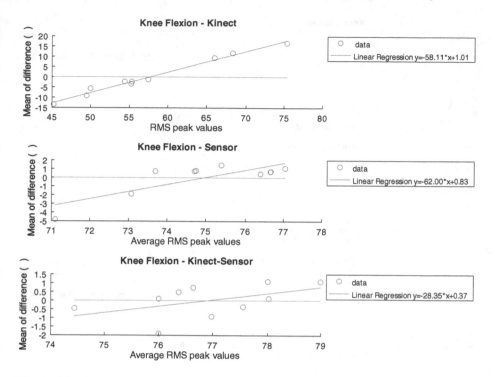

Fig. 7. The X axes are the average peak angles of knee flexion in the frontal plane. The Y axes are the average of the differences in degrees with respect to the goniometer technique. The green line (average) is used to indicate a perfect agreement between devices. The red line is a line of linear regression. (Color figure online)

The results found for knee flexion in the frontal plane, in session 1 the average knee angle for the subjects was 56(12) for the Kinect measurement, 76(4) for the measurement of IMU and 70(3) for the reference system as can be seen in Table 2. For session 2, the average of the subjects was 52(18) for the Kinect measure, 72(4) for the measurement of IMU and 73(3) for the reference system. For knee flexion in the sagittal plane, in session 1 the average knee angle for the subjects was 89(5) for the measurement with Kinect device, 75(4) for the measurement of IMU and 72(3) for the reference system.

The level of error can be represented from a dispersion curve, which represents the difference between the proposed technique with respect to the reference technique. In addition, a linear regression is included that represents the proportion of the error with respect to the maximum angle reached for each squat. Figures 7 and 8 describe the error differences for the frontal and sagittal plane respectively. Finally, the values obtained for the merged Kinect + IMU system show lower error values with respect to the IMU and Kinect techniques for the different configurations and sessions. In this way, with the fused system, measurements can be obtained with an accuracy of 5.5° and an average consistency

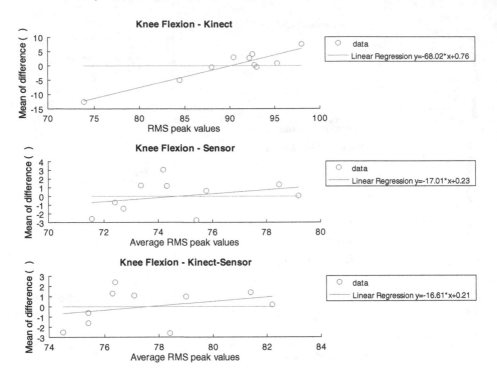

Fig. 8. The X axes are the average peak angles of knee flexion in the sagital plane. The Y axes are the average of the differences in degrees between Kinect and goniometer. The green line (average) is used to indicate a perfect agreement between devices. The red line is a line of linear regression. (Color figure online)

of 92.5%. In contrast, the IMU system without data fusion moves away from the acceptable range for measuring knee angles, since it is approx. 8°. This aspect is of great importance since the medical experts, interested in analyzing the angles of the joints, require a precision of six degrees for the upper extremities 4.5° and 5.5° for the lower extremities. It is necessary to clarify that the errors associated with the IMU sensor are also related to the positioning of the sensors on the body segments, reaching a variability of up to 3.34% when placed with the help of the goniometer. It is necessary to highlight that the fusion of data from this preliminary study has some limitations in relation to the occlusion of some movements due to the configuration used (frontal and sagittal), which implies that for clinical use it is necessary to explore other variables that may influence Obtaining a reliable measure. In addition, the objective of this study is not to replace a method as precise as the use of the universal goniometer (used to measure angles in static positions), what it seeks is to provide a tool that allows the dynamic measurement of angles. A potential use of this tool is the monitoring and monitoring of supervised therapeutic treatments.

4   Conclusions

In summary, a quantitative comparison was made between our fusion results with methods commonly used in the clinical setting. This work presents a methodology that allows the improvement of knee angle measurement through a fusion system between Kinect and IMU sensors for movements in the sagittal and frontal planes for two speeds of movement. A method of synchronization and characterization of both signals is proposed. The approach adopted is to merge the low frequency angle measurement of the Kinect sensor and the angle measurement of the high frequency IMU sensors. This requires the application of a Kalman filter. The experimental results show that the Kalman filter helps to improve the accuracy of the estimation of the state of the system, helping to stabilize the angle measurement for the selected movements. The methods used make it possible to obtain a measurement with an acceptable minimum RMS error in comparison with traditionally used instruments such as the goniometer.

The IMU and Kinect-IMU approaches are within the minimum acceptable range for measurement of lower limb angles. In general, the therapist requires more precision for a certain part of the body during a specific rehabilitation movement, and the use of Kinect alone can not provide such precision. This method will allow future correction of the data delivered by kinect and obtain a skeleton with greater precision. This study incorporated the use of IMU sensors to estimate the angle measurement and not the position of the joints. Therefore, these results must be taken with great care, and a broader exploration is necessary at different distances from the device and the different orientations in which the movement can be performed, the frontal and sagittal planes being studied in this investigation. Additionally, this work suggests a future work, such as obtaining a 3D corrected skeleton from the data obtained by the IMU device, and expanded to other joints of the human body.

Acknowledgements. This research work is supported by the seed group 'SIngBio Seedbed of Research in Engineering and Biomedical Sciences' of the Universidad de Caldas. In the same way, this work was supported by the Mechatronic Engineering research Group of the Mariana University. Also the authors are very grateful for the valuable support given by SDAS Research Group (www.sdas-group.com).

References

1. Rienk, P., Jensen, P.L., Tony, L.: Los trastornos musculoesqueléticos de origen laboral en los Estados miembros de la Unión Europea (2010)
2. Asociación internacional de la Seguridad Social, La prevención de las enfermedades profesionales (2013)
3. De Jaén, U.: Tratamiento de la tendinopatía rotuliana
4. D'Souza, J., Franzblau, A., Werner, R.: Review of epidemiologic studies on occupational factors and lower extremity musculoskeletal and vascular disorders and symptoms. J. Occup. Rehabil. **15**(2), 129–165 (2005)
5. Cifuentes, C., Martínez, F., Romero, E.: Análisis teórico y computacional de la marcha normal y patológica: una revisión. Rev. Med. **18**(2), 182 (2010)

6. Mariana Haro, D.: Laboratorio de análisis de marcha y movimiento, Rev. Médica Clínica Las Condes, **25**(2), 237–247 (2014)
7. Støvring, N.M., et al.: Multi-kinect skeleton fusion for enactive games. In: Brooks, A.L., Brooks, E. (eds.) ArtsIT/DLI -2016. LNICST, vol. 196, pp. 173–180. Springer, Cham (2017). https://doi.org/10.1007/978-3-319-55834-9_20
8. Li, S., Pathirana, P.N., Caelli, T.: Multi-kinect skeleton fusion for physical rehabilitation monitoring. In: 2014 36th Annual International Conference of the IEEE Engineering in Medicine and Biology Society, EMBC 2014, pp. 5060–5063 (2014)
9. Moon, S., Park, Y., Ko, D.W., Suh, I.H.: Multiple kinect sensor fusion for human skeleton tracking using Kalman filtering. Int. J. Adv. Robot. Syst. **13**(2) (2016)
10. Bravo, D.A., Rengifo, C.F., Agredo, W.: Comparación de dos sistemas de captura de movimiento por medio de las trayectorias articulares de marcha. Rev. Mex. Ing. Biomédica **37**(2), 149–160 (2017)
11. Calderita, L.V., Bandera, J.P., Bustos, P., Skiadopoulos, A.: Model-based reinforcement of kinect depth data for human motion capture applications. Sensors (Switzerland) **13**(7), 8835–8855 (2013)
12. Dao, T.T., Pouletaut, P., Gamet, D., Christine Ho Ba Tho, M.: Real-time rehabilitation system of systems for monitoring the biomechanical feedbacks of the musculoskeletal system. In: Nguyen, V.-H., Le, A.-C., Huynh, V.-N. (eds.) Knowledge and Systems Engineering. AISC, vol. 326, pp. 553–565. Springer, Cham (2015). https://doi.org/10.1007/978-3-319-11680-8_44
13. Connork, P., Ross, P.: Biometric recognition by gait: a survey of modalities and features. Comput. Vis. Image Underst. **167**, 1–27 (2018)
14. Brandão, A.F., Dias, D.R.C., Castellano, G., Parizotto, N.A., Trevelin, L.C.: RehabGesture: an alternative tool for measuring human movement. Telemed. e-Health **22**(7), 584–589 (2016)
15. Napoli, A., Glass, S., Ward, C., Tucker, C., Obeid, I.: Performance analysis of a generalized motion capture system using microsoft kinect 2.0. Biomed. Signal Process. Control **38**, 265–280 (2017)
16. Pérez-Alba, K., León-Aguilar, A., Salido-Ruiz, R.: Estudio comparativo de métodos para el análisis del movimiento en 2D: ventajas y desventajas del uso de marcadores. Memorias del Congr. Nac. Ing. Biomédica **4**(1), 294–297 (2017)
17. Lin, C.H., Liu, J.C., Lin, S.Y.: 3-dimension personal identification and its applications based on kinect, pp. 143–146 (2016)
18. Destelle, F., et al.: Low-cost accurate skeleton tracking based on fusion of kinect and wearable inertial sensors. In: 2014 22nd European Signal Processing Conference (EUSIPCO), Portugal, pp. 371–375 (2014)
19. Bo, A., Hayashibe, M., Poignet, P., Padilha, A.: Joint angle estimation in rehabilitation with inertial sensors and its integration with Kinect. In: Conference Proceedings IEEE Engineering in Medicine and Biology Society, Boston, pp. 3479–3483 (2011)
20. Diebel, J.: Representing attitude: euler angles, unit quaternions, and rotation vectors, Stanford (2006)
21. Glonek, G., Wojciechowski, A.: Hybrid orientation based human limbs motion tracking method, Standford, Switzerland, vol. 17, no. 12, p. 2857 (2017)
22. Chen, S., Brantley, J., Kim, T., Lach, J.: Characterizing and minimizing synchronization and calibration errors in inertial body sensor networks. In: Proceedings of the Fifth International Conference on Body Area Networks - BodyNets, Corfu, Greece, p. 138 (2010)

23. Wåhslén, J., Orhan, I., Lindh, T.: Local time synchronization in bluetooth piconets for data fusion using mobile phones. In: 2011 International Conference on Body Sensor Networks, pp. 133–138. IEEE Xplore, Dallas (2011)
24. Tannous, H., Istrate, D., Benlarbi-Delai, A., Sarrazin, J.: A new multi-sensor fusion scheme to improve the accuracy of knee flexion kinematics for functional rehabilitation movements sensors, vol. 16, no. 11. MEDLINE, Switzerland (2016)
25. Brosseau, L., et al.: Intra-and intertester reliability and criterion validity of the parallelogram and universal goniometers for measuring maximum active knee flexion and extension of patients with knee restrictions. Arch. Phys. Med. Rehabil. **82**(3), 396–402 (2001)
26. Lesmes, J.D.: Evaluación clínico-funcional del movimiento corporal humano. Ed. Médica Panamericana (2007)

Eye-Tracking Data Analysis During Cognitive Task

Rafael Nobre Orsi$^{(\boxtimes)}$, Davi Araujo Dal Fabbro ,
and Carlos Eduardo Thomaz

Centro Univesitario FEI, Sao Bernardo do Campo, SP, Brazil
{rafaelorsi,ddfabbro,cet}@fei.edu.br

Abstract. This work investigates the use of eye-tracking as a method for analysis of mental effort in cognitive tasks. From a trivial task of counting objects, the proposal of this work is to present a study on the reactions of the nervous system through visual stimuli to the cognitive system. Our experimental results show that there is a relationship between the cognitive load and pupillary diameter variation, reinforcing the idea that the pupil is a sensitive indicator of mental effort. We believe that pupil diameter measurement can be used as a performance descriptor in cognitive tasks.

Keywords: Mental effort · Eye-tracking · Cognitive counting

1 Introduction

Most of the studies involving human cognition are based on local mapping methods, acquired on a spatial and temporal scale about brain activity, such as, for example, the mapping of brain activity by functional Magnetic Resonance Imaging (fMRI) and the mapping of electrical activity measured on the scalp by means of electroencephalography (EEG) [11]. However, from an approach still little used in studies of the science of cognition, arise the eye tracking devices, which through the measurement of the pupil diameter, offer a promising measure of the workload of the cognitive system, [16,36], opening a window to more accurate interpretations when combined with most common methods (local mapping) [8] or until conceiving alternatives to studies of cognition in environments less invasive and uncomfortable for the individuals, thus enabling, as in this work, to apply simplified experimental protocols to of measuring the performance of individuals in basic cognitive tasks, such as counting objects and multiplying numbers [12,18,43].

The method of study of cognition through pupil measurement arose in 1960 [19]. From then on, Eckhard Hess, precursor of this method, initiated a series of studies about the pupillary reactions coming from mental activities [17,20, 21]. He found that pupils dilate substantially when people perform arithmetic operations of multiplication, dilating to a greater degree for difficult tasks and to a lesser degree for easy tasks [18].

V. R. Cota et al. (Eds.): LAWCN 2019, CCIS 1068, pp. 200–219, 2019.
https://doi.org/10.1007/978-3-030-36636-0_15

From the findings of Hess and still manually, that is, without an automated mechanism for acquisition of the pupillary signal, Beatty and Kahneman (a Nobel laureate in economics) helped to disseminate this method [4–7,15,22–28]. They showed in a cognitive experiment involving memorization and arithmetic operations, whose name was "Add-1" [23], that the pupil can dilate up to 50% of its original size in just 5 s.

The main problems reported in pupillary measurement experiments were related to the exhaustive manual work of measuring each eye photograph, but from the year 2000 arose the first automated equipment to perform the eye tracking. The first patent was filed by Sandra Marshall [31] and, since then, has substantially increased the publications of studies on human cognition involving eye tracking and the automated pupillary measurement.

Some of these studies, such as the detection of psychological stress [33], the observation of physiological signs in decision making [9], the comparison of learning methods [29] and the analysis of cognitive engagement in mental tasks [2], provide indications that it is possible quantitatively to estimate the mental effort intensity in cognitive tasks, pointing the index of variation pupil as an indicator sensitive to the mental workload.

In this work, the cognitive test proposal was based on an object counting task. The main studies about how people do count indicates that there are two main methods that are used to in different situations. In the first method, the counting is fast, accurate and done instantly for small groups (perceptive) or by the arithmetic of units for larger (progressive) groups. Already in the second method is done by approximation of the quantity based on known and convenient patterns [43]. Thus, with the glimpse that the use of counting strategies can reduce the intensity of mental effort employed in a task, an experiment was developed involving the counting of large quantities of objects, arranged in geometric formats that induce the use of mathematical operations to speed up the process.

The objective of this work is to present a study about the reactions of the nervous system through visual stimuli to the cognitive system and, more specifically, verify the intensity of mental effort of individuals in tasks of counting objects. In this study two hypotheses were tested. The first investigates whether counting tasks with multiplication operations stimulate dilation of the pupils in proportion to the complexity of the calculation. In this study two hypotheses were tested. The first investigates whether counting tasks with multiplication operations stimulate dilation of the pupils in proportion to the complexity of the calculation. This hypothesis has already been partially evidenced by [19] when mentioning the increase of the mental workload in multiplication tasks with more than 1 digit and by [1] when mentioning the sensitivity of the pupillary signal in multiplication tasks, but, in an unprecedented way, in this experiment this hypothesis will be tested in a task that includes the counting of objects, which consequently increases the degree of difficulty due to the need to memorize the quantities for the calculation [12,29,41]. In a complementary way, the second hypothesis investigates whether there is alteration in pupillary diameter variation when grouping the objects for counting in subsets or in geometric formats, facilitating the association of other skills such as the multiplication of numbers or the sum of smaller subsets.

2   Fundamentals of Human Vision

Vision is the dominant sense among the five senses of the human body, for the eyes concentrate about 70% of the sensory receptors of the whole human body and, the cognitive processes mobilize about 40% of the cerebral cortex to process visual information [30].

The eye, for being a visceral organ, is a key point in this work, because besides being a receiver sensor that allows the individual to see what happens around them, it is also an emitter sensor that reflects the sympathetic and parasympathetic activations of the nervous system [30].

2.1   Eye Movement

Eye movements can be divided into internal movements, which are dilations and pupillary constrictions, and external movements, which are classified into fixations and saccades. Fixation is a time interval in which the eyes remain fixed at one point and saccades are the eye movements between the fixation from one point to another. These external movements are controlled by six extrinsic muscles of the eye bulb and, as shown in Fig. 1, the actions of each muscle can be easily deduced from their names and locations [30].

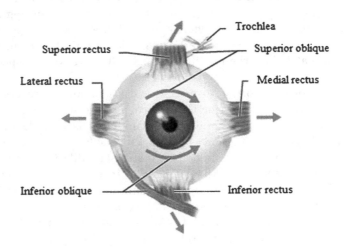

Fig. 1. Eye movements (right eye) [30].

In the counting test proposed in this work, the eye tracking was classified into fixations, with saccades and their respective duration times was timed and organized sequentially, allowing to analyze all the action of the participants during the test.

2.2   Pupil Size

Constriction and the dilation of the pupil are controlled by the muscles of the iris, which is composed of the sphincter and dilator muscles [3]. The iris is responsible for internal eye movements and its function is to regulate the amount of light entering the eye. However, may occur pupillary constrictions and dilations unrelated the light control functions, because the iris muscles are innervated by the parasympathetic and sympathetic fibers of the nervous system (as shown in Fig. 2), which allows actions resulting from of other stimuli or inhibitions of the Autonomic Nervous System (ANS), such as dilations caused by mental effort [30].

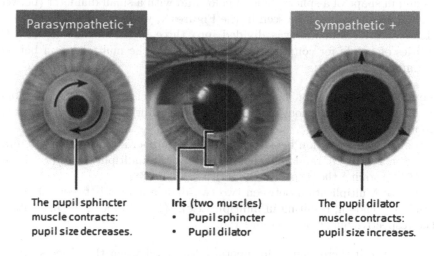

Fig. 2. Dilation and constriction of the pupil [30].

3   Materials and Method

This section presents the set of materials and methods used in the experiment and is divided into eight subsections:

1. Task and stimulus;
2. Participants;
3. Signal acquisition;
4. Data processing;
5. Analysis of the pupillary variance;
6. Analysis of the pupillary signal in the time domain;
7. Analysis of the counting strategy by eye tracking;
8. Performance rating.

3.1   Task and Stimulus

Considering that pupil size is a sensitive indicator of mental workload and that arithmetic operations require relative mental effort [1,19], in this experiment it was proposed a task of counting objects distributed in geometric formats, so that it would be possible to simplify counting using arithmetic skills such as multiplication, addition, and subtraction. The visual stimuli were carefully designed so that the eye fixations obtained were only from the counting of each object, that is, were used uniform objects and without unnecessary details that could distract the individual during the count. Other criteria such as the background in white color to increase the accuracy of the lighting system [40], object size for precise fixations [38] and contrast index for good visual perception [37], resulted in stimuli in shape of a sphere, blue in color and with a small diameter (between 5 mm and 10 mm), as can be seen in the Figures x, y and z.

The cognitive stimulus was divided into three levels of difficulty and the quantities of points for counting were defined from the multiplication between two numbers, such that:

- **Level 1**: Multiplication between two randomly chosen one digit numbers, resulting in multiplications (4×5 and 7×8), totaling the respective quantities 20 and 56.
- **Level 2**: Multiplication between a one-digit number and a two-digit number between 10 and 20, randomly chosen, resulting in multiplications (7×12 and 8×11), totaling the respective quantities 84 and 88.
- **Level 3**: Multiplication between two two-digit numbers between 10 and 20, randomly chosen, resulting in multiplications (11×14 and 12×13), totaling the respective quantities 154 and 156.

To analyze if there change in mental effort level when the objects are distributed in known geometric patterns, beyond of the number of digits for multiplication, each of the six quantities were arranged in three distinct patterns (A, B, C), totaling 18 counting tasks, such that:

- The first pattern (A), shown in Fig. 3, is the matrix pattern (in rectangle format) and stimulates the participant to perform multiplication;

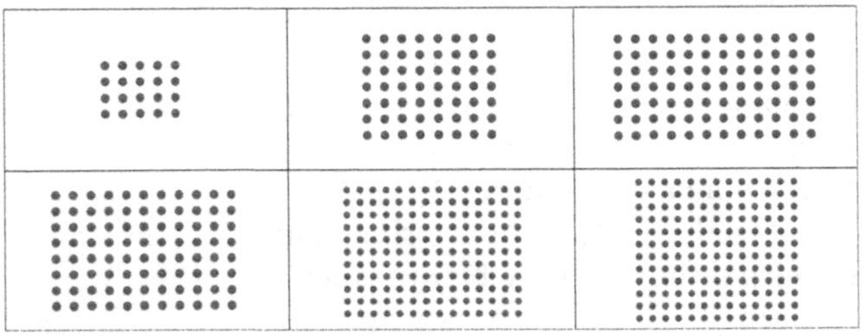

Fig. 3. Quantities arranged in pattern A. (Color figure online)

– The second pattern (B), shown in Fig. 4, divides the total amount into smaller subgroups and stimulates the participant to perform multiplication and addition;

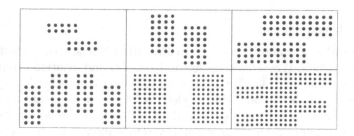

Fig. 4. Quantities arranged in pattern B. (Color figure online)

– The third pattern (C), shown in Fig. 5, includes an empty region in the center of the set and stimulates the participant to perform multiplication and subtraction.

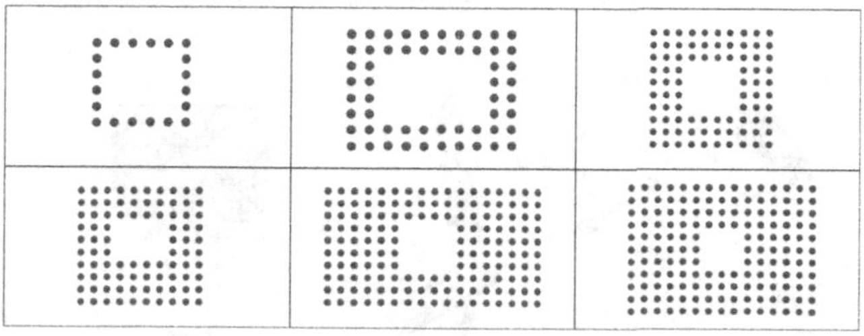

Fig. 5. Quantities arranged in pattern C. (Color figure online)

To not induce the test participant to an estimated response, these 18 tasks were presented in a random sequence. And to unlink the eye fixation between the tasks, was inserted, between each task, a screen without stimulus with a duration of 1 s.

At the start of the experiment, on the equipment screen, the participant receives the instructions and a preview of the task to be performed. Then, after certifying the understanding of the instructions, the count task is started.

Additionally, it is important to know that the participant had no time constraint to perform the tasks, but it was emphasized in the instructions that the counting should be done as soon as possible because time is a performance criterion.

3.2   Participants

The sample used consisted of 35 adult volunteers (29 men and 6 women) aged 19–40 years. None of the participants had an uncorrected vision problem and all demonstrated basic knowledge in arithmetic.

3.3   Signal Acquisition

Signal acquisition was done in a closed room, with artificially controlled lighting within ideal specifications (between 300 and 1000 lx) and positioned outside the participant's visual field [40]. For acquisition of the signal was used an eye tracking equipment, of the brand Tobii, model TX300, with data capture capacity of 300 Hz, a common keyboard (standard ABNT) and a notebook with core i7 processor, 16 GB of RAM and operational system Windows 7. The accuracy and precision tests were performed according to the manufacturer's specifications [38].

Before beginning the experiment, the participant is accommodated in front of the eye tracking equipment and oriented to look only at the screen in front of him, avoiding closing his eyes or making sudden movements with his head to avoid losing the signal. With the aid of Tobii Studio application software, the equipment is calibrated at each collect, adjusting the position of the participant within the range of the equipment (as shown in Fig. 6) and adjusting the focus of the eye fixation by means of a calibration grid [39].

Fig. 6. Range parameters of the equipment.

In this phase an application protocol was used with the following steps:

1. Selection of volunteers;
2. Explanation to the volunteers about the experiment;
3. Fill of the free and informed consent form;
4. Positioning of the volunteer in the eye tracking equipment;
5. Calibration of the equipment adjusted to the volunteer;
6. Presentation of the initial instructions (on equipment screen);
7. Application of test task to verify the understanding;
8. Initiation of the experiment with 18 tasks, presented randomly and sequentially conducted by the volunteer himself;
9. Closure of the test (after the volunteer performs the 18 tasks);
10. Presentation of the result of the data recording to the volunteer.

3.4   Data Processing

In this step were done the quality analysis, the preprocessing and the treatment of the signal, as shown in Fig. 7.

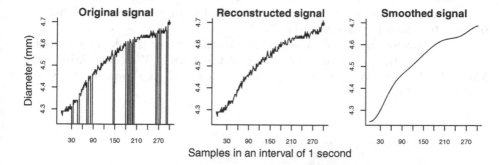

Fig. 7. Preprocessing of the signal.

In the quality analysis the samples capture rate was verified, because there are several factors inherent to each individual that contribute to the loss of the signal, such as winks or blink of an eye [32]. The minimum capture rate adopted as criterion in this experiment was 60% and only 2 of the 35 participants did not reach this rate and were discarded from the database.

The remaining data were treated and preprocessed to remove signal loss intervals and isolated samples *(outliers)*. In this step a filter with a cut-off factor was made based on the standard deviation of the neighboring samples, because when there is a loss of signal it is common for some samples to accompany the decay of the real measurement until the value zero. Then was done linear interpolation to reconstruct the loss intervals and the signal smoothing to correctly estimate the pupil size [32].

3.5   Analysis of the Pupil Variance

The calculation of the pupillary diameter variance was performed based on the sample population variance of each task [34], calculating the coefficient of variation by means of the mean of the square of the deviations (σ^2), which is given by Eq. (1):

$$\sigma^2 = \frac{1}{N} \sum_{i=1}^{N} (y_i - \mu)^2, \tag{1}$$

where N is the number of samples, i is the index of each sample, y_i is the value of each sample and μ is the global mean of the samples.

From the calculation of the variance, a matrix was generated with the coefficients of variation of the pupillary diameter in each task, composing a set of 18 coefficients that supposedly describe the performance of each of the 33 participants.

3.6   Analysis of the Signal in the Time Domain

Due to the time for the counting task to be free, when analyzing the signal in the time domain, was observed a large difference in the amount of time used by each volunteer. This time difference, although it was used as an indirect criterion for performance evaluation, made it impossible to compare direct performance (sample to sample) as described by [32].

To circumvent this problem and allow visualization of the data as a whole, that is, in the time domain, was computed the Locally Weighted Arithmetic Mean (LWAM) according to the length of each signal, as shown in Fig. 8 and described by Eq. 2.

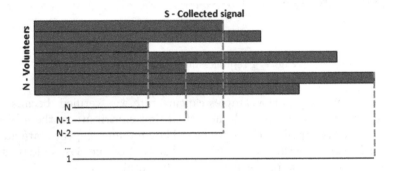

Fig. 8. Example of signals with different lengths.

$$S(N) = \frac{\sum_{i=1}^{N} S(i)}{N}, \frac{\sum_{i=1}^{N} S(i)}{N-1}, \frac{\sum_{i=1}^{N} S(i)}{N-2}, ..., \frac{\sum_{i=1}^{N} S(i)}{1}. \tag{2}$$

where $S(N)$ is LWAM of the pupil signal computed sample to sample, N is the number of volunteers and S is the signal of each volunteer.

Thus, although limited by the particularities of the signal of each volunteer, when calculating LWAM it was possible to obtain the mean signal of overall performance, as shown in Figs. 14 and 15, in the results section.

3.7   Analysis of the Counting Strategy

The strategy that each volunteer used to perform the task of counting can be estimated, or even deduced, from how each one looked at the proposed problem, that is, sequentially computing all the eye fixations it is possible to review the visual paths used for obtain information and verify whether the objects were counted "one by one" or whether some specific strategy was used for counting.

The consolidation of these eye fixations can be represented graphically by means of a heat map, which takes into consideration two measures: the space threshold that indicates maximum area in pixels to compute a fixation; and the time threshold that indicates the minimum time to account for each fixation [10]. In this work, the heat maps were generated with the Tobii Studio (proprietary software of the Tobii TX300 equipment) and these thresholds were configured with an area of 40 pixels and a time of 60 ms, generating a points mask that accumulates each fixation for generate the graduations of the heat map, which as shown in Fig. 9, go from red (points of highest incidence) to green (points of least incidence) [35].

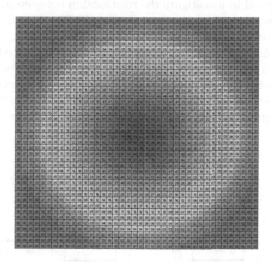

Fig. 9. Example of a points mask to generate a heat map on areas with eye fixation [35]. (Color figure online)

Thus, applying the points mask on the images presented as stimulus in this experiment is possible to measure the regions of greatest visual attention and, consequently, to estimate the strategy used for the counting as shown in Fig. 16 in the results section.

3.8 Performance Rating

The performance of the participants was ranked taking into consideration the number of correct answers, the time spent by each participant on each task and the average time spent of all participants. The criterion used for classification was an adaptation of the equation proposed by [42], given by Eq. (3):

$$H = \left(N_{correct} - \frac{N}{2} \right) \cdot \frac{RT_m}{RT_s}, \tag{3}$$

where H is the performance index, $N_{correct}$ is the number of hits, N is the number of tasks, RT_m is the average time of all participants and RT_s is the reaction time of the individual.

The performance of the participants was ordered in a list by Eq. (3). Then the list was partitioned into quartiles, generating 4 groups with distinct performance, the first quartile being the best performing group and the fourth quartile the worst performing group.

4   Results

Based on the proposal to investigate the relationship between pupil dilation and mental effort in counting tasks, the data presented below were based on the pupil diameter measurement and the performance of each volunteer in each task.

The first hypothesis raised by this study, which investigated the relation of pupillary dilatation to mental effort, was confirmed. We could see that as the task complexity increased, the degree of pupil dilation also increased. This relation can be seen in Fig. 10, in which the pupillary variation of all the volunteers grouped by the number of objects arranged for counting is presented.

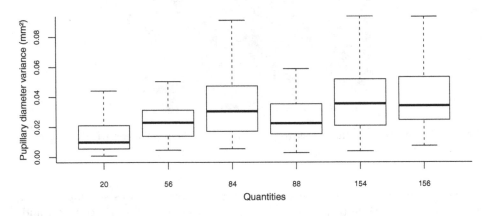

Fig. 10. Pupillary variance by quantity of objects.

The difference between the complexity levels of the tasks was evaluated by means of the variance analysis "ANOVA" and Tukey Test [13]. In this step the *p-values* obtained in the comparison between counting quantities was $2.07e^{-13}$, that is, if consider that *p-values* less than 0.05 mean that there is a statistically significant difference between each quantity, it can be inferred that in most comparisons it is possible to reject the null hypothesis (H_0) and indicate that the mental effort is proportional to the degree of complexity of the tasks.

The details of the hypothesis test by quantity can be seen in Fig. 11, where Tukey's multiple comparison is presented. It is observed that when the confidence interval crosses the zero axis, the null hypothesis is not rejected.

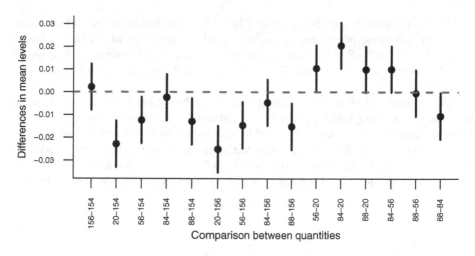

Fig. 11. Tukey's multiple comparisons with 95% family-wise confidence level.

From the evaluation between tasks, the performance quartiles (modeled by the 3 equation) were also compared. In this step, was calculated the locally weighted polynomial regression from the mean variance distribution of each quartile, as can be seen in Fig. 12.

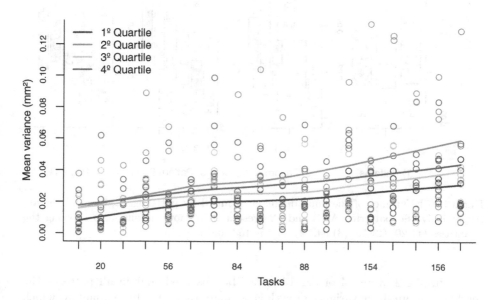

Fig. 12. Mean variance by performance quartile. Each line represents the polynomial regression locally weighted from the mean pupillary variance of each volunteer, which are indicated by the circles.

212   R. N. Orsi et al.

The trend line of the first quartile (the of best performance) stood out from the other quartiles, presenting a smaller pupillary variation along the 18 tasks. However, the test of statistical significance performed between each quartile revealed *p-values* greater than 5% in all cases, not allowing to reject the null hypothesis H_0.

The second hypothesis that investigates whether there is alteration in pupil dilation in counting tasks with different patterns for the same amount has not been confirmed. The *p-value* obtained in this step was *0.151* and as can be seen in the graph 1 of the Fig. 13, the mean variance of the pupil diameter by pattern shows a very similarity between the patterns (A, B e C), which indicates that the difference between the patterns was not an impact factor in the load of mental effort.

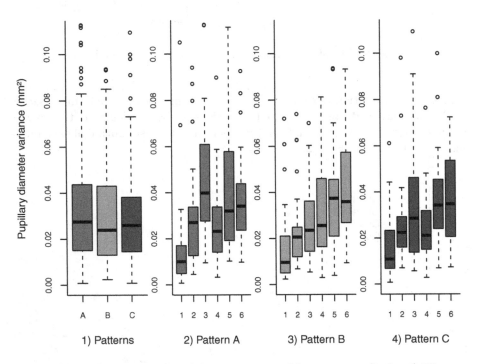

Fig. 13. (1) Variance of the pupil diameter grouped by patterns. (2, 3 e 4) They are respectively the patterns, A, B and C, presented in more details, also showing the quantities (1) 20, (2) 56, (3) 84, (4) 88, (5) 154 and (6) 156.

In graphs 2, 3 and 4 of Fig. 13 it can be observed that in all patterns the tendency of pupillary variance growth is strongly related only to quantity, which reinforces the first hypothesis, indicating the quantity as a impact factor to the mental workload.

4.1   Signal Analysis in the Time Domain

With the artifice of calculating the signal by segments it was possible to find an average signal by means of the weighted composition of all the other signals, as can be seen in Fig. 14.

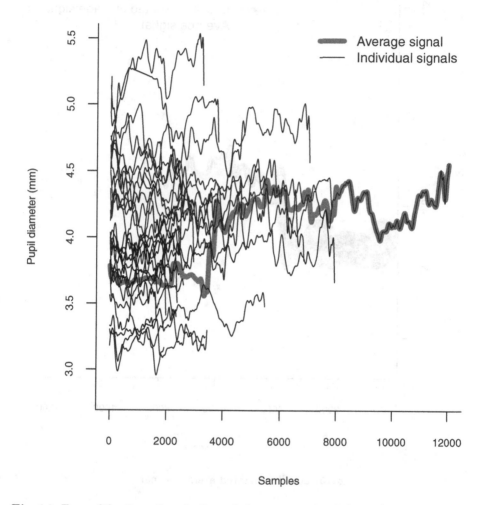

Fig. 14. Exemplification of projection of the average signal (in red) from all signals acquired in a task. This data are of the task 4×5 pattern C. (Color figure online)

From this, the length of each signal was adjusted to the average signal, transforming the Fig. 14 into the Fig. 15, where the global participation of the volunteers is represented by thickness of the locally weighted average signal, that is, line thickness decreases as the shorter length signals stop of to contribute to the average signal. In this example (Fig. 15), there is little pupillary variance at the beginning of the signal (thicker black line), where there is greater participation of volunteers and, when the average signal begins to be composed of few volunteers, the variance increases.

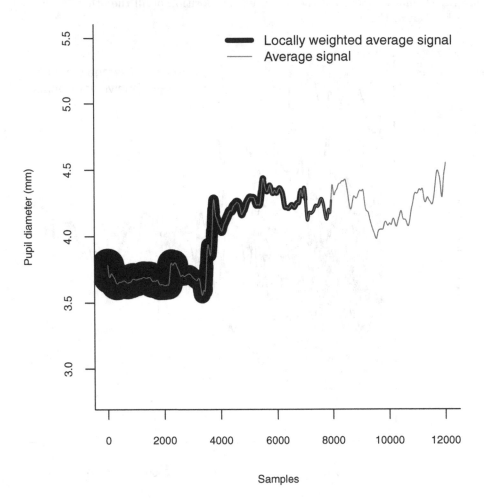

Fig. 15. Locally weighted average signal.

This analysis, of the signal in the time domain, revealed that the pupillary variance measure can lead to hasty conclusions, because as can be seen in Fig. 15, the global variance (of all volunteers) is affected by the few remaining volunteers exposed to the stimulus for longer.

4.2   Visual Attention Map

The visual attention map, obtained from the eye fixations, allowed us to reveal the counting strategy used by each of the 33 volunteers participating in the experiment. As can be seen in Fig. 16, the regions of greatest interest and, consequently, that concentrated the greatest amount of eye fixations, were the sides of the geometric distributions, which shows a strong evidence that the counting was based on arithmetic operations.

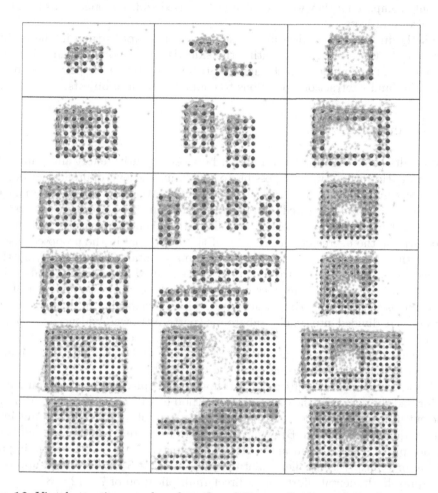

Fig. 16. Visual attention map based on the relative eye fixations of all volunteers. The colored regions highlight the amounts of fixations in a color gradation that ranges from red (more fixings) to green (less fixings). (Color figure online)

In the individual analysis of each volunteer, was not detected manual counting (one by one) in any task, that is, somehow all volunteers found a way to speed up the counting process.

In the rectangular object distributions (pattern A), the volunteers quickly recognized the geometric shape and then counted the sides (most of the volunteers counted the left side and the upper side), clearly indicating that they performed multiplication operations to count the total of objects.

In the subdivided rectangular distributions (pattern B), the same behavior is perceived (counting of the sides) for counting of the first subset. However, there was a large reduction in the number of fixations in the other subsets, which supposedly indicates that the volunteers did not count all the subsets separately, but only compared if they were equal and then used addition operations to count the total of objects.

Lastly, in the rectangular distributions with an empty region in the center (pattern C), the strategy of counting the sides is perceived again, in this case, the outer and inner sides, which supposed to indicate that they performed multiplication and subtraction operations to count the total of objects.

5   Discussion

The results show that there is a relation between cognitive effort and pupillary dilatation. However, it was not possible to determine the level of proficiency of the volunteers by the degree of variation, as expected. We believe that the analysis of variance is an exaggerated simplification of cognitive performance, because although it indicates the degree of mental effort, it is not a measure that allows to determine the degree of performance of the individual in the proposed task.

On the other hand, the visual attention map, obtained by quantifying the eye fixations, clearly shows the counting strategy used by the individuals, who in their entirety counted the sides of the objects to perform the multiplication calculations without counting each object. More specifically, in tasks in which objects were divided into smaller subgroups (pattern B), was evidenced the strategy of counting by sense of magnitude [14], showing that individuals give up exact counting to increase the speed of response, based on only on the size and geometric shape of the distribution of the objects.

Besides revealing the subjectivity of thought in expressing how the individual performed the counting, the eye tracking method has also been shown to be quite efficient in mental effort comparison tasks. For example, dividing the count into smaller quantities (pattern B), while seeming to be more advantageous and fast, did not prove to be a significantly effective strategy. The need for regrouping by adding or multiplying smaller quantities, such as $(7 \times 3) \times 4 = 84$, is supposed to require both mental effort and a direct multiplication of $7 \times 12 = 84$.

Within the already existing results in the literature, the main scientific contributions of this work are:

1. Presentation of a method for analysis of signals with different lengths;
2. Presentation of evidence that pupil variance is not a good measure to determine cognitive performance;
3. Comparison of mental effort in tasks of counting large quantities of objects;
4. Presentation of visual attention maps of tasks of counting large quantities of objects.

6   Conclusion

In this work it was evidenced, experimentally, that the pupil is an indicator sensitive to the mental workload. The results confirmed the first hypothesis, indicating that there is an increase in pupillary dilation in cognitive tasks that involve multiplication operations and that the pupillary variance is proportionally related to the complexity of the calculation. The second hypothesis was not confirmed, because the results indicated that there is no statistically significant difference in object counting tasks when they are subdivided into smaller sets.

It was also possible to highlight the strategy used to count large quantities when arranged in known geometric formats. The individual (visual) review of the visual attention map of each participant showed that 100% of participants used arithmetic resources to count all objects, avoiding exhaustive "one-by-one" manual counting.

We believed that such results are promising for the area of Neuroengineering as a whole and especially for research involving neural signal processing, because they help to clarify subjective information of cognitive exercise, such as the mental effort in a cognitive task and the strategy used to solve the problem.

Acknowledgment. This study was financed in part by the Coordenação de Aperfeiçoamento de Pessoal de Nível Superior – Brasil (CAPES) – Finance Code 001.

References

1. Ahern, S., Beatty, J.: Pupillary responses during information processing vary with scholastic aptitude test scores. Science **205**(4412), 1289–1292 (1979)
2. Ales, F., Giromini, L., Zennaro, A.: Complexity and cognitive engagement in the Rorschach task: an eye-tracking study. J. Pers. Assess. 1–13 (2019)
3. Alexandridis, E., Telger, T.: The Pupil. Springer, New York (1985). https://doi.org/10.1007/978-1-4612-5086-9
4. Beatty, J.: Phasic not tonic pupillary responses vary with auditory vigilance performance. Psychophysiology **19**(2), 167–172 (1982)
5. Beatty, J.: Task-evoked pupillary responses, processing load, and the structure of processing resources. Psychol. Bull. **91**(2), 276 (1982)
6. Beatty, J., Kahneman, D.: Pupillary changes in two memory tasks. Psychon. Sci. **5**(10), 371–372 (1966)
7. Beatty, J., Legewie, H.: Biofeedback and behavior: introduction to the proceedings. In: Beatty, J., Legewie, H. (eds.) Biofeedback and Behavior. NATOCS, vol. 2, pp. 1–5. Springer, Boston (1977). https://doi.org/10.1007/978-1-4684-2526-0_1
8. Bodala, I.P., Li, J., Thakor, N.V., Al-Nashash, H.: Eeg and eye tracking demonstrate vigilance enhancement with challenge integration. Front. Hum. Neurosci. **10**, 273 (2016)
9. Cavanagh, J.F., Wiecki, T.V., Kochar, A., Frank, M.J.: Eye tracking and pupillometry are indicators of dissociable latent decision processes. J. Exp. Psychol. Gen. **143**(4), 1476 (2014)
10. Duchowski, A.T.: Eye Tracking Methodology. Springer, Cham (2017). https://doi.org/10.1007/978-3-319-57883-5

11. Eysenck, M.W., Keane, M.T.: Manual de Psicologia Cognitiva, 7th edn. Artmed Editora, Porto Alegre (2017)
12. Fabbro, D.A.D., Thomaz, C.E.: Contagem e Cognição Numérica: experimentos com eye-tracking. In: Proceedings of the 4th Symposium on Knowledge Discovery, Mining and Learning, Recife, Brazil, pp. 186–193 (2016)
13. Faraway, J.J.: Practical regression and ANOVA using R (2002)
14. Ganor-Stern, D., Weiss, N.: Tracking practice effects in computation estimation. Psychol. Res. 80(3), 434–448 (2016)
15. Gross, J.J.: Emotion regulation. In: Handbook of Emotions, vol. 3, pp. 497–513 (2008)
16. Hayhoe, M., Ballard, D.: Eye movements in natural behavior. Trends Cogn. Sci. 9(4), 188–194 (2005)
17. Hess, E.H.: Attitude and pupil size. Sci. Am. 212, 46–55 (1965)
18. Hess, E.H.: The role of pupil size in communication. Sci. Am. 233(5), 110–119 (1975)
19. Hess, E.H., Polt, J.M.: Pupil size as related to interest value of visual stimuli. Science 132(3423), 349–350 (1960)
20. Hess, E.H., Polt, J.M.: Pupil size in relation to mental activity during simple problem-solving. Science 143(3611), 1190–1192 (1964)
21. Hess, E.H., Polt, J.M.: Reply to "Critique of a pupillary response experiment" by Roger P. Dooley and Donald J. Lehr. Percept. Mot. Skills 25(2), 659–660 (1967)
22. Kahneman, D.: Attention and Effort, vol. 1063. Prentice-Hall, Upper Saddle River (1973)
23. Kahneman, D.: Thinking, Fast and Slow. Farrar Straus and Giroux, New York (2011)
24. Kahneman, D., Beatty, J.: Pupil diameter and load on memory. Science 154(3756), 1583–1585 (1966)
25. Kahneman, D., Onuska, L., Wolman, R.E.: Effects of grouping on the pupillary response in a short-term memory task. Q. J. Exp. Psychol. 20(3), 309–311 (1968)
26. Kahneman, D., Peavler, W.S.: Incentive effects and pupillary changes in association learning. J. Exp. Psychol. 79(2p1), 312 (1969)
27. Kahneman, D., Tursky, B., Shapiro, D., Crider, A.: Pupillary, heart rate, and skin resistance changes during a mental task. J. Exp. Psychol. 79(1p1), 164 (1969)
28. Kahneman, D., Wright, P.: Changes of pupil size and rehearsal strategies in a short-term memory task. Q. J. Exp. Psychol. 23(2), 187–196 (1971)
29. Korbach, A., Brünken, R., Park, B.: Differentiating different types of cognitive load: a comparison of different measures. Educ. Psychol. Rev. 30, 1–27 (2017)
30. Marieb, E.N., Wilhelm, P.B., Mallat, J.: Anatomia Humana, 7th edn. Pearson Education do Brasil, São Paulo (2014)
31. Marshall, S.P.: Method and apparatus for eye tracking and monitoring pupil dilation to evaluate cognitive activity. US Patent 6,090,051, 18 July 2000
32. Orsi, R.N., Thomaz, C.E.: Classificação automática do desempenho humano em tarefas cognitivas por meio da mensuração do diâmetro pupilar. In: XXII Congresso Brasileiro de Automática - Sistemas Inteligentes. Congresso Brasileiro de Automática, CBA2018, João Pessoa - PB, Brasil (2018)
33. Pedrotti, M., et al.: Automatic stress classification with pupil diameter analysis. Int. J. Hum.-Comput. Inter. 30(3), 220–236 (2014)
34. Pinheiro, J.: Estatística Básica. Em Portuguese do Brasil, Elsevier Acadêmico (2009)

35. Silva, L.: Um estudo sobre mapeamento cerebral e análise de movimentos oculares em jogadores de xadrez. Master's thesis, Centro Universitário FEI, São Bernardo do Campo - SP, Brazil (2017), 65.f. Dissertação (Mestrado em Engenharia Elétrica) - Centro Universitário FEI, São Bernardo do Campo (2017)
36. Sirois, S., Brisson, J.: Pupillometry. Wiley Interdisc. Rev. Cogn. Sci. 5(6), 679–692 (2014)
37. Souza, G.D.S., Lacerda, E.M.D.C.B., Silveira, V.D.A., Araújo, C.D.S., Silveira, L.C.D.L.: A visão através dos contrastes. estudos avançados 27(77), 45–60 (2013)
38. Tobii: Accuracy and precision test method for remote eye trackers. Tobii Technology, 2.1.1 edn. (2011)
39. Tobii Technology: User Manual - Tobii Studio, 3.2 edn. (2012). rev A
40. Tobii Technology: Accuracy and precision test report, 2.1.7 edn. (2013). rev AB
41. Van Gerven, P.W., Paas, F., Van Merriënboer, J.J., Schmidt, H.G.: Memory load and the cognitive pupillary response in aging. Psychophysiology 41(2), 167–174 (2004)
42. Volke, H.J., Dettmar, P., Richter, P., Rudolf, M., Buhss, U.: On-coupling and off-coupling of neocortical areas in chess experts and novices as revealed by evoked EEG coherence measures and factor-based topological analysis-a pilot study. J. Psychophysiol. 16(1), 23 (2002)
43. Warren, H.: The reaction time of counting. Psychol. Rev. 4, 569 (1897)

Brain-Computer Interfaces and Neurostimulation

Towards a Roadmap for Machine Learning and EEG-Based Brain Computer Interface

Taline Nobrega[1(✉)], Severino Netto[2], Rommel Araujo[2], Allan Martins[1], and Edgard Morya[2]

[1] Post-Graduation Program in Electrical and Computer Engineering (PPGEEC), Federal University of Rio Grande do Norte, Natal, RN 59064-741, Brazil
taline.nobrega@gmail.com
[2] Neuroengineering Program, Edmond and Lily Safra International Neuroscience Institute, Santos Dumont Institute, Macaiba, RN 59280-000, Brazil

Abstract. The technological revolution of the last decades allowed the development of algorithms to perform tasks computationally demanding. Electroencephalography (EEG) signal processing typically requires complex protocols for feature extraction. Machine learning emerged as a potential tool to demystify these complications. Brain-computer interface (BCI) researchers have already implemented machine learning techniques to solve complicated paradigms. These studies achieved significant results and suggested that machine learning could accelerate complex data analysis. This study aims to develop quantitative bibliometric research, i.e., a roadmap, to evaluate the development of studies involving machine learning and BCI applications, especially motor imagery protocols. The results showed that machine learning provides innovative solutions for motor imagery studies. Although, there were few publications related to machine learning and BCI, it is clear that the scientific applications are growing fast, and are developing higher-performance EEG-based approaches.

Keywords: Machine learning · BCI · Motor imagery · Roadmap

1 Introduction

In the past years, the increase in computational capacity contributed to the machine learning algorithms and the exponential growth on research applications of brain-computer interfaces (BCI) [12]. BCI contributions comprehend several fields, such as rehabilitation, remote control applications, marketing, games, and educational programs [1].

BCI systems can recover or even improve human capabilities by communicating the brain with external devices or virtual reality environments [21,33]. This communication is accomplished by capturing electrical, magnetic, or chemical brain activities. EEG-based BCI is preferred and largely used due to its lower

© Springer Nature Switzerland AG 2019
V. R. Cota et al. (Eds.): LAWCN 2019, CCIS 1068, pp. 223–235, 2019.
https://doi.org/10.1007/978-3-030-36636-0_16

cost, size and safety compared to other techniques. The first human EEG was recorded by Hans Berger in 1924 [11]. Electroencephalographic signals have small amplitudes (in the order of 10–100 μV) [6] and, thus, need proper amplification and filtering to extract specific attributes, such as time-locked potentials [10].

1.1 EEG Based BCI

In the past few years, studies have shown that the ability of mentally rehearsing a movement recruits similar brain structures involved in planning and executing the same movement, what is broadly known as motor imagery (MI) [15, 28]. In terms of brain activity, this can be detected as sensorimotor rhythm (SMR) (8–15 Hz) or beta rhythm (18–25 Hz) desynchronizations (ERD, event-related desynchronization) or synchronizations (ERS, event-related synchronization) [23, 29].

Subjects can be trained to imagine and, consequently, desynchronize these rhythms to interact with orthotic, prosthetic or assistive devices even though they are no more capable of voluntarily execute the movement. This has provided opportunities to develop MI-based BCI to help recovering lost functions in disabled patients [8, 9, 33]. MI paradigms are also useful for healthy people to improve their motor skills in sports competitions [24] or to control virtual objects in a gaming environment [19].

Even patients suffering from brain damages in motor cortex or related pathways are still capable of executing MI tasks [8, 27, 36]. A preliminary study developed by [8] showed that chronic hemiplegic stroke patients with complete paralysis of the hand were able to control an orthotic device in a few weeks. Although this work did not reveal any motor recovery after a short period of MI training tasks, it motivated more extensive studies such as [33]. In this last work, 32 chronic stroke patients underwent a more intensive training protocol to control an orthosis from EEG signals. After the intervention, these patients improved their motor skills significantly.

However, EEG signals represent electrical potentials from neurons firing together in a large brain area. These signals reach the scalp with very low amplitudes and therefore can be easily contaminated with muscle activities and external noises. Hence, decoding and processing these electrical potentials to detect a large number of degrees of freedom (DOF) in MI paradigms is still challenging. The advance of machine learning techniques has supported neuroengineering researchers to develop new decoding methods to better predict different classes in EEG signals. An increasing number of papers in this topic have been published seeking to develop new algorithms to improve accuracy rates [5, 18, 25, 31].

1.2 Machine Learning

Technological advances brought bigdata generation with challenges of extracting information from large datasets. The term machine learning is based on the automated detection of relevant features in data. Nowadays, machine learning based technology integrates many daily life tools, such as antispam, ads, fraud detector, credit card, cameras, smartphones, and cars [34].

Machine learning algorithms are usually divided into two main groups. Unsupervised learning focuses on grouping and interpreting data based only on input data, basically a clustering process. Alternatively, supervised learning uses two approaches, regression, and classification, but both uses predictive models based on input and output data. Due to the popularization and comprehensiveness of the techniques in machine learning, many examples are available in different programming languages: Matlab, Python, C and others.

Machine learning is widely used in academic fields such as bioinformatics, finances, and neuroengineering. It can also be used to diagnostics, e.g., Alzheimer, Parkinson, schizophrenia, depression diagnosis, and seizures detection [2,3,26,35,38]. Furthermore, there is a growing number of works regarding EEG-based brain-machine interfaces. Machine learning applications in this area are expected to enable a large number of attributes detection or, more specifically, to detect more human intentions.

Over the years, many BCI protocols were established to detect EEG signal patterns, such as P300, SSVEP, Motor Imagery, and other [7,14,20]. Machine learning aims to optimize or improve detection performance. Unsupervised neural networks is used in motor imagery paradigms to cluster the acquired data [13] and supervised learning methods were applied to classify the data [4,22].

This work focused on developing a roadmap, i.e, a quantitative analysis about a specific topic on databases. Numerical analysis were performed concerning machine learning techniques applied to motor imagery protocols. Results obtained from machine learning in BCI were also considered to contextualize how machine learning is able to bring solutions for complex purposes such as motor imagery. The roadmap was based on the results from two platforms: Web of Science and Scopus. Patentscope platform was applied for searching topic-related patents.

2   Methodology

Science and technology roadmaps can be a tool to analyze the technological and scientific development of a certain technology, technique or area [37]. They are widely used in academic research and industry to portray the relationships between technology, science and their applications [16]. Roadmaps help to define the development level of an application or technology and their probability of growth in different fields [30]. They are employed as decision aids to improve the arrangement of resources and activities in progressively uncertain and complex areas [16]. Therefore, results obtained by roadmaps analyses help to identify potential areas to research and invest.

The first step to build the roadmap consisted of a literature review to obtain a general overview of the topic of interest. In this stage, the taxonomy that better unify the broad spectrum of the roadmap applications and objectives was defined. Surveys and whitepapers were used to extract this information, for instance, the research papers [28] and [32]. The abstract and keywords of these papers were used to define the taxonomy implemented. This taxonomy will be presented as a group of keywords.

Two keyword groups and two databases were selected. The two groups were labelled as A and B. Tables 1, and 2 present the keywords used and their logical connectivity. The databases chosen were Web of Science and Scopus. Just title, abstract, and keywords were considered during searching. These databases provide bibliometric research of different types of information and they are widely used to access research from various fields of interest.

Table 1. Group A. Keywords and logical connectivity used for searching in databases.

Group A - Keywords
"motor imagery" AND "machine learning" AND "eeg"
"motor imagery" AND "machine learning" AND "electroencephalography"
"motor imagery" AND "machine learning" AND "electroencephalogram"

Table 2. Group B. Keywords and logical connectivity used for searching in databases.

Group B - Keywords
"bci" AND "machine learning" AND "eeg"
"bci" AND "machine learning" AND "electroencephalography"
"bci" AND "machine learning" AND "electroencephalogram"
"bmi" AND "machine learning" AND "eeg"
"bmi" AND "machine learning" AND "electroencephalography"
"bmi" AND "machine learning" AND "electroencephalogram"

The sentences presented in Tables 1 and 2 were connected using the logical operator OR, which imposes that it is necessary to satisfy at least one of the sentences. In other words, the research considered three EEG term variations: EEG, electroencephalography and electroencephalogram. The same occurred for the term BCI, which is equivalent to BMI for some researchers. These considerations ensured that important results were not excluded.

Group A was used in the databases to evidence which articles and studies about machine learning, motor imagery, and EEG signals were published over the years. This analysis provides consistent bases to comprehend the development of the topic inside academic fields, which is also directly related to business, industry, and market interest. Group B considers the term BCI (or BMI) instead of motor imagery. The results from this group were used to contextualize applications with motor imagery using machine learning, once BCI studies involving machine learning have already achieved relevant outcomes.

Besides Scopus and Web of Science platforms, patents analysis was also considered. The Patentscope database by World Intellectual Property Organization

(WIPO) was used. This platform has international patent registrations since 1978. The keywords applied for searching were those previously defined in Group A (Table 1) and Group B (Table 2).

3   Results and Discussion

The first analysis was made considering results from Group A. Besides being excellent platforms for searching scientific publications, the databases Web of Science and Scopus also provide statistical data about the articles. These data were considered in the results. The following section discusses the statistical results obtained considering Group A. In addition, Sect. 3.4 addresses results for Group B.

3.1   Database Overview

The keywords represented by Group A and B were used on Web of Science and Scopus. The number of papers presented from each platform is showed in Table 3.

Table 3. Number of papers from Web of Science and Scopus databases for keywords - Group A and B

	Number of papers	
	Web of Science	Scopus
Group A	82	121
Group B	275	443

Intersections between databases were identified. Same papers were considered for both platforms. However, this consideration did not affect the analysis, once Web of Science and Scopus results were observed in simultaneously.

The methodology did not define an exclusion criteria for the search. However, the keywords used for searching on databases were defined considering logical operator AND. Tables 1 and 2 show the logical connectivity between the keywords. Results were analyzed from both databases. In general, the majority considered machine learning as an efficient tool for complex data analyzing. Table 3 shows that—in terms of machine learning—there are more BCI research (Group B) than motor imagery studies (Group A). This was expected, once machine learning for motor imagery was recently explored.

3.2   Statistical Analyses

Document Type. The results provided by Web of Science and Scopus regarding document type show that most documents are published in article format. These results are presented in Fig. 1.

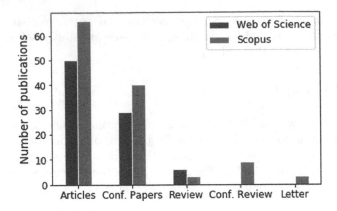

Fig. 1. Bar plot showing the distribution of type of publications on Web of Science and Scopus databases for the topic searched.

Research Areas. The analysis of research areas indicates the main fields for publication. The Figs. 2 and 3 show, respectively, the results obtained from Web of Science and Scopus. It is possible to state that Computer Science, Engineering and Neuroscience are areas that receive greater interest from the scientific community for the topic. These results were already expected since they are directly related to the topic. However, the graphs also indicate that distinct areas have also been interesting for publication, for example, Mathematical Computational Biology and Physic and Astronomy.

Temporal Analysis. According to the databases, [17] was the first publication focused on machine learning to classify human brain signals while performing motor imagery tasks. This paper was published in 2005 and the authors considered it as a "proof of concept". Figure 4 presents the distribution of articles per years. It is evident that the interest of the research on the topic is increasing over the years and the academic production is fairly recent. The two databases showed that since the first publication in 2005, the number of publications is expanding.

Geographical Analysis. The distribution of publications around the world is presented on Figs. 5 and 6. The results indicate that China, Germany, the USA, Australia and India holds higher number of publications. According to SCOPUS, China is the leader country with 31 papers, Germany is in the second position with a total of 15 papers. WOS platform reveals a similar pattern, except that China appeared in the second position with 11 papers and Germany at first with 17 papers. In both platforms, the USA appears in the third position. Databases showed no papers from South America and Africa. These facts may be related to the novelty of this research field.

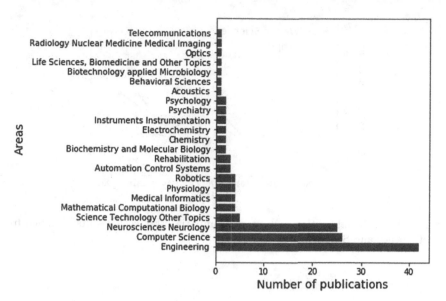

Fig. 2. Bar graph showing research areas for Web of Science database and the distribution for each of them considering results from Group A.

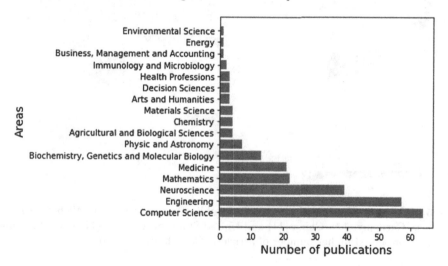

Fig. 3. Bar graph showing research areas for Scopus database and the distribution for each of them considering results from Group A.

3.3 Patent Analysis

The platform Patentscope was used in order to analyse patents registered around the world about motor imagery, BCI and machine learning. Table 4 shows results

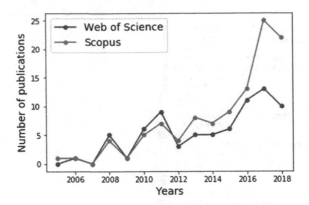

Fig. 4. Number of publication over years. Comparison between results obtained from Web of Science and Scopus.

Fig. 5. Color map showing the number of publications according to Web of Science database. Germany (17), China (11) and United States of America (11) were the countries that presented higher number of articles. (Color figure online)

about the number of patents registered in the last 10 years. These data considered Group A and Group B during searching.

According to Patentscope, the majority of the patents was registered in the United States of America, accounting more than 50% of all patents. Comparing the results obtained from Group A and Group B it is possible to identify that Group B, which involves BCI (or BMI), it has a greater number of patents. This result was expected. BCI associates other applications fields and therefore it is more general than motor imagery. However, the results from both groups show

Fig. 6. Color map showing the number of publications according to Scopus database. China (31), Germany (15) and United States of America (13) were the countries that presented higher number of articles. (Color figure online)

that the development of research and projects involving motor imagery and BCI are increasing.

3.4   BCI and Motor Imagery in Terms of Machine Learning

Section 3.2 presented statistical data regarding Group A, which involves publications about motor imagery, machine learning and EEG signal. As previously discussed, Group B addresses publications related to BCI (or BMI). Motor imagery and BCI are directly related topics. However, applications in these two research areas in terms of machine learning show different aspects.

Figure 7 presents a comparison between data collected from Web of Science and Scopus for Group A (MI papers) and Group B (BCI papers). The first analysis is about the number of publications, represented on Y-axis. There are more papers involving BCI and machine learning than motor imagery. Additionally, making an analysis on X-axis it is possible to note that the first papers related to motor imagery were in 2005 whereas papers about BCI started in 1991.

These results show a recent and crescent development of research about machine learning applied in motor imagery protocols. Studies involving BCI are more developed and, as expected, there are more publications. Machine learning has been improving many scientific areas. Research has been achieving better results after machine learning techniques. Figure 7 presents a regression analysis regarding the data. It is evident that both research areas are growing. This proves the constant growth of the scientific community interest on the topic.

Table 4. Number of patents registered between 2009 and the first semester of 2019.

Year	Number of patents	
	Group A	Group B
2009	25	6
2010	0	4
2011	5	16
2012	3	12
2013	1	11
2014	5	118
2015	1	66
2016	2	63
2017	1	50
2018	4	62
2019	8	61
	58	**508**

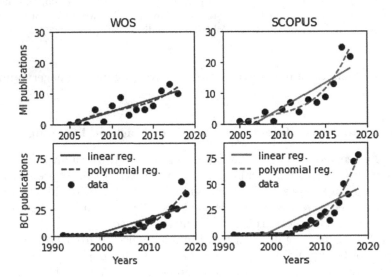

Fig. 7. Scatter plots show correlation between Web of Science and Scopus data for Group A (top row - MI papers) and Group B (bottom row - BCI papers) over the years. Linear and polynomial regression lines adjust data representation and provide clearer analysis.

3.5   Database Limitations

Web of Science and Scopus are well known worldwide platforms used for searching scientific contents. These databases index scientific journals, books and conference proceedings, and they provide relevant material for bibliography review.

However, it is impossible to assure that these platforms have all scientific ever published in the world. In other worlds, the discussions made in this paper were based on the results obtained from these two databases. Therefore, the results represents a significant overview about the topic, but probably they did not consider all publications.

3.6 Applications and Future

As previously discussed, roadmap provides interesting analyses regarding metrics and quantitative paper assessment. These considerations are extremely useful to comprehend the development stage of a certain topic or area, for instance. However, it is also crucial to qualitatively assess papers to identify and determine fundamental characteristics of this development. For future studies, we suggest to combine the results obtained here with a qualitative analysis about machine learning and motor imagery.

4   Conclusion

Machine learning in BCI applications shows an increase of interesting outcomes in recent years. This roadmap highlights an impressive growth of researches related to machine learning and BCI, and evidences that machine learning could significantly improve motor imagery signal processing. The bibliometric results present that machine learning was not widely explored by the BCI scientific community. Therefore, machine learning is a potential tool to accelerate EEG based BCI performance.

References

1. Abdulkader, S.N., Atia, A., Mostafa, M.S.: Brain computer interfacing: applications and challenges. Egypt. Inform. J. 16(2), 213–230 (2015)
2. Acharya, U.R., Oh, S.L., Hagiwara, Y., Tan, J.H., Adeli, H.: Deep convolutional neural network for the automated detection and diagnosis of seizure using EEG signals. Comput. Biol. Med. 100, 270–278 (2018)
3. Acharya, U.R., et al.: A novel depression diagnosis index using nonlinear features in EEG signals. Eur. Neurol. 74(1–2), 79–83 (2015)
4. An, X., Kuang, D., Guo, X., Zhao, Y., He, L.: A deep learning method for classification of EEG data based on motor imagery. In: Huang, D.-S., Han, K., Gromiha, M. (eds.) ICIC 2014. LNCS, vol. 8590, pp. 203–210. Springer, Cham (2014). https://doi.org/10.1007/978-3-319-09330-7_25
5. Ang, K.K., Guan, C.: EEG-based strategies to detect motor imagery for control and rehabilitation. IEEE Trans. Neural Syst. Rehabil. Eng. 25(4), 392–401 (2017)
6. Aurlien, H., et al.: EEG background activity described by a large computerized database. Clin. Neurophysiol. 115(3), 665–673 (2004)
7. Aznan, N.K.N., Bonner, S., Connolly, J., Al Moubayed, N., Breckon, T.: On the classification of SSVEP-based dry-EEG signals via convolutional neural networks. In: 2018 IEEE International Conference on Systems, Man, and Cybernetics (SMC), pp. 3726–3731. IEEE (2018)

8. Buch, E., et al.: Think to move: a neuromagnetic brain-computer interface (BCI) system for chronic stroke. Stroke **39**(3), 910–917 (2008)
9. Caria, A., et al.: Chronic stroke recovery after combined BCI training and physiotherapy: a case report. Psychophysiology **48**(4), 578–582 (2011)
10. Duncan, C.C., et al.: Event-related potentials in clinical research: guidelines for eliciting, recording, and quantifying mismatch negativity, P300, and N400. Clin. Neurophysiol. **120**(11), 1883–1908 (2009)
11. Haas, L.F.: Hans Berger (1873–1941), Richard Caton (1842–1926), and electroencephalography. J. Neurol. Neurosurg. Psychiatry **74**(1), 9 (2003)
12. Hamadicharef, B.: Brain-computer interface (BCI) literature - a bibliometric study, pp. 626–629, June 2010. https://doi.org/10.1109/ISSPA.2010.5605421
13. Hsu, W.Y., et al.: Unsupervised fuzzy C-means clustering for motor imagery EEG recognition. Int. J. Innov. Comput. Inf. Control **7**, 4965–4976 (2011)
14. Isa, N.M., Amir, A., Ilyas, M., Razalli, M.: Motor imagery classification in brain computer interface (BCI) based on EEG signal by using machine learning technique. Bull. Electr. Eng. Inform. **8**(1), 269–275 (2019)
15. Jeannerod, M.: Mental imagery in the motor context. Neuropsychologia **33**(11), 1419–1432 (1995)
16. Kostoff, R.N., Schaller, R.R.: Science and technology roadmaps. IEEE Trans. Eng. Manag. **48**(2), 132–143 (2001). https://doi.org/10.1109/17.922473
17. Lai, T., et al.: A brain computer interface with online feedback based on magnetoencephalography. In: ICML 2005 - Proceedings of the 22nd International Conference on Machine Learning, pp. 465–472 (2005)
18. Lee, H.K., Choi, Y.S.: A convolution neural networks scheme for classification of motor imagery EEG based on wavelet time-frequecy image. In: 2018 International Conference on Information Networking (ICOIN), pp. 906–909. IEEE (2018)
19. Li, T., Zhang, J., Xue, T., Wang, B.: Development of a novel motor imagery control technique and application in a gaming environment. Comput. Intell. Neurosci. **2017**, 1–16 (2017)
20. Liu, M., Wu, W., Gu, Z., Yu, Z., Qi, F., Li, Y.: Deep learning based on batch normalization for P300 signal detection. Neurocomputing **275**, 288–297 (2018)
21. Lotte, F., et al.: Combining BCI with virtual reality: towards new applications and improved BCI. In: Allison, B., Dunne, S., Leeb, R., Millán, J.D.R., Nijholt, A. (eds.) Towards Practical Brain-Computer Interfaces. Biological and Medical Physics, Biomedical Engineering, pp. 197–220. Springer, Heidelberg (2012). https://doi.org/10.1007/978-3-642-29746-5_10
22. Lu, N., Li, T., Ren, X., Miao, H.: A deep learning scheme for motor imagery classification based on restricted Boltzmann machines. IEEE Trans. Neural Syst. Rehabil. Eng. **25**(6), 566–576 (2016)
23. McFarland, D.J., Krusienski, D.J., Wolpaw, J.R.: Brain-computer interface signal processing at the Wadsworth center: mu and sensorimotor beta rhythms. Prog. Brain Res. **159**, 411–419 (2006)
24. Murphy, S.M.: Imagery interventions in sport. Med. Sci. Sports Exerc. **26**(4), 486–494 (1994)
25. Oganesyan, V.V., Agapov, S.N., Bulanov, V.A., Biryukova, E.V.: Comparison of results obtained using brain-computer interface classifiers in a motor imagery recognition task. Neurosci. Behav. Physiol. **48**(9), 1164–1168 (2018)
26. Oh, S.L., et al.: A deep learning approach for Parkinson's disease diagnosis from EEG signals. Neural Comput. Appl., 1–7 (2018)
27. Page, S.J., Levine, P., Leonard, A.C.: Effects of mental practice on affected limb use and function in chronic stroke. Arch. Phys. Med. Rehabil. **86**(3), 399–402 (2005)

28. Pfurtscheller, G., Neuper, C.: Motor imagery and direct brain-computer communication. Proc. IEEE **89**(7), 1123–1134 (2001). https://doi.org/10.1109/5.939829
29. Pfurtscheller, G., Brunner, C., Schlögl, A., Da Silva, F.L.: Mu rhythm (de) synchronization and EEG single-trial classification of different motor imagery tasks. NeuroImage **31**(1), 153–159 (2006)
30. Phaal, R., Farrukh, C.J., Probert, D.R.: Technology roadmapping - a planning framework for evolution and revolution. Technol. Forecast. Soc. Chang. **71**, 5–26 (2004)
31. Prakaksita, N., Kuo, C.Y., Kuo, C.H.: Development of a motor imagery based brain-computer interface for humanoid robot control applications. In: 2016 IEEE International Conference on Industrial Technology (ICIT), pp. 1607–1613. IEEE (2016)
32. Rabha, J., Nagarjuna, K.Y., Samanta, D., Mitra, P., Sarma, M.: Motor imagery EEG signal processing and classification using machine learning approach. In: 2017 International Conference on New Trends in Computing Sciences (ICTCS), pp. 61–66, October 2017. https://doi.org/10.1109/ICTCS.2017.15
33. Ramos-Murguialday, A., et al.: Brain-machine interface in chronic stroke rehabilitation: a controlled study. Ann. Neurol. **74**(1), 100–108 (2013)
34. Shalev-Shwartz, S., Ben-David, S.: Understanding Machine Learning: From Theory to Algorithms. Cambridge University Press, Cambridge (2014)
35. Shim, M., Hwang, H.J., Kim, D.W., Lee, S.H., Im, C.H.: Machine-learning-based diagnosis of schizophrenia using combined sensor-level and source-level EEG features. Schizophr. Res. **176**(2–3), 314–319 (2016)
36. Sirigu, A., et al.: Congruent unilateral impairments for real and imagined hand movements. Neuroreport **6**(7), 997–1001 (1995)
37. de Souza, L.B., M.D.F.C., Borschiver, S.: Formas de onda e o programa rds-defesa: Proposta e resultados do roadmap tecnológico do lte para aplicações militares. In: XXXVI Simposio Brasileiro de Telecomunicações e Processamento de Sinais - SBrt2018 (2018)
38. Trambaiolli, L.R., Lorena, A.C., Fraga, F.J., Kanda, P.A., Anghinah, R., Nitrini, R.: Improving alzheimer's disease diagnosis with machine learning techniques. Clin. EEG Neurosci. **42**(3), 160–165 (2011)

Considerations on the Individualization of Motor Imagery Neurofeedback Training

Carlos A. Stefano Filho[1,2](✉) (iD), Romis Attux[2,3] (iD),
and Gabriela Castellano[1,2] (iD)

[1] Neurophysics Group, "Gleb Wataghin" Institute of Physics,
University of Campinas, Campinas, Brazil
cstefano@ifi.unicamp.br
[2] Brazilian Institute of Neuroscience and Neurotechnology (BRAINN),
Campinas, Brazil
[3] Signal Processing Department, School of Electrical Engineering and Computing,
University of Campinas, Campinas, Brazil

Abstract. Motor imagery (MI), the mental rehearsal of a movement task, is known to activate similar brain areas to the ones related to actual motor execution. Based on this, MI has been used in many brain-computer interface (BCI) applications, ranging from motor rehabilitation to the actual control of external hardware and other devices. Although great improvement has been made in the field, MI-BCIs still face several issues that limit their applicability to the clinical environment. The aim of this work was to improve on the understanding of one of these issues - namely, the inter and intra-subject variability regarding the electroencephalography (EEG) signals produced by MI tasks. EEG data from 10 healthy subjects who underwent 12 hands-MI sessions, without any feedback, were collected. Differently than most current studies in the field, we screened our analysis into small frequency intervals, from 5–26 Hz, at 4 Hz steps. We then computed how often a given (electrode, frequency interval) pair was optimal for BCI classification, across all sessions, attempting to identify features that would maximize reproducibility. Although similar electrodes are most recurrent across all subjects, each participant displayed their own particularities. Also, these individual patterns did not necessarily reflect the traditional locations over the primary sensorimotor cortex of most EEG-MI studies. Furthermore, our classification results suggested that identifying the best spectral intervals, and not just electrodes, is crucial for improving results. Given the reduced number of existing training protocols supporting individualization, we emphasize that considering subjects' particularities is essential.

Keywords: Motor imagery · Feature selection · Training individualization

Supported by FAPESP (São Paulo Research Foundation; grants 2016/22116-9, 2017/10341-0 and 2013/07559-3) and CNPq (National Council for Scientific and Technological Development; grant no. 142229/2016-4).

V. R. Cota et al. (Eds.): LAWCN 2019, CCIS 1068, pp. 236–248, 2019.
https://doi.org/10.1007/978-3-030-36636-0_17

1   Introduction

Brain-computer interfaces (BCIs) are systems that aim to translate brain states into commands for an external device, having already being employed, for example, in studies involving the control of robotic components or orthoses [5–7]. Motor imagery (MI) has been extensively explored as an approach for generating signals for BCIs [1–4]. BCIs, however, are not restricted to MI, as they can also be driven by other types of approaches that rely on event-related potentials such as the P300 wave and the steady-state visually evoked potential (SSVEP): the former is an electrophysiological response that has been mainly employed in designing BCI-based spellers (see, for example, [8,9]); the latter has been used in many different applications, such as spatial navigation [10] and robot control [11]. Although such systems usually yield good accuracy performances, they require external stimulation, whereas MI could, in principle, be initiated at any time by the user. On the other hand, MI-BCIs generally present poorer performance when compared to other types of BCIs, especially regarding the time needed for learning to control the system, as well as its operation time [12].

Nevertheless, MI-BCIs have been successfully employed in studies involving motor rehabilitation of post-stroke patients, with a wide range of combinations with other technologies, including virtual or augmented reality, as well as several modalities of MI signal feedback to the user (for a review on these topics, the reader may refer to [13,14]). Some studies have also investigated the effect of MI on cognitive tasks, such as working memory, showing that MI training could induce larger activations on the related areas at the prefrontal cortex, when compared to controls who did not perform the imagery tasks [15]. Such works, then, suggest that MI training could be an efficient task for inducing both motor and cognitive improvements.

Even with considerable recent advances in the designing and implementation of MI-BCIs (see, for example, the preprocessing and classification methodologies reviewed in [16,17]), their use has been mainly restricted to research environments, as there are still several challenges that make their implementation in a real clinical operation difficult. The large intra-subject variability, for example, imposes several limitations on seeking a unified feature for large ensembles of subjects, or even for applying the same methodology from one user to another. Additionally, not all users are able to evoke high-quality and recognizable MI responses, thus becoming virtually unable to control a MI-BCI - a problem that has been described in the literature as BCI illiteracy [17–19]. Recently, however, some authors have criticized the usage of this term, claiming that it "is an inadequate concept for explaining many cases of poor user performance in BCI systems. The concept of BCI illiteracy relies on poor assumptions and fails to consider key aspects about BCI systems and their relationship to their users" [20]. Furthermore, the authors suggest that BCI research should also address the underlying causes of the so-called BCI illiteracy, rather than merely labeling users as not being able to operate them.

Concomitantly, other studies have suggested that proper MI training could improve BCI performance. In 2009, for example, Hwang, Kwon and Im developed a system for neurofeedback (NFB) MI training that showed users their cortical activation maps in real time. In this case, the study's participants, aware of the sensorimotor cortex location, were instructed to attempt to generate cortical activations in this region. The authors found a larger number of significant activations during MI for this group compared to their control group, which argued in favor of their methodology usage for both BCI applications and MI functional mapping studies [21]. In another work, Xia, Zhang, Xie and Li (2012) developed an NFB system whose feedback was related to the strength of the MI event, arguing that the type of feedback also influenced the development of the user's skill [22]. Furthermore, in 2013, Lotte, Larrue and Mühl analyzed several flaws for BCI training, particularly the ones involving spontaneous control (such as those controlled by MI), concluding that not only the type of feedback, but several other training protocol design considerations, could largely impact its outcome [23].

Thus, motivated by the idea that MI-NFB training could aid to better understand the generating factors of BCI illiteracy, the goal of this study was to investigate issues directly related to the inter and intra-subject variability regarding the electroencephalography (EEG) signals produced by MI tasks. We addressed the reproducibility of feature selection techniques' results for subjects that underwent 12 MI sessions, without feedback - the choice for a no-feedback approach allows us to disregard any contributing alterations that may be induced by the feedback modality. We also explored how classification accuracy rates could be affected by selecting multiple electrodes within a given frequency interval, or by gathering distinct intervals, as well as electrodes, attempting to investigate whether some of these approaches would be more favorable. Although individualization of MI protocols have been increasingly employed in the field, our results provide descriptions of the MI response over a relatively large time frame, of about a month - which, to the best of our knowledge, does not exist in the literature.

2   Materials and Methods

2.1   Subjects, Data Acquisition and Pre-processing

Ten healthy subjects (2 female, mean age 22 ± 4 years old; 9 right-handed) participated in this study, signing an informed consent term provided by our university's ethical comitee (CAAE: 53041616.6.0000.5404). All subjects underwent 12 MI data acquisition sessions, with no feedback, and they were all instructed to attend from two to three MI training sessions per week. Data were acquired with the g.tec amplifier g.SAHARA box, with a 16 dry-electrodes ensemble, at 256 Hz, placed at the following positions: AF3, AF4, F3, F4, Fz, Cz, C1, C2, C3, C4, C5, C6, P3, P4, P5 and P6.

During each session, subjects were placed sitting comfortably on a chair, facing a computer screen, which showed them the data acquisition interface: a black

screen displaying instructions on its center. When nothing was shown, participants should remain at rest; a cross cued MI onset occurrence, and the subsequently display of an arrow indicated that they should begin to imagine the hand
movement corresponding to the arrow's direction. Each session was divided into
five 128-seconds runs, with each run consisting of alternating rest/task blocks,
lasting 8 seconds each (Fig. 1). Task blocks also randomly alternated between
right and left hand MI, and, as shown in Fig. 1, only 6 s of the task block corresponded to actual MI. The data were analyzed considering one-second samples;
thus, each session yielded a total of 120 one-second samples/subject (5 runs x 4
blocks/run x 6 seconds/block) for either right or left hand MI.

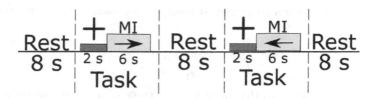

Fig. 1. Experimental protocol scheme. Rest and task blocks lasted 8 s each and were
alternated. The corresponding hand to perform the imagery action was determined
randomly.

Due to the highly noisy nature of the EEG signal, preprocessing steps are
necessary to increase the signal-to-noise ratio. Initially, the signals were band-
passed to the 5–26 Hz interval, since this frequency interval has been commonly
reported as containing the EEG-MI response. Also, a common average reference
filter [25] was used to cope with common artifacts arising at all channels at
the same time. An independent component analysis (ICA)-based method was
employed for excluding the contribution of eye blinks from the signal [26]. The
general idea of this method is to compute the correlation between each signal's
independent component and the most frontal electrodes (in our case, we considered AF3 and AF4), proceeding to exclude the component with the highest
score.

Finally, possible frequency bands optimization was explored by further sub-
dividing the initial 5–26 Hz interval into smaller sub-bands, using a 3 Hz step -
that is, 5–8 Hz, 8–11 Hz, 11–14 Hz, 14–17 Hz, 17–20 Hz, 20–23 Hz and 23–26 Hz.

2.2 Feature Calculation and Selection

Since MI has been reported to induce power changes in specific frequency bands
[27], the first step was to calculate the signal's power differences between rest
and task blocks as (Eq. 1):

$$\Delta P_{sub}(t) = \frac{1}{4} \sum_{f=1}^{4} \frac{P_{MI}(f,t) - P_R(f)}{P_R(f)}; \tag{1}$$

in which $\Delta P_{sub}(t)$ corresponds to the power change at a given sub-band for time instant t within a given block, and f refers to a frequency bin within the corresponding sub-band range. P_{MI} indicates the power during the MI task and P_R represents the average power at the corresponding previous rest block, respectively. All power values were estimated by the Welch's periodogram amplitude at frequency bin f.

The next step was to explore two feature selection approaches to rank the best electrodes and frequencies for each subject: the Fisher ratio and a wrapper coupled to a support vector machine (SVM) classifier.

Fisher's Discriminant Ratio. The Fisher ratio (F) was computed to rank the best electrodes within frequency sub-bands, for each subject, according to Eq. 2 [28]:

$$F_{sub} = \frac{(\mu_1 - \mu_2)^2}{\sigma_1 + \sigma_2};$$

(2)

in which μ_i and σ_i indicate the mean and variance of a given feature for data class i. Hence, the higher the score yielded by Eq. 2, the larger the difference between the means is in relation to the total data variance. In other words, features with the highest F's will tend to best discriminate between both data classes. In our case, each class corresponded to a given hand data (that is, either to the left or right hand MI).

Wrapper for Feature Selection. The wrapper was designed under a sequential forward selection approach: starting from an empty subset of optimal features, it continuously gathered possible attributes, for each frequency band, testing all possible electrode combinations until a subset of four optimal sensors for classification was reached.

Electrode Recurrence Between Sessions. For both feature selection methods, the electrodes' recurrence (ER) was then analyzed by computing how often a given electrode was selected amongst the four top-ranked electrodes for each session, normalized by the total number of MI sessions. Therefore, the ER of each electrode, per frequency interval, should be normalized within the [0,1] range. Computationally:

$$ER(sub, electrode) = \frac{1}{12} \sum_{n=1}^{12} x_n;$$

(3)

with $x_n = 1$ if the electrode satisfied the aforementioned feature selection criteria, and $x_n = 0$, otherwise. Note that an additional restriction of adding to x_n only up to our choice of four electrodes should be accounted for in Eq. 3. Generally, maximum ERs tend to increase as this tolerance choice also becomes looser. Our option for considering the best four electrodes per session was based on our experimentation with the data, and emerged as a value that was neither so restrict nor so loose.

2.3 Data Classification Analysis

An SVM with Gaussian kernel was used for classifying between right and left hand MI tasks, independently of the feature selection method used. Results were computed for each session, testing two approaches for data classification: (A) by employing a 10-fold cross validation scheme, with 70% of the data being randomly assigned to the training dataset and the remaining 30% for testing the then-trained classifier; and (B) by testing the classification output by gathering the first 70% of data for training and allocating the remaining 30% for testing the classifier, without performing any random permutations, attempting to maintain the temporal structure of our data and confront the classifier with non-stationarities. Results, however, were very similar, and we chose to display only the ones obtained through strategy (A). In addition, unlike for the previous ER computation, in these analyses, the best 6 features were used for data classification.

Finally, classification tests were two-folded: (1) it was investigated whether a given frequency sub-band improved accuracy; and (2) it was evaluated whether single-band or multi-band features produced the best classification results (that is, whether the best approach was to combine multiple frequency sub-intervals features, or to restrict the analyses to a single sub-band, and gather only distinct electrodes).

3 Results and Discussion

3.1 Maximum ERs - Spectral and Scalp Location

First, the spectral and scalp locations of the maximum ER for each subject (S) were explored. Results are displayed in Table 1, for both the Fisher and wrapper scenarios, listing the sub-band(s) and the respective electrode(s) in which ER was maximum. Note that, for some cases, more than one spectral interval and scalp location occurred for the same subject. Regardless, all results are shown as pairs (SUB-BAND (Hz), ELECTRODE).

Largest maximum ERs were generally observed for the wrapper method, of 0.75, with most of them remaining at about 0.67. On the other hand, the Fisher criterion yielded maximum ERs of 0.67, with most of the other values remaining around 0.58. This may be due to the wrapper being coupled to the classifier and, therefore, yielding more reproducible results, since it is already linked to the classification scheme.

Regardless, results for both methods indicate that, despite a degree of reproducibility, the large intra-subject variability still limits the use of the same features for all MI sessions. A hypothesis is that subjects may learn to adapt in

Table 1. Electrodes that presented the largest ERs, as well as the corresponding frequency intervals in which they occurred. Results are shown for each subject (S).

S	(Sub-band(Hz),electrode)		Maximum ER	
	Fisher	Wrapper	Fisher	Wrapper
S1	(8-11,P6);(11-14,P6);(20-23,P4)	(11-14,P5)	0.58	0.75
S2	(8-11,C1+Fz)	(20-23,P3)	0.58	0.75
S3	(5-8,C6);(8-11,C6);(11-14,C5)	(23-26,P4)	0.58	0.67
S4	(11-14,F3);(14-17,F3)	(23-26,P5)	0,58	0,67
S5	(8-11,P5);(14-17,P5) (23-26,P3)	(5-8,C1+Fz);(8-11,C1+P3) (14-17,P6);(17-20,P6);(20-23,Cz)	0.58	0.58
S6	(8-11,C5)	(5-8,P3+P4);(11-14,P6);(23-26,Cz)	0.58	0.58
S7	(8-11,AF3)	(11-14,P5);(20-23,P4)	0,67	0,75
S8	(17-20,C6);(20-23,C5)	(14-17,C1)	0.58	0.67
S9	(23-26,P4)	(14-17,P5);(23-26,P5)	0.67	0.67
S10	(5-8,C5);(20-23,C6)	(23-26,P6)	0.58	0.67

order to increase this reproducibility, should they be given the appropriate feedback. Nonetheless, since in this work they did not have feedback, this remains a conjecture yet to be tested.

Also, although the MI task has been commonly reported to induce event-related desynchronizations (ERDs) in the contralateral primary motor cortex (M1), mostly on C3 and C4 for hands movement imagery [27], our results highlight that there is relevant information for distinguishing hands MI activity on other cortical regions as well. Despite EEG central electrodes being associated with M1's surroundings, mainly encompassing the pre and post-central gyri [29–31], a considerable fraction of our results displayed maximum ERs on other areas as well, with some subjects even not displaying any central electrode at all (such as S1, S4, S7 and S9, which accounts for 25 % of this study's participants). Furthermore, aside from these central electrodes, when scrutinizing each approach, the Fisher's ratio seemed to extract relevant information with a larger prominence for frontal areas, when compared to the wrapper.

Despite the underlying electrophysiological response of MI for these areas not being well-established, previous network studies with functional magnetic resonance imaging (fMRI) have implicated both frontal and parietal areas in the MI skill [32]. Also, previous EEG functional connectivity studies from our group have both displayed significant correlations between the MI-induced ERDs and alterations in the functional networks [33], and evidenced the occurrence of frontal and parietal electrodes in providing relevant features for classification of hands MI tasks for some network metrics [34]. Moreover, other MI-BCI works which did not consider functional networks have also found relevant features for classification on electrode areas similar to the ones implied in Table 1 [35,36].

Although these frontal and parietal areas are not traditionally evident in the EEG-MI literature, they are actually anatomically accurate, since anterior areas to the precentral gyrus include the premotor cortex and the supplementary motor area, which have already been described as participating in the generation of motor commands in motor rehearsal tasks [37]. Moreover, the parietal cortex has also been bilaterally implicated in fMRI studies to be involved in this type of activity [36, 38].

Regardless, despite the aforementioned evidences for the participation of other cortical sites in MI, to the best of our knowledge, many EEG-BCI and MI-training studies are still restricted to the sensorimotor cortex, thus disregarding the other areas involvement, which could limit improvements on these systems. Therefore, our results also reinforce the importance to seek the exact electrophysiological mechanisms underlying the occurrence of frontal and parietal electrodes as output of the feature selection methodologies.

3.2 Classification Accuracy

Comparison Between Frequency Sub-bands. Since different frequency sub-bands were shown to contain the highest ERs (see Table 1), we investigated whether a specific frequency interval could provide the best classification outcome. Results are shown in Fig. 2 as a bar graph, with the error bars corresponding to the standard error across subjects and sessions, for a given frequency range. Also, the distinct colors indicate the two feature selection approaches: the Fisher ratio (blue) and the wrapper methodology (green).

As can be seen in this figure, statistically significant differences (t-test; $p < 0.05$) were found between the Fisher and Wrapper approaches for all frequency bands. Such differences were also observed when comparing across some frequency intervals, and are displayed as indicating asterisks: for the Fisher criterion, results from 11–14 Hz were generally significantly larger than for the first two intervals. Also, for the wrapper methodology, the same can be stated from 17–20 Hz (note that not all significantly distinct results are displayed as asterisks, to avoid convoluting the figure). These findings agree with results from Table 1, since frequencies in the β range displayed the largest accuracies, and they were also present more often in the maximum ERs - approximately 53% and 67% of the frequency intervals in Table 1 were located within this band for the Fisher and wrapper methods, respectively. Hence, these results suggest that: (1) frequencies that provided the most recurrent electrodes across sessions tended to also be the intervals that yielded the better classification accuracies; and that (2) classification outcome for ranges in the β band were sligtlhy better than for those in the μ rhythm.

Nevertheless, this type of analysis becomes more meticulous as participants are analyzed separately, since Table 1 indicates that each subject presents optimum spectral bands favoring ER, as well as its own scalp locations.

Single and Multi-band Comparison. We also evaluated whether classification outcome would be favored by selecting electrodes from just one frequency

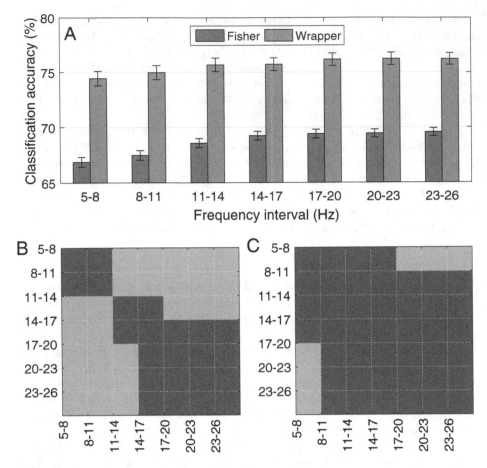

Fig. 2. (A) Average classification accuracy rates across subjects and MI sessions for both feature selection methods. Error bars represent the standard error across samples. Results for the wrapper always presented a statistical significance below the 0.05 threshold, through a t-test. The bottom row display matrices of statistical significance between each frequency sub-band pair for the (B) Fisher and (C) wrapper approaches. The matrix elements colored in green indicate that the t-test returned a significant difference between those specific conditions. (Color figure online)

interval (which we are labeling as *single-band* approach), or by combining distinct ranges (*multi-band*). Figure 3 displays the corresponding results, also in the form of a bars graph, with error bars representing the standard error across subjects for a given frequency band. Also, each studied approach is shown in a different color: the single-band methodology is displayed in lighter tones, whereas the multi-band is shown in darker colors, for both the Fisher ratio (blue) and the wrapper (red).

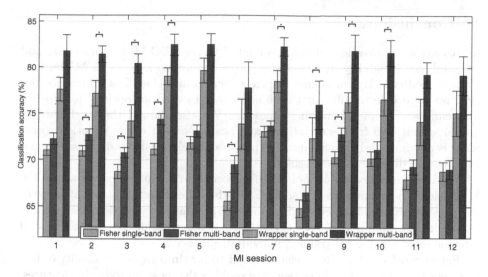

Fig. 3. Average classification accuracy rates over subjects across sessions. Results are shown for both feature selection methods, employing both features from the 23–26 Hz sub-interval (Fisher in light blue; and wrapper in light red) and by combining distinct frequency intervals (Fisher in dark blue; and wrapper in dark red). Stars placed above the bars indicate the sessions in which statistically significant differences were observed ($p < 0.05$; t-test) between the single and multi-band methods, for each feature selection technique. (Color figure online)

For both feature selection scenarios, the multi-band approach provided the largest classification accuracies: since each subject presented optimal frequency intervals for favoring ERs (see Table 1), it is expected, then, that combining frequency intervals would result in a better performance than testing electrodes combinations on a given, fixed range. Note, however, that statistically significant differences ($p < 0.05$; t-test) were only found between the single and multi-band methods at sessions 2 through 4, 6 and 9, for the Fisher approach, and 2 through 4, and 7 to 10, for the wrapper criterion. On the other hand, basically all testing between the Fisher and wrapper methodologies yielded the latter as being superior in terms of classification accuracy.

Finally, on average, no improvement trend was observed across MI sessions, which we attribute to the lack of appropriate feedback. The choice for absence of feedback, however, was important to allow the investigation of variability issues without including bias factors from the type of feedback. Therefore, we propose that a naive MI-BCI user should undergo one or two no-feedback sessions whose aim is to identify the best frequency and electrodes ensembles particular to that subject that would maximize the training efficiency.

4   Conclusions

In this work, we investigated features related to the EEG MI response inter and intra-subject variability in 10 healthy subjects that underwent 12 MI sessions without feedback. By combining feature selection and classification methodologies, we were able to infer that each subject presented an optimal feature set that can vary in an MI training timescale. We also showed that each subject presents their own frequency interval and scalp location where selection recurrence is maximal and, for classification purposes, seeking such individual optimal features can directly impact results.

We also associated the lack of classification accuracy improvement across the MI sessions to the absence of feedback. On the other hand, this was a choice of the present study, which enabled us to perform this investigation disregarding feedback biases and related issues. Therefore, it was possible to suggest a general pipeline for designing MI training individual protocols.

Future works may address issues related to maximizing the reliability of feature selection approaches, in the sense of seeking the most reproducible features, and developing strategies to induce the subject on adapting themselves to the system, not relying only on the system's adaptation to its user (since adaptive methods, which essentially adapt the system to the user, are already more developed than user-adaptation studies).

Hence, by investigating the recurrence of electrodes gathered by the feature selection approaches, and by combining this information with classification algorithms, we argue on the individualization of MI training protocols. Although similar issues have been previously addressed [24], to the best of our knowledge, protocol individualization is still not a common practice, nor does it attract the appropriate attention from the research community. Besides, as far as we have been able to investigate, we provided an analysis of the MI response at a timescale (several weeks) that is currently not to be found in the literature.

Thus, in this work, we provide additional data to enhance the existing evidence for individualization protocols in a BCI-context analysis pipeline, also indicating possible roles of the involvement of frontal and parietal areas in MI, as well as highlighting the potential benefits of frequency intervals individualization in such protocols.

References

1. Nicolas-Alonso, L.F., Gomez-Gil, J.: Brain computer interfaces, a review. Sensors **12**(2), 1211–1279 (2012)
2. Ahn, M., Jun, S.C.: Performance variation in motor imagery brain-computer interface: a brief review. J. Neurosci. Meth. **243**, 103–110 (2015)
3. Alonso-Valerdi, L.M., Salido-Ruiz, R.A., Ramirez-Mendoza, R.A.: Motor imagery based brain-computer interfaces: an emerging technology to rehabilitate motor deficits. Neuropsychologia **79**, 354–363 (2015)
4. Ortner, R., Irimia, D.C., Scharinger, J., Cuger, C.: A motor imagery based brain-computer interface for stroke rehabilitation. Stud. Health Technol. Inform. **181**, 319–323 (2012)

5. Barbosa, A.O.G., Achanccaray D.R., Meggiolaro, M.A.: Activation of a mobile robot through a brain computer interface. In: 2010 IEEE International Conference on Robotics and Automation, Anchorage, Alaska, USA (2010)
6. King. C.E., et al.: Noninvasive brain-computer interface driven hand orthosis. In: 33rd Annual Conference of the IEEE EMBS Boston, Massachusetts, USA (2011)
7. Meyer, T., et al.: A brain–robot interface for studying motor learning after stroke. In: IEEE/RSJ International Conference on Intelligent Robots and Systems (2012)
8. McCane, L.M., et al.: P300-based Brain-Computer Interface (BCI) Event-Related Potentials (ERPs): People with Amyotrophic Lateral Sclerosis (ALS) vs Age-Matched Controls. Clin. Neurophysiol. **126**(11), 2124–2131 (2015)
9. Fazel-Rezai, R., Allison, B.D., Guger, C., Sellers, E.W., Kleih, S.C., Kübler, A.: 300 brain computer interface: current challenges and emerging trends. Front. Neuroeng. **5**, 14 (2012)
10. Chen, J., Zhang, D., Engel, A.K., Gong, Q., Maye, A.: Application of a single-flicker online SSVEP BCI for spatial navigation. PLoS One **12**(5), e0178385 (2017)
11. Cabestany, J., Sandoval, F., Prieto, A., Corchado, J.M.: Bio-Inspired systems: computational and ambient intelligence. In: 10th International Work-Conference on Artificial Neural Networks (IWANN), Salamanca, Spain. Proceedings, Part I (2009)
12. Rak, R.J., Kolodziej, M., Majkowski, A.: Brain-computer interfaces as a measurement and control system the review paper. Metrol. Meas. Syst. **XIX**(3), 427–444 (2012)
13. Abdulkader, S.N., Atia, A., Mostafa-Sami, M.: Brain computer interfacing: applications and challenges. Egypt. Inform. J. **16**(2), 213–230 (2015)
14. Cervera, M.A., et al.: Brain-computer interfaces for post-stroke motor rehabilitation: a meta-analysis. Ann. Clin. Transl. Neurol. **5**(5), 651–663 (2018)
15. Moriya, M., Sakatani, K.: Effects of motor imagery on cognitive function and prefrontal cortex activity in normal adults evaluated by NIRS. Adv. Exp. Med. Biol. **977**, 227–231 (2017)
16. Zhang, W., Tan, C., Sun, F., Wu, H., Zhang, B.: A review of EEG-based brain-computer interface systems design. Brain Sci. Adv. **4**(2), 156–167 (2018)
17. Padfield, N., Zabalza, J., Zhao, H., Masero, V., Ren, J.: Brain-computer interfaces using motor imagery: techniques and challenges. Sensors **19**, 1423 (2019)
18. Vidaurre, C., Blankertz, B.: Towards a cure for BCI illiteracy. Brain Topogr. **32**(2), 194–198 (2010)
19. Dickhaus, T., Sannelli, C., Müller, K.R., Curio, G., Blankertz, B.: Predicting BCI performance to study BCI illiteracy. Eighteenth Ann. Comput. Neurosci. Meeting BMC Neurosci. **10**(1), P84 (2009)
20. Thompson, M.: Critiquing the Concept of BCI Illiteracy. Science and Engineering Ethics (2018)
21. Hwang, H.J., Kwon, K., Im, C.H.: Neurofeedback-based motor imagery training for brain-computer interface (BCI). J. Neurosci. Meth. **179**(1), 150–156 (2009)
22. Xia, B., Zhang, Q., Xie, H., Li, J.: A Neurofeedback training paradigm for motor imagery based Brain-Computer Interface. IEEE World Congress on Computational Intelligence, Brisbrane (2012)
23. Lotte, F., Larrue, F., Mühl, C.: Flaws in current human training protocols for spontaneous Brain-Computer Interfaces: lessons learned from instructional design. Front. Hum. Neurosci. **7**, 568 (2013)
24. Attina, V., Maby, E., Bouet, R., Gibert, G., Mattout, J., Bertrand, O.: The importance of individual features for motor-imagery based BCI. In: 4th International Brain-Computer Interface Workshop and Training Course (2008)

25. Alhaddad, M.J.: Common average reference (CAR) improves P300 speller. Int. J. Eng. Technol. **2**(3), 451–464 (2012)
26. Kong, W., Zhou, Z., Hu, S., Zhang, J., Babiloni, F., Dai, G.: Automatic and direct identification of blink components from scalp EEG. Sensors **13**(8), 10783–10801 (2013)
27. Pfurtscheller, G.: Spatiotemporal ERD/ERS patterns during voluntary movement and motor imagery. In: Ambler, Z., Nevšímalová, S., Kadaňka, Z., Rossini, P.M.: Supplements to Clinical Neurophysiology 53, 196–198 (2000)
28. Andrew, W.: Statistical Pattern Recognition, 2nd edn. Willey and Sons, Hoboken (2002)
29. Kabedon, C., Leroy, F., Simmonet, H., Perrot, M., Dubois, J., Dehaene-Lambertz, G.: Anatomical correlations of the international 10–20 sensor placement system in infants. NeuroImage **99**, 342–356 (2014)
30. Towle, V.L., et al.: The spatial location of EEG electrodes: locating the best-fitting sphere relative to cortical anatomy. Electroencephalogr. Clin. Neurophysiol. **86**, 1–6 (1993)
31. Okamoto, M., et al.: Three-dimensional probabilistic anatomical cranio-cerebral correlation via the international 10–20 system oriented for transcranial functional brain mapping. NeuroImage **21**(1), 99–111 (2004)
32. Oostra, K.M., Bladel, A.V., Vanhoonacker, A.C.L., Vingerhoets, G.: Damage to fronto-parietal networks impairs motor imagery ability after stroke: a voxel-based lesion symptom mapping study. Front. Behav. Neurosci. **10**, 5 (2016)
33. Stefano Filho, C.A., Attux, R., Castellano, G.: EEG sensorimotor rhythms' variation and functional connectivity measures during motor imagery: linear relations and classification approaches. PeerJ:e3983 (2017)
34. Rodrigues, P.G., Stefano Filho, C.A., Attux, R., Castellano, G., Soriano, D.C.: Space-time recurrences for functional connectivity evaluation and feature extraction in motor imagery brain-computer interfaces. Medical & Biological Engineering & Computing. https://doi.org/10.1007/s11517-019-01989-w (2019)
35. Ge, S., Wang, R., Yu, D.: Classification of four-class motor imagery employing single-channel electroencephalography. PLoS One **9**(6), e98019 (2014)
36. Aflalo, T., et al.: Decoding motor imagery from the posterior parietal cortex of a tetraplegic human. Neurophysiology **348**(6237), 906–910 (2015)
37. Tong, Y., et al.: Motor imagery-based rehabilitation: potential neural correlates and clinical application for functional recovery of motor deficits after stroke. Aging Dis. **8**(3), 364–371 (2017)
38. Fleming, M.K., Stinear, C.M., Byblow, W.D.: Bilateral parietal cortex function during motor imagery. Exp. Brain Res. **201**(3), 499–508 (2010)

The Muscle-Machine Interface After Stroke in Improvement of Hand Extension: Case Report

Jessika M. Fiusa[1]($\boxtimes$), Gabrielly S. Yonamine[2] (iD),
Giovanna L. C. Fumagali[2] (iD), Gabriela F. Moraes[3] (iD),
Percy Nohama[4] (iD), and Eddy Krueger[5] (iD)

[1] Programa de Pós-Graduação em Ciências da Reabilitação UEL-UNOPAR,
Laboratório de Engenharia Neural e Reabilitação – LENeR,
Universidade Estadual de Londrina – UEL, Londrina, PR, Brazil
jessikamehret@gmail.com

[2] Graduação em Fisioterapia UEL, Laboratório de Engenharia Neural
e Reabilitação – LENeR, Universidade Estadual de Londrina – UEL,
Londrina, PR, Brazil

[3] Residência em Fisioterapia Neuro-Funcional UEL, Laboratório de Engenharia
Neural e Reabilitação – LENeR, Universidade Estadual de Londrina – UEL,
Londrina, PR, Brazil

[4] Programa de Pós-Graduação em Tecnologia em Saúde – PPGTS,
Pontifícia Universidade Católica do Paraná – PUCPR, Curitiba, PR, Brazil

[5] Laboratório de Engenharia Neural e Reabilitação – LENeR,
Universidade Estadual de Londrina – UEL, Londrina, PR, Brazil

Abstract. The muscle-machine interface assists in the neuroplasticity of healthy with lesions during the combination of electromyography techniques and functional electrical stimulation (EMG-FES). This case report aimed to evaluate this interface for rehabilitation in a post-stroke participant. For the treatment, an EMG-FES interface was associated with functional exercises for wrist and finger extension. This case report aimed to evaluate this interface for rehabilitation in a post-stroke participant. The protocol was applied 3x/week during 12 sessions. Were applied eliminatory tests (Mini mental exam, active range of motion and Ashworth modified scale), functional tests (Fugl Meyer scale and 9 hole peg test) and electromyography evaluation in time (EMG_{RMS}) and frequency (EMG_{MDF}) domain. In the functional tests occurred increase in sensibility, mobility, oriented tasks and pain reduction (18/48 to 23/48) and the electromyography showed an increase 35.12 V_{RMS} in EMG_{RMS} and 123 Hz in EMG_{MDF}. This interface is effective for improving voluntary movement of hand extension after stroke.

Keywords: Neuroplasticity · Electromyography · Functional electrical stimulation · Rehabilitation

© Springer Nature Switzerland AG 2019
V. R. Cota et al. (Eds.): LAWCN 2019, CCIS 1068, pp. 249–257, 2019.
https://doi.org/10.1007/978-3-030-36636-0_18

1   Introduction

Conventional treatment methods for rehabilitation after a stroke may produce effective correction of abnormal motor patterns [1]. However, mainly in ischemic post stroke, the execution of wrist and hand movements are the last body regions that achieve improvement, often partially [2].

Surface electromyography (EMG) records the activation of motoneuron and can be used as a biofeedback mechanism or to trigger a device [3]. Functional electrical stimulation (FES) is a technique that evokes functional movements in muscles affected by neurological alterations [4]. The EMG-FES interface allows the activation of the neuromuscular apparatus close to the human physiology, promoting neuroplasticity [5].

The EMG-FES interface used as therapy does not necessarily have standard parameters regarding to its application [5, 6], as well its effectiveness in people with partial motor impairments after stroke. Based on these gaps, the goal of this research is to analyze the response of this interface for a post stroke volunteer with motor deficit in the extension movement of wrist and fingers.

2   Methods

2.1   Participant

This study was approved by the Ethics and Research Committee in Humans of the State University of Londrina, under the protocol number 3.004.069 and in Registro Brasileiro de Ensaios Clínicos n° RBR-4dnqys. It was performed with one volunteer, female, 69 years old, 5–6 months of injury and motor deficit in the left hand, with the onset of a spastic pattern (modified Ashworth scale (MAS) level 3).

2.2   Functional Assessments

To functional assessments were performed Fugl Meyer functional test, MAS, 9 hole peg test (9HPT) and neuromuscular activation by surface electromyography (Fig. 1). All tests were performed by the same blind evaluator.

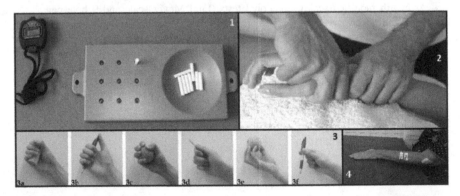

Fig. 1. Examples of tests applied during assessments: (1) 9HPT; (2) MAS; (3) Fugl Meyer; (4) surface electromyography.

2.3 EMG Evaluation

The equipment used for the signal acquisition was Bitalino®. The amplification was 2000x, and sampling frequency was 1 kHz. The pair of bipolar EMG surface electrodes (Ag/Ag-Cl) were positioned on extensor digitalis muscle. The participant performed 5 s submaximal contraction through the verbal command "open your hand".

EMG Signal Processing

The signal processing was performed by a customized routine in MatLab® (Mathworks, Inc, version 2013). For EMG analysis, 2 s (in the middle of 5 s) were used. The EMG signals were filtered using a 3rd order Butterworth band-pass filter (10–450 Hz) with notch filters on power line harmonics (60, 120, 180, 240, 300, 360 and 420 Hz). The root mean square (EMG_{RMS}) and median frequency (EMG_{MDF}), to temporal and spectral domain, respectively, were calculated.

Cauchy Wavelet Transform

The signals were processed using the Cauchy wavelet transform (CaW) [7] with scale factor modified to 0.9. Thus, eighteen EMG frequency bands were selected (20, 30, 42, 56, 72, 90, 110, 131, 155, 180, 207, 237, 268, 300, 335, 372, 410 and 450 Hz).

2.4 EMG-FES Interface

The EMG-FES equipment used was built in the Neural Engineering and Rehabilitation Laboratory (LENeR) of the State University of Londrina, Brazil. The EEG-FES interface device was custom built through Arduino Uno® hardware with a 24 V battery to avoid power line interference. The Ag/Ag-Cl electrodes for EMG were positioned between the electrodes of the FES, with 1 mm of distance between them and a reference electrode in the lateral epicondyle of the humerus bone. The 5 × 5 cm self-adhesive electrodes for FES were positioned in the region of wrist and finger extensors of the left upper limb (Fig. 2).

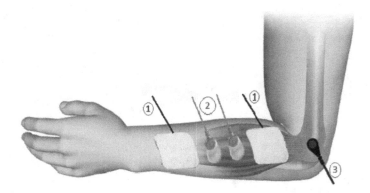

Fig. 2. Electrodes configuration. 1: FES electrodes. **2 and 3**: EMG electrodes.

EMG to Muscle-Machine Interface

The EMG sensor used to interface was Myoware, SparkFun®. Gain pre-defined, signal was filtered 2–106 Hz rectified and smoothed. A potentiometer (multi turn 10 kΩ) was used to adjust the baseline, changing the difficult to trigger the FES (Fig. 3).

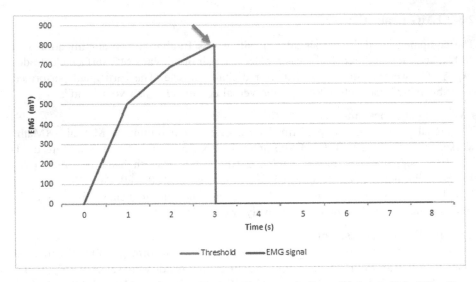

Fig. 3. Threshold for the FES activation. The arrow indicate the threshold in 800 mV.

FES to Interface

The carrier frequency was ∼1.3 kHz and pulse width divided with ∼200 μs positive, ∼200 μs negative and ∼600 μs off pulse. The amplitude was pre-defined with a potentiometer. The FES modulation to evoke the contraction was adjusted through frequency according to Fig. 4. The FES amplitude (V) was increase in order to achieve a quasi-maximal extension of wrist and fingers. When the FES is EMG triggered, the EMG acquisition was paused to avoid the interference between the techniques.

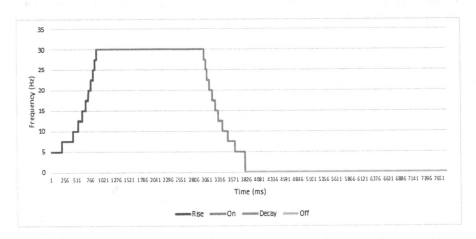

Fig. 4. Period to FES frequency modulation.

2.5   Description of the Protocol

The functional training associated with the EMG-FES interface consisted of exercises for wrist and fingers extension, with 30-min sessions for 3 times a week (Fig. 5). The grasping activity occurred during FES time off. Functional activities such as free hand extension; support the hand in soft object; abacus manipulation in horizontal position; geometric shapes fitting; placing and removing parts of wood from a small box; pick up and drop off a glass were performed during twelve sessions.

Fig. 5. EMG-FES interface application. Biofeedback on the computer screen.

3   Results and Discussion

This case report have shown positive results on hand functionality after twelve sessions of the muscle-machine interface. There was a progressive reduction of 12% in the magnitude of FES between the first and twelfth exercises session. Ambrosini (2017) also obtained improvements after the EMG-FES interface application. In his study, the need for electrical activation to perform the exercises suffered a reduction of 34.5% [3].

The results are show in Figs. 6 and 7.

Tests	Before		After	
Ashworth modified	3		N/A	
9HPT	Does not perform		Does not perform	
Electromyography	RMS	Fmed	RMS	Fmed
	14.28 V_{RMS}	106 Hz	49.40 V_{RMS}	229 Hz
Fugl Meyer for wrist and fingers:	18/48		24/48	
Hand hold	3/14		7/14	
Handle Functionality	4/10		5/10	
Thick Sensitivity/Kinesthesia	5/8		7/8	
Passive ADM	5/8		5/8	
Pain	1/8		0/8	

Fig. 6. Evaluation. N/A: not applicable. RMS: root mean square, MDF: median frequency.

According to the functional assessments applied, it is perceived that the muscle-machine interface corroborated with the improvement in the movement of the wrist extension and the fingers of the hand. Through Fugl Meyer scale there was a functional improvement of 5 points (18/48 to 23/48), among the activities of holding object, functional tasks, sensibility/kinesthesia and pain. Jeon [8] used EMG-FES in 20 subjects after stroke in the upper limb and tested the functionality by the Fugl Meyer scale. In comparison with a control group (only using FES), improvement in functionality and reduction of shoulder subluxation of these individuals was obtained. Regarding the EMG_{RMS} values, the experimental group also obtained significant improvement (p = 0.022), suggesting the use of interfaces as adjuvant therapy in the treatment of individuals with post stroke motor sequelae [9].

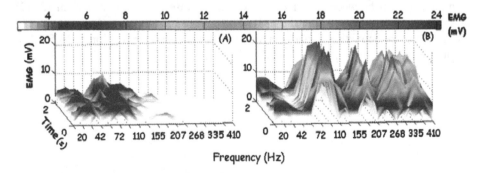

Fig. 7. EMG wavelet-based response to extensor digitalis muscle. The color bar shows the maximum EMG magnitude in dark red color and the values below 10% of maximum EMG magnitude are in white color. (Color figure online)

Our EMG results have presented an increase of 14.28 to 49.40 V_{RMS}, and 106 to 229 Hz in EMG_{RMS} and EMG_{MDF}, respectively. Through the possibility of verifying the EMG in real time, it is possible to demonstrate the intention of movement and trigger the FES, simultaneously [10]. Belardinelli [11] have used EMG to evaluate a robotic orthosis controlled by the brain-machine interface for the movement of the finger extensors with post AVE (n = 9). As result, five subjects obtained gains in muscle activity (EMG_{RMS}: $p < 0.001$), two subjects had loss of muscle activity (EMG_{RMS}: $p < 0.001$) and one subject did not obtain significative change (RMS: $p = 0.08$). We hypothesized that the use of the robotic prosthesis uses a passive neuromuscular activation system, and in the EMG-FES interface the movement occurs voluntary. The active movement stimulates neuroplasticity and maintains gains after therapy.

Through the experimental protocol, there was greater recruitment of muscle fibers and greater activation of motoneuron, observed by surface electromyography. These results indicate that neuroplasticity has probably occurred, which may be central or peripheral. One study evaluated neuroplasticity in a post stroke patient using electroencephalography and electromyography as evaluation methods. The author observed that there is a correlation between central and peripheral neural excitability. The central activity increases, the peripheral also increases, respectively [12].

This study had limitations regarding the participant ability to concentrate. The environment needed to be in silence and the objects of the activities could not be of different colors at the same time. The patient needed to be concentrated to perform the movement and activate the interface. When I was having a personal problem, she couldn't get the treatment either. Batista (2017) indicates the theory of flow to explain and assist in the task effectively. The individual should forget that he is in treatment, that is, the therapist should provide a playful and attractive environment to the patient [13].

In the grip amplitude movement tests, as in the 9HPT there was no difference in results, probably because a short period of treatment was performed and with greater focus for the realization of the finger extension. It is believed that if the same technique (EMG-FES) is used for the fine grip movement, results like the present study can be found. An essay [14] to restore the function with feedback system was performed in the year 2017. Its result after the training was $P = 0.002$ for the clamp/hold movement. The use of 9HPT may be more effective when used as an intervention. Gillentine [15] have used the 9HPT as a method of treatment during the intervention with transcranial magnetic stimulation (TMS) and evaluated by EMG in the movement of the fingers of the hand. According to the authors, a significant effect was achieved in the movement during TMS and 9HPT, simultaneously ($p = 0.03$).

4 Conclusion

The EMG-FES interface showed improvement of functionality for the Fugl Meyer test in the hand hold aspects (3/14–7/14), wrist functionality (4/10–5/10), sensitivity/kinesthesia (5/8–7/8) and pain reduction (1/8–0/8). Moreover, the greatest benefit obtained in this study was the improvement in the neuromuscular response of

35.12 mV$_{RMS}$ in EMG$_{RMS}$ and 123 Hz in EMG$_{MDF}$. This response of the electromyographic signal explains the development in the functional movements tested. Therefore, it can be affirmed that EMG is an effective alternative for use in the evaluation in patients with sequelae of neuronal injuries.

We also observed that the use of the muscle-machine interface associated to activities can be a resource used to rehabilitation to active movement. It is believed in a possible neuroplasticity, observed by the possibility of reducing the parameters of the EMG-FES interface during the treatment period. Therefore, the continuity of this study using this methodology with a longer treatment time and a larger number of participants will be perform.

Acknowledgements. This study was financed in part by the Coordenação de Aperfeiçoamento de Pessoal de Nível Superior – Brasil (CAPES) – Finance Code 001. EK and PN thanks CNPq - National Council for Scientific and Technological Development for financial support processes n. 151210/2018-7 and 314241/2018-3, respectively. We thank Taimara Zimath for her collaboration in this study with the realization of the assessments, and Carla Rinaldin for draw the Fig. 5.

References

1. Dąbrowski, J., et al.: Brain functional reserve in the context of neuroplasticity after stroke. Neural Plast. **2019**, 1–10 (2019)
2. Persch, A.C., Gugiu, P.C., Velozo, C.A., Page, S.J.: Rasch analysis of the wrist and hand fugl-meyer. J. Neurol. Phys. Ther. **39**(3), 185–192 (2015)
3. Ambrosini, E., et al.: The combined action of a passive exoskeleton and an EMG-controlled neuroprosthesis for upper limb stroke rehabilitation: first results of the RETRAINER project. In: IEEE International Conference on Rehabilitation Robotics, pp. 56–61 (2017)
4. Camona, C., Wilkins, K.B., Drogos, J., Sullivan, J.E., Dewald, J.P.A., Yao, J.: Improving hand function of severely impaired chronic hemiparetic stroke individuals using task-specific training with the rein-hand system: a case series. Front. Neurol. **9**, 923 (2018)
5. Bae, S., Kim, K.Y.: Dual-afferent sensory input training for voluntary movement after stroke: a pilot randomized controlled study. NeuroRehabilitation **40**(3), 293–300 (2017)
6. Piyus, C.K., Cherian, V.A., Nageswaran, S.: EMG based FES for post-stroke rehabilitation. In: IOP Conference Series: Materials Science and Engineering, vol. 263, no. 5 (2017)
7. von Tscharner, V.: Intensity analysis in time-frequency space of surface myoelectric signals by wavelets of specified resolution. J. Electromyogr. Kinesiol. **10**(6), 433–445 (2000)
8. Jeon, S., Kim, Y., Jung, K., Chung, Y.: The effects of electromyography-triggered electrical stimulation on shoulder subluxation, muscle activation, pain, and function in persons with stroke: a pilot study. NeuroRehabilitation **40**(1), 69–75 (2017)
9. Tabernig, C.B., Lopez, C.A., Carrere, L.C., Spaich, E.G., Ballario, C.H.: Neurorehabilitation therapy of patients with severe stroke based on functional electrical stimulation commanded by a brain computer interface. J. Rehabil. Assist. Technol. Eng. **5**, 205566831878928 (2018)
10. Zhou, Y., Fang, Y., Zeng, J., Li, K., Liu, H.: A multi-channel EMG-driven FES solution for stroke rehabilitation. In: Chen, Z., Mendes, A., Yan, Y., Chen, S. (eds.) ICIRA 2018. LNCS (LNAI), vol. 10984, pp. 235–243. Springer, Cham (2018). https://doi.org/10.1007/978-3-319-97586-3_21

11. Belardinelli, P., Laer, L., Ortiz, E., Braun, C., Gharabaghi, A.: Plasticity of premotor cortico-muscular coherence in severely impaired stroke patients with hand paralysis. NeuroImage Clin. **14**, 726–33 (2017). http://dx.doi.org/10.1016/j.nicl.2017.03.005
12. Dias, M.P.F.: Efeito imediato da realidade virtual sobre a atividade eletroencefalográfica e eletromiográfica no membro superior parético após acidente vascular encefálico (2018)
13. Batista, T.V.V.: Reconhecimento de gestos por sinais eletromiográficos para um jogo voltado à reabilitação de mãos e punho, vol. 549. UFPB (2017)
14. César, J., Costa, S., Catarina, T., Clementino, A., Campos, T.F., De Melo, L.P.: Função motora melhora em pacientes pós-acidente vascular cerebral submetidos à terapia espelho. Rev. de Terapia Ocupacional da Universidade de São Paulo **28**(3), 333–339 (2017)
15. Gillentine, M.A., et al.: Enhanced motor function and its neurophysiological correlates after navigated low-frequency repetitive transcranial magnetic stimulation over the contralesional motor cortex in stroke. J. Autism. Dev. Disord. **47**(3), 549–562 (2017)

Electrographic Spectral Signatures of Animals Submitted to Pentylenetetrazole-Induced Seizures and Treated with Bilateral Asynchronous Non-periodic Stimulation

Wenderson de Souza Silva[1] (ID), Renato M. Maciel[2] (ID), and Vinícius Rosa Cota[1(✉)] (ID)

[1] Laboratório Interdisciplinar de Neuroengenharia e Neurociências (LINNce), Departamento de Engenharia Elétrica, Universidade Federal de São João Del-Rei, São João Del-Rei, Brazil
vrcota@ufsj.edu.br
[2] Instituto do Cérebro, Universidade Federal do Rio Grande do Norte (UFRN), Natal, Brazil

Abstract. Non-periodic stimulation (NPS) has been shown to be an alternative to the treatment of epilepsy due to its anticonvulsant power. In this work, we analyzed the effects of NPS in the amygdalae of animals submitted to pentylenetetrazole (PTZ), a convulsant drug. We used the power spectrum density (PSD) to compare the energy bands and spectral signatures of Wistar rats under the effects of NPS, PTZ, and the use of NPS and PTZ together to characterize each of the agents and to be able to understand therapeutic mechanisms of NPS. All the animals underwent a surgical procedure for implantation of bipolar stimulation electrodes in both amygdalae and of monopolar recording electrodes in thalamus, hippocampus, and cortex. On the experiment day, NPS was applied in the amygdalae of animals in NPS and PTZ + NPS groups. In the PTZ and PTZ + NPS group, animals received a bolus injecion of PTZ (20 mg/Kg). After the experiment, energy bands for the electrophysiologic data were analyzed with Fourier transform performed in a bin with 15 min. Results showed that the spectrum of the PTZ group is deformed to lose energy at lower frequencies (<100 Hz) and gain power at higher (>100 Hz) when compared with the control group. Animals submitted to PTZ + NPS has a spectral signature with less changes, indicating that NPS acts in a way that forces the PTZ-changed spectrum back to its normal state. Moreover, NPS did not show any effect in the activity of a healthy brain.

Keywords: Epilepsy · Non-periodic stimulation · Spectral signatures

1 Introduction

Epilepsy is the third most common neurological disorder, affecting approximately 65 million people worldwide [1]. Besides the risk of death, patients with epilepsy suffer from other limitations due to seizures impairing their quality of life, such as the

© Springer Nature Switzerland AG 2019
V. R. Cota et al. (Eds.): LAWCN 2019, CCIS 1068, pp. 258–266, 2019.
https://doi.org/10.1007/978-3-030-36636-0_19

impossibility of driving, the frequent risk of falling, difficulties in work, anxiety, depression, and others [1, 2].

Unfortunately, pharmacological treatment only is not effective for all patients. Approximately one-third of these fails to control epileptic seizures using pharmacotherapy [1]. In these cases, ablation surgery for removal of the epileptic focus or electrostimulation are some of the most common alternative treatments.

In 2009, Cota and colleagues introduced a novel electrostimulation approach called NPS (Non-Periodic Stimulation) with anticonvulsive power, by imposing a non-rhythmic firing of four pulses per second [3]. This treatment transfers less energy to the brain tissue when compared to high-frequency stimulation (>100 pulses per second). Since then, several other studies in our laboratory (LINNce) have demonstrated the anticonvulsant effects of NPS when applied unilaterally and bilaterally in the amygdala. This stimulation seems to break the hypersynchronized activity of neural tissue [4, 5], a main characteristic of epileptic seizures with no adverse effects in baseline neural function [6].

The objective of this work was to analyze the effects of NPS stimulation and chemical induction of epileptic seizures on the Local Field Potential (LFP) energy bands in the cortex, hippocampus, and thalamus. We found changes in the energy levels of the spectrogram, observing what happens with the energy bands regarding the excitation of neural tissue after the injection of pentylenetetrazole (PTZ) and the use of NPS in tissues with and without PTZ. For this, we used both the traditional energy bands (delta, theta, alpha, beta, low and high gamma) and the concept of spectral signature.

The spectral signature or spectrogram is used in most areas of science, from optics [7] and mechanical engineering [8] to astronomy [9]. Its main goal is to obtain the dynamic characteristics of a system based on its spectral density.

In this work, we used the spectral signature of the LFP data for animals submitted to PTZ, NPS, and PTZ and NPS together to define and analyze the energy bands behavior against the application of these variables and to compare them with the standard behavior of energy bands in a healthy animal.

2 Methods

2.1 Groups

Data used in this study were supplied by Dr. Renato Maciel, the source of which is his Ph.D. thesis [10]. All experiments were performed under Protocol License no. 024/2015 and 17/2013 approved by Ethical Committee for use of Animals in Research (CEUA) of Federal University of São João del-Rei (UFSJ).

The animals used were male albino Wistar rats (n = 18; weighing 248 g–375 g) supplied by the vivarium of UFSJ. They were kept with free access to food and water, in a clear cycle between 7 am and 7 pm, dark cycle between 7 pm and 7 am and room temperature of 24 °C ± 2 °C.

Animals were divided in three groups, one group (n = 6) submitted to pentylenetetrazole injection (20 mg/Kg), one group (n = 6) received only NPS stimulation and physiologic serum in similar quantities of the PTZ group, and one group (n = 6) received PTZ injection (20 mg/Kg) and NPS stimulus; see Fig. 1.

In addition to the groups mentioned above, on the first experimental day of all animals, no PTZ nor electrostimulation was applied, and only electrographic data were collected. In this work, the first day of the experiment was used as a control group (n = 18), serving as a reference for the standard patterns of the spectral signature and the LFP bands.

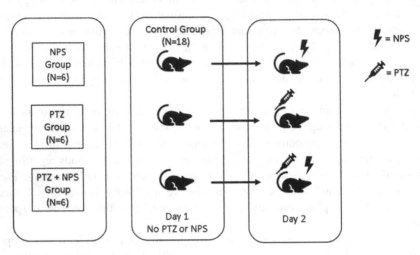

Fig. 1. Experimental protocol: animals were separated in 3 groups NPS (n = 6), PTZ (n = 6) and PTZ + NPS (n = 6). On the first day of the experiment, no drug or electrostimulation was used to generate a control group (n = 18). On Day 2, experiments were carried according to the group.

2.2 Surgical Procedures

All animals underwent a surgical procedure for implantation of bipolar stimulation electrodes made of stainless-steel Teflon-coated wires (# 7914, A-M Systems, California, USA) in right and left amygdalae (coordinates from bregma: AP = 2.8 mm, ML = ±5.0 mm, DV = −7.2 mm) and of monopolar recording electrodes made of stainless-steel Teflon-coated wire (# 7916, A-M Systems, California, USA) at the right thalamus (coordinates from bregma: AP = 3.0 mm, ML = +2.6 mm, DV = −6.4 mm) and right hippocampus (coordinates from bregma: AP = 2.8 mm, ML = +1.5 mm, DV = −3.3 mm). In the cortex (coordinates from bregma: AP = 6.0 mm, ML = +2.6 mm, DV = 0.3 mm), the recording electrode was a screw made of stainless-steel (Fine Science Tools®) bonded to a monopolar electrode.

The electrodes were fixed to the bone with zinc cement and soldered to an ethernet jack (RJ-45), which was fixed onto the skull with dental acrylic. The correct placement was verified by visual inspection of histology after the experiment.

Each of the animals underwent a post-surgery recovery period of 7 to 10 days before being subjected to the experimental procedures. One day before the experiment (day 0), animals received an electrostimulation to determine the current threshold for each animal. The test started with 50 μA in a low frequency stimulation (0.5 Hz) and gradually increased by 50 μA steps until a twitching behavior or a limit of 600 μA occurred. Upon reaching the twitching behavior, the electric current was reduced to the closest lower level.

On day 2 of the experiment, animals from PTZ and PTZ + NPS group received a bolus injection of pentylenetetrazole (20 mg/Kg) diluted in saline at a concentration of 10 mg/ml intraperitoneally. Animals of the NPS group received the same amount of only saline.

2.3   Non-periodic Stimulation

The stimulation protocol used is the NPS-IH which has been demonstrated to be an electrostimulation with anticonvulsant power in Cota [3]. NPS-IH has 4 pulses per second distributed in a pseudo-randomized fashion. The inter-pulses intervals have restrictions that results in an inverse decay histogram, as it can be seen in Fig. 2. The stimulation signal is a biphasic square wave that has amplitude ranging from 50 to 600 μA and duration of 100 μs. In this work, the stimulation was applied in a bilateral way in the amygdalae with biphasic signals and in an asynchronous way like it is shown in Oliveira et al. [4]. The randomization of the pulses in each amygdala occurs independently. Thus, the probability of the pulses occurring on both sides at the same time is minimal [10].

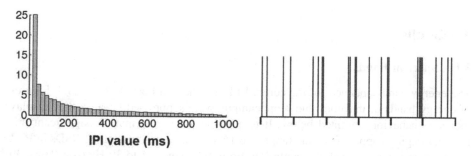

Fig. 2. Histogram (left) of inter-pulses intervals (IPI) used in NPS-IH stimulation (right); figure was adapted from Cota (2009) [3].

2.4   Pentylenetetrazole-Induced Seizures

Pentylenetetrazole (PTZ) is a known convulsant drug, responsible for causing an imbalance between the inhibitory and excitatory tonus, leading the neural tissue to a condition of hyperexcitability. PTZ can induce an animal model of acute seizures widely used in the study of epileptic seizures, both to unravel the mechanisms of hyperexcitability, hypersynchronism, and also the action of antiepileptic drugs in the central nervous system [11].

2.5 Spectral Bands

After data recording, the energy bands for the cortex, thalamus, and hippocampus for each animal were analyzed. The Fourier transform was performed in a bin with 15 min, starting after the application of PTZ while the animal (rat) was awake. For each of the frequency bands, the Power Spectral Density (PSD) was calculated based on the proportion of energy in the band divided by the total power of the signal.

In this way, we analyzed the following bands: Delta (0 to 4 Hz), Theta (4 to 7 Hz), Alpha (7 to 15 Hz), Beta (15 to 30 Hz), Low Gamma (30 to 60 Hz), High Gamma (60 to 100 Hz), and the bands 100 to 200 Hz and 200 to 300 Hz.

The results were analyzed using ANOVA parametric test plus Tukey's post hoc test, comparing the same bands between the different groups: Control, PTZ, NPS, and PTZ + NPS. Data were considered statistically significant at $p < 0.05$.

2.6 Spectral Signatures

To calculate the spectral signature, a window with 15 min was used, in the same way of the experiment with energy bands. The main difference was that instead of looking at the frequency ranges, calculation was accomplished with resolution of 1 Hz. Then the frequency spectrum from 0 to 300 Hz for each animal was obtained. Finally, all curves were normalized in reference to control animals, the curve of which became a flat line at value 1.

3 Results

3.1 Spectral Bands

The energy bands obtained for the cortex LFP are show in Figs. 1, 2, 3 and 4. Figures of energy bands of thalamus and hippocampus were suppressed because they display the same behavior presented below. It is possible to observe that the significant differences begin to appear from the range 7 to 15 Hz with a decrease of the PSDs in PTZ group when compared with the control group in the ranges 15 to 30 Hz ($p < 0.05$), 30 to 60 Hz ($p < 0.001$), and 60 to 100 Hz ($p < 0.05$). Above 100 Hz, there is an inversion in this trend and the animals with PTZ display an increase of energy from the control group in the bands 100 to 200 Hz ($p < 0.05$) and 200 to 300 Hz ($p < 0.05$). When compared with NPS, the PTZ group showed differences in 15 to 30 Hz ($p < 0.05$) and 30 to 60 Hz ($p < 0.01$).

The NPS, PTZ + NPS, and control groups did not show significant statistical differences compared among themselves.

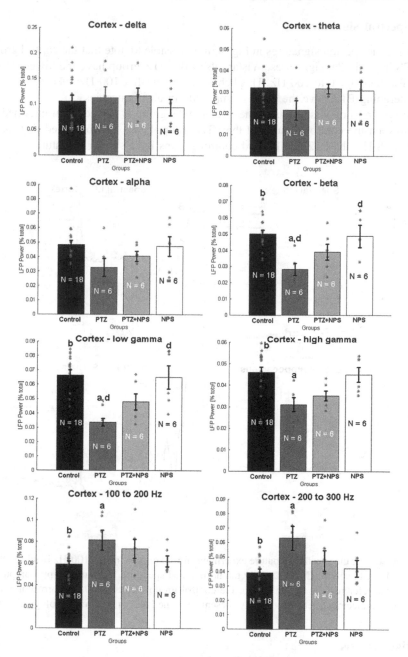

Fig. 3. Results of the experiment in all groups for bands: delta, theta, alpha, beta, low gam, high gamma, 100 to 200 Hz, and 200 to 300 Hz in panels A to H respectively. The panels show the PSD of all groups for the given frequencies, the data used are represented by *. The error bars are the standard deviation and the letters on the bars indicate groups with significant statistical difference (p < 0.05) to a = Control; b = PTZ; c = PTZ + NPS; d = NPS.

3.2   Spectral Signatures

Looking at the spectral signatures in Fig. 4, it is possible to note that the control groups and NPS have similar signatures. Wistar rats in the PTZ group have the lowest energy values for the range 0 to 100 Hz. This behavior reverts after 100 Hz, where the Wistar rats undergoing PTZ have the highest amplitude in all frequencies.

The spectrum of Wistar rats in the PTZ + NPS group is placed in an intermediary way, between the control group and the PTZ group, being also observed that, in the range 0 to 8 Hz, the PTZ + NPS and control groups have similar signatures.

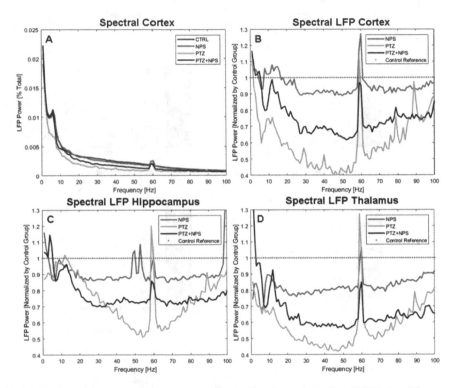

Fig. 4. Results of the spectral signature experiment for all groups in 0 to 100 Hz band for cortex LFP (panel A). Panels B, C and D show the normalized spectrum for cortex, hippocampus and thalamus; the reference are the values for the control group. Peaks at 60 Hz correspond to the noise from the electrical network, usually present in some level in electrophysiological data.

4   Discussions

4.1   Spectral Bands

Injection of PTZ in low subliminal doses (20 mg/kg) induces detectable changes in the energy bands, shifting the energy to higher frequencies (>100 Hz), which may indicate increased brain activity due to the hyperexcitability of the neural tissue [11].

Apparently, NPS does not modify the energy bands of the brain; the results obtained do not show statistical significance in comparison to control animals. This indicates that NPS does not interfere with the "normal" activity of the brain corroborating locally published results of our group that showed NPS does not modify base level anxiety, motor function, object recognition, and social interaction [6].

When we compared the results obtained with those observed for hippocampal Deep Brain Stimulation (DBS) [12], nucleus accumbens stimulation [13], and limbic DBS [14] with different patterns of stimulation, we observed that despite other stimulation patterns that change the energy on theta, delta, alpha and beta bands, in particular, the lower bands (Theta and Delta) in the NPS group tested in this study did not show statistical differences to control group.

Although NPS does not interfere with the activity of a healthy brain, results obtained for the NPS + PTZ group show that the use of NPS in a brain hyperexcited by pentylenetetrazole minimizes the effects caused by the PTZ [4, 5], "decreasing" the impacts of hyperexcitability which may be one of the reasons underlying the anti-convulsant power of NPS.

4.2 Spectral Signatures

The results observed in the energy bands are maintained when analyzing the signal spectrum. Spectral energies of the NPS and control groups remain close throughout the range, indicating that possibly NPS does not alter the "normal" electrophysiological functioning of the brain.

The spectrum of the PTZ group is deformed to lose energy at lower frequencies (<100 Hz) and gain power at higher ones (>100 Hz) showing the greatest difference for the control group in the range of 10 to 60 Hz.

The PTZ + NPS group does not differ statistically from the control group in the range 0 to 8 Hz and its signature is placed in an intermediate position between the control group and the PTZ group. This suggests that NPS acts in a way that forces the PTZ-changed spectrum back to its normal state, a possible mechanism of action of this novel therapeutic.

References

1. Monteiro, G., Aroca, I., Margarit, B., Herán, I.: Epilepsy, vol. 3, pp. 4222–4231. Springer, New York (2019)
2. Epilepsy Society. https://www.epilepsysociety.org.uk/risks-epilepsy. Accessed 06 Aug 2019
3. Cota, V.R., de Castro Medeiros, D., da Páscoa Vilela, M.R.S., Doretto, M.C., Moraes, M.F. D.: Distinct patterns of electrical stimulation of the basolateral amygdala influence pentylenetetrazole seizure outcome. Epilepsy Behav. **14**, 26–31 (2009)
4. de Oliveira, J.C., Maciel, R.M., Moraes, M.F.D., Cota, V.R.: Asynchronous, bilateral, and biphasic temporally unstructured electrical stimulation of amygdalae enhances the suppression of pentylenetetrazoleinduced seizures in rats. Epilepsy Res. **146**, 1–8 (2018)
5. Cota, V.R., Drabowski, B.M., de Oliveira, J.C., Moraes, M.F.: The epileptic amygdala: toward the development of a neural prosthesis by temporally coded electrical stimulation. J. Neurosc. Res. **94**(6), 463–485 (2016)

6. Réboli, L.A., Oliveira, J.C., Maciel, R.M., Tilelli, C.Q., Cota, V.R.: Avaliação do comportamento social em animais submetidos à estimulação elétrica em distintos padrões temporais. In: XVI Congresso de produção científica e acadêmica 2018, São João del-Rei. XXV SIC (2018)
7. Akturk, S., Couairon, A., Franco, M., Mysyrowicz, A.: Spectrogram representation of pulse self compression by filamentation. Opt. Express 16(22), 17626–17636 (2008)
8. Léonard, F.: Phase spectrogram and frequency spectrogram as new diagnostic tools. Mech. Syst. Sig. Process. 21(1), 125–137 (2007)
9. Millman, P.M., Cook, A.F.: Photometric analysis of a spectrogram of a very slow meteor. Astrophys. J. 130, 648 (1959)
10. Maciel, R.M.M.: Efeitos da estimulação elétrica para tratamento das crises epiléticas e suas influencias sobre a neurodinâmica do ciclo sono-vigília. Ph.D. thesis– UFSJ. São João del-Rei (2018)
11. Velisek, L., Kubová, H., Pohl, M., Stanková, L., Mares, P., Schickerovi, R.: Pentylenetetrazol-induced seizures in rats: an ontogenetic study. Naunyn-Schmiedeherg's Arch. Pharmacol. 346(5), 588–591 (1992)
12. Quinkert, A.W., Schiff, N.D., Pfaff, D.W.: Temporal patterning of pulses during deep brain stimulation affects central nervous system arousal. Behav. Brain Res. 214(2), 377–385 (2010)
13. Ewing, S.G., Grace, A.A.: Long-term high frequency deep brain stimulation of the nucleus accumbens drives time-dependent changes in functional connectivity in the rodent limbic system. Brain Stimul. 6(3), 274–285 (2013)
14. Neumann, W.J., et al.: Different patterns of local field potentials from limbic DBS targets in patients with major depressive and obsessive compulsive disorder. Mol. Psychiatry 19(11), 1186 (2014)

Seizure Prediction

On the Validity of Using Probing Stimuli for Seizure Prediction in the Epileptor Model

Vinícius R. Carvalho[1,2(✉)] ⓘ, Márcio F. D. Moraes[2] ⓘ,
and Eduardo M. A. M. Mendes[1,2] ⓘ

[1] Programa de Pós-Graduação em Engenharia Elétrica - Universidade Federal de Minas Gerais, Belo Horizonte, MG, Brazil
vrcarva@ufmg.br
[2] Núcleo de Neurociências, Departamento de Fisiologia e Biofísica, Instituto de Ciências Biológicas, Universidade Federal de Minas Gerais, Belo Horizonte, MG, Brazil

Abstract. Epilepsy is characterized by transitory recurrent disturbances to the functioning of the brain. Methods of forecasting the occurrence of seizures could alleviate some of the burden of this disease, which is the unpredictability of these events. One of the proposed approaches for achieving this is the use of stimuli that could highlight otherwise unobservable abnormal changes that would alert patients on impending seizures. This work aims to evaluate the value of a probing approach in seizure prediction, using the Epileptor. Composed by five state variables, which represent three coupled ensembles, the Epileptor is a phenomenological model that replicates transitions involved in onset and offset of seizures, as well as electrographical signatures such as fast discharges and spike and wave events. A slow permittivity variable is responsible for very slow timescale dynamics and affects the likelihood of the occurrence of seizure-like events. Stimuli were defined as biphasic pulses applied every two seconds to perturb the system. The model was configured to generate "normal" dynamics and was simulated with and without stimuli, but slowly shifting the excitability parameter towards seizure activity. Features such as statistical moments, Lag-1 autocorrelation and Hjorth parameters are successively extracted from the model output. Results show decreases in feature values (except for Hjorth Complexity and lag-1 autocorrelation, which increase) as the system approaches the transition from normal to ictal activity, only when probing stimuli are used. This confirms the initial hypothesis and encourages further studies on probing approaches for seizure prediction in different models and configurations.

Keywords: Epileptor · Seizure prediction · Probing · Excitability · Modelling

1 Introduction

1.1 Epileptic Seizures

Epilepsy is a neurological disease that affects approximately 50 million people around the world, 80% of whom live in developing countries (World Health Organization 2012). It is marked by the occurrence of recurrent spontaneous seizures, which are

V. R. Cota et al. (Eds.): LAWCN 2019, CCIS 1068, pp. 269–281, 2019.
https://doi.org/10.1007/978-3-030-36636-0_20

transient abnormalities in the neuronal activity of the brain, usually in a synchronous and hyper-excitable way (Engel and Pedley 1989).

The study of ictogenesis (the dynamics which lead to a seizure episode) and epileptogenesis (changes in the brain that lead to the occurrence of recurrent seizures) is a challenging task, in part due to the great variety of epilepsy and seizure types, as well as the number of possible causes for this disease, such as dysplasias, genetic factors, traumas and infections in the nervous system, ischemia, tumors, among others (Sander 2003). Understanding and characterizing the mechanisms of various forms of epilepsy, and defining the common factors in most types are important steps in order to devise better treatment options, especially considering the high rates of refractory epilepsy, which are still near 30%, despite the development of new drugs in the last decades (French 2007).

1.2 Seizure Forecasting

Part of the study of ictogenesis deals with detecting changes in signals preceding seizures. Devising an alarm system that warns the patient of an impending seizure would ease part of the burden of epilepsy, which is the unpredictability of seizures. Initially, the advent of several of promising methods made it seem that this problem would be solved in a few years. However, an important review (Mormann et al. 2007) made clear that this would be far from the truth; most methods would perform poorly when confronted with different, more recent datasets. Some recommendations for the development and evaluation of new methods were made, such as to consider the underlying mechanisms of seizure generation, the use of long-term recordings and more robust validation methods.

The last years have been encouraging for research in seizure prediction or forecasting. We have seen a clinical trial showing that this task is possible (Cook et al. 2013), increased availability of Electroencephalogram (EEG) databases, such as EPI-LEPSIAE (Ihle et al. 2012) or IEEG.org, as well as seizure prediction competitions that serve as platforms for evaluating a diverse range of methods proposed by the community (Kuhlmann et al. 2018). Improved understanding about epilepsy, which is increasingly seen as a network disorder (Jiruska et al. 2013), and availability of multi-channel iEEG data has also encouraged the use of methods that take into account aspects such as network connectivity and topology (Rubinov and Sporns 2010; Kramer and Cash 2012; Van Diessen et al. 2013). Computational neuronal models with widespread use in the study of epilepsy (Lytton 2008) may also offer insights and test hypotheses regarding seizure prediction (Freestone et al. 2015; Kuhlmann et al. 2018). Finally, alternative approaches such as probing are also considered promising venues towards seizure forecasting (Freestone et al. 2017).

1.3 Probing

Probing strategies are considered as the ones that use relatively subtle stimuli applied to a system in order to extract or highlight information that would be otherwise not available through passive observation. In the case of seizure prediction, stimuli would provide responses (with increasing or decreasing features from post-stimuli epochs) that would help to detect impending seizures.

The first use of a probing approach for assessing transitions to ictal states was done with intermittent photic stimulation (IPS) in 2002 (Kalitzin et al. 2002). This was used to test the hypothesis that response changes to IPS would precede the transition to seizure activity in photosensitive patients. This was verified by the increase of the Relative Phase Clustering Index (rPCI), reflecting the hyperexcitability of the underlying dynamical system. Other works used cortical or deep brain stimulation (DBS) in epilepsy patients (Kalitzin et al. 2010; Freestone et al. 2011) and in canines (Freestone et al. 2013). In a pentylenetetrazol (PTZ) model with rats, electrical stimulation was used to detect electrographic changes as the ictal state approached (Medeiros et al. 2014). Recently, this method was improved by pairing stimuli with a PTZ-induced seizure in order to devise a programmable surrogate marker for seizure detection (Medeiros et al. 2018).

So far, only two works have combined the use of computational models with probing approaches. In (Suffczynski et al. 2008), a neural mass model with seizure-generating dynamics related to the hippocampal region (Wendling et al. 2002) is stimulated. Excitability changes towards ictal activity were tracked with the relative Phase Clustering Index (rPCI), that showed excitability and inhibitory alterations with stimuli, but not with passive observation. Another work (O'Sullivan-Greene et al. 2017) used Kuramoto Oscillators to show that synchrony measurements are improved when active probing is employed, as long as sufficiently dense recordings are made.

1.4   Computational Models and Ictal Dynamics

Neuronal computational models may be used to interpret experimental data, formulate and test hypotheses about neuronal functions and make predictions about changes and perturbations to systems, thus providing important information for linking behavior and neuronal mechanisms (Suffczynski et al. 2006). Models may represent microscopic or detailed dynamics, such as the Hodgkin-Huxley (Hodgkin and Huxley 1952) neuron model for action potential generation, to macroscopic behavior, through neural mass models (macro or lumped models) like the Wilson & Cowan model (Wilson and Cowan 1972). Alternative approaches can focus on reproducing general dynamical behaviors instead of being built upon purely biological constraints, such as the Epileptor model (Jirsa et al. 2014).

A large part of neuronal computational models is based on differential equations, in which states may represent specific system properties, such as membrane voltage. With few state variables, complex behaviors may arise, from simple oscillations to chaotic dynamics. Parameters may be varied slowly to search for abrupt output changes in the form of bifurcations, such as transitions from resting to bursting. In the work of Jirsa and colleagues (Jirsa et al. 2014), a taxonomy of seizures is established, where the combination of four types of bifurcations of equilibria and four bifurcations of oscillations result in 16 possible classes, following Izhikevich's classification (Izhikevich 2000). For the most common seizure class (saddle-node at seizure onset and homoclinic bifurcation at offset), a five-state variable model is developed, called Epileptor. This model reproduces the behavior of experimental seizures *in vitro* (low MG^{2+} hippocampal slices) and has similar patterns with *in vivo* seizures, such as in patients with temporal lobe epilepsy and hyperthermia-induced seizure-like events in zebrafish.

The Epileptor has been used to investigate seizure recruitment and propagation (Proix et al. 2014). Recently, this approach has been further developed by associating the Epileptor with patient-specific virtual brain models, where connectivity matrices are constraining by structural information obtained by diffusion-weighted magnetic resonance imaging (DW-MRI or DWI) (Proix et al. 2017). A detailed bifurcation analysis of this model is done by El Houssaini and colleagues (El Houssaini et al. 2015). The Epileptor has also been used in a network model that links both neuronal and network (or population) representations to describe brain dynamics and parameter changes involved in the development of epilepsy (Naze et al. 2015).

1.5   Objectives

This work aims to evaluate the value of probing stimuli in seizure forecasting, using the Epileptor. Features are extracted as the model is shifted towards seizure states. It is expected that with stimuli, feature trends would be highlighted with the use of probing, indicating the imminence of transition to ictal states.

2   Methods

2.1   Epileptor Model

With five state variables, the Epileptor (Jirsa et al. 2014) model comprises two coupled oscillators linked together by a slow permittivity variable. It enables the simulation of the recurrence, onset, time-course and offset of ictal-like events.

The first oscillator ensemble is composed of two state variables (x_1 and y_1) and is responsible for the generation of fast discharges, which are analogous low voltage fast activity (Jiruska et al. 2013). With an intermediate time scale, Spike and wave events (SWEs) are generated by the second ensemble with variables x_2 and y_2. The first ensemble is adapted from the Hindmarsh-Rose neuronal model (Hindmarsh and Rose 1984) and the second from the Morris-Lecar (Morris and Lecar 1981; Roy et al. 2011). In a slower timescale, a permittivity variable z is responsible for the alternation between 'normal' and ictal period. This variable would play the role of representing certain extracellular processes that influence the likelihood of seizures and deals with ultra-slow timescales.

$$\dot{x}_1 = y_1 - f_1(x_1, x_2) - z + I_{rest1}$$

$$\dot{y}_1 = y_0 - 5x_1^2 - y_1$$

$$\dot{z} = \frac{1}{\tau_0}(4(x_1 - x_0) - z) \tag{1}$$

$$\dot{x}_2 = -y_2 + x_2 - x_2^3 - I_{rest2} + 0.002g(x_1) - 0.3(z - 3.5)$$

$$\dot{y}_2 = \frac{1}{\tau_2}(-y_2 + f_2(x_1, x_2)),$$

where

$$g(x_1) = \int_{t_0}^{t} e^{-\gamma(t-\tau)} x_1(\tau) d\tau \tag{2}$$

$$f_1(x_1, x_2) = \begin{cases} x_1^3 - 3x_1^2 & \text{if } x_1 < 0 \\ \left(x_2 - 0.6(z-4)^2\right) x_1 & \text{if } x_1 \geq 0 \end{cases} \tag{3}$$

$$f_2(x_1, x_2) = \begin{cases} 0 & \text{if } x_2 < -0.25 \\ 6(x_2 + 0.25) & \text{if } x_2 \geq -0.25 \end{cases} \tag{4}$$

Based on (Jirsa et al. 2014) and (Naze et al. 2015), brief parameter descriptions and values used are shown in Table 1.

Table 1. Parameter descriptions and values.

Name	Description	Value
x_0	Degree of excitability or epileptogenicity	$[-4.0\ -1.6]$
y_0	–	1.0
τ_0	Time constant of permittivity variable	2857
τ_2	Time constant of second ensemble (SWE-generating)	10
I_{rest1}	Input to first ensemble	$3.1 + u_{stim}$
I_{rest2}	Input to second ensemble	$0.45 + u_{stim}$
γ	Timescale of low-pass filtered excitatory coupling	0.01
u_{stim}	Periodic input probing stimulus	± 4 every 2 s

The output of this model is defined as $-x_1 + x_2$ for its resemblance to field potential recordings (Jirsa et al. 2014). Figure 1 illustrates the output of a short simulation, revealing the alternation between seizure-like events (SLEs) and normal activity. This alternation is dictated by the slow permittivity variable z, plotted in the same Figure.

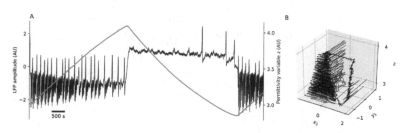

Fig. 1. (A) Epileptor output $(-x_1 + x_2)$ for one simulation without stimuli, with parameters described in Table 1 and $x_0 = 1.6$. This shows alternating normal activity and SLEs of the Epileptor model (in black) and the slow permittivity variable z (orange). Changes in activity are accompanied by abrupt DC shifts. (B) 3D trajectory of the simulation. (Color figure online)

In this work, probing stimuli (u_{stim}) were applied to this model, summed to the periodic input series to I_{rest1} and I_{rest2}. More specifically, biphasic brief pulses with 0.02 s of duration and 4 (AU) of amplitude were applied every 2 s.

Ictal activity can be achieved with two approaches: in the first, the parameter x_0 can be set to specific values (such as −2.0) which elicits alternating periods of seizure and "normal" activity. An alternative approach used in this work, involves varying x_0 throughout the simulation. This was done linearly, starting with −4.0, related to normal activity, up to −1.6, thus eliciting a seizure at the end of the simulation.

The model was simulated using the Euler-Maruyama method with an integration step of 0.002. It was implemented in Python 3.7, with SciPy and NumPy packages. All codes are available at https://github.com/vrcarva/LAWCN_2019.

2.2 Features

Univariate features were extracted from post-stimuli epochs with duration of 400 ms. Simulations were carried out with and without stimuli and the resulting evolution of features was compared. The following features were computed: statistical moments (variance, skewness and kurtosis), Hjorth mobility and complexity (Hjorth 1970) and lag-1 autocorrelation. These features reflect changes to response shape and amplitude, which are expected to be altered as a seizure approaches.

$$Variance(x) = \sigma^2 = E\left[(x(t) - \mu)^2\right] \tag{5}$$

$$Skewness(x) = E\left[\left(\frac{x(t) - \mu}{\sigma}\right)^3\right] \tag{6}$$

$$Kurtosis(x) = E\left[\left(\frac{x(t) - \mu}{\sigma}\right)^4\right] \tag{7}$$

$$Hjorth\, Mobility(x) = \sqrt{\frac{Var\left(\frac{dx(t)}{dt}\right)}{Var(x(t))}} \tag{8}$$

$$Hjorth\, Complexity = \frac{Mob\left(\frac{dx(t)}{dt}\right)}{Mob(x(t))} \tag{9}$$

$$lag1AC = \frac{cov(x_t, x_{t-1})}{\sigma_{x_t}\sigma_{x_{t-1}}}, \tag{10}$$

where $x(t)$ are post-stimuli epochs, $cov(x_t, x_{t-1})$ is the covariance between $x(t)$ and its lagged version, $Mob(x)$ is Hjorth mobility and σ is the standard deviation. An additional extracted feature is the response amplitude, defined as the maximum value of $x(t)$.

The simulated LFP signal presents slow trends and DC shifts prior to seizures, which would make these more easily predictable. However, signal acquisition systems usually apply highpass filters which exclude such components. Thus, the resulting signals were zero-phase filtered with a 3rd order butterworth highpass of 0.05 Hz for the control (no stimuli) and 1.5 Hz for the simulation with stimulus. Furthermore, in order to smooth the resulting predictors, responses were first averaged (N = 20 and overlap = 75%), and then features were extracted.

3 Results

Representative simulated signals are plotted in Fig. 2. It shows the Epileptor output, from simulations with and without periodic probing stimuli, as the excitability parameter x_0 varies linearly from -4 to -1.8 throughout the simulation. This elicits Seizure-like events (SLEs) at the end.

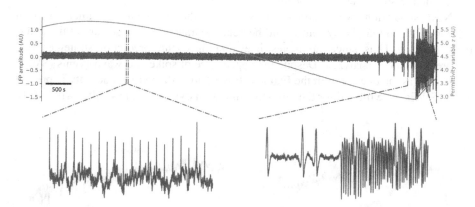

Fig. 2. Simulated LFP and z with probing stimuli. Parameter x_0 was varied linearly from -4 to -1.8, eliciting a seizure at the end. Insets show normal activity with stimuli responses and the beginning of ictal activity with sustained discharges or SLEs. This transition is preceded by the occurrence of inter-ictal spikes.

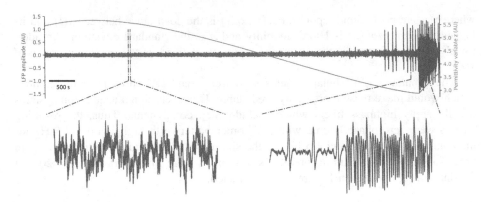

Fig. 3. Simulated LFP and z without probing stimuli. Parameter x_0 was varied linearly from -4.0 to -1.8, eliciting a seizure at the end. Insets show normal activity and the beginning of ictal activity with sustained discharges or SLEs. This transition is preceded by the occurrence of inter-ictal spikes.

It is important that the stimuli serve as predictors, but not at the cost of being proictal. This could be verified from Figs. 2 and 3. That is, seizures begin at the same time, whether stimuli are used or not.

Next, simulations were carried out by varying the excitability parameter x_0 from -4.0 to -2.0, so that the system would be near the transition to a seizure at the end of the simulation. Thus, since the interest is evaluating seizure prediction strategies, only the preictal state is analyzed. Despite the appearance of spike and wave events (SWEs) at the end (as the ones seen in the Figures above), no sustained ictal activity is present. These SWEs were filtered for the probing simulation (with a highpass filter with 1.5 Hz

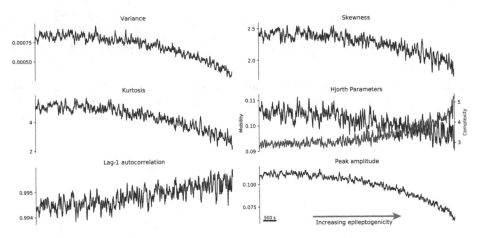

Fig. 4. Features calculated as the Epileptor approaches the ictal state, **with** probing stimuli. The excitability parameter x_0 varies linearly from -4 from the beginning (leftmost parts) to -2 (near the ictal threshold). These changes are highlighted by probing.

cutoff frequency), in order to highlight stimuli response changes. Figures 4 and 5 show the extracted features as a seizure approaches, with and without probing.

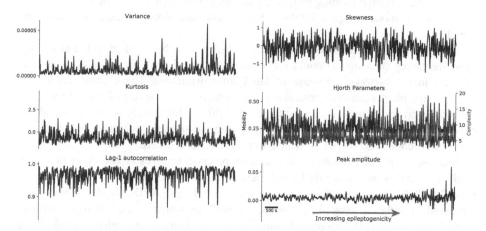

Fig. 5. Features calculated as the Epileptor approaches the ictal state, **without** probing stimuli. The excitability parameter x_0 varies linearly from -4 from the beginning (leftmost parts) to -2 (near the ictal threshold). These changes are not visible with the passive observation of the system.

Probing results from Fig. 4 show that Hjorth Complexity increases as a seizure approaches, while decreases in all other features are observed. This was not observed in the control simulation, where feature series are noisy and show no visible increasing or decreasing trends, with the exception of increases in amplitude at the very end of the simulation, due to the occurrence of SWEs. These events indicate that the Epileptor is getting close to the separatrix or seizure threshold, and may be considered as warning signals for the imminence of a seizure. However, probing provides warning signals much earlier with all extracted features.

Results were analyzed qualitatively, without quantification of how good a feature or stimulus condition is for predicting such transitions. Nonetheless, the initial hypothesis was confirmed; the observed trends and changes in features observed with probing are not observed in the control simulation. These changes would indicate transitions towards ictal states and could be used as predictors for the imminence of a seizure. For future works, the use of measures for comparing different stimulating parameters and patterns should address the issue of quantification of probing and seizure prediction effectiveness.

4 Discussion and Conclusion

In this work, a well-known dynamical model that replicates topology and trajectory of seizures is used to verify the use of probing stimuli to identify changes prior to the occurrence of ictal onset. This would provide further evidence for the use of this approach for seizure prediction.

Interpretation of the results and relating these with experimental models is partially hampered by the nature of the output signal of the simulations, which are calculated as $-x_1 + x_2$ simply for its resemblance to some experimental LFPs. Nevertheless, the observed and expected probing response changes are here discussed for some features, which could provide insights for the behavior and transitions to seizures in different models.

The slight decrease observed in Hjorth mobility (which is related to the slope and mean frequency of a signal) could reflect slower stimuli responses. This can also be reflected in the observed increase of lag-1 autocorrelation. These results could be related to the phenomenon of critical slowing, which would be one of the hallmarks of impending critical transitions (Scheffer et al. 2009). Other early warning signals of these catastrophic bifurcations or tipping points would be increased variance and skewness (Scheffer et al. 2012), which were not observed here.

Increased cortical excitability is found to precede seizures (Badawy et al. 2009; Cook et al. 2013), which would be reflected in increased stimuli responses (Freestone et al. 2011). Excitability reduction by antiepileptic drugs (AEDs) is also observed in decreased stimulation-evoked responses, as well as intrinsic excitability measures (Meisel et al. 2015). Increased time-locked responses are also found in a Pentylenetetrazole model just before seizure onset (Medeiros et al. 2014). However, the observed results in this work are decreased variance and response amplitude as seizures approached, instead of expected increases. A possible cause for this is the fact that the variables composing the Epileptor output ($-x_1 + x_2$) are the same that are subject to the stimulus. This highlights one of the drawbacks of this model, which is lack of a straightforward way to interpret its variables and parameters (El Houssaini et al. 2015). Despite this, the ability to capture dynamical transitions involved in the majority of seizures makes the Epileptor an interesting model for evaluating the validity of using probing approaches for seizure prediction. Detailed microscopic neuronal models such as the one in (Demont-Guignard et al. 2009), or even neural mass models such as Wendling's (Wendling et al. 2002) can offer a greater interpretability of the evolution of response features.

The interpretation of the parameter x_0 and how it was shifted to generate seizures in this work should also be considered when discussing the results. It is initially defined as "degree of epileptogenicity" (Proix et al. 2014), and the model enters continuous epileptogenic conditions if it is goes beyond a critical value. That is, alternating between ictal and inter-ictal cycles. Thus, x_0 could be related to neuronal tissue properties (Jirsa et al. 2017), which would imply that the results are more applicable in the context of presurgical evaluation for removal of epileptogenic regions. However, x_0 could also correspond to the combined effect of a set of factors modulating neural excitability, such as ATP availability, oxygenation and extracellular ion concentrations (Naze et al. 2015). These factors also fluctuate on faster timescales (in relation to scales involved in epileptogenesis) and would be related to periods of heightened seizure susceptibility. This implies that changing the x_0 parameter could also be used in the context of seizure forecasting.

Altogether, despite the limitations regarding the physiological interpretation of the Epileptor's outputs and parameters, the results motivate the further evaluation of active probing as a viable tool for seizure prediction, with further possible diagnostic applications for identifying epileptogenic regions. The latter is in accordance with (Valentin 2002), which used single pulse electrical stimulation (SPES) to identify regions of hyperexcitable cortex in humans.

Using a computational model which replicates the onset dynamics of SLEs, the results in this work support the value of probing approaches to highlight features that warn about imminent dynamical transitions to seizure states. This drives further exploration of the repertoire of possible stimuli types and configurations, which could provide improvements for seizure forecasting, while being relatively subtle and innocuous for system behavior.

Acknowledgements. This work was supported by the agencies CAPES, FAPEMIG and CNPq.

References

Badawy, R., MacDonell, R., Jackson, G., Berkovic, S.: The peri-ictal state: cortical excitability changes within 24 h of a seizure. Brain **132**, 1013–1021 (2009). https://doi.org/10.1093/brain/awp017

Cook, M.J., O'Brien, T.J., Berkovic, S.F., et al.: Prediction of seizure likelihood with a long-term, implanted seizure advisory system in patients with drug-resistant epilepsy: a first-in-man study. Lancet Neurol. **12**, 563–571 (2013). https://doi.org/10.1016/S1474-4422(13)70075-9

Demont-Guignard, S., Benquet, P., Gerber, U., Wendling, F.: Analysis of intracerebral EEG recordings of epileptic spikes: insights from a neural network model. IEEE Trans. Biomed. Eng. **56**, 2782–2795 (2009). https://doi.org/10.1109/TBME.2009.2028015

El Houssaini, K., Ivanov, A.I., Bernard, C., Jirsa, V.K.: Seizures, refractory status epilepticus, and depolarization block as endogenous brain activities. Phys. Rev. E – Stat. Nonlinear Soft Matter Phys. **91**, 2–6 (2015). https://doi.org/10.1103/PhysRevE.91.010701

Engel, J., Pedley, T.: Epilepsy - A Comprehensive Textbook. Lippincott Williams & Wilkins, Philadelphia (1989)

Freestone, D.R., Karoly, P.J., Cook, M.J.: A forward-looking review of seizure prediction. Curr. Opin. Neurol. **30**, 167–173 (2017). https://doi.org/10.1097/WCO.0000000000000429

Freestone, D.R., Karoly, P.J., Peterson, A.D.H., et al.: Seizure prediction: science fiction or soon to become reality?. Curr. Neurol. Neurosci. Rep. **15**: 73 (2015). https://doi.org/10.1007/s11910-015-0596-3

Freestone, D.R., Kuhlmann, L., Grayden, D.B., et al.: Electrical probing of cortical excitability in patients with epilepsy. Epilepsy Behav. **22**, S110–S118 (2011). https://doi.org/10.1016/j.yebeh.2011.09.005

Freestone, D.R., Long, S.N., Frey, S., et al.: A method for actively tracking excitability of brain networks using a fully implantable monitoring system. In: Conference Proceedings Annual International Conference of the IEEE Engineering in Medicine Biology Society, pp. 6151–6154 (2013). https://doi.org/10.1109/embc.2013.6610957

French, J.A.: Refractory epilepsy: clinical overview. In: Epilepsia, pp 3–7 (2007)

Hindmarsh, J.L., Rose, R.M.: A model of neuronal bursting using three coupled first order differential equations. Proc. R. Soc. London Ser. B. Biol. Sci. **221**, 87–102 (1984). https://doi.org/10.1098/rspb.1984.0024

Hjorth, B.: EEG analysis based on time domain properties. Electroencephalogr. Clin. Neurophysiol. **29**, 306–310 (1970)

Hodgkin, A.L., Huxley, A.F.: A quantitative description of membrane current and its application to conduction and excitation in nerve. J. Physiol. **117**, 500–544 (1952). https://doi.org/10. 1113/jphysiol.1952.sp004764

Ihle, M., Feldwisch-Drentrup, H., Teixeira, C.A., et al.: EPILEPSIAE - A European epilepsy database. Comput. Methods Programs Biomed. **106**, 127–138 (2012). https://doi.org/10.1016/ j.cmpb.2010.08.011

Izhikevich, E.M.: Neural excitability, spiking and bursting. Int. J. Bifurcat. Chaos **10**, 1171–1266 (2000). https://doi.org/10.1142/S0218127400000840

Jirsa, V.K., Proix, T., Perdikis, D., et al.: The virtual epileptic patient: individualized whole-brain models of epilepsy spread. Neuroimage **145**, 377–388 (2017). https://doi.org/10.1016/j. neuroimage.2016.04.049

Jirsa, V.K., Stacey, W.C., Quilichini, P.P., et al.: On the nature of seizure dynamics. Brain **137**, 2210–2230 (2014). https://doi.org/10.1093/brain/awu133

Jiruska, P., de Curtis, M., Jefferys, J.G.R., et al.: Synchronization and desynchronization in epilepsy: controversies and hypotheses. J. Physiol. **591**, 787–797 (2013). https://doi.org/10. 1113/jphysiol.2012.239590

Kalitzin, S., Parra, J., Velis, D.N., Lopes da Silva, F.H.: Enhancement of phase clustering in the EEG/MEG gamma frequency band anticipates transitions to paroxysmal epileptiform activity in epileptic patients with known visual sensitivity. IEEE Trans. Biomed. Eng. **49**, 1279–1286 (2002). https://doi.org/10.1109/TBME.2002.804593

Kalitzin, S.N., Velis, D.N., da Silva, F.H.L.: Stimulation-based anticipation and control of state transitions in the epileptic brain. Epilepsy Behav. **17**, 310–323 (2010). https://doi.org/10. 1016/j.yebeh.2009.12.023

Kramer, M.A., Cash, S.S.: Epilepsy as a disorder of cortical network organization. Neuroscientist **18**, 360–372 (2012). https://doi.org/10.1177/1073858411422754

Kuhlmann, L., Lehnertz, K., Richardson, M.P., et al.: Seizure prediction—ready for a new era. Nat. Rev. Neurol. **14**, 618–630 (2018). https://doi.org/10.1038/s41582-018-0055-2

Lytton, W.W.: Computer modelling of epilepsy. Nat. Rev. Neurosci. **9**, 626–637 (2008). https:// doi.org/10.1038/nrn2416

de Castro Medeiros, D., Raspante, L.B.P., Mourão, F.A.G., et al.: Deep brain stimulation probing performance is enhanced by pairing stimulus with epileptic seizure. Epilepsy Behav. **88**, 380–387 (2018). https://doi.org/10.1016/j.yebeh.2018.09.048

Medeiros, D.D.C., Oliveira, L.B., Mourão, F.A.G., et al.: Temporal rearrangement of pre-ictal PTZ induced spike discharges by low frequency electrical stimulation to the amygdaloid complex. Brain Stimulation **7**, 170–178 (2014). https://doi.org/10.1016/j.brs.2013.11.005

Meisel, C., Schulze-Bonhage, A., Freestone, D., et al.: Intrinsic excitability measures track antiepileptic drug action and uncover increasing/decreasing excitability over the wake/sleep cycle. Proc. Natl. Acad. Sci. U.S.A. **112**, 14694–14699 (2015). https://doi.org/10.1073/pnas. 1513716112

Mormann, F., Andrzejak, R.G., Elger, C.E., Lehnertz, K.: Seizure prediction: the long and winding road. Brain **130**, 314–333 (2007). https://doi.org/10.1093/brain/awl241

Morris, C., Lecar, H.: Voltage oscillations in the barnacle giant muscle fiber. Biophys. J. **35**, 193–213 (1981). https://doi.org/10.1016/S0006-3495(81)84782-0

Naze, S., Bernard, C., Jirsa, V.: Computational modeling of seizure dynamics using coupled neuronal networks: factors shaping epileptiform activity. PLoS Comput. Biol. **11**, 1–21 (2015). https://doi.org/10.1371/journal.pcbi.1004209

O'Sullivan-Greene, E., Kuhlmann, L., Nurse, E.S., et al.: Probing to observe neural dynamics investigated with networked Kuramoto oscillators. Int. J. Neural Syst. **27**, 1650038 (2017). https://doi.org/10.1142/S0129065716500386

Proix, T., Bartolomei, F., Chauvel, P., et al.: Permittivity coupling across brain regions determines seizure recruitment in partial epilepsy. J. Neurosci. **34**, 15009–15021 (2014). https://doi.org/10.1523/JNEUROSCI.1570-14.2014

Proix, T., Bartolomei, F., Guye, M., Jirsa, V.K.: Individual brain structure and modelling predict seizure propagation. Brain **140**, 641–654 (2017). https://doi.org/10.1093/brain/awx004

Roy, D., Ghosh, A., Jirsa, V.K.: Phase description of spiking neuron networks with global electric and synaptic coupling. Phys. Rev. E – Stat. Nonlinear Soft Matter Phys. **83**, 1–10 (2011). https://doi.org/10.1103/PhysRevE.83.051909

Rubinov, M., Sporns, O.: Complex network measures of brain connectivity: uses and interpretations. Neuroimage **52**, 1059–1069 (2010). https://doi.org/10.1016/j.neuroimage.2009.10.003

Sander, L.: The epidemiology of the Epilepsies revisited. Curr. Opin. Neurol. **16**, 165–170 (2003). https://doi.org/10.1097/01.wco.0000063766.15877.8e

Scheffer, M., Bascompte, J., Brock, W.A., et al.: Early-warning signals for critical transitions. Nature **461**, 53–59 (2009). https://doi.org/10.1038/nature08227

Scheffer, M., Carpenter, S.R., Lenton, T.M., et al.: Anticipating critical transitions. Science **338**, 344–348 (2012)

Suffczynski, P., Kalitzin, S., Da Silva, F.L., et al.: Active paradigms of seizure anticipation: Computer model evidence for necessity of stimulation. Phys. Rev. E – Stat. Nonlinear Soft Matter Phys. **78**, 1–9 (2008). https://doi.org/10.1103/PhysRevE.78.051917

Suffczynski, P., Wendling, F., Bellanger, J.-J., Da Silva, F.H.L.: Some insights into computational models of (patho)physiological brain activity. Proc. IEEE **94**, 784–804 (2006). https://doi.org/10.1109/JPROC.2006.871773

Valentin, A.: Responses to single pulse electrical stimulation identify epileptogenesis in the human brain in vivo. Brain **125**, 1709–1718 (2002). https://doi.org/10.1093/brain/awf187

Van Diessen, E., Diederen, S.J.H., Braun, K.P.J., et al.: Functional and structural brain networks in epilepsy: what have we learned? Epilepsia **54**, 1855–1865 (2013). https://doi.org/10.1111/epi.12350

Wendling, F., Bartolomei, F., Bellanger, J.J., Chauvel, P.: Epileptic fast activity can be explained by a model of impaired GABAergic dendritic inhibition. Eur. J. Neurosci. **15**, 1499–1508 (2002). https://doi.org/10.1046/j.1460-9568.2002.01985.x

Wilson, H.R., Cowan, J.D.: Excitatory and inhibitory interactions in localized populations of model neurons. Biophys. J. **12**, 1–24 (1972). https://doi.org/10.1016/S0006-3495(72)86068-5

World Health Organization (2012) Fact Sheet about Epilepsy. http://www.who.int/mediacentre/factsheets/fs999/en/. Accessed 17 Mar 2015

Author Index

Printed in the United States
By Bookmasters